The Mythmaking Frame of Mind

Social Imagination and American Culture

James Gilbert
University of Maryland

Amy Gilman
Montclair State College

Donald M. Scott
New School for Social Research

Joan W. Scott
Institute for Advanced Study

Wadsworth Publishing Company
Belmont, California
A Division of Wadsworth, Inc.

For William R. Taylor
Teacher and Friend

History Editor: Peggy Adams
Editorial Assistant: Amy Havel
Production Editor: The Book Company
Print Buyer: Diana Spence
Designer: Andrew Ogus
Copy Editor: Laura Kenney
Cover: Andrew Ogus
Compositor: Scratchgravel Publishing Services
Printer: Edwards Bros.

1 2 3 4 5 6 7 8 9 10—97 96 95 94 93

Library of Congress Cataloging-in-Publication Data

The Mythmaking frame of mind : social imagination and American culture / [edited by] James Gilbert . . . [et al.].
p. cm.
Includes bibliographical references.
ISBN 0-534-19038-3
1. United States—Civilization. I. Gilbert, James Burkhart.
E169.1.M989 1992
973—dc20 92-22739
CIP

Contents

❧

Introduction

THE ESSAYS IN THIS VOLUME ILLUSTRATE SOME OF THE DIRECTIONS OF CULtural and intellectual history as currently practiced in the United States. They touch on many themes, but they have some common preoccupations. One is the varied manifestations of the rise of commercial culture; another is the city in its many guises and representations, including the institutions that constitute the culture of urban-industrial life; yet another is the way in which social myths function to interpret the meanings of modern life. The essays do not offer a unified commentary on these questions; indeed, their interest and excitement come from their different and sometimes conflicting perspectives.

If the essays do not produce a single interpretation, neither do they exemplify a single theoretical or methodological approach. In this they reflect the necessary eclecticism of the field. They are linked, however, by a certain ingenuity that gives a distinctive cast to their work: their innovative choice of subject matter, their ability to draw rich historical insight from unusual sources, to read those sources with a kind of daring and imagination, and in so doing to expand our understanding of the texture of life in the past.

That the essays share this distinctive quality has something to do with the influence of William R. Taylor, Distinguished Professor of History at the State University of New York at Stony Brook, and formerly Professor of History at the University of Wisconsin, Madison, in whose honor these essays have been written. With the exception of Christopher Lasch and William Leach, all of the authors have been his students, either at Wisconsin or Stony Brook. They have been moved by his questions and criticisms, enticed by his mischievous provocations, challenged by his curiosity, and inspired by his writing. Bill Taylor is not the kind of teacher who turns out carbon copies of himself, nor does he direct students to topics that are pieces of his own project. Rather, he has taught by engaging in conversations that are open ended and continuing, playful and far ranging. These are conversations that draw in others; Bill is a relay for the exchange of ideas among his students and friends. In addition, he attends to and appreciates all kinds of imaginative work. As one of the authors puts it, "We acknowledge that sometimes uncomfortable, but ultimately reassuring recognition, that he is a keen audience for the work we do."

One of the ongoing conversations Bill has had over the years is about the rise of commercial culture in America. The subject is one of great interest to the field of cultural history generally; the essays in this volume go far in illuminating its many and conflicting dimensions. The growth of a capitalist market in the nineteenth century was not a uniform or singular phenomenon, nor was it confined simply to the buying and selling of goods. Its manifestations were diverse, as shown in the essays by Donald Scott, Susan Strasser, and William Leach. Scott details the way in which knowledge itself became a commodity. He follows the careers of some of the most famous purveyors of "useful knowledge" in the 1840s and 1850s. By focusing on a debate about Henry Ward Beecher's exorbitant lecture fees, Scott manages to reveal how the ethos of profit entered the marketplace of ideas. Susan Strasser discusses the agents of commercial capital, traveling salesmen, at the end of the nineteenth century. Her account lays bare the structure of the distribution of goods and the extent to which, in the early twentieth century before the rise of national advertising, it depended on a personal relationship between wholesalers and retailers. Interestingly, too, the culture of salesmanship was unique, and many of its values were not direct reflections of the commercial exchange involved in the work. William Leach analyzes the marketing strategies of American merchants who targeted children as consumers at the turn of the century. He shows how their plans drew on and fed into a larger discourse on children, in which the National Consumer League participated along with child psychologists and social workers. In Leach's essay we see Santa Claus transformed from the mythic domestic figure of the early nineteenth century (described in Stephen Nissenbaum's article) to the centerpiece of merchandising extravaganzas.

The rise of commercial culture was most evident in urban centers, so it is not surprising that the essays that focus on the city also touch on this theme. Nissenbaum's essay locates Clement Moore's famous poem "The Night Before Christmas" in the context of early nineteenth-century urban social politics. Fear of mingling with the rough and irreverent lower classes led middle-class representatives to redefine Christmas as a private, family celebration. Older rituals that revolved around the patron-client relationships of rich and poor were reenacted as domestic rituals involving parents and their children. In Nissenbaum's reading, the myth of Santa Claus is a story about city life. So, too, is Amy Gilman's reading of Edgar Allan Poe's urban detective stories. But while Nissenbaum argues that

Moore's poem is part of a movement to bring the dangers of the new urban world under control, Gilman suggests that Poe believed such control to be futile. The violence tracked by Poe's detectives was meant to show that cities were the site of "natural" forces of unpredictable and uncontainable chaos.

Visions of the city were more varied and conflicting than these two discussions suggest. In Peter Buckley's essay, the question of cities as centers of sexual immorality emerges. Buckley suggests that debates about burlesque dancing in New York in the period after the Civil War were a way of expressing middle-class anxieties about the changing composition of the city and about feminism, which somehow seemed connected to urban growth. James Gilbert takes us on a tour of Chicago at the time of the World's Columbian Exposition of 1893. Following the guidebooks produced for middle-class visitors to the city reveals a Chicago of historic landmarks and isolated neighborhoods. Nothing is mentioned of the indigenous (often immigrant) cultural life that late twentieth-century tourists value. Rather, the image produced for outsiders in the 1890s erased from view all traces of ethnic, class, and racial diversity. Gilbert concludes that these books express the hostility of Chicago's middle classes to the growing alliance of commercial culture with immigrant and lower-class populations. They are an attempt to represent the city as white, nativist, and middle class.

One after another of these essays takes up the question of representation. They suggest that the reality of urban life is constructed through its representation, that representation is not epiphenomenal but constitutive, and that social tensions are often expressed as conflicts about representation. What could be called "the formation of the middle class" is treated here as an issue of representation; the essays by Nissenbaum, Scott, Buckley, and Gilbert all show how crucial representation was to the articulation of class identities and class relationships. Peter Hall's article adds another dimension to the discussion of representation by focusing on the organization and management of the New Haven Water Company. Hall argues that historians must learn to read visual manifestations—machinery, buildings, interior layout and design—as the symbolic self-representations of urban administrators and industrialists. Such self-representations are artifacts that must be interpreted, he suggests, for they deepen our understanding of the "reality" of the very structures of urban-industrial life.

Some of the essays on commercial culture and the city also take up the theme of social myth, another aspect of representation. In this they follow a direction pointed out by Bill Taylor in his important study of North and South before the Civil War, *Cavalier and Yankee* (New York, 1961). There he wrote of his interest in those who projected the images and stories that gave meaning to the diverse and changing lives of Americans: "It is the mythmaking frame of mind, the social imagination of mythmakers and the circumstances which have molded them that has interested me most." The essays by Nissenbaum, Leach, and Gilbert offer insight into these questions, as does the piece by Joyce Antler, who looks at myths surrounding educated women in the 1920s. In searching for an explanation for the institutional isolation of these women, Antler points out how difficult it was for women to argue against prevailing beliefs about suitable activities for females and to fashion myths of their own. Mary Beard and Mary Austin were far more limited and far less successful in their attempts to present genius (typically defined as male) as a female trait. By reading Antler's essay one gains perspective on the ways in which gender figures in the making of myths.

Gender is one of the several themes that recur in these essays, cross-cutting others. We understand how significant issues of sexual difference were when we read of the anxieties of the critics of burlesque described by Buckley, of the importance attributed to brotherhood by Strasser's traveling salesmen, and of the difficulties Antler recounts were experienced by those seeking to reevaluate women's intellectual capacities. The experiences of immigrant women in Connecticut is the theme taken up in Laura Anker's paper. Anker uses the archives of the Federal Writer's Project to explore the ways in which immigrant women represented themselves to social investigators. She is interested in the interactions between the investigators and their informants, in the ways in which perceived differences of class and education affected the quality of the interviews and responses. These exchanges shaped the stories, the ways in which women's lives in the immigrant experience were represented.

Christopher Lasch's paper is also about gender, although it makes a very different argument from the others. It uses material from early modern Europe to argue directly with contemporary American feminists about the history of gender relations. Insisting that patriarchy has had a history and that it has been significantly different at different times, Lasch nostalgically evokes a time when the battle between the sexes took the form of ritualized play. We have included this paper, despite its European materials, in a volume that is otherwise devoted to American history for two reasons. First, Lasch is an American historian who once collaborated with Taylor on an article on the history of women in America (" 'Two

Kindred Spirits': Sorority and Family in New England, 1839–1846," *New England Quarterly* 36 [1963], 25–41). Lasch's essay in this volume is meant to evoke that early partnership. Second, Lasch's essay is a document for the history of our own times, a piece that uses an interpretation of the past to comment on contemporary American cultural politics.

Another theme that cross-cuts these essays has to do with the culture of professions in nineteenth-century America. In Scott's essay we learn of the lecturing "profession"; in Strasser's we read about the codes governing salesmanship. In Steven Stowe's essay we get a close look at how southern doctors understood their work. Stowe shows that these committed men of science do not fit into modernist notions that see science and religion as binary opposites. Instead, they understood their calling in religious terms, and these were in no way taken to undermine the practice of medicine. In fact, in their understanding of themselves and in their self-representation, religion enhanced their ability as doctors.

The essays in this book are arranged chronologically. This seemed the wisest course because they are so interconnected thematically, interpretively, and substantively. Each is enriched by reading the others; one offers implicit commentary on another. Reading them chronologically deepens our understanding of the changes that occurred over the course of about a century and a half. Reading them against one another generates impressions and patterns that sometimes resonate and sometimes conflict, pointing out new directions for future research. The essays document the richness, variety, partiality, and incompleteness of our knowledge of the past. They take up the question of culture as a question of representation and, in so doing, they exemplify a method of reading for historians. Finally, in their inventiveness and imagination, they are testimony to the effects of an inspiring teacher on the practice of the historian's craft.

Joan W. Scott
Princeton, N.J.

Acknowledgments

We would like to thank the following reviewers for their comments: Susan Porter Benson, University of Missouri; Richard Fox, Boston University; David Nasaw, City University of New York; and David J. Walkowitz, New York University.

Contributors

Laura Anker is associate professor and chair of the American Studies Program at SUNY Old Westbury. Most recently she has published articles on women and immigration and is working on a book based on the Connecticut Federal Writers Project life histories of immigrants, primarily women.

Joyce Antler is associate professor of American studies at Brandeis University. She is author of *Lucy Sprague Mitchell: The Making of a Modern Woman; The Educated Woman and Professionalization: The Struggle for a New Feminine Identity, 1890–1920;* and coauthor of *Year One of the Empire: A Play of Politics, War and Protest.* She has edited *America and I: Short Stories by American Jewish Women Writers* and coedited *Change in Education: Women as Radicals and Conservators* and *The Challenge of Feminist Biography.*

Peter Buckley is assistant professor of history in the Faculty of Humanities and Social Sciences at the Cooper Union for the Advancement of Science and Art in New York City. He is also a fellow of the New York Institute for the Humanities at New York University.

James Gilbert is professor of American history at the University of Maryland and the author of several books, most recently *Perfect Cities: Chicago's Utopias of 1893.*

Amy Gilman is associate professor of history at Montclair State College, where she teaches history and women's studies. She has written on women and culture in nineteenth-century America and is currently completing *The Death of Mary Rogers: Sex and Culture in Nineteenth-Century New York.*

Peter Dobkin Hall is research scientist at the Institute for Social and Policy Studies, Yale University. His published works include *The Organization of American Culture, 1700–1900, Inventing the Nonprofit Sector,* and (with George E. Marcus) *Lives in Trust: The Fortunes of American Dynastic Families in the Late Twentieth Century.*

Christopher Lasch teaches history at the University of Rochester. He is the author, most recently, of *The True and Only Heaven: Progress and Its Critics.* In 1960, he and William R. Taylor embarked on a historical study of American women. Needless to say, they never finished it; but their article, "Two Kindred Spirits: Sorority and Family in New England, 1839–1846" is sometimes mentioned as an early contribution to the history of women, a field of study then just beginning to take shape.

William Leach is author of *Land of Desire, American Culture in the New Age of Consumption* (forthcoming, 1993); *True Love and Perfect Union, The Feminist Reform of Sex and Society;* and editor of *The Wonderful Wizard of Oz* by L. Frank Baum.

Stephen Nissenbaum teaches history at the University of Massachusetts, Amherst. He has written *Salem Possessed: Social Origins of Witchcraft in America* (with Paul Boyer) and *Sex, Diet and Debility in Jacksonian America.* He is writing a book about the battle for Christmas.

Donald M. Scott is a member of the faculty and dean of Eugene Lang College of the New School for Social Research. His publications include *From Office to Profession: The New England Ministry, 1750–1850* and *America's Families: A Documentary History.* He is currently at work on a study of democracy and knowledge in nineteenth-century America.

Joan W. Scott is professor of social science at the Institute for Advanced Study. She is author, most recently, of *Gender and the Politics of History.*

Steven M. Stowe is associate professor of history at Indiana University, Bloomington, and the author of *Intimacy and Power in the Old South: Ritual in the Lives of the Planters.*

Susan Strasser is associate professor of history and American civilization, and director of the University Honors Program, at George Washington University. She is author of *Never Done: A History of American Housework* and *Satisfaction Guaranteed: The Making of the American Mass Market.*

❧

Religion, Science, and the Culture of Medical Practice in the American South, 1800–1870

Steven M. Stowe

AT THE CLOSE OF HIS FIRST FEW DAYS OF MEDICAL PRACTICE IN PORT Jackson, Florida, in December 1848, the young physician Charles A. Hentz sat down on his front stoop and wrote a page in his diary. Though in later years he was to look back on the rough village on the Chattahoochie River as "one of the worst, whisky drinking, fighting, horse racing, gambling communities to be found on this side of Texas," Hentz's initial reflections were optimistic. And they reveal something important about how a young doctor in the rural South expected his new career to embody personal and professional goals. "I am becoming *acclimated* to my solitude," he wrote.

> I pray that my isolation may be beneficial to me. God guiding me, I know that it will, in temporal, as well as spiritual affairs. I hope to discipline myself for a much higher sphere of action, than that in which I have been compelled to launch my bark. I will have ample time to think, concoct,

> and mature my course in after life—God granting his blessing, and enlightening my understanding. . . . Oh! glorious privilege of thought—to dive into the weighty things of creation and eternity—illimitable as their Author, God.

Solitude, self-discipline, and the expectation of intellectual growth were common themes in the hopes of young country doctors in the mid-nineteenth century. So, too, was the striking religious tone of Hentz's language: plain, devout, anchored in self-worth, and as such wholly in the stream of Protestant evangelicalism. Well schooled in medicine by nineteenth-century standards, Hentz like many of his fellow M.D.'s nonetheless relied on religious language to sum up his hope for success and satisfaction. Science and religion—"creation and eternity"—were inseparable at the heart of the young doctor's view of his backwoods life.[1]

In this essay I explore a culture of medical practice importantly shaped by this link between science, religion, and the work of doctoring. My aim is to characterize the cultural setting of medical practice immediately prior to the drastic changes wrought by "scientific medicine" at the turn of the century. Appreciated as an emotional as well as an intellectual setting, the culture of medical practice was significantly problematic for rural southern physicians. It sustained them in their work, yet it also unsettled their self-image. It embodied a way to make humdrum practice answer to higher ends, but it also uncovered disturbing truths about medical crisis, knowledge, and the doctor's role. Two key tensions in physicians' experience appear most frequently in this respect: a tension between the intellectual satisfactions of science and the often crude realities of doctoring, and a tension between two conflicting images of the physician—as healer and as artisan. I hope to suggest here the importance of understanding the culture of medical practice through these tensions drawn from doctors' own reflections. The tensions were, I believe, central to the continuity of practice and also to the change that would come.

Although the tie between religion and science was a fundamental one for southern physicians, informing both the common sense of doctoring and more elevated values, it was not a uniquely "southern" phenomenon. And because historians of southern medicine generally have followed well-established historiographical themes that stress southern uniqueness, it has been overlooked. Studies of slavery, race, and sectionalism have commanded attention instead. Yet certain conditions of medical practice that obtained both South and North—the isolated rural setting, for example, with its lack of institutions and its tenuous collegial networks, or the routine ethics of daily practice that preceded and survived the sectional crisis—were as fundamental to southern medicine as the slave system or sectional politics. Indeed, the former provided a cultural setting for understanding the significance of the latter.[2]

Richard Shryock's classic essay "Medical Practice in the Old South" typifies the strength and weakness of the traditional historiographical focus. Still much cited, this essay's strength is its broad synthesis of distinctively southern themes—medical care of slaves, regional epidemics, standards for professional life and letters. Yet Shryock's discussion of medical practice in terms of the southern "disease situation" begins by assuming southern "backwardness" in comparison with the North. And because southern backwardness, an archetypal theme in southern studies, is the organizational premise of the essay, crucial aspects of ordinary medical practice—the daily routine of a rural practitioner's work, his apprenticeship, collegial relations, and self-education; the vagaries of drugs, travel, income—simply do not receive attention. Moreover, when Shryock portrays a typical doctor in the closing paragraphs of the essay, the idealized image of a kindly, beloved physician is such that no questions are raised about the texture of meaning doctors found in the fluctuations of their practice—the understandings they shared that made sense of the hardships and the successes.[3]

If traditional themes in southern historiography have circumvented aspects of the culture of medical practice, so too have traditional perspectives in the historiography of science and medicine. Although this is a vast body of work, the part that recounts the emergence of a scientifically oriented medicine in the mid-nineteenth century usually has described this emergence in terms of a conflict between scientific values and older, religious ones. This perspective may be traced to the extraordinary influence of writers such as Andrew Dickson White and his image of a "warfare" between religion and science in which the encounter is depicted as linear and complete: historical change moves "from miracles to medicine," "from fetich to hygiene," and so on. Even though White invoked "Christendom" in his title, implying a religiously based culture, he portrays religion merely as a force for ignorance and error. Recent scholarship has modulated this view, but it is still possible to find "theology, astrology, and witchcraft" lumped together in a single atavistic group that was "phased out" of medical science in the nineteenth century. Physicians still are portrayed as finding their religious beliefs superfluous to their medical work. "By the 1830s and 1840s," two historians of medicine have written recently, "physicians had already ceased to air their theological views . . . in medical publications. Whatever their private religious beliefs, they now kept them to themselves; as physicians, they dealt only with natural causes."[4]

Some important matters are raised by such judgments: the nature of nineteenth-century science as a unique epistemology, as opposed to one that possessed common roots with other ways of knowing; the character of nineteenth-century medicine as an emerging "modern" science rather than as a craft concerned more with effective healing than with "causes"; and the simultaneous rise of science (including popular scientific fashions) and a vigorous evangelical Christianity. With regard to the last, we know that popular science and evangelical Protestantism frequently went hand-in-hand in American communities. We know that both academic science and Protestantism branched out with great energy (and some confusion) into sectarian worlds with well-developed medical preferences, as in the case of the Millerites, the Emmanuel Movement, and even mainstream Presbyterianism. Implied in these developments is a complicated and various relationship between medical common sense and religious belief that we are only beginning to comprehend.[5]

In terms of the South, then, neither traditional southern historiography, with its emphasis on the region's uniqueness, nor the main themes in the history of science and medicine, with their emphasis on dichotomy and progress, have taken into consideration a local culture of medical practice in the mid-nineteenth century rooted in both religious and scientific beliefs. A threshold on that culture is the actual *work* of medical practice. We must look at doctoring itself as a particular blend of craft, science, and livelihood, which means looking at the shared conditions under which most southern physicians found themselves practicing, conditions not all uniquely southern but all typically so. These include the difficulties that rural isolation and distances held for medical efficacy and knowledge; the intimacy and multiple social ties that marked small communities; and the complications of a biracial patient population. It also means looking at the shared understandings through which physicians approached the meaning of their work—the expectations and aspirations that comprised "good medicine" and made it satisfying.[6]

Much of the meaning doctors hoped to find in practicing medicine revolved around the expectation that medicine would provide intellectual stimulation. In a time of therapeutic uncertainty, doctors had conflicting things to say about healing patients. But they spoke with one voice about medicine's link to the values of science that "serve to enlighten, refine, & elevate their possessor," and they had a broadly inclusive sense of which sciences mattered. Dr. Joseph Milligan, for example, told his medical-student son to take up the study of geology and mineralogy with a view to his intellectual improvement. Milligan's friend Henry M. Bruns wrote admiringly, "With your telescope, microscope, thermom[eter], barometer, quadrant, &c, and your diligence in the use of them, you will come to be looked upon as the Lion of Hamburg [S.C]." Physicians' interest in broad areas of study such as meteorology, based upon the premise that disease was lodged quite specifically in local ecology, accounted for many studies of the climate and geography of the South. Most country doctors also set aside some time to record descriptions of fevers and seizures, both considered to be associated with the local "atmosphere" of disease. Journals frequently made mention of characteristic southern conditions discovered by "inductive" observation, the keystone of the scientific perspective. Southern climate, for example, was seen by many doctors as "less oxygenated and invigorating" than northern climate, causing southerners, particularly "soft" women, to become lax and weak. Northern women who moved to the South, however, found their health, particularly in childbirth, much improved in the relaxed southern air.[7]

Grand theories aside, many doctors found intellectual satisfaction in discovering facts about the natural world, such as the anatomy of the human fetus or the toxicity of water passed through lead pipe. Opportunities for such studies did not arise each day of practice, of course, but it is clear that intellectual stimulation, often as a hedge against the boredom of rural doctoring, remained central to physicians' interest in their work. Samuel H. Dickson advised a fellow M.D. who had decided to quit his practice to go into cotton factoring to keep up his medical studies because "your mind will & *must be actively* employed." Outright passion for intellectual activity runs throughout doctors' accounts of their work. Many saw themselves not only as naturalists but almost as visionaries, feeding on the belief that "it does a poetic imagination good to gaze at such marvellous works of nature," as a Mississippi doctor told his diary. Another doctor was said by a friend to be "almost crazy about [the study of] human bones & in fact about everything relating to medicine."[8]

Whether large scale or minute, intellectual work provided physicians with an important measure of the value of doctoring. It permitted them to feel part of an unfolding human potential for knowledge. It allowed them to join a large, if scattered, group of fellow scientists who believed in the same values despite being bogged down in the uncertain work of healing. In their most elevated public talk, doctors liked to speak of medicine, in Joseph LeConte's words, "in the only sense in which it can lay any claim to the rank of science, and define it to be the science of Life or Biology." The intellectual curiosities and discoveries revealed in medical encounters were potentially the most significant of all, "embracing a knowledge of all science," as Joseph Jones declared. The intellectual challenge was to see the enormous scope of medicine, including both bedside intimacy and the impersonal natural world, as part of the same endeavor. This vision stimulated many physicians' attempts to heal and linked "physicking" to the highest imperatives of mental activity.[9]

The difficulty of this challenge, however, was exposed in the very intensity of the doctors' hope. Intellectuals like LeConte and Jones were forced to admit that the "practical" side of medicine, that is, actual patient care, appeared to take away from its scientific standing. Often medicine was simply a remedial craft. Despite LeConte's insightful observation that even "common-sense" clinical skills in fact depended upon "general notions or theories of some kind" that doctors should strive to better understand, many people skeptical of the doctor as scientist argued that the crude dosing and gouging that marked therapeutics scarcely merited a claim to science. Moreover, sick people expected doctors to *act,* not to seek remote knowledge. Indeed, even those doctors who most passionately argued for medicine as the science of life frequently relied not on medical examples but on examples from other fields with uncontested scientific status, chiefly astronomy and geology. Physicians, the argument went, should embrace these solidly scientific fields because they hold models of what medicine might become and because physicians were, as scientists, by definition interested in the larger natural world. The vagaries of bedside care did not permit systematic experimentation and otherwise confounded even the most careful inductive observer. Of necessity, the actual practice of medicine dealt with "conditions of life . . . so nicely balanced, that in attempting to modify, we destroy," and yet doctors continued to invoke the kinship between medicine and all science.[10]

In part, many physicians attempted to get around the disparity between their love for science and the questionable scientific standing of medicine by making a virtue of medicine's weakness. Admitting that the uncertainties of diagnosis, prescription, and prevention were serious obstacles to the science of medicine, doctors nevertheless maintained that this very drawback underscored what made medicine important. The doctor occupied a social position unique among scientists. He was not aloof among the constellations, but squarely in the center of social life. His science was a social science; his duty was to a range of social experience and personal variation. He was the man entrusted with interpreting nature to his neighbors, whether through the course of a fever, the timing of a childbirth, or the fluctuations of seasonal health. Unlike the astronomer, the physician "comes into contact with all classes. . . . He has the most familiar admission to the entire range of human society." A doctor sees everyone and everything, and even though he is not always effective, as William Holcombe reflected, the doctor proceeds "dispensing light and hope and comfort wherever he comes, anxiously expected, cordially welcomed, admitted to the private heart-stories of man, to the confidence of all." The physician was singularly responsive in his social duties to the immediate, pressing obligations of life and death. A rural physician typically was described as duty-bound to "always be found when wanted." He was a constant adviser in times of crisis. By his constancy he entered into a bond with his patients in which the trust he drew from them was nicely balanced by the hopefulness he returned, contributing "to the success of the one and the cure of the other."[11]

This social feature of doctoring reflected back upon the character of the man who aspired to practice medicine. Probably not a few physicians at one time or another were struck by the realization, as was Joseph LeConte, of "my want of preparation to undertake the awful responsibilities of a medical practitioner," given the little that was known about disease and health. A man of strong character helped to make up for this want. The doctor as scientist, one physician wrote, "should cultivate that strength of mind which will enable him to separate the probable from the improbable . . . , never allowing what we do know to be disturbed by what we do not know." In this way, medicine called upon and witnessed the moral strength of a man. "The hard service you speak of having to go through, is the very thing for you," a North Carolina doctor wrote to his physician son, "it will make a man of you." And yet the unique demands of a socially oriented science, exposing the deepest character of the scientist, were extreme in their very moral quality. Samuel H. Dickson took note of this when he observed to his friend Joseph A. S. Milligan that while medicine required exclusive intellectual concentration, intellectual effort was not sufficient to produce a good doctor: "The success of a Physician is . . . attributable to a peculiar set of habits, not only of thought, reading &c, but also of manner & conduct. [This] theory assists me in accounting for the comparative failure of so many good intellects & the elevation of so many inferior ones."[12]

Dickson's observation points to another way in which doctors sought meaning in their practice, apart from striving for the intellectual satisfaction of science. This was the meaning—often contradictory and only partly conscious—a doctor fashioned from the routine of doctoring itself. It was the meaning at the center of his daily rhythm of work, the travel by horseback alone, the compounding of drugs, the examination of patients of all ages in their homes, the occasional patient at the door, the struggle to find time to read outdated journals, rewrite case notes, collect fees. Given the rise of modern medicine as the preeminent profession, it is difficult to appreciate the prosaic toil of nineteenth-century doctoring without either sentimentalizing it or discounting it. Yet the ordinary, rote work of doctors, broken by episodes of sudden crisis, had a profound effect on what meaning they were able to make of their calling. One young physician in northern Florida, only recently taking on patients, spent a typical week recopying his medical school notes, setting a young girl's broken bone, figuring out how to make his office appear homelike yet professional, reading articles on gastritis, dissecting a hawk he had shot, attending a party in order to meet people in the neighborhood, and reading *The Vicar of Wakefield.* Rural practice included almost no hospital experience, only sporadic contact with other doctors, long hours of lonely travel, and the performance of a wide range of duties, from sweeping the office to physically restraining a maniac. There were rewards in the routine: "Give me a bright, bracing day, a fine road, and a lonely one, an active, stirring horse—and a certain mood of mind, and nothing is more pleasant," one physician wrote in his diary. Yet he also noted, a few months later, a deluge of emergency: "Called up at daybreak to three severe cases. . . . After breakfast visited four obstinate cases of dysentery and several minor affairs. . . . Before night had pneumonia and puerperal convulsions to treat. Out since supper twice, and promised to call at one place again between one and two o'clock in the night. Afternoon nap interrupted. Wife sick in bed. Thermometer 90° in deep shade. Dust almost insufferable. A little indisposed myself. *Finis.*"[13]

Returning from his rounds, a physician would find patients or notes from them requesting his advice or his presence. Doctors were asked to prescribe by letter, to rewrite patients' descriptions of their illnesses in "scientific" language so that other doctors might credit it, and to examine slaves sent by their masters. People's letters voiced their suffering and anxiety: "Dear Dr, My wife shows no symptoms of convalescence yet," "My mouth & tongue will be constant drye and no spittle on it," "The little Negro Mary has had a cough and has been unwell for some day [*sic*]. . . . She threw-up thick bile and Saturday she threw up 2 worms about a foot long each," "Dier Sir My wife had hur baby last night [and] the child was dead," "I send for you in a case of emergency. I want you to come as soon as you can get here. My wife cannot live 24 hours without relief. . . . I do not know anything I can do." Thus physicians experienced the eruption of urgent need into their routine drudgery. There were successes. James Cross, an Alabama doctor, attended a woman in childbirth convulsions one afternoon. He marshalled contradictory textbook knowledge, followed the author he respected the most, tried a variation by prescribing opium, and concluded triumphantly, "It worked." Charles Hentz spent hours improvising a splint from clapboards and felt quite pleased with the result, noting with pride his "surgery in the backwoods." The young J. Marion Sims wrote his fiancé after his first few months of practice, "I have the glorious consolation of knowing (to a certainty) that by a very simple operation I have saved one man's life," and less grandly, a North Carolina doctor recounted his feelings in a difficult case: "I was scared . . . but the little shaver got well and I was glad." But patients also got sicker, suffered, and died. Physicians' daybooks recount failures like William Holcombe's efforts to help a girl with scarlet fever "on the very pivot of life or death." He sat up two nights with her and watched her die. Exhausted and depressed, Holcombe wrote that being both doctor and nurse was surely too much for a sane man to bear.[14]

The shifting back and forth between rote task and urgent necessity, in the context of solitary practice and rural isolation, made up the fundamental rhythm of a doctor's work. But country practice also was marked by the circumstances of a doctor's personal relationship with his community. Rural doctors were not choosy about whom they treated, taking on patients of both races and all social classes; they could not afford to be too particular, nor was it considered ethical to turn down a case. Charles Hentz recorded a typically wide variety of patients, one day beginning with a visit by a Mrs. R., a planter woman, who came to "talk with me about her ailings," followed immediately by a visit from a slave woman named Huldey who, "poor thing, had a desperately sick turn in my office—rolled over the floor, vomited & spewed." Like most doctors, Hentz appears not to have altered his care according to the race of his patient, at least not the terms of ordinary diagnosis and prescription. But he was quite clear in his dislike for poor white people, considered to be the least desirable patients by far. "Ignorant, vacillating, prejudiced," is how another doctor described his "pauper calls." A physician's own fears and class prejudices, coupled with the fact that most care given to the poor was given free, convinced most doctors that treating poor whites was at best an opportunity to gain experience and demonstrate Christian charity.[15]

A community's opinion of a doctor, more than any other single factor, nevertheless established or finished his practice. Physicians who tried to look at country practice as only the first step in their careers were well aware that most doctors never practiced anywhere else. Enduring talkative hypochondriacs, "reckless, drunken men" demanding chloroform for "its wonderful effects," and landlords who expected free care in addition to rent added to the vexations of practice. Physicians resolved to please people by a "sincere desire to make them happy," good manners, and by work habits that would prove them to be something more than the "Carpet Knight" practitioner who hugged his office and rarely ventured abroad. Yet this effort to be not only employed but "beloved," as one doctor admitted, caused many doctors to resent a community's hold over their fortunes. As one doctor wrote, medicine is practiced among people who like to argue law or politics but become mute when health is at issue, expecting the physician to do everything in just the way that will meet their wishes.[16]

Physicians commiserated with and inspired each other, yet collegiality was marred by rivalries and one-upsmanship in the competitive world of rural practice. With so much of medicine so uncertain, a doctor inevitably fell back on his own judgment and his sense of his own self-worth, which often put him at odds with other doctors who did the same thing. Looking at his work, a doctor might conclude simply that the clutter of his office, the mysteries of treatment, and the fatigue of travel made him "at times wearied, at times satisfied, with my calling," and leave it at that. But many doctors, in struggling to assess what they felt about the habits and values of their work, returned again and again to how medical practice did not realize either intellectual satisfaction or scientific promise. There were too many "plodding things relating to physic" that undercut its pleasures and gains. A young doctor who at first feared that his learning would stagnate and his grasp of healing wither in the stillness and loneliness of country practice settled down at last "into the contemptible character of a routine practitioner—with opium and antimony for the care of all diseases." At first concerned that it took months to receive books or to write an article, a southern doctor ended his career by not caring about books at all, content to ride his "professional hobbies." And perhaps worse, doctors became over time impatient and disappointed with their own minds. William Holcombe abandoned his daily journal in 1855, begun with high expectations of intellectual pilgrimage, because it had "degenerated into a sham affair," a mere catalogue of "my fatigues, troubles, &c, &c." More than a few doctors would have agreed with one South Carolinian that "It is with much regret that I am forced to make the same acknowledgment that you do in regard to the 'Noble Art of Healing'; no great profit and precious little honour, in being an M.D."[17]

If such tensions of practice were not trivial, neither were they incapacitating for most physicians. Doctoring went on in spite of them and indeed embraced them to some extent as badges of hard service. The personal difficulties of doctoring, worried over, written about, tirelessly examined, channeled the flow of professional achievement and ambition. Finding their way repeatedly into the consciousness of physicians, the tensions of doctoring could become a kind of self-indulgence. But they also initiated self-reflection and were the stimuli of professional change, however tedious and groping. Key tensions, as we have seen, were first, a conflict between the anticipated intellectual satisfaction of medicine and the discovery that doctoring itself was only with great difficulty perceived as a science, and second, a conflict between what amounted to two images of the doctor: as a healer in the crucible of medical crisis and as a "plodding" artisan burdened with the routines of medical maintenance. Premodern medicine from the country practitioner's viewpoint, not from the vantage point of twentieth-century hindsight, was defined precisely by tensions such as these.

The meaning of these tensions may be explored a bit further. When southern doctors faced them most squarely and eloquently, they frequently relied on the images and understandings of religion. Religion provided the breadth and intensity equal to the conflicts in medical practice. Appreciating what was encompassed by religious forms (meaning for the most part, of course, the expressions and usages of Protestantism) reveals the extent to which doctors were able to establish an ethic for their work. It was an ethic that summoned the aspirations of science and invoked the moral bonds of the community. It gave a language to the confrontation with death.

To an important extent, religious meanings served to tie medicine more firmly to scientific values. It will be recalled that for many American scientists the study of nature was the study of the order and wisdom of God. So, too, for many physicians. "It is universal law," one physician told the assembled medical students at the Medical College of Georgia, "that all the component parts of the

Universe have not in themselves the entire aim or reason of their existence . . . [but] form the essential conditions for the manifestations of the great designs of the Creator." If likening medicine to the "pure" science of astronomy stretched credibility, placing medicine in God's natural world was beyond question. To know God was no less an effort of science than to study the stars or human biology; observational powers and inductive methods were not confined to the material world. And in God's plan, medicine was no less a science for all of its mystery and messiness. Charles Caldwell put a nice turn on the argument when he told medical students at Transylvania University: "Theology is the science of Deity, . . . The science of medicine may be truly denominated a *branch* of theology; for, taken in its entire scope, it communicates very amply a knowledge of the Deity, his attributes and laws, through the medium of his works." Religious understanding validated medicine as a science as no other form of knowledge could do.[18]

This perspective did not completely solve the difficulty of medicine's problematic nature as science, however; in fact, old tensions arose in a new, more complicated way for some doctors. It was all very well to assert the ultimate unity of medicine with both science and theology, but, as one medical-school lecturer noted ruefully with regard to the actual work of the scientist, "The fact . . . that religious truths are so little involved in scientific pursuits, causes the minds of scientific men to lose sight of them." The materialism of a Thomas Cooper was always available to the scientific skeptic, stressing humans' likeness to all other creatures and the superfluity of religion in the effort to understand any particular creature. Though many doctors asserted the bond between medicine and religion on the one hand and science on the other, they were also perplexed when forced to return to a more pragmatic view. "What advantage has your road over mine?" physician William Forwood asked a religious correspondent. "The whole subject [of faith] dwindles down to mere *opinions* and *beliefs*. . . . The attainable and knowable should be sought after in preference to the unattainable and unknowable." Yet in the same letter he described intellect as God-given and acknowledged that "[we] are answerable to God for the proper use of the talents that he has bestowed upon us."[19]

This counterpoint between a practical relativism that threatened to shrink belief into opinion and an overarching faith that joined individual effort to God's judgment sheds light on the complexity of physicians' attraction to religious explanation of doctoring. A reductive individualism certainly did not square with an enlarged sense of God's law. Yet if theology were a science, and if medicine, too, could be so identified, doctors puzzled anew over who should be accepted as most knowledgeable in such matters. One sign of the uncertainty was the conflict between physicians and clergy that appears in both medical and church publications throughout the antebellum years. Even those writers who strove to depict doctors and ministers working together observed the uneasiness of the relation. Doctors tended to exclude clergy from sickrooms with greater frequency, it was said, and clergy bitterly opposed being seen as the undertaker's assistants. Doctors, for their part, increasingly criticized clergy for being medically uninformed, even to the point of sponsoring quackery, and for depressing patients' spirits as often as lifting them.[20]

Particularly vexing was the question of whether physicians' work compelled them to be irreligious. Was there something about medical practice that alienated faith even as it fell short of science? As one minister told a medical audience, there is no necessary contradiction between science and religion, but "medical men have a . . . formidable difficulty in their case, in their frequent want of the Sabbath." Not science but doctoring posed a threat to an individual's faith, and to public worship as well. A busy practice did not excuse absence from church, this minister continued, for to be so consumed by work was a proscribed form of selfishness. Many M.D.'s agreed that this drift toward unbelief was a significant problem. It was a problem for all practitioners because it distorted the medical profession's role as caregivers. Worrying this problem clarified a set of issues and gave physicians a language with which to confront an uneasiness over self-image and the meaning of medical practice. Aspiring to the unified and uplifting awareness of the world promised by religious worship and scientific knowledge alike, the physician could not ignore the requirement that he act, that he *doctor*. The argument had to be advanced that there was no necessary conflict between acting and aspiration. There was no impassable gulf between a man's faith and his work. It was not true, one doctor asserted, that "the study and practice of medicine tends to infidelity." That a doctor does not weep at every patient's death or fall to his knees in prayer at every bedside "is no evidence that these sacred feelings do not exist and powerfully affect the medical man." The scientific mien was not what it appeared. It is increasingly fashionable, wrote another doctor, for people to assume "that the medical man has no peculiar sympathy with the sufferings he is called upon to witness . . . that death is but the 'diverting the course of a little red fluid.'" But this image was superficial. "There is feeling in [the doctor's] breast—intense sympathy—but it vents itself in doing: it is the truest kind of sympathy—a sympathy of action." Charles Caldwell enlarged upon the image of the doctor as worshipping by doing. A doctor's work is testimony to his belief, he asserted, and "in the performance of the functions of his profession . . . he is discharging his duty to God." Even if medical practice, as opposed to pure science, offered unique opportunities for irreligion (overwork, overevaluation of the material world, calloused feelings, and urban-trained values were the temptations to unbelief most frequently cited), it also offered possibilities for Christian expression not available to anyone else. The physician "has access to individuals whom no clergyman can reach. . . . He can choose his opportunities for bringing forward the subject of religion, and select the most suitable mode and form for presenting it. . . . The feeling of dependence, which reveals itself in the lighting up of the invalid's countenance, ... shows that his physician has an ascendancy over him which no other person can have." For a doctor like homeopathic physician William Holcombe, the fit between belief, evangelism, and healing was exact. Reflecting on a slip of the tongue in which he said "Allopathic mummeries" instead of "Catholic mummeries," Holcombe decided that in misspeaking he had uttered a truth: "The difference between Old and New Church are [*sic*] very similar to those between Old and New Medicine. Indeed I am a Homeopath . . . because I was previously a new Churchman. And it is impossible for the old bottles to contain our *new wine*."[21]

Fear of the irreligious doctor thus was countered by hope for a man of practical faith, a man more equipped to save souls than even the clergy. Medical work was not a distraction, it was a doxology. Tensions still abounded, however: physicians' self-doubt balanced by grandiose visions of the healer as supreme Christian; the nature of worship as either church-going (a communal but passive image) or as vigorous good works among the community; what God required of the faithful and what that had to do with possessing medical knowledge. Each of these tensions might pull in many directions, but in the writings of southern doctors they fundamentally embodied an effort to see doctoring in relation to the community. Speaking of belief, work, and self, doctors drew upon the most powerful language at hand, a religious language held in common. For it was the community, more than the doctor's other worldly ties, that defined the standards and expectations he held most dear.

Of course, this effort at definition could seem merely self-serving, as in those accounts rhetorically bedecked with the suffering of the bedside healer waiting "through the noontide heats, the darkening twilights and all the gloomy hours, until the grey dawn." Yet this rhetoric was no simple screen; it served to counter the doctor's alienation with a chance for heroism within the community. The doctor was loved when he healed. And whether successful or not in a given case, in Joseph Jones's words, the doctor always "works with deadly knives, and still more deadly medicines" and thus needs—for his spiritual sake and for the trust of the community—"the highest self-command, the loftiest moral training, and the purest religious belief." Medicine was practiced among people known to the physician on the most ordinary terms and through the most routine transactions. Then, in times of general illness or in a sudden explosion of mysterious, individual sickness, this same doctor would know his neighbor, creditor, or kin in the terms of greatest intimacy and dependence. Such times were not always straightforwardly dramatic, and doctors acknowledged the temptations to absurdity in such instances as the one in which William Holcombe found himself one afternoon, struggling to relieve the "fits" of a pious neighbor woman who had been taken with seizures while praising God. But the good doctor in such a case was the man who could treat the woman, love the neighbor, and respect the faith that shouted to the Lord. "When I speak of a good physician," as one southern doctor wrote, "I wish you to understand me as meaning *a good man,* possessing medical information." The community set the standards for goodness, and there was little question that those standards required the scope and coverage of religion. "In such a science as Medicine," one doctor wrote without irony, "where it is impossible to prescribe any fixed rules of treatment, everything . . . depends on the judgment of the physician." A community, and a good doctor, would want—would require—that judgment grounded in the deepest web of values; for, in the words of another physician, "it is only religion that can center in a man all the graces, and finish him for the walks of life."[22]

Privately as well as publicly, doctors attested to the power of religion as the model of shared knowledge and collective well-being. The most satisfying, and sustaining, self-image of a medical worker was that of a man who is "diligent in the acquisition of knowledge, and [who] faithfully & honestly discharges his duty" while reminding himself in times of crisis, "Trust in God, and everything will come out alright." The trials of the world are both shared and intimate, a young doctor was reminded, and in the times of greatest difficulty the physician gathers strength "by reflecting that we are in the care of an all powerful God." Whether inspiring themselves to work harder at medical studies, at "charity care" for poor neighbors, or at understanding the surges of feeling that accompany a doctor on his rounds—his own emotion and his patients'—religious understandings quieted anxiety and explained purposes by tying the doctor to his community and locale. By working hard among his neighbors and friends, even to the point of exhaustion, a Mississippi doctor discovered that he was more willing to work; "the propriety of our being kept *constantly* at work in our sphere," he was convinced, was God's plan revealed in the lives of friends and neighbors as plainly as if it were handwriting on a wall.[23]

The themes of faith, work, and community in doctoring were perhaps most complicated when death occurred. Physicians had little to say on a grand scale about birth, but death called up the full complexity of doctoring. In one sense, a religious understanding of death acknowledged the doctor's helplessness in mortal cases without either claiming or avoiding his responsibility for it. "Do everything that science can do, for your patients, carefully & kindly by admonishing them to adhere to your directions, and leave the event with God," Dr. Joseph Milligan advised his physician son. But the good doctor went beyond this, the elder Milligan wrote on another occasion, by making "it a matter of conscience to direct all your patients (who may be in such a state as to lead you to look for their death at no late day) to trust alone in the Savior & not to look to any merits . . . of their own."[24]

It was part of medical care, in the view of many physicians, not only to refresh dying patients' spiritual fortitude but also to glorify death. Medical attention alone was not enough to bid farewell to the dying. Only religious expressions sealed the transition from this to the next world. Young John Richardson, studying medicine with his physician uncle, described with clinical detail the prolonged death of a patient and concluded by observing that on "Friday morning half past 12 o'clock the chariot of the Lord came, and his spirit took its flight for eternal worlds, on the pinions of faith it soared high above the the [*sic*] things which impale mortal vision, leaving terrestrial objects at an incommensurable distance, with an eye fixed with an undying gaze on the throne of the Eternal God." Later, rereading his account, Richardson observed, "I may have dealt too much hyperbole in my description of his death, but if true piety and an inflexible will to do the commands of God insure immortal life, [this patient] most certainly deserves it." Some months later, Richardson "felt awfully" when a young slave girl named Lindy died after he spent many hours attending her. He consoled himself and honored her memory by writing, "She has . . . been cut off before the temptations of earth allured her from the path of rectitude. . . . I knew her well, . . . a better disposed, more modest girl I never knew. Her manners were so lady-like. She has been raised in the house from a babe. The Lord does all things well."[25]

Consoling, achieving closure, explaining—religious understanding combined these for physicians and their patients. In the intimacy that a death brings, everyone at the bedside shared a single meaning. Charles Hentz, losing the infant of one of his slaves, "felt deep emotions of sadness," but encouraged by the mother's own Christian belief in the face of her child's death, and recalling that death favors no one, he resolved to "pursue my calling as I ought . . . for a higher sphere of action." Similarly, John Richardson reflected upon the death of one of his patients, that death itself revealed the kinship of all people, the importance of shared belief. "Death is a fearful thing," he wrote in his journal. "It cuts off all connection with sublunary things. . . . The old, the young, the rich & the poor have to yield to its incessant blow." Such reflections did not always resolve matters, however; religious meaning sometimes cut in more than one way, consoling yet reminding physicians of their own mortality and loss. Desperately ill himself, "worn down by disease & covered with cold clammy perspiration, with a mind correspondingly prostrated," J. Marion Sims learned a valued lesson of sickness: "This is the time that death appears in all its terrors to the mind of him who feels conscious that his course of life has not been in consistence with all the first principles of moral & religious rectitude." Seeing his own death from consumption approaching, John Young Bassett exchanged several letters with a religious friend who implored him to join the church before it was too late. Sometimes ironic, sometimes impassioned, Bassett wrote that he did not "expect any miracles to be wrought in my favour," but that he nevertheless wondered why he was not religious. "I am living in a religious community," he observed. "My wife is a truly religious woman, my pastor is pious and learned, a most refined gentleman and my personal friend. I keep no irreligious company, am not afraid of the opinion of any man, and desire to be religious. I do not understand why I am not religious any more than I do why others are."[26]

Thus, even as he expressed his puzzlement at his own lack of faith, Bassett underscored the ways religion anchored medicine in a wider knowledge of personhood, community, and meaning. Medicine alone was too feeble to provide a world view of sickness and health. Or, rather, medicine in the antebellum years was so firmly rooted in the common sense understandings of the community—of which religion was a major one—that religious meanings were drawn easily from medical events. That these features of the culture of medical practice changed drastically by the twentieth century has been almost axiomatic. But perhaps we have too hastily assumed what the change means. In fact, medicine remains in many ways more a craft than a science, and the personal beliefs of physicians—especially religious beliefs—remain at the center of any penetrating view of what doctoring entails. For southern doctors, the meaning of their world would change only as their sense of it changed, a sense given shape by the tensions deeply bound up in the work of doctoring itself.

Notes

1. Charles A. Hentz autobiography (typed copy), Southern Historical Collection, University of North Carolina, Chapel Hill (hereafter SHC), 159; Charles A. Hentz diary, December 17, 1848, SHC.

2. Studies that emphasize the associations among medicine, race, slavery, and sectionalism in the South include Todd Savitt, "The Use of Blacks for Medical Experimentation and Demonstration in the Old South," *Journal of Southern*

History 48 (August 1982), 331–48; John Harley Warner, "The Idea of Southern Medical Distinctiveness: Medical Knowledge and Practice in the Old South," in Ronald Numbers and Judith Leavitt, eds., *Sickness and Health in America: Readings in the History of Medicine and Public Health,* 2d ed. (Madison, Wisc., 1985), and "A Southern Medical Reform: the Meaning of the Antebellum Argument for Southern Medical Education," *Bulletin of the History of Medicine* 57 (Fall 1983), 364–81; John Duffy, "A Note on Ante-bellum Southern Nationalism and Medical Practice," *Journal of Southern History* 34 (May 1968), 274–76 and "Sectional Conflict and Medical Education in Louisiana," *Journal of Southern History* 23 (August 1957), 289–306; Joseph I. Waring, "Charleston Medicine, 1800–1860," *Journal of the History of Medicine and Allied Sciences* 31 (July 1976), 320–42; John S. Haller, "The Negro and the Southern Physician: A Study of Medical and Racial Attitudes, 1800–1860," *Medical History* 16 (July 1972), 238–53; Lucie Bridgforth, "Medicine in Antebellum Mississippi," *Journal of Mississippi History* 46 (May 1984), 82–107; Walter J. Fisher, "Physicians and Slavery in the Antebellum Southern Medical Journal," *Journal of the History of Medicine and Allied Sciences* 23 (January 1968), 36–49; James O. Breeden, "Statesrights Medicine in the Old South," *Bulletin of the New York Academy of Medicine* 52 (1968–69), 29–45; Martha C. Mitchell, "Health and the Medical Profession in the Lower South, 1845–1860," *Journal of Southern History* 10 (November 1944), 424–46; Mary Louise Marshall, "Samuel A. Cartwright and States' Rights, Medicine," *New Orleans Medical and Surgical Journal* 93 (1940), 74–78. A sophisticated study of health and race among North American blacks is Kenneth Kiple and Virginia H. King, *Another Dimension to the Black Diaspora: Diet, Disease, and Racism* (Cambridge, England, 1981).

3. Richard H. Shryock, "Medical Practice in the Old South," in *Medicine in America: Historical Essays* (Baltimore, 1966).

4. Andrew Dickson White, *A History of the Warfare of Science with Theology in Christendom,* 2 vols. (New York, 1932 [first published 1896]); Richard H. Shryock, "Empiricism and Rationalism in American Medicine, 1650–1950," *Proceedings of the American Antequarian Society,* n.s. 79, part I (April, 1969), 106; Ronald L. Numbers and Ronald C. Sawyer, "Medicine and Christianity in the Modern World," in Martin Marty and Kenneth L. Vaux, eds., *Health/Medicine and the Faith Traditions: an Inquiry into Religion and Medicine* (Philadelphia, 1982), 139. For broad views of the relationships among science, religion, and (at times) medicine in antebellum America, see Theodore Dwight Bozeman, *Protestants in an Age of Science: The Baconian Ideal and Antebellum Religious Thought* (Chapel Hill, N.C., 1977); Herbert Hovenkamp, *Science and Religion in America, 1800–1860* (Philadelphia, 1978); Conrad Wright, "The Religion of Geology," *New England Quarterly* 14 (June 1941), 335–58; James C. Whorton, "'Christian Physiology': William Alcott's Prescription for the Mellennium," *Bulletin of the History of Medicine* 49 (Winter 1975), 466–81.

5. See, for example, Raymond J. Cuningham, "The Emmanuel Movement: A Variety of American Religious Experience," *American Quarterly* 14 (Spring 1962), 48–63; Ronald L. Numbers and Janet S. Numbers, "Millerism and Madness: A Study of 'Religious Insanity' in Nineteenth-Century America,"

Bulletin of the Menninger Clinic 40 (1985), 289–320; Theodore Dwight Bozeman, "Inductive and Deductive Politics: Science and Society in Antebellum Presbyterian Thought," *Journal of American History* 64 (December 1977), 704–22. Also suggestive are A. J. Youngson, *The Scientific Revolution in Victorian Medicine* (New York, 1979); E. Brooks Holifield, *Health and Medicine in the Methodist Tradition: Journey toward Wholeness* (New York, 1986); Paul H. Kocher, "The Idea of God in Elizabethan Medicine," *Journal of the History of Ideas* 11 (January 1950), 3–29.

6. For studies of southern medical practice, varying in degree of detail and interpretation, see Todd L. Savitt, *Medicine and Slavery: The Diseases and Health Care of Blacks in Antebellum Virginia* (Urbana, Ill., 1978); William D. Postell, *The Health of Slaves on Southern Plantations* (Baton Rouge, La., 1951); Reginald Horsman, *Josiah Nott of Mobile: Southerner, Physician, and Racial Theorist* (Baton Rouge, La., 1987); Diane Sydenham, "Practitioner and Patient: The Practice of Medicine in Eighteenth-Century South Carolina" (Ph.D. diss., Johns Hopkins University, 1979); John Duffy, "Medical Practice in the Ante Bellum South," *Journal of Southern History* 25 (February 1959), 53–72; David O. Whitten, "Medical Care of Slaves: Louisiana Sugar Region and South Carolina Rice District," *Southern Studies* 16 (Summer 1977), 153–80; Bennett H. Wall, "Medical Care of Ebenezer Pettigrew's Slaves," *Mississippi Valley Historical Review* 37 (December 1950), 451–70; Thomas B. Jones, "Calvin Jones, M.D.: A Case Study in the Practice of Early American Medicine," *North Carolina Historical Review* 49 (January 1972), 56–71. See also the extraordinarily rich series of articles on a folk practitioner by Weymouth T. Jordan, "Martin Marshall's Book: Introduction," *Alabama Historical Quarterly* 2 (Summer 1940), 156–68, "Martin Marshall's Book: Herb Medicine," *Alabama Historical Quarterly* 2 (Winter 1940), 443–59, "Martin Marshall's Book: Homemade Medicine," *Alabama Historical Quarterly* 2 (Spring 1941), 117–29. Helpful in suggesting questions of practice and livelihood are Ian Inkster, "Marginal Men: Aspects of the Social Role of the Medical Community in Sheffield, 1790–1850," in John Woodward and David Richard, eds., *Health Care and Popular Medicine in Nineteenth-Century England* (New York, 1977), and Ruth Purtilo and James Sorrell, "The Ethical Dilemmas of a Rural Physician," *Hastings Center Report* 16 (August 1986), 24–28.

7. A. M. Clemens to John Y. Bassett, December 10 [1846], Bassett papers, SHC; Joseph Milligan to Joseph A. S. Milligan, July 9, 1846, Milligan papers, SHC; Henry M. Bruns to Joseph Milligan, March 27, 1835, ibid.; Henry J. Peck, "On the Sanative Influence of a Southern Residence on Northern Patients," *Transylvania Journal of Medicine and the Associated Sciences* 3 (August 1830), 405–10. For accounts of fever, seizures, and therapies, see John M. Richardson diary, June 10, 1854, SHC; William Holcombe diary, May 6 and May 8, 1855, SHC. On women and southern climate, see, for example, Samuel K. Jennings, *A Compendium of Medical Science, or Fifty Years' Experience in the Art of Healing* (Tuscaloosa, Ala., 1847), 134–35; John S. Wilson, *Woman's Home Book of Health: A Work for Mothers and for Families* (Philadelphia, 1860), 153–55. For discussion of science in the antebellum southern

context, see Thomas Cary Johnson, Jr., *Scientific Interests in the Old South* (New York, 1936); James O. Breeden, *Joseph Jones, M.D.: Scientist of the Old South* (Lexington, Ky., 1975); Theodore D. Bozeman, "Joseph LeConte: Organic Science and a 'Sociology for the South,'" *Journal of Southern History* 39 (November 1973), 565–82; William H. Longton, "The Carolina Ideal World: Natural Science and Social Thought in Ante-Bellum South Carolina," *Civil War History* 20 (June 1974), 118–34; Reginald Horsman, *Josiah Nott of Mobile*, passim. See also Isabella Porcher, plantation prescription book, ca. 1834, Waring Historical Library, Medical University of South Carolina, Charleston (hereafter Waring), for a mix of folkways and science.

8. Samuel H. Dickson to Joseph Milligan, February 10, 1835, Milligan papers, SHC; William Holcombe diary, January 23, 1855, SHC; J. [Milliman ?] to Joseph A. S. Milligan, March 13, 1844, Milligan papers, SHC. See also Henry M. Bruns to Joseph Milligan, April 24, 1835, ibid.; Joseph A. S. Milligan to Joseph Milligan, September 8, 1844, ibid.; Charles A. Hentz diary, September 19, 1860, Hentz papers, SHC; Lunsford Yandell diary, 1843, The Filson Club, Louisville, Ky., 3.

9. Joseph LeConte, "On the Science of Medicine and the Causes which have Retarded its Progress," *Southern Medical and Surgical Journal* n.s. 6 (1850), 461; Joseph Jones, "Suggestions on Medical Education: Introductory Lecture to the Course of 1859–60, in the Medical College of Georgia . . ." (Augusta, Ga., 1860), 5. For LeConte's instructive career, see Lester D. Stephens, *Joseph LeConte: Gentle Prophet of Evolution* (Baton Rouge, La., 1982). See also Joseph Jones to "Dear Cousin," June 16, 1853, Joseph Jones collection, Manuscripts Department, Howard-Tilton Memorial Library, Tulane University, New Orleans, La. (hereafter Tulane).

10. LeConte, "On the Science of Medicine," 459, 470. See also LeConte, untitled ms. on Nature, LeConte-Furman papers, SHC; Jones, "Suggestions on Medical Education," 23–25. For the thoughts and reading of a young man moving toward a career in medicine, see Francis P. Porcher, commonplace book, 1843–1845, South Carolina Historical Society, Charleston.

11. T. V. Moore, "Religion and Medicine," *Maryland and Virginia Medical Journal* 14 (1860), 96; William Holcombe diary, January 19, 1855, SHC; Joseph A. S. Milligan to Octavia Camfield, December 20, 1847, Milligan papers, SHC; William Holcombe, "The Elements of Professional Success," *United States Medical and Surgical Journal* 9 (April 1874), 302. See also Hugh L. Hodge, "A Lecture, Introductory to the Course on Obstetrics . . ." (Philadelphia, 1835).

12. Joseph LeConte ms. autobiography, SHC, 143; Charles Quintard, "An Address Delivered Before the Graduating Class of the Medical College of Georgia" (Augusta, Ga., 1851), 10; Joseph Milligan to Joseph A. S. Milligan, June 25, 1846, Milligan papers, SHC; Samuel H. Dickson to Joseph A. S. Milligan, August 27, 1844, ibid.

13. William Holcombe diary, January 28, 1855, SHC; ibid., May 11, 1855. See also Charles A. Hentz diary, 1848–49, Thomas O'Dwyer diary, 1825, and Joseph A. S. Milligan daybook, 1857, SHC; Courtney Clark papers, notebook, 1844–

74, Manuscripts Department, Duke University Library, Durham, N.C., for typical accounts of practice routine.

14. H. R. Kingly to John Lyle, April 19, 1856, Lyle-Siler papers, SHC; Thomas Brewer to James S. Smith, May 4, 1833 (inserted in Smith's account book for 1828–32, vol. 2, p. 155), James S. Smith papers, SHC; M. Speer to James S. Smith, n.d. (inserted in Smith's account book for 1828–32, vol. 2, p. 90), ibid.; William N. Jordan to James S. Smith, November 3, 1831 (inserted in Smith's account book for 1828–32, vol. 1, p. 183), ibid.; A. B. Johnson to Beverley Jones, August 17, 1854, Jones family papers, SHC; James Conquest Cross, "Cases and Observations on Convulsive Affections," *Transylvania Journal of Medicine and the Associated Sciences* 1 (1828), 161–62; Charles A. Hentz diary, December 23, 1848, Hentz papers, SHC; J. Marion Sims to Theresa Jones, December 31, 1835, Sims papers, SHC; R. A. Edmonston to John Lyle, November 2, 1851, Lyle-Siler papers, SHC. For Holcombe's case, see Holcombe diary, May 6–8, 1855, SHC. See also George Colmer papers, medical journal, 1859–78, Tulane, esp. 261, 310–11.

15. Charles A. Hentz diary, February 1, 1849, Hentz papers, SHC; William Holcombe diary, February 3, 1855, SHC. See also Hentz diary, December 11–12, 1848; E. R. Calhoun to Joseph A. S. Milligan, June 4, 1847, Milligan papers, SHC; William Blanding diary, 1807–11, South Caroliniana Library, University of South Carolina, Columbia (hereafter SCL).

16. Charles A. Hentz ms. autobiography, Hentz papers, SHC, 168; Joseph Milligan to Joseph A. S. Milligan, June 11, 1846, Milligan papers, SHC; ibid., January 4, 1846. See also Hentz autobiography, 165; E. D. Fenner to John Y. Bassett, September 18, 1849, Bassett papers, SHC; James Ewell, *The Planter's and Mariner's Medical Companion* (Philadelphia, 1807), 1–3.

17. Charles A. Hentz diary, February 2, 1849, Hentz papers, SHC; ibid., January 20, 1849; Quintard, "An Address," 8; William Holcombe diary, June 1, 1855, SHC; [?] Elliott to Joseph Milligan, August 8, 1835, Milligan papers, SHC. See also John Y. Bassett to Theodore Parker, December 15, 1849 (copy on reverse of Parker's letter to Bassett, November 25, 1849), Bassett papers, SHC; Josiah C. Nott to J. M. Gage, July 28, 1836, Gage papers, SHC.

18. Jones, "Suggestions on Medical Education," 11; Charles Caldwell, "An Introductory Address, Intended as a Defence of the Medical Profession . . ." (Lexington, Ky., 1826), 11. See also Matthew Boyd Hope, "A Discourse Designed to Show that Physiological Inquiries are Not Unfriendly to Religious Sentiment . . ." (Philadelphia, 1845).

19. Moore, "Religion and Medicine," 90; William Forwood to S[usan] R. L[yons], July 26, 1860, Forwood papers, SHC. Typical of Cooper's skeptical medical essays is "A View of the Metaphysical and Physiological Arguments in Favour of Materialism, by a Physician" (Philadelphia, 1824).

20. For the relationship of doctors and clergy, see Moore, "Religion and Medicine," esp. 94–97; William M. Boling, "Remarks on the Importance of Good Health in Ministers of the Gospel, and on the Best Means of Attaining it," *Western Journal of Medicine and Surgery* 2d ser., 3 (1845), 283–313; Charles A.

Hentz autobiography, 168, 176, Hentz papers, SHC. For discussion, see James H. Cassedy, "An American Clerical Crisis: Ministers' Sore Throat, 1830–1860," *Bulletin of the History of Medicine* 53 (Spring 1979), 23–38; Theron Kue-Hing Young, "A Conflict of Professions: The Medical Missionary in China, 1835–1890," *Bulletin of the History of Medicine* 47 (May–June 1973), 250–72.

21. Moore, "Religion and Medicine," 91; C. Tate Murphy, "The Heroic Character of the True Physician," *Transactions of the Medical Society of North Carolina* 17 (1870), 18–35; Quintard, "An Address," 9; Caldwell, "Introductory Address," 8; H. A. Boardman, "The Claims of Religion Upon Medical Men" (Philadelphia, 1844), 4; William Holcombe diary, April 4, 1855, SHC. See also Samuel Leland diary, September 5, 1852 and January 23, 1853, SCL; Dandridge A. Bibb, "Essay on the Effects of the Study and Practice of Medicine . . . ," M.D. thesis, 1846, Waring; Jeptha McKinney notebook, 1856–57, Special Collections, Louisiana State University, Baton Rouge, La.

22. Murphy, "Heroic Character," 30–31; Jones, "Suggestions on Medical Education," 25; Alfred M. Folger, *The Family Physician, being a Domestic Work, Written in Plain Style* . . . (Spartanburg, S.C., 1845), 219; Wilson, *Woman's Home Book,* 217; Thomas S. Powell, *A Colloquy on the Duties and Elements of a Physician* (Atlanta, Ga., 1860), 32–33. See also William Holcombe diary, May 13, 1855, SHC.

23. Joseph Milligan to Joseph A. S. Milligan, June 11, 1846, Milligan papers, SHC; John Gage to James Gage, August 2, 1835, Gage papers, SHC; William Holcombe diary, May 4, 1855, SHC.

24. Joseph Milligan to Joseph A. S. Milligan, July 8, 1848, Milligan papers, SHC; ibid., January 4, 1846. See also Moore, "Religion and Medicine," 97, and the many reflections on death in Leland, diary, SCL.

25. John M. Richardson diary, August 10, 1853, and November 1–2, 1853, SHC. Compare the sentiments in Powell, *Colloquy on the Duties,* 66.

26. Charles A. Hentz diary, January 3, 1849, Hentz papers, SHC; John M. Richardson diary, July 2, 1853, SHC; J. Marion Sims to Theresa Jones, October 10, 1836, Sims papers, SHC; John Y. Bassett to George Wood, April 6, 1851, Bassett papers, SHC. See also William Forwood to S[usan] R. Lyons, June 8, 1860; Joseph LeConte to Emma LeConte, July 21, 1866, LeConte-Furman papers, SHC; Joseph LeConte to Caroline LeConte, July 17, 1866, Elizabeth Talley papers, SHC.

Revisiting "A Visit from St. Nicholas": The Battle for Christmas in Early Nineteenth-Century America

Stephen Nissenbaum

THE CHRISTMAS SEASON WAS ALWAYS AN IMPORTANT OCCASION IN THE LIFE of John Pintard, a prominent New York City merchant and civic leader of the early nineteenth century. As Pintard went to bed on the evening of December 31, 1820, he was looking forward to the schedule he had carefully laid out for the celebration of New Year's Day, the season's end. First, he would get up early for a private chat with his daughter (married but still living in the household). Next, there would be a devotional morning service at a nearby church. The middle hours of the day would be devoted to an extended round of "ceremonial and friendly visits" with acquaintances and colleagues around the city. Finally, in mid-afternoon Pintard would return to his Wall Street home, where the entire household would, as he put it, "assemble round our festive boards" for a "little family party"—a meal of venison and other holiday dishes that had been prepared weeks in advance and punctuated by a series of toasts "drunk with all affection and old fashioned formality."

Pintard managed, the next day, to get through most of the activities he had planned, but only after his night's sleep had been interrupted—twice. First, in the middle of the night, with the household sound asleep, Pintard's daughter was awakened when she heard "someone take [a] key and deliberately open the door." The family knew that New Year's Eve marked the peak of rowdy Christmas revels in New York, so Pintard had reason to fear the presence of an intruder. He roused his wife ("mama," as he referred to her in a letter written very early the next morning). "I threw on my clothes in haste, and down we sallied [to investigate,] found the back parlor door ajar, but nothing out of place." As it turned out, the noise was only a false alarm—the family's servant had merely arisen early in order to light a fire in the study. So John Pintard returned to bed. But no sooner had he fallen asleep than he was roused again, this time by bands of loud revelers marching down Wall Street and directly outside his house, banging on drums, blowing on fifes and whistles, and all the while loudly proclaiming the New Year. The revelers did not leave and in fact kept Pintard up for the rest of the night: they "interrupted all repose until daylight, when I arose, leaving mama . . . to take a little rest till nine, when I shall call [her]." [1]

What this little episode reveals is two incompatible styles—two "traditions," if you like—of celebrating the holiday season. One of them, that of John Pintard, was a daytime affair, genially formal, mostly domestic, and quiet. The other, that of the revelers in the street, was nocturnal, aggressively public, and just as noisy as they could make it. The two traditions came into conflict in John Pintard's household only two years before Pintard's friend Clement Clarke Moore wrote his poem "A Visit from St. Nicholas"—the account of a rather different kind of nighttime visitation during the Christmas season. The connection is not artificial: John Pintard himself played a role in the development of Christmas as we know it today. One might even say that his role was that of John the Baptist to the figure of Santa Claus that Moore would soon perfect.

❧

The Christmas season has often been a focus of struggle. From Puritans in seventeenth-century England and North America to Communists in twentieth-century eastern Europe, different groups have had their own reasons to suppress its observance altogether. And other groups have chronically contested the timing and the manner of its celebration.

There is, of course, no biblical or historical reason to place the birth of Jesus on December 25. The Church officially decided to observe it on that date only in the fourth century. And the December 25 date was chosen not for any Christian reasons but simply because it happened to mark the approximate arrival of the winter solstice, an event celebrated long before Christianity. The Puritans were correct when they pointed out—and they pointed it out often—that Christmas was nothing but a pagan festival covered with a Christian veneer. Most cultures (outside the tropics) have long marked with rituals involving light and greenery those dark weeks of December when the daylight wanes, culminating in the winter solstice—the return of sun and light and life itself. Thus Chanukah, the "feast of lights." And thus the yule log, the holly, the mistletoe, and the Christmas tree—pagan traditions all, with no direct connection to the birth of Jesus.[2]

There was another reason for marking this season with festivity. December was the major "punctuation mark" in the rhythmic cycle of work in northern agricultural societies, a time when there was a minimum of work to be performed. The deep freeze of mid-winter had not yet set in; the work of gathering the harvest and preparing it for winter was done; and there was plenty of fresh meat from newly slaughtered animals, meat that had to be consumed before it spoiled. St. Nicholas, for example, is associated with the Christmas season chiefly because his "name-day," December 6, coincided in many European countries with the end of the harvest and slaughter season.[3]

So our own culture is by no means the first in which "Christmas" has meant an entire *season* rather than a single day. In early modern Europe and colonial America, the Christmas season could begin as early as late November and continue past New Year's Day. (We still sing about the twelve days of Christmas, and the British still celebrate Twelfth Night.) In England, the season might open as early as December 16 and last until the first Monday after January 6 (dubbed "Plough Monday," the return to work).[4] In early nineteenth-century New York, seasonal festivities generally peaked at New Year's—as the experience of John Pintard suggests.[5] But it isn't very useful, finally, to try to pin down the exact boundaries of a "real" Christmas in times past or the precise rituals of some "traditional" holiday season; these seem to have changed over time and to have varied by region, by locality, even from one household to another. What is more useful, in any one setting, is to look for the dynamics of an ongoing contest—sometimes a real "battle"—between those who wished to expand the season and those who wished to contract and restrict it. (In our own day, the contest may pit merchants on one side—together with children—against grownups who for various reasons resent seeing Christmas displays go up earlier and earlier each year.)

❧

In early modern Europe, the years between 1500 and 1800, the Christmas season was a time for emotional and social release, an opportunity to let off steam. But reveling could easily become rowdiness; making merry could edge into making trouble. The season sanctioned a kind of behavior that was not tolerated at most other times of the year.

Christmas was a season of "misrule," a time when ordinary behavioral restraints could be violated with impunity. It was part of what one historian has called "the world of carnival." (The word *carnival* is rooted in the Latin *carne*, meaning "flesh"—referring both to meat and to sex.) Indeed, Christmas "misrule" meant that hunger, sexual lust, and even anger could be acted out openly and in public. Here is how an English Puritan, writing in the 1580s, saw it:

> What dicing and carding, what eating and drinking, what banqueting and feasting is then used, more than in all the year besides. . . . What more mischief is that time committed . . . ; what masking and mumming, whereby robbery, whoredom, murder and what not is committed?[6]

People might don the masks of animals and act under cover of anonymity (a practice known as "mumming"). And the social hierarchy itself might be symbolically turned upside down, inverting designated roles of age, gender, and class. A boy might be chosen "bishop" and take on for a brief time some of a real bishop's authority. Men might dress like women; and women might dress (and act!) like men. A peasant or apprentice might become "Lord of Misrule" and mimic the authority of a *real* "gentleman."[7]

This was exactly the kind of behavior the Puritans tried hard to suppress when they came to power in England (and New England) in the middle of the seventeenth century. One unhappy Englishman referred to such Christmas rituals as nothing more than "liberty and harmless sports . . . [by] which the toiling plowswain and labourer were wont to be recreated, and their spirits and hopes revived for a whole twelve month." But the Puritans had made these innocent customs "extinct and put out of use . . . as if they never had been. . . . Thus are the merry lords of misrule suppressed by the mad lords of bad rule at Westminster [i.e., the Parliament]."[8]

One rather common nighttime Christmas ritual was known in England as "wassailing." Here poor people marched rowdily to the houses of the local gentry, demanding entry and calling for gifts to be presented on the spot—gifts of food, drink, even money. There was always the threat of damage if the demands were not met—wassail could always turn into charivari—but there was also the promise of "good will" if the wassailers were treated well. One surviving wassail song contains this blunt demand and threat:

> We've come here to claim our right. . . .
> And if you don't open up your door,
> We will lay you flat upon the floor.

Another begins with a promise: "Come, butler, draw us a bowl of the best/Then we hope your soul in heaven shall rest"; but the threat follows quickly: "But if you draw us a bowl of the small,/ Then down will come butler, bowl, and all." Other wassail songs simply demanded cash.[9] All in all, the custom was a far cry from its prettified modern reincarnation, where well-dressed carolers stroll amiably through neighborhoods resembling their own, singing cheerily but pounding on no doors, demanding no favors, uttering no threats. The same contrast holds true for most of the familiar "old" Christmas rituals we practice today.

In an agricultural economy, this kind of "misrule" did not really challenge the authority or the position of the gentry. E.P. Thompson has noted that landed gentlemen could always try to use a generous handout at Christmas as a way of making up for a year's accumulation of small injustices, regaining in the process their tenants' "good-will." In fact, episodes of misrule were widely tolerated by the elite. Some historians argue that role inversions actually functioned as a kind of safety valve that contained class resentments within clearly defined limits, and that by *inverting* the established hierarchy (rather than simply ignoring it), role inversions actually served to reaffirm the existing social order.[10] It was all a little like Halloween today—when, for a single evening, children "assume" the right to enter the houses of neighbors and even strangers, to *demand* of their elders a gift (or "treat"), and to threaten them, should they fail to provide one, with punishment (or "trick").

But the eighteenth-century upper classes, at least in England, severed the paternalist bonds that may have allowed "misrule" rituals to operate as a safety valve. E.P. Thompson has argued that in eighteenth-century England both the gentry and the established church abandoned their control over holiday rituals; these now became distinctly "plebeian" cultural expressions, purged of Christian references. In this new setting, rituals of misrule began to assume a more clearly *oppositional* form. Thompson describes these eighteenth-century protests as a kind of political "theater" directed at the gentry "audience" before whom it was "performed"—something less than a full-fledged radical "movement," but more than sheer unfocused rowdiness.[11] For example, in eighteenth-century England there appeared a kind of late-night serenade on New Year's Eve known as the "Callithumpian band"—possibly derived from the Greek word *calli* (meaning "beautiful"). But the music these bands played was hardly beautiful. It was meant to be loud and offensive, characterized by "beating on tin pans, blowing horns, shouts, groans, catcalls," and it was performed as a gesture of deliberate mockery—the general term in England for such things was "rough music." (This was not wholly new; "rough music" is simply the British term for what in France was called *charivari*. But the Callithumpian bands seem to have directed their "rough music" against those who seemed to be claiming too much dignity, or abusing their power.)

By the early nineteenth century, with the spread of wage labor and other modes of capitalist production in England and the United States, what I have chosen to call the "battle for Christmas" entered an acute phase. For some urban workers, the Christmas season no longer entailed a lull in the demand for labor; their employers insisted on business as usual.[12] (It was this impulse that Charles Dickens caricatured in the behavior of his character Ebenezer Scrooge.) For other urban workers, the coming of winter brought the prospect of being laid off, as the icing-up of rivers brought water-powered factories to a seasonal halt; December's leisure thus meant not relative plenty—but forced unemployment and want. The Christmas season, with its traditions of wassail, misrule, and Callithumpian "street theater," could easily become a vehicle for social protest, an instrument to express powerful ethnic or class resentments. Little wonder, then, that the upper classes displayed little interest in making the season into a major holiday. The turn of the nineteenth century seems to have marked a historic low point in the celebration of Christmas among the elite.

❧

Let me return, then, to New York City, where John Pintard's neighborhood was subjected to the "rough music" of a Callithumpian band in 1821, and where our modern American Christmas was invented the following year with the composition of Clement Clarke Moore's poem "A Visit from St. Nicholas." New York in the early nineteenth century was a fast-growing place. As late as 1800, the urbanized part of the city covered only a small area at the southern tip of Manhattan Island—the area to the south of what are now the numbered streets. But the size of the city's population had begun a rapid, almost geometrical, increase—from 33,000 in 1790 to 200,000 in 1830 and 270,000 just five years later. In order to accommodate the rapid increase in population, the city in 1811 started implementation of a plan to construct a regular grid system of numbered streets (and avenues) that would crisscross the entire island. (I shall have something to say shortly about the effects of this plan on Clement Clarke Moore.)

This numerical growth was accompanied by a change in the composition of the city's population: an influx of immigrants, especially Irish Catholics, and the appearance of an impoverished under class living for the first time in its own "poor" districts (generally divided up by ethnicity and race) along with a wealthy upper class living for the first time in *its* fashionable ones.[13] In the second decade of the nineteenth century, New York underwent an explosion of poverty, vagrancy, and homelessness followed in the third decade by the persistent danger of serious public violence. In the eyes of New York's "respectable" citizens, to quote a recent historian of the subject, "the entire city appeared to have succumbed to disorder. . . . [It] seemed to be coming apart completely."[14] Many well-to-do New Yorkers began to move out to new uptown estates, which they enclosed with fences or hedges. In turn, those fences were sometimes pulled down and hedges uprooted by poor and homeless people who persisted in regarding the new estates as "common land" open to their own use. By the 1820s these estates were commonly guarded by private watchmen, drawn from the same under class.

The city's streets became the center of a different version of the same conflict. As Elizabeth Blackmar has written, the city's poorest residents—"peddlers, ragpickers, prostitutes, scavengers, beggars, and . . . criminals"—depended for subsistence on the freedom of the streets and the unregulated opportunity to accost strangers at will, whether for legal or illegal purposes. By the 1820s the propertied classes were making systematic efforts to protect themselves from such "unwanted intrusions from the streets."[15]

John Pintard, for one, was deeply troubled by the increasing visibility of poor people and by the danger their aggressive behavior posed to "respectable" New Yorkers.[16] Pintard was the moving force behind the establishment in 1817 of the Society for the Prevention of Pauperism, an organization designed to put both a cap on the skyrocketing costs of poor relief and a stop to the public begging and drinking of the poor themselves—in order to make the city streets a safe place for people like himself.[17] Needless to say, all these efforts failed. By 1828 Pintard was acknowledging that the problems of poverty, drinking, and street crime had, "I confess, baffled all our skill. . . . The evil is obvious, acknowledged by all, but a sovereign remedy appears to be impossible."[18]

It should not be a surprise that all this was reflected in the transformation of the Christmas season. What Susan G. Davis has demonstrated in her study of Philadelphia holds equally true of New York. By the 1820s, bands of roaming young street toughs, members of the emerging urban proletariat, were no longer restricting their seasonal reveling to their own neighborhoods; they had begun to travel freely, and menacingly, wherever they pleased. Often carousing in disguise (a holdover from the old tradition of "mumming"), these street gangs marauded through the city's wealthy neighborhoods, especially on New Year's Eve, in the form of Callithumpian bands that resembled (and may have overlapped with) the street gangs that were now vying for control of the city's poorer neighborhoods. Throughout the night these bands made as much noise as they could, sometimes stopping deliberately at the houses of the rich and powerful.[19] In 1826, for example, such a gang stopped in front of the Broadway house of the city's mayor; there they "enacted" what a local newspaper termed "a scene of disgraceful rage."[20] The next year, another newspaper sarcastically described these same gangs as "a number of ill-bred boys, chimney sweeps, and other illustrious and aspiring persons" whose sole purpose was "to perambulate the streets all night, disturbing the slumbers of the weary . . . by thumping upon tin kettles, sounding penny[whistles] and other martial trumpets."[21] John Pintard would have understood.

In 1828 there occurred an extensive and especially violent Callithumpian parade, complete with the standard array of "drums, tin kettles, rattles, horns, whistles, and a variety of other instruments." This parade began along the working-class Bowery, where the band pelted a tavern with lime; then it marched to Broadway, where a fancy upper-class ball was being held at the City Hotel; then to a black neighborhood, stopping at a church where the Callithumpians "demolished all the windows, broke the doors [and] seats," and beat with sticks and ropes the African-American congregants who were holding a "watch" service; next, the band headed to the city's main commercial district, where they smashed crates and barrels and looted at least one shop; still unsatisfied, they headed to the Battery (at the southern tip of the city), where they broke the windows of several of the city's *wealthiest* residences and tried to remove the iron fence that surrounded Battery Park; finally they headed back to Broadway for a second visit. This time a group of hired watchmen were waiting for the Callithumpians; but the band stood down the watch-force, and, in the words of a local newspaper, "the multitude passed noisily and triumphantly up Broadway."[22]

What are we to make of scenes like this? I would agree with E.P. Thompson that it would be misleading to interpret them either as wholly conscious political protest *or* as mere revelry that had gotten out of hand, a kind of nineteenth-century frat party. Susan G. Davis, in her study of Christmas disorders in Philadelphia, has put it like this: "Riotous disorder, racial violence, and jolly foolery for neighbors and audiences existed side by side . . . for decades. . . . Customary Christmas license combined with seasonal unemployment made the winter holiday a noisy, drunken, threatening period in the eyes of the respectable." And Paul Gilje suggests that New York's Callithumpians, too, can be considered "a bridge between the traditional youth group misrule of the English village . . . and a more direct challenge to authority."[23]

John Pintard offered his own interpretation of the situation in December 1823. He mused that it might be the culture of Protestantism itself that was to blame for New York's problems. Protestants, he argued, unlike Catholics and even pagans, had systematically suppressed the kind of "religious festivals" at which "mechanics and laborers" could find officially sanctioned and organized "processions" that would allow them to release their "pent up" energies in satisfying but orderly ways.[24]

In fact, Pintard himself was drawn almost compulsively to ceremony, ritual, and tradition—for himself and his family, for New York City, even for the United States as a nation. And when he could not find such things, he devised them. (One of the nation's first antiquarians, Pintard was the founder of the New-York Historical Society in 1804; and he even played a role in the establishment of Washington's Birthday, the Fourth of July, and Columbus Day as national holidays.[25]) In fact, it was John Pintard who brought St. Nicholas to America, in an effort to make that figure both the icon of the New-York Historical Society and the patron saint of New York City. In 1810 Pintard paid for the publication of a broadside, sponsored by the historical society, that featured a picture of St. Nicholas bringing gifts to children at the Christmas season (actually, on St. Nicholas's Day, December 6). The picture was accompanied by a short poem, "Sancte Claus goed heylig man."[26]

In his letters, Pintard regularly expressed nostalgia for what he called the "old customs" and "ancient usages" of New York, and particularly for the forgotten spirit of the old Christmas season, when rich folk and poor, old and young, would mingle together in genial harmony in the streets of the city.[27] But Pintard never managed to discover or devise any way of observing the Christmas holidays that actually involved working-class people. All of his own carefully planned seasonal rituals were restricted to the members of his own social class (recall, for example, the formalized New Year's Day I described at the very beginning of this essay). The reason for this constriction was clear: It had simply become impossible for New York's respectable citizens to continue participating in the rowdy old cross-class celebrations that Pintard recalled fondly from his own youth. (Those celebrations involved public drinking; and, as Pintard put it in 1827, "since staggering through the streets on New Years day is out of fashion, it is impossible to drink drams at every house as of old.") And while Pintard sorely regretted the disappearance of the good will evident in those days on such occasions of public drinking—he referred to these as "the joyous older fashion"—he also understood that the social price to be paid for that good will had become impossibly high. Sobriety had become a necessity: "It is well," Pintard acknowledged with what I take to be a kind of sigh—"for formerly New Years was a riotous day." And he quickly added, as if suddenly recalling that the *real* problem was a *present-day* one, that "the beastly vice of drunkenness among the lower laboring classes is growing to a frightful excess. . . . Thefts, incendiaries, and murders—which prevail—all arise from this source."[28] After all, that is why he had founded the Society for the Prevention of Pauperism.

Since there existed no Christmas rituals that were socially acceptable to the upper class, Pintard took on the responsibility for inventing them—characteristically enough, in the name of restoring that which had been forgotten. For more than 20 years, roughly between 1810 and 1830, he tried almost every year to come up with the perfect holiday. (Before the late 1820s these did not involve Christmas day itself; until 1827, Pintard always observed that day in simple fashion, as a time of prayer and private religious devotion.)

In the 1810s, Pintard organized and led elaborate St. Nicholas's Day banquets for his fellow members of the New-York Historical Society, held at the society's office in city hall. But in 1820 his celebration of St. Nicholas's Day was interrupted: "At six [P.M.] I attended [a meeting of] the Pauperism Society, for even festivity must not interfere with works of benevolence." That, as it happens, is the last mention of St. Nicholas's Day in Pintard's published correspondence. By this time, and with increasing intensity of commitment through most of the 1820s, he had turned to New Year's Day: holding lavish dinners for his extended family and making formal visitations with old friends and relatives around the city. On

January 1, 1821 Pintard engaged, apparently for the first time, in what he called "the good old custom of mutual visitings and cordial greetings." Pintard devoted each year for the rest of the decade to his attempts to establish New Year's as a day of mutual visitation in New York, describing it (as he did in 1822) as "the custom of the simple Dutch settlers." Pintard sometimes referred to this custom with the phrase "open house," but his use of the phrase is clear: houses were "open" only to old friends and kin—to members of his own class. And in 1828 Pintard ruefully admitted that the phenomenon was fading away in New York—"the joyous older fashion [of visitation] has declined gradually." Two years later he explained why: the practice was becoming "irksome" because "our city grows so extensive, and friends so scattered."[29] But by *then*, as we shall see, Pintard had discovered Christmas.

Pintard was not the only New Yorker interested in restoring the old customs of the Christmas season. In 1819 and 1820 there appeared a book written by a fellow member of the New-York Historical Society—Washington Irving. Irving had actually written parts of *The Sketch Book*, as he titled his new publication, *at* the historical society. The book was a smashing success, one that propelled Irving into sudden transatlantic celebrity. *The Sketch Book* contained two stories that were destined to become classics: "Rip Van Winkle" and "The Legend of Sleepy Hollow." But it also included five stories about Christmas. Unlike "Rip Van Winkle," these Christmas tales were not about the Dutch heritage of New York; instead, they were set on a gracious estate in the modern British countryside, Bracebridge Hall. In these stories Irving used Christmas to imagine a culture in which all the classes joined together in paternalist harmony. Irving's narrator is hosted at Christmas by old Squire Bracebridge, an antiquarian-minded gentleman who is obsessed with the past and who wields the social authority that he is able to recruit the neighboring peasantry to join him in a reenactment, under his direction, of "the holyday customs and rural games of former times." Irving's narrator waxes eloquent as he contemplates "the quaint humours, the burlesque pageants, the complete abandonment to mirth and good fellowship with which this [Christmas] festival was celebrated." The occasion "seemed to throw open every door, and unlock every heart. It brought the peasant and the peer together, and blended all ranks in one warm generous flow of joy and kindness."

At the climax of the Bracebridge Hall stories, the Squire presents a Christmas banquet at which are displayed, along with "brawn and beef, and stout home brewed," all the archaic customs of the season, including a wassail bowl, a Lord of Misrule, and a group of peasants—the old Squire's trusty dependents—who perform an old dance and then mingle gratefully with the Squire's household:

> There is something genuine and affectionate in the gayety of the lower orders, when it is excited by the bounty and familiarity of those above them; the warm glow of gratitude enters into their mirth, and a kind word, and a small pleasantry frankly uttered by a patron, gladdens the heart of the dependant more than oil and wine.

It was, of course, an invention—"the invention of tradition," as historian Eric Hobsbawm has dubbed this kind of self-conscious recreation of ostensibly oldtime customs[30]—and Irving knew that. In fact, he not only knew it, he even took pains to let us in on the secret. The narrator's description of the Squire's Christmas celebration is larded with such terms as "odd and obsolete," "quaint," "ancient," even "eccentric," and in a later edition of *The Sketch Book* Irving admitted that at the time he wrote "Bracebridge Hall" he had never actually seen the kind of Christmas he described in it. Even the Lord of Misrule is fictive: the role is taken by a real gentleman.

Nor is this all. As Squire Bracebridge is driving home from church just before his great dinner party, he engages in a bit of nostalgic commentary. The Squire begins by lamenting

> the deplorable decay of the games and amusements which were once prevalent at this season among the lower orders, and countenanced by the higher. When the old halls of castles and manor houses were thrown open at daylight; . . . and when rich and poor were alike welcome to enter and make merry.

As he continues, the Squire's nostalgia spills over into a confession of his inability to recreate the real rituals of Christmases past. And at precisely this moment, the Squire moves from antiquarianism into political theory—*Tory* political theory:

> The nation . . . is altered; we have almost lost our simple true-hearted peasantry. They have broken asunder from the higher classes, and seem to think their interests are separate. They have become too knowing, and

> begin to read newspapers, listen to ale house politicians, and talk of reform. I think one mode to keep them in good humor in these hard times, would be for the nobility and gentry to pass more time on their estates, mingle more among the country people, and set the merry old English games going again.

At this point, Irving's own narrative voice takes over from Squire Bracebridge. "Such," Irving writes, "was the good Squire's project for mitigating public discontent; and, indeed, he had once attempted to put his doctrine in[to] practice, and a few years before had *kept open house during the holidays in the old style*" [italics added]. But the open house experiment had failed:

> The country people . . . did not understand how to play their parts in the scene of hospitality: many uncouth circumstances occurred [these Irving does not describe]; the manor was overrun by all the vagrants of the country, and more beggars [were] drawn into the neighborhood in one week than the parish officers could get rid of in a year.

So the Squire was forced to back off his original "project." Nowadays, Irving tells us, he "contented himself with inviting the *decent part* of the neighboring peasantry to call at the hall on Christmas day" [italics added]. It is that select group, and not the entire "neighborhood," which comes to Bracebridge Hall (at the stipulated time) to entertain and mingle with the Squire's *real* guests.

But so self-conscious is this scene—so close to the edge of silliness—that Irving himself suspected it might ring false to his contemporary readers. For as the Squire "mingled among the rustics" and was "received with awkward demonstrations of deference and regard," Irving's narrator observes something that escapes the notice of his host, Squire Bracebridge: "I perceived two or three of the younger peasants, as they were raising their tankards to their mouths, when the Squire's back was turned, making something of a grimace, and giving each other the wink, but the moment they caught my eye they pulled grave faces, and were exceedingly demure." Irving surely wrote this little scene to protect his credibility with an 1820 audience, and his meaning would have been clear enough to the knowing reader: Despite all the precautions Squire Bracebridge had taken to do the job right, he had been unable to keep even the "decent part" of the local peasantry in "good humor" on Christmas Day.

The Bracebridge Hall stories proved immensely popular, and they played an important part in restoring the interest of "respectable" Americans (and Britishers) in celebrating Christmas. Indeed, it was Irving's Bracebridge Hall sketches, together with the stories of Charles Dickens, that provided much of what a recent book terms the "enduring imagery of Christmas which is annually reiterated in Christmas cards and festive illustrations, where jovial squires entertain friends and retainers by roaring fires, and stout coachmen, swathed in greatcoats, urge horses down snow-covered lanes as they bring anticipatory guests and homesick relations to their welcoming destinations."[31]

Irving's vision of Christmas did not exactly offer a practical model for anyone who was tempted—and many must have been—to celebrate Christmas in this fashion. How could John Pintard, say, reproduce a ritual that Washington Irving himself found difficult even to *imagine* for his readers? It is easy to sympathize with Pintard, who, I am confident, read *The Sketch Book* and felt the power of Irving's vision. But it was easier for Irving to imagine such a scene than for John Pintard to duplicate it, even though it may have been the Bracebridge Hall stories that inspired—and finally frustrated—Pintard's elaborate efforts during the 1820s to recreate an oldtime New Year's Day. Pintard would not be satisfied until he discovered what had happened, in the hands of his friend Clement Clarke Moore, to a figure that he himself had originally introduced—that is, of course, the figure of St. Nicholas.

As late as 1826, Pintard did not associate Christmas itself with St. Nicholas (or with anything at all except attending church and what Pintard termed "solemni[ty]" and "devotional feelings"). Pintard went to church on Christmas in 1827, too; but there was something new that year: "We had St. Claas in high snuff," Pintard noted, and he referred briefly to the "bon bons" his grandchildren had received. The next year, 1828, Pintard's description was more elaborate:

> All due preparations having been made by the children the preceding evening, by placing hay for his horses [!] and invoking "St. Claas, Gude Heylig Man," he came accordingly during the night, with most elegant toys, bon bons, oranges, etc., all which, after filling the stockings suspended at the sides of mother's chimney, were displayed in goodly order on the mantle, to the ecstatic joy of [the children] in the morning, whose exhaltations resounded through the house.[32]

Pintard's letters from each of the years 1830 through 1832 contain descriptions at least this extensive. By 1831, Pintard was characteristically referring to the ritual as an "ancient usage," adding that "St. Claas is too firmly riveted in this city ever to be forgotten." And in 1832, Pintard concluded a very lengthy account of the children's reactions to Santa's visit with these words: "Happy golden age. All was joy and gladness."[33] That was all there would be; Pintard lived another dozen years (dying at age 85), but he was becoming blind and seems to have stopped writing letters.

❧

Over the two decades from 1810 to 1830, while Pintard shifted his energies from December 6 to January 1, then from January 1 to December 25, this much remained constant: The season was to be celebrated with members of his own social class. But one thing had changed nevertheless, and something more important than the simple date of the celebration. What had changed was this: Pintard had gradually moved from a celebration that took place in public (first at city hall, with the New-York Historical Society; then on the city streets, and in the houses of kinsmen and old acquaintances) to one that took place in private, in his own home, with his immediate family, and—just as important—a celebration that was focused on a single group within the family: young children.

Such a child-centered event was new. Before the nineteenth century, children were merely dependents, miniature adults who occupied the bottom of the hierarchy within the family. But perhaps that was exactly the point. Making children the center of joyous attention marked an inversion of the social hierarchy. In essence, the structure of an older Christmas ritual *was being precisely preserved:* people in positions of social and economic authority were offering gifts to their dependents. The ritual of social inversion was still there, but now it was based on age and family status alone. The children of a single household had replaced a larger group of the poor and powerless as the symbolic objects of charity and benevolence. It was those children who became the temporary centers of the attention and deference at Christmas, and the joy and gratitude on those children's faces and in their voices as they opened their presents was a vivid recreation of the exchange of gifts for "good will" that had long constituted the emotional heart of the Christmas season.

It was just such an exchange that Washington Irving had evoked in "Bracebridge Hall" when he insisted that "there is something genuine and affectionate in the gayety of the lower orders, when it is excited by the bounty and familiarity of those above them; [how] the warm glow of gratitude enters into their mirth, and a kind word, and a small pleasantry frankly uttered by a patron, gladdens the heart of the dependant more than oil and wine." Such an exchange had particular appeal during the 1820s for the urban upper classes, precisely because they were still residually sensitive to the need to demonstrate noblesse, especially during the Christmas season. But Irving, who continued to place the patron-client exchange in the older context of social class, was able to imagine it only with difficulty. Clement Clarke Moore, by translating the patron-client exchange from one between the classes to one between the generations, helped transform it into a practical, simple ritual that almost any household could perform. And eventually, as we know only too well, almost every household *would*.

❧

Nowadays, many Americans believe that there was nothing new about "the night before Christmas" described in Moore's poem—that the story it told was simply an old Dutch tradition brought to the New World in the seventeenth century and then, in the natural course of things, gradually "Americanized." That is just what John Pintard would wish us to believe (and he may even have believed it himself).

But the preeminent scholar of St. Nicholas in our own day has shown that this could not have been the case. In an article published in 1954, Charles W. Jones argued forcefully that "there is no evidence that [the cult of Santa Claus] existed in New Amsterdam, or for [more than] a century after British occupation." Jones pointed out that *nobody* has ever found any contemporary evidence of such a St. Nicholas "cult" in New York during the colonial period.[34] Instead, the familiar Santa Claus story appears to have been devised in the early nineteenth century, over the two decades that ended in the early 1820s. It seems likely that a similar ritual, along with others, was sometimes practiced in seventeenth-century Holland, on St. Nicholas's Day, December 6; but I am persuaded by Charles Jones that the "Santa Claus" devised in early nineteenth-century New York was in any case a conscious reconstruction of that ritual, and not its natural continuation.

I do not mean that "the night before Christmas" belongs to Clement Clarke Moore alone. In fact, it was the work of a small group of antiquarian-minded New York gentlemen—men who knew each other and who were members of a distinct social set. Collectively, those men became known as the Knickerbockers; the name comes from an immensely popular book published in 1809 by the single best-known member of the group, Washington Irving. That book, commonly known as the *Knickerbocker History of New York*, was a brilliantly satirical allegory about life in the contemporary city that Irving lived in but was written in the guise of a history of New Amsterdam in old Dutch times. Irving himself mentioned St. Nicholas 25 times in the *Knickerbocker History*, including references to his wagon, his pipe (more of that later), and a line that went: "laying his finger beside his nose." Irving even chose to have the *Knickerbocker History* published on St. Nicholas's Day. If it was John Pintard who introduced the figure of St. Nicholas, it was Washington Irving who popularized it. In the words of Charles W. Jones, "Without Irving there would be no Santa Claus. . . . Santa Claus was *made* by Washington Irving."[35]

The real Knickerbockers were men—and men they all were—who inhabited a special niche in the world of early nineteenth-century New York. As a rule, they were of British, not Dutch, descent. They were members of the Episcopal Church, and of its "High Church" faction. They belonged to the wealthy old aristocracy of the city (or they identified themselves with it). And they were politically conservative, reactionary even—opposed to democracy (which they identified with mob rule) and fearful of both the working class and the new bourgeoisie. Indeed, they often failed to distinguish between the two, sometimes lumping them together with the general yet quite telling word *plebeian*.

For example, in his *Knickerbocker History of New York*, Washington Irving disdainfully summarized in a single sentence an episode that clearly represented to his readers the Jeffersonian revolution of

1800: "[J]ust about this time the mob, since called the sovereign people . . . exhibited a strange desire of governing itself."[36] And in 1822 (the year "A Visit from St. Nicholas" was written), John Pintard explained to his daughter just why he was opposed to a new state constitution adopted that year, a constitution that gave men without property the right to vote: "All power," Pintard wrote, "is to be given, by the right of universal suffrage, to a mass of people, especially in *this* city, which has no stake in society. It is easier to raise a mob than to quell it, and we shall hereafter be governed by rank democracy. . . . Alas that the proud state of New York should be engulfed in the abyss of ruin."[37]

In short, the Knickerbockers felt that they belonged to a patrician class whose authority was under siege. From that angle, their invention of Santa Claus was part of a larger, ultimately quite serious cultural enterprise: forging a pseudo-Dutch identity for New York, a placid "folk" identity that could provide a cultural counterweight to the commercial bustle and democratic "misrule" of early nineteenth-century New York. The best-known literary expression of this larger enterprise is Irving's classic story "Rip Van Winkle" (published a full decade after the *Knickbocker History*). But in the *Knickerbocker History*, too, Irving pictured old New Amsterdam as a place of "filial piety" in which people thought and acted "with characteristic slowness and circumspection . . . ; who adhere . . . to the customs . . . of their revered forefathers." New Amsterdam was a serene place in which people (watched over by good St. Nicholas himself) "did not regulate their time by hours, but by [the smoking of] pipes."[38]

Which finally brings me to Clement Clarke Moore, the author of "A Visit from St. Nicholas." *Clement Clarke Moore:* If we have any image of the man at all, it is apt to be of a benevolent figure, a scholarly but genial professor of Hebrew who stepped, just this once, out of his ivory tower to write for his children those magical verses about what happened on "the night before Christmas." He is a man who would seem to be as distant from the wider currents of history and politics as the figure of Santa Claus himself.

The image is not necessarily false, and it is not my intention to dispel it. Still, Moore *did* have a real existence: He was born in 1779 (during the American Revolution) and died 84 years later, in 1863 (during the Civil War). He fits perfectly the Knickerbocker mold—Episcopalian, conservative, and upper-class. Moore's father was for

35 years the Episcopal bishop of the diocese of New York, and Moore himself, though a layman, was an active and influential figure in the Episcopal Church. (In fact, Moore held his professorship in a seminary that he himself had helped set up.)

Moore was also conservative. His parents and grandparents had been closet Tories during the American Revolution, and open Federalists afterwards. Moore's own brand of conservatism took the form of an agrarian paternalism not far removed from that of some wealthy Virginia planter of the same generation. As a young man, Clement Clarke Moore himself published a series of tracts attacking both Jeffersonian radicalism and urban commerce, and to the end of his life he remained suspicious of democracy and other "reforms." For example, in his middle age Moore opposed the movement to abolish slavery. Indeed, at the time Moore wrote "A Visit from St. Nicholas" in 1822, he owned five slaves.[39]

Moore's ideology was well suited to his social position. He was an old-style country gentleman, a patrician man of leisure who inherited so much land (and the income it brought) that he never needed to take a job. (Moore accepted his professorship when he was past 40, and for a token salary, in a seminary constructed on land he himself had donated for the purpose.[40] He was also wealthy enough to be the subject of no fewer than four commissioned portraits.) Moore inherited his mother's large Manhattan estate, originally located well to the north of New York City. This estate, which bore the name "Chelsea," extended all the way from what is now Nineteenth Street to Twenty-fourth Street, and from Eighth Avenue to Tenth. (The estate gave its name to the present-day Chelsea district of the city, just north of Greenwich Village.)

But when Moore was a young man, this area was isolated and pastoral.[41] John Pintard, who knew Moore well, wrote in 1830 that his Chelsea estate alone was worth $500,000. Pintard acknowledged Moore as his own social superior: Pintard wrote that even though he and Moore "have been always on the most friendly terms, . . . I have resisted all hospitalities when sitting in [his] elegantly furnished drawing room, for *he* is *wealthy.*"[42]

Still, Moore's great wealth did not prove sufficient to insulate him from the pressures that were transforming New York in the first decades of the nineteenth century. In 1811 the New York City Council approved a grid system of numbered streets and avenues to crisscross the island above Fourteenth Street. By the time Moore wrote "A Visit from Saint Nicholas," New York was expanding north through "Chelsea" itself. In fact, late in 1818, something called "Ninth Avenue" was dug right through the middle of his estate (the land having been taken from him by eminent domain).[43] The 1821 city directory lists Moore as residing not at "Chelsea" but near the corner of Ninth Avenue and Twenty-first Street.[44] Eleven years later, in 1832, John Pintard visited Chelsea and mused about the changes that had overtaken the neighborhood, filled now (as Pintard put it) with "streets that have become regularly built up . . . where, but a few years ago, all was open country. It really surprised me to notice a dense population and contiguous buildings in what only 10 years since was merely a sparse city."[45] By the 1850s the entire hill on which Moore's house stood had been leveled to make new land and bulkheads along the Hudson River waterfront, and Moore had built new homes for himself and his family.[46] (See Figure 1.)

Moore was disturbed by the transformation of his city and the cutting-up of his estate. In 1818, the very year that his property was bisected by Ninth Avenue (and just four years before he wrote "A Visit from St. Nicholas"), Moore published a pamphlet that protested against the relentless development of New York. In it he expressed a fear that the city's beauty and tranquility would be lost forever and that its future was already in what he termed "destructive and ruthless hands," the hands of men who did not "respect the rights of property." City politics and policy were controlled by men Moore described as "mechanics and persons whose influence is principally among those classes of the community to whom it is indifferent what the eventual result of their industry may be to society." New York was being turned over to a conspiracy, and Moore named its members: "cartmen, carpenters, masons, pavers, and all their host of attendant laborers." Moore doubted that the city could be (as he put it) "save[d] from ruin." And he was pessimistic about the future of his class: "We know not the amount nor the extent of oppression which may yet be reserved for us."[47]

It was at this difficult juncture, in 1822, that Clement Clarke Moore wrote "A Visit from St. Nicholas." I have already noted that Moore did not invent "the night before Christmas" out of whole cloth. In the distant background was the old Dutch ritual. John Pintard and Washington Irving offered more immediate models.

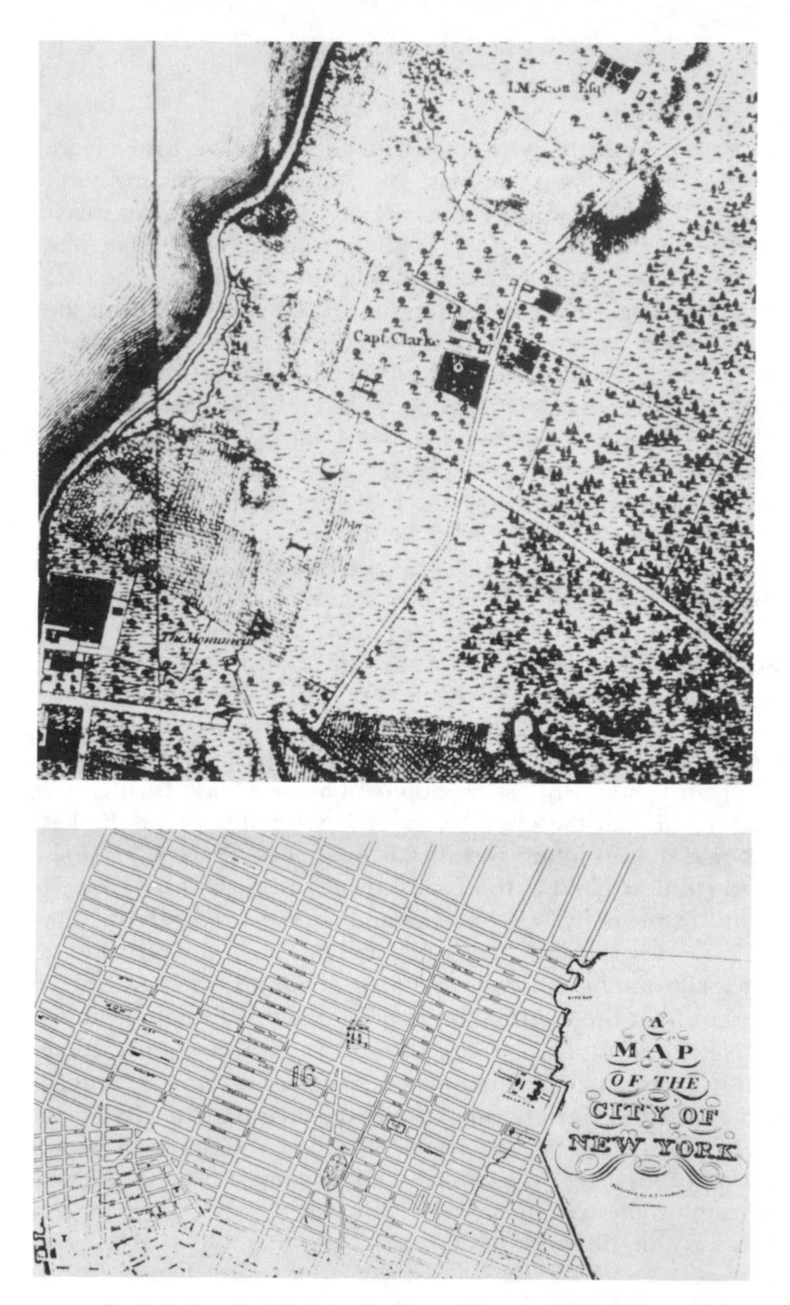

FIGURE 1. "Chelsea" in 1767 (above) and 1837 (below). (Courtesy of the New-York Historical Society.)

And three other poems, two from 1810 and the third from 1821, would provide still further materials, such as Santa's sleigh and reindeer, and even the poetic meter that Moore would employ. Moore's own contributions may have been small ones, but I believe they were crucial to the creation of a myth that suited the needs of Moore's own Knickerbocker set. It finally proved malleable enough to transcend those needs and eventually to be appropriated by other groups of Americans. Let me demonstrate what I mean by examining more closely the sources Moore had at his disposal.

First, Washington Irving. Yes, there *were* 25 references to St. Nicholas in the *Knickerbocker History*. But Irving represented St. Nicholas not as a figure who appeared during the Christmas season but rather in the way that John Pintard had *originally* introduced him to the New-York Historical Society—that is, as the mythic patron saint of New Amsterdam. Early in the *Knickerbocker History*, Irving wrote that "the great and good St. Nicholas . . . took . . . New Amsterdam under his peculiar patronage, and has ever since been . . . the titular saint of this excellent city." In this role, St. Nicholas (he never actually *appears*, except once in a dream-scene and again as the figurehead of a ship) was essentially an amusing caricature of the old-time Dutch gentry who inhabited Irving's imaginary New Amsterdam: a genial yet obviously patrician saint, dressed in a broad hat and invariably smoking a long pipe.[48] (Clement Clarke Moore would later pick *that* up, but with one difference.)

Next, the 1810 broadside picture that John Pintard commissioned (together with the verse that accompanied it); then the two anonymous poems, one from 1810 and the other from 1821. In each of those the pipe disappeared, and so did the satire, and St. Nicholas himself finally became a figure who distributed gifts to children during the Christmas season. But in all these sources, St. Nicholas was still very much a figure of majesty and authority—or at least of benevolent, kindly dignity. (The *real* St. Nicholas, if he existed at all, was an actual bishop, and in any case he was an official saint, the *real* patron saint of both Russia and Greece.) As a bishop, St. Nicholas was the direct representative of God and a figure of great authority as well as great charity. So it is not surprising that John Pintard would wish him to be represented in such a "serious" fashion in the broadside he commissioned and not, as

Washington Irving had irreverently done, as a humorous figure. (See Figure 2.)

In this picture, St. Nicholas comes not just to reward but also to punish. In the right-hand panel stand two children: a pleased little girl who has received a present and a tearful little boy who has not (perhaps he has received a caning instead). St. Nicholas himself is a figure of authority: We see him with his halo, ecclesiastical robes, and bishop's scepter. John Pintard confirmed the image in a short poem placed beneath the picture, a child's poem that begins "St. Nicholas, good holy Man" and concludes, "St. Nicholas, my dear good friend, / To serve you ever was my end. / If you will now, me, something give, / I'll serve you ever while I live."

St. Nicholas retained his air of authority in a poem that appeared in a New York newspaper just two weeks after Pintard's broadside. This poem, essentially a longer, more elaborate version of Pintard's, opens in similar fashion, with a child hailing St. Nicholas, this time not in awkward iambic but in a more tripping meter—in fact, the exact meter that Moore would employ 12 years later, anapestic tetrameter. It opens: "Oh good holy man! whom we Sancte Claus name, / The Nursery forever your praise shall proclaim." The poem goes on to catalog the presents St. Nicholas might be hoped to leave, followed by a "prayer" that St. Nicholas not come for the purpose of punishment. ("[I]f in your hurry one thing you mislay, / Let that be the Rod—and oh! keep it away.") The poem concludes with a promise of future good behavior:

> Then holy St. Nicholas! all the year,
> Our books we will love and our parents revere,
> From naughty behavior we'll always refrain,
> In hopes that you'll come and reward us again.

The pattern of authority and judgment holds even in the poem that was Clement Clarke Moore's most immediate source. Published in 1821, only a year before Moore wrote "A Visit from St. Nicholas," this poem appeared as a little illustrated book called *The Children's Friend.* Here, for the first time, we even find St. Nicholas appearing not on December 6 but on Christmas Eve; and we even find him traveling on a sleigh that is pulled by a reindeer—a single reindeer. But he is still a bishop (a "child's bishop," perhaps), a fig-

FIGURE 2. "St. Nicholas," 1810. John Pintard commissioned this woodcut (by Alexander Anderson), which was published as a broadside by the New-York Historical Society. It was accompanied by a short poem beginning "St. Nicholas, good holy man." (Courtesy of the New-York Historical Society.)

ure who metes out punishments along with rewards, and whose visit is designed to inspire anxiety along with hope (see Figure 3):

> Old SANTECLAUS with much delight
> His reindeer drives this frosty night,
> O'er chimneytops, and tracks of snow,
> To bring his yearly gifts to you.

FIGURE 3. "St. Nicholas," 1821. One of eight illustrations for *The Children's Friend.* This St. Nicholas, like the one in Figure 2, is holding a bishop's scepter (as well as wearing a bishop's hat and robe).

The steady friend of virtuous youth,
The friend of duty, and of truth,
Each Christmas eve he joys to come
Where love and peace have made their home.

Through many houses he has been,
And various beds and stockings seen,
Some, white as snow, and neatly mended,
Others, that seem'd for pigs intended.

Where e'er I found good girls or boys,
That hated quarrels, strife and noise,
I left an apple, or a tart,
Or wooden gun, or painted cart;

To some I gave a pretty doll,
To some a peg-top, or a ball;
No crackers, cannons, squibs, or rockets,
To blow their eyes up, or their pockets.

No drums to stun their Mother's ear,
Nor swords to make their sisters fear;
But pretty books to store their mind
With Knowledge of each various kind.

But where I found the children naughty,
In manners rude, in temper haughty,
Thankless to parents, liars, swearers,
Boxers, or cheats, or base tale-bearers,

I left a long, black, birchen rod,
Such, as the dread command of GOD
Directs a Parent's hand to use
When virtue's path his sons refuse.

This kind of Christmas can be thought of as a mini version of the Day of Judgment. Insofar as the history of gift giving on St. Nicholas's Day can be traced back to Europe (and much of the evidence here strikes me as ambiguous or dubious), it is this kind of "judgmental" ritual that seems to have been involved. It can be seen in a seventeenth-century picture, "St. Nicholas Day," by the Dutch painter Jan Steen, in which there is also a smiling girl (in the foreground) and a tearful boy (on the left); see Figure 4. Even today some Americans celebrate Christmas a little bit in this fashion: it can be found, for example, in the song that begins, "You'd better watch out . . . Santa Claus is coming to town," and goes on, "He knows if you've been sleeping, he knows if you're awake; he knows if you've been bad or good—so be good for goodness' sake!"

To be sure, this kind of Christmas ritual was designed largely for children, while Judgment Day was for adults. Christmas took place once a year, Judgment Day once an eternity. The "judge" at Christmas was St. Nicholas, on Judgment Day it was God himself. Both

FIGURE 4. Jan Steen, "St. Nicholas Day," a seventeenth-century Dutch painting. Observe the bad little boy who is crying at the left (and the two other children who are mocking him) as well as the good little girl in the foreground. (Courtesy of the Rijksmuseum, Amsterdam.)

the rewards and the punishments that were meted out on Christmas—a cookie on the one hand or a birch rod on the other—were far less weighty than those of eternal joy or eternal damnation. But the parallel was always there, and always (I believe) meant to be there. Christmas was a child's version of Judgment Day, and its ambiguous prospects of reward or punishment (like those of Judgment Day itself) were a means of regulating present behavior—and of preparing children for the greater judgment that was to come.

Indeed, *The Children's Friend* even speaks of the birch rod as a product of "the dread command of GOD."

The threat of judgment was gone the next year, when Moore wrote "A Visit from St. Nicholas." Moore's St. Nicholas, as we all know, leaves only presents and good will, and he makes no threats—not even gentle ones. There is no warning of the birch rod, no hints about messy rooms or bad behavior. There is no stick to join the carrot. There is no little Day of Judgment. There is only a "happy Christmas to *all*."

This shift is all the more striking because the *structure* of "A Visit from St. Nicholas" (unlike that of its immediate sources) parallels the structure of a seventeenth-century American poem about the *real* judgment day. That poem, written by Massachusetts clergyman Michael Wigglesworth, was published in 1662 with the title "The Day of Doom." It was nearly as popular in its own time as "A Visit from St. Nicholas" is today, and it retained its popularity into the early nineteenth century.

Both poems begin with people sleeping serenely on a still night, dreaming of good things to come. It is "the night before Christmas" in the one case; "the evening before [Doomsday]" in the other:

Still was the night, Serene and Bright, when all Men sleeping lay;	'Twas the night before Christmas, when all through the house
Calm was the season, and carnal reason thought so 'twould last for ay.	Not a creature was stirring, not even a mouse;
Soul, take thine ease, let sorrow cease, much good thou hast in store:	The stockings were hung by the chimney with care
This was their Song . . . the Evening before.	In hopes that St. Nicholas soon would be there.
Virgins unwise . . . had closed their eyes . . .	The children were nestled all snug in their beds, While visions of sugarplums danced in their heads;
Yea, and the wise through sloth and frailty slumbered.	And mama in her kerchief, and I in my cap,
	Had just settled our brains for a long winter's nap.

Then, suddenly, the slumbering calm is shattered by a sudden interruption that rouses the sleepers, causing them to rush out of bed and run to the window:

For at midnight brake forth a
Light, which turn'd the
night to day,
And speedily an hideous cry
did all the world dismay.
Sinners awake, their hearts
do ache, trembling their
loins surprizeth;
Amazed with fear, by what
they hear each one of them
ariseth.
They rush from Beds with
giddy heads, and to their
windows run,

When out on the lawn there
arose such a clatter,
I sprang from my bed to see
what was the matter.
Away to the window I flew
like a flash,
Tore open the shutters and
threw up the sash.

Through the window they witness the arrival of an unexpected supernatural visitor, a visitor who has arrived through the air to approach them, accompanied by other magical creatures:

Viewing this light, which
shines more bright than
doth the Noonday Sun.

Straightway appears (they
see't with tears) the Son
of God most dread;
Who with his Train comes on
amain to Judge both Quick
and Dead.

His winged Hosts flie through
all coasts, together
gathering
Both good and bad, both quick
and dead, and all to
Judgement bring.

The moon, on the breast of
the new-fallen snow,
Gave a luster of midday to
objects below
When, what to my wondering
eyes should appear,
But a miniature sleigh and
eight tiny reindeer,
With a little old driver so
lively and quick
I knew in a moment it must be
St. Nick.
More rapid than eagles his
coursers they came,
And he whistled and shouted
and called them by name. . . .

These parallels make the contrasts between the two poems all the more acute. In "The Day of Doom," the supernatural visitor has come as a pitiless judge; he causes everyone to come before his "throne," to separate those who can look forward to eternal happiness from those filled with the "dreadful expectation" of "endless pains and scalding flames." In "A Visit from St. Nicholas," he is a jolly fellow who reassures his startled company that they have "nothing to dread," and who departs from the house wishing happiness "*to all.*"

I am not sure that Clement Clarke Moore read "The Day of Doom." But such are the parallels between the two poems that it is difficult to avoid speculating that the one was written with the other somewhere in mind. If so, then "The Day of Doom" constitutes another source of "A Visit from St. Nicholas."

What Moore has evoked, in any case, is Christmas *without* the prospect of judgment. Without such a prospect, St. Nicholas himself loses his authority—indeed, he loses his very identity as a bishop. And Moore's lengthy physical description of St. Nicholas reinforces the point (such a description is not to be found in *any* of Moore's sources, but here it takes up four of the poem's fourteen stanzas): Santa's eyes "twinkle," his cheeks are "rosy" and his dimples "merry," his mouth is "droll," his figure "chubby and plump," his manner "jolly." He is tiny—the size of an "elf." His appearance and manner actually cause the narrator to laugh out loud, "in spite of [him]self."

In all these ways Moore's St. Nicholas has lost his authority, his majesty, even his patrician dignity. He carries no bishop's scepter. He is clothed not in a bishop's red robes (despite the illustrations we may recall from modern editions of the poem) but in ordinary fur. *This* St. Nicholas is no bishop at all. He has effectively been defrocked.

But if Moore has defrocked St. Nicholas, he has effectively *declassed* him, too. It is not only his authority that has vanished; his gentility is gone, too. Consider how St. Nicholas is pictured in the first illustrated edition of Moore's poem, dating from 1848 (and probably issued with Moore's approval). He looks like a plebeian; and that's also how he is described in the text. Remember that Moore says "he looked like a pedlar"—"a pedlar just opening his pack"—something, that is, between a beggar and a petty tradesman. (See Figure 5.)

FIGURE 5. Clement Clarke Moore's St. Nicholas (from the illustrated edition of 1848).

And he smokes "the stump of a pipe." Now, that little detail comes directly from Washington Irving—and from none of Moore's other sources. Irving invariably associated St. Nicholas with a pipe. But there was a difference: *that* pipe was always referred to as a *long* pipe (indeed, flamboyantly long—in Irving's word, a "mighty" pipe).

Something should be said here about the history and politics of pipes, if only because Irving himself does so. Indeed, there is a chapter in the *Knickerbocker History* that bears the title "Of the Pipe Plot." This chapter has nothing to do with St. Nicholas; what it deals with is the moment at which New Amsterdam (that is, New York) was transformed from a community characterized by "ease, tranquillity, and sobriety of deportment" into "a meddlesome and factious" city. Irving associated this transformation with the Jeffersonian revolution of 1800, the same political upheaval in which "the mob, since called the sovereign people . . . exhibited a strange desire of governing itself." What happened, Irving reported, was that the citizens of New York organized themselves for the first time into two opposing parties. The terms Irving chose to identify these parties are intriguing: "[T]he more wealthy and important . . . formed a kind of aristocracy, which went by the appellation *Long Pipes,* while the lower orders . . . were branded with the plebeian name of *Short Pipes.*"[49]

Clearly, Irving was suggesting that short pipes were associated with working-class radicalism in the early nineteenth century. My own investigation of the question bears Irving out. For example, a recent paper delivered by a historical archaeologist who has been studying artifacts from the boarding houses of the cotton mills in Lowell, Massachusetts, bears the improbable subtitle "Clay Pipes and Class Consciousness." It seems that by the early nineteenth century gentlemen smoked long pipes (some as long as two feet), known as "aldermen" or "church wardens"; workers smoked short pipes (or "cuddies"). It was not out of economic necessity—because short pipes were cheaper—that working-class men (and women) smoked them; rather, they did so as a public gesture of class identity. In fact, the archaeological evidence (in the form of numerous broken-off pipe stems) suggests that workers often purchased longer pipes and then proceeded immediately, before smoking them, to break off the stems. The evidence seems compelling: few of the broken-off stems recovered from the Lowell mills bear any telltale toothmarks.[50] Workers *chose* to smoke "the stump of a pipe." (See Figure 6.)

Which finally brings me to connect literary history with social history, the analysis of genteel mythology with the description of the social change that helped to generate it. Remember what was actually *happening* in the streets of early nineteenth-century New York at the Christmas season: the presence there of marauding bands of revelers who threatened peace and property, whose revelry often turned into riot, who used this annual opportunity to

FIGURE 6. Long pipes and short pipes. In this caricature, drawn by Washington Allston for the frontispiece to Irving's *Knickerbocker History*, the two gentlemen seated on the left are smoking long pipes, while the servant standing behind them is smoking a short one.

symbolically reclaim as their own the fashionable residential territory that had become the private preserve of the well-to-do. Remember the example of John Pintard's unsettling experience on New Year's Eve 1821, when he was kept awake until dawn by the noise of a Callithumpian band that stayed outside his door. Remember Clement Clarke Moore's own anxiety, in the same period, about the slicing-up of his own pastoral estate into city streets for rapid development, the result of a conspiracy of artisans and laborers. Remember that Moore wrote "A Visit from St. Nicholas" in 1822, when the streets had just been dug and the development begun.

Viewed from this angle, there is something resonant about the choices Moore made in writing his little poem—and especially his decision to "defrock" St. Nicholas and to "de-class" him, to take away his clerical authority and his patrician manner, and to represent him instead as a plebeian. Moore's decision meant that his St. Nick resembles, after all, the kind of man who *might* have come to "visit" a wealthy New York patrician on Christmas Eve—to startle him out of his slumber with a loud "clatter" outside his door, perhaps even to enter his house, uninvited and unannounced.

But with this one dramatic difference: The working-class visitor feared by the patrician would come in a different way, for a different purpose. Such a visitor would have inhabited that murky ground between old-style village "wassailing" and new urban political violence. He would have been youthful and full-sized, not a tiny "old elf." He would very likely have been part of a roving gang (perhaps a Callithumpian band), not a single individual. He would have come to make all the noise he could rather than to speak "not a word"; to demand satisfaction, not to give it; to harass or threaten his host, not to reassure him that he "had nothing to dread." And, if he had finally departed in a genial spirit, wishing a "happy Christmas to all, and to all a good night," it would have been because he had *received* satisfaction, not because he had *offered* it. In contrast, the household visitor *Moore* portrays has come neither to threaten his genteel host nor to make any demands on his generosity. The narrator of "A Visit from St. Nicholas" is openly fearful when St. Nicholas first appears—but his fears have been assuaged by the time St. Nicholas departs.

If "A Visit from St. Nicholas" spoke to the physical fears of its upper-class readers, it also addressed their moral *guilt*. What it suggested was that this was one Christmas visitor to whom one owed no obligations, none at all. *This* visitor asks for nothing; by implication, his host owes him nothing. An important point, if one is willing to believe (as I do) that as late as the 1820s many patrician New Yorkers still felt a strong, if inchoate, obligation to be generous to the poor during the emotionally resonant holiday season.

If Moore's upper-class readers were to be comfortable at Christmastime, they needed to have at their disposal a class of dependents whose palpable "good will" would assure them that they had fulfilled their obligations after all. They did this in part, as I have suggested earlier, by substituting their own children for the needy and homeless outside their household. In that way they were preserving the structure of an older Christmas ritual, in which people occupying positions of social and economic authority offered gifts to their dependents. The children in their own households had replaced the poor outside it as the symbolic objects of charity and deference, and the gratitude those children displayed as they opened their presents was a vivid recreation of the exchange of gifts for "good will" that had long constituted the emotional heart of the Christmas season. The ritual of social inversion was still there, but now it remained securely within the household.

Still, *that* change could easily have been implemented without changing St. Nicholas from a bishop and a patrician into a plebeian (indeed, it could have been achieved without the presence of St. Nicholas at all). By representing him as a plebeian, Moore allowed something else to happen. It's a fascinating transformation. Without losing his role as the bringer of gifts, St. Nicholas has assumed an additional role: that of a grateful, nonthreatening, old-style dependent. In the first of these roles (as gift-bringer), St. Nicholas is purely imaginary—a fiction devised for children, a private joke among adults (more about that in a moment). In the second role (as grateful dependent), St. Nicholas is imaginary in a different way, and only in part—a fiction devised for adults, and hardly as a joke; and imaginary only to the degree that, say, the old Dutch yeomanry nostalgically described by Washington Irving in "Rip Van Winkle" or the *Knickerbocker History* were imaginary, or the loyal peasants that Irving presented in his Bracebridge Hall Christmas stories. Like those fictional characters, Moore's St. Nicholas may not have existed; but (in this second role) he too was based on a social prototype that meant a great deal to the upper-class New Yorkers who very much wished to believe that he still *did* exist.

In this way, Moore managed to evoke what had eluded his fellow Knickerbockers, Washington Irving and John Pintard, in their own efforts to recapture the spirit of Christmas past: that is, the integration of the social classes in shared festivity where the poor posed no threat and gratefully accepted their place. Moore did this by replacing the cheerful poor of cherished memory not just with the children of the household but also with the magical figure of St. Nicholas himself. With this tricky maneuver, Moore managed to transform what had been merely archaic and sentimental (and also patronizing) into something I would call mythic.

In order to negotiate that transformation, to create that myth, Moore had to make two simple yet crucial changes: he had to present St. Nicholas as a figure who would evoke in his listeners and readers a working-class image (and not a patrician one) and also a figure who would act the patrician's part (and not the worker's). He had to present St. Nicholas in the *role* of a bishop, but without a bishop's authority to stand in judgment. In short, Moore had to present St. Nicholas as both a bishop and a worker—without either the power of the one or the animosity of the other. He had to devote fully one-third of his poem to offering the reassurance that the people who received visits from this figure of the night would have "nothing to dread."

St. Nicholas first offers that reassurance by giving "a wink of his eye and a twist of his head." And a little later, when St. Nicholas has filled all the stockings and is about to depart, he turns abruptly to face the narrator—the head of the household, or the reader—and places his finger "aside of his nose." A meaningless phrase today—but in the late eighteenth and early nineteenth century, this gesture seems to have represented the equivalent of a secret wink—a visual way of saying something like, "I'm only kidding" or "Let's keep it between the two of us." For example, in Figure 5, the man seated on the left is making this very gesture to the man on the right, who is laughing so hard at the other man's joke that he has dropped his long pipe. In fact, the source of Santa's gesture in "A Visit from St. Nicholas" was a passage in Irving's *Knickerbocker History*, a passage in which St. Nicholas appears in a dream to a character named Van Kortland. The dream concludes with these words: "And when St. Nicholas had smoked his pipe, he twisted it in his hat-band, and *laying his finger beside his nose*, gave the astonished Van Kortland *a very significant look*, then, mounting his wagon, he returned over the tree-tops and disappeared" [italics added]. Since Clement Clarke Moore was obviously alluding to this very passage, St. Nicholas's gesture in his poem can be understood as a signal to the narrator (and to all *adult* readers of the poem): *This is all a dream.* As if to say: "*We* know I don't exist; but let's keep *that* between you and me!"

❧

All a dream. For the upper-class New Yorkers who collectively "invented" Christmas, Moore's quiet little achievement was especially resonant. It offered a Christmas scenario that took a familiar ritual (the exchange of generosity for good will) and transfigured it with a symbolic promise to release them from both the fear of harm and the pressure of guilt. A generation earlier, one might argue, the parents of these men were firmly enough in control of their social world that they yet did not require such a catharsis. A generation later, their children were sufficiently purged of a sense of direct social obligation that they required it no longer.

By the 1850s, in any event, there were other ways of being generous at Christmastime, ways that involved no contact at all with the poor. Charitable agencies had been created that acted as middlemen between the needy and the well-to-do and kept the two sides at a safe distance from each other. Charles Dickens's 1843 book *A Christmas Carol* had a double effect: It rekindled the impulse to assuage the suffering of the needy, and it simultaneously offered people the assurance that they could fulfill this impulse without getting their hands dirty.

By then, "A Visit from St. Nicholas" was taking on new meanings. Santa Claus himself would lose his plebeian character as time passed and as the poem (and the new kind of holiday it helped create) was taken over by the middle classes and even by the poor themselves. Still "plebeian" in the 1840s, Santa and his "team" soon cease being portrayed as miniatures ("eight tiny reindeer," a "miniature sleigh," and a "tiny old elf"). He becomes full-sized, even large. His beard turns into the full gray beard of the late Victorian bourgeoisie. He appears increasingly avuncular. In the hands of Thomas Nast, the famous cartoonist who was responsible for much of this change, over a period of 18 years even his pipe grows long once again. (See Figure 7.) Still, for all these changes, Santa Claus recovers none of the episcopal dignity that Clement Clarke Moore had taken from him in 1822. Between being a tiny plebeian elf and a jolly fat uncle, the "real" St. Nicholas would surely have found it difficult to choose.

❧

Clement Clarke Moore wrote "A Visit from St. Nicholas" on what could be called the cusp of his life. The expansion of New York affected him in a direct way, breaking up his estate into city blocks. Before 1820 he saw this change as a threat, and he protested it accordingly. But after 1820 Moore changed his strategy. He stopped protesting the new conditions and began instead to protect his economic and social position by systematically controlling the development of the Chelsea district. In 1818 he donated an entire city block adjacent to his own house for the construction of an Episcopal theological seminary, and he gave another large parcel for a new and very lavish Episcopal church.[51] By doing so, Moore protected the value of the rest of his holdings in Chelsea. Over the following years he consciously controlled the development of those holdings by leasing lots rather than selling them and by putting restrictive covenants in the deeds he gave builders.[52] Under Moore's careful direction, Chelsea became a fashionable district, an oasis of respectability on New York's west side.

As a great Manhattan landowner, Clement Clarke Moore played a part in the emergence of a new urban landscape, a landscape that stratified and segregated the city by wealth and class, and in which housing itself became a commodity.[53] What I have tried to suggest

FIGURE 7. How Thomas Nast transformed Santa Claus. The illustration above (1864) was Nast's first published Santa Claus picture; here Santa is still a plebeian, and he is smoking a short pipe. By the time Nast published the illustration on the facing page in 1881, Santa had become obese and smug, and his pipe had grown quite long.

in this essay is less easy to prove: It is that Moore helped to bring about a parallel change on the American cultural landscape, in the role for which he is known to most Americans today—as the poet of Christmas Eve. If my reading is correct, it was *that* which constituted his most important contribution to the history of American capitalism.

Notes

1. The episode is recorded by Pintard in a letter written in stages between December 8, 1820, and January 4, 1821 (the passage I have used was written on January 1): *Letters from John Pintard to his Daughter 1816–1833,* vol. I (New York, 1940), 359. I have modernized Pintard's spelling and punctuation. The revelers who disturbed Pintard's sleep would have constituted a Callithumpian band, consisting of young working-class men; by the 1820s these bands had become a menace to more prosperous New Yorkers. See Paul A. Gilje, *The Road to Mobocracy: Popular Disorder in New York City, 1763–1834* (Chapel Hill, N.C., 1989), 254–55.

2. The best account of the non-Christian origins of Christmas rituals is Clement A. Miles, *Christmas in Ritual and Tradition, Christian and Pagan* (London, 1912; reissued by Dover Publications, New York, 1976, as *Christmas Customs and Traditions: Their History and Significance*), 159–360 passim.

3. Ibid., 173–74.
4. See for example John Ashton, *A Right Merrie Christmasse: The Story of Christ-Tide* (New York and London, 1968), 6–8, 45, 246–50. The situation was similar in colonial America: see James H. Barnett, *The American Christmas: A Study in National Culture* (New York, 1954), 9, 11.
5. Charles W. Jones, "Knickerbocker Santa Claus," *The New-York Historical Society Quarterly,* 38 (October 1954), 273.
6. Philip Stubbes, *The Anatomie of Abuses,* quoted in Chris Durston, "Lords of Misrule: The Puritan War on Christmas, 1642–60," *History Today* 35 (1985), 7–14.
7. From this perspective, the real Jewish equivalent of Christmas is not Chanukah but Purim. Purim entails the same ritualized inversion of the social hierarchy (students playing the role of rabbis), the same mockery of the sacred (biblical texts recited in nonsensical juxtaposition), the same carnival atmosphere (parade and masquerade), even a "commandment" to drink until intoxicated. Purim is also a time of charitable giving. See Michael Strassfeld, *The Jewish Holidays, A Guide and Commentary* (New York, 1985), 187–96. This chapter bears the title "Purim: Self-Mockery and Masquerade."
8. John Taylor, *The Complaint of Christmas,* quoted ibid.
9. For example: "Wissal, wissal through the town; / If you've got any apples throw them down; / Up with the stocking, and down with the shoe, / If you've got no apples, money will do." Or these two stanzas from a children's wassail song (only slightly less threatening): "We are not daily beggars / That beg from door to door, / But we are neighbors' children / Whom you have seen before. . . . / We have got a little purse / Made of stretching leather skin, / We want a little of your money / To line it well within." For accounts of wassailing that suggest "misrule," see Ashton, *A Right Merrie Christmasse,* 50–52, 111–12, 120, 125–26, 143–58 passim, 202–4, 214–15, 220–21, 226–27. See also T.G. Grippen, *Christmas and Christmas Lore* (London and Glasgow, 1929), 66, 84–87, 94–104.
10. See Peter Burke, *Popular Culture in Early Modern Europe* (London, 1978), 199–203; Natalie Zemon Davis, "The Reasons of Misrule: Youth Groups and Charivaris in 16th-Century France," *Past and Present* (1971), 41–75.
11. E.P. Thompson, "Patrician Society, Plebeian Culture," *Journal of Social History* 7 (1974), 382–405 (see esp. 390–94). The resurgence of paganism in England during this period has often been noted; Thompson's splendid article places that resurgence in a richly subtle context.
12. Such employers collectively resisted the ongoing tendency of their workers to treat the month of December as a period of leisure and festivity. An instance of English worker resistance to celebrating Christmas on a single day is reported in J.M. Golby and A.W. Purdue, *The Making of the Modern Christmas* (Athens, Ga., 1986), 76. This book offers the best overall history of Christmas I have found.
13. For the transformation of New York, see Gilje, *The Road to Mobocracy;* Christine Stansell, *City of Women: Sex and Class in New York, 1789–1860* (New York,

1986); Elizabeth Blackmar, *Manhattan for Rent, 1785–1850* (Ithaca, N.Y., and London, 1989); Sean Wilentz, *Chants Democratic: New York City & the Rise of the American Working Class, 1788–1850* (New York, 1984); Raymond A. Mohl, *Poverty in New York, 1783–1825* (New York, 1971). The recorded population of New York City increased from 33,131 in 1790 to 202,589 in 1825.

14. Gilje, *The Road to Mobocracy,* 239; see also 135–213. The best brief account of the transformation of early nineteenth-century New York is Stansell, *City of Women,* 4–10.

15. Blackmar, *Manhattan for Rent,* 170–72. According to Blackmar, the poor "used the streets as a common landscape" that provided an opportunity for unregulated, spontaneous encounters with others, encounters that made it possible for them "to gain or supplement subsistence by peddling fruits, oysters, hardware, used clothing, or sexual favors" (or by scavenging, gambling, shoplifting, or fencing stolen goods). "No less than foraging on rural common land, the 'liberty' of the streets supported the city's poorest residents." See also 41–42.

16. See for example letter of December 17, 1828, in Pintard, *Letters,* vol. III, 51–52.

17. October 28, 1818, in Pintard, *Letters,* vol. I, 151. For the Society for the Prevention of Pauperism, see Stansell, *City of Women,* 30–36 (also 18, 71, 164) and Mohl, *Poverty in New York,* ch. 5. The SPP's purposes included the discouragement and "prevention of mendicity and street begging"; the group argued that existing relief policies only served to encourage laziness and dependence on charity (Mohl, *Poverty,* 245). Pintard himself wrote that the SPP was intended to stem the growth of "the present system of relieving the poor," by providing "not . . . alms but labor, so that there shall be no pretext for idleness," and "to expel the drones from society" (Pintard, *Letters,* vol. I, 151).

18. December 16, 1828, Pintard, *Letters,* vol. III, 51–52.

19. Gilje, *The Road to Mobocracy,* 130–33, 253–60. See also Susan G. Davis, "'Making Night Hideous': Christmas Revelry and Public Order in Nineteenth-Century Philadelphia," *American Quarterly* 34 (Summer 1982), 185–99; esp. 186–92. This is the best study of the battle for Christmas in a nineteenth-century city. See also Susan G. Davis, *Parades and Power: Street Theatre in Nineteenth-Century Philadelphia* (Philadelphia, 1986), 38–39, 76–78, 103–9, 158–59.

20. Ibid., 255. The mayor was Philip Hone. In 1837 Hone recorded in his diary a New Year's Day scene at the house of a subsequent mayor: "[T]he rabble . . . use his house as a Five Points tavern. . . . [T]he scene . . . defies description. . . . the tables were taken by storm, the bottles [of wine and punch] emptied in a moment. Confusion, noise, and quarreling ensued, until the Mayor, with the assistance of his police, cleared the house and locked the doors. . . . Every scamp . . . considers himself authorized to use him and his house and his furniture at his pleasure; to wear his hat in his presence, to smoke and spit upon his carpet, to devour his beef and turkey, and wipe his greasy fingers upon the curtains, to get drunk with his liquor." Hone suggests that similar scenes had happened before. Allan Nevins, ed., *The Diary of Philip Hone, 1828–1851,* vol. I (New York, 1927), 235–36.

21. Quoted in Gilje, *The Road to Mobocracy*, 254.
22. Gilje, *The Road to Mobocracy*, 257–59.
23. Davis, *Parades and Power*, 108; Gilje, *The Road to Mobocracy*, 260.
24. May 27, 1823, in Pintard, *Letters*, vol. II, 137–38.
25. See Jones, "Knickerbocker Santa Claus," 367–71.
26. Ibid., 370–71.
27. For example see December 18, 1827, in Pintard, *Letters*, vol. II, 382.
28. January 2, 1828, in Pintard, *Letters*, vol. III, 1. Two weeks earlier Pintard had noted that "intemperance, among the higher classes of our city, is no longer the order of the day. Among the hospitable circles . . . , a man would be marked who should retire intoxicated; indeed, convivial parties are all decent and sober" (December 16, 1827, in Pintard, *Letters*, vol. II, 381–82).
29. For the St. Nicholas's Day banquets, see Pintard, *Letters*, vol. I (1816), 38; (1818), 156. For New Year's Day, see ibid. (1817), 44; (1819), 161; (1821), 358–59; vol. II (1822), 117; (1827), 320, 324; vol. III (1828), 1; (1830), 117. In 1832 Pintard anonymously published in the *New-York Mirror* (December 29, 1832, 207) an essay lamenting the decline of New Year's open houses among the New York elite and attributing it to the nouveaux riches. (I am indebted to Elizabeth Blackmar for bringing the essay to my attention.) Pintard's authorship of this anonymous essay is indicated ibid., vol. IV, 114–15, 117.
30. Eric J. Hobsbawm and Terence Ranger, eds., *The Invention of Tradition* (Cambridge, 1983).
31. Golby and Purdue, *Making of the Modern Christmas*, 43.
32. For Christmas as a day of prayer, see Pintard, *Letters*, vol. I (1820), 356; vol. II (1821), 114; (1825), 210. For "St. Claas": ibid., vol. II (1827), 384; vol. III (1828), 53–54; (1829), 115; (1830), 206; (1831), 305; vol. IV (1832), 116.
33. While Pintard's basic Santa Claus ritual remained essentially the same after he first devised it, Pintard did continue to tinker with the details. From 1827 to 1829, the family's presents were placed in stockings hung by the chimney, but in 1830 they were placed on a table. The presents themselves changed, too: candies and fruit at first, toys added in 1828 (a drum), and in 1832 the toys replaced with books (because toys "cost much and are soon broken").
34. There were allusions to St. Nicholas's Day in 1773 and 1774, but Jones explains these in reference to the American Revolution (i.e., as a patriot alternative to St. George's Day) and not as precursors of the St. Nicholas cult that would develop a generation later. (Jones, "Knickerbocker Santa Claus," 362–64.)
35. Ibid., 374, 376. In another study Jones even suggests that the Dutch themselves took up the St. Nicholas cult from America—in the twentieth century, and largely for the sake of the tourist trade. See Charles W. Jones, *St. Nicholas of Myra, Bari, and Manhattan: Biography of a Legend* (Chicago, 1978), 307–8.

36. Washington Irving, *A History of New York* (second edition: 2 vols., New York, 1812), vol. I, 247 (book 4, ch. 5).
37. January 15, 1822, in Pintard, *Letters,* vol. II, 121–122.
38. Irving, *A History of New York* (1812 ed.), vol. I, 116 (book 4, ch. 5–6); "with characteristic slowness . . ." appears only in the first edition (New York, 1809), vol. I, 116 (book 2, ch. 5); Irving deleted the passage in the 1812 edition.
39. Sean Wilentz terms Moore a "level-headed Episcopalian conservative." (See *Chants Democratic,* 79.) The only book-length study of Moore, short and hagiographic, is Samuel W. Patterson, *The Poet of Christmas Eve: A Life of Clement Clarke Moore, 1779–1863* (New York, 1956). For Moore's ancestral background (and the Tory sympathies of his family) see 22–29, 31–36, 48–51. His wife, whom he married in 1813, was a member of the Cortland family (64–66). For Moore's slaves, see 5, 48. The political tracts Moore published include *Observations upon Certain Passages in Mr. Jefferson's Notes on Virginia* (New York, 1804), a critique of Jefferson's irreligion; and *A Sketch of Our Political Condition* (New York, 1813), condemning the Jefferson/Madison administrations (and the War of 1812) for their destruction of rural life. A shorter biographical sketch is Arthur N. Hosking, "The Life of Clement Clarke Moore," appended to the 1934 reprint of a facsimile edition of Moore's "A Visit from St. Nicholas" (New York, 1934); this edition has since been reprinted in a paperback edition by Dover Publications.
40. Moore's professorship initially paid a token $750, a figure that eventually increased to $2000. See Patterson, *The Poet of Christmas Eve,* 77–79.
41. Hosking, "The Life of Clement Clarke Moore," in Moore, "The Night Before Christmas" (New York, 1934), 23.
42. April 8, 1830, in Pintard, *Letters,* vol. III, 137. For Moore's wealth, see Charles Lockwood, *Manhattan Moves Uptown: An Illustrated History* (Boston, 1976), 205; Patterson, *The Poet of Christmas Eve,* 106–110.
43. Isaac N. Phelps Stokes, *The Iconography of Manhattan Island, 1498–1909* (6 vols., New York, 1915–28), vol. V, 1602. Moore writes of eminent domain in *A Plain Statement, Addressed to the Proprietors of Real Estate in the City and County of New-York* (New York, 1818), 13–18. A few years later, the city made plans to fill in an area under the Hudson River, in the process moving the river away from Moore's estate (Phelps Stokes, *Iconography,* vol. V, 1603). By the 1830s, some of that land was occupied by the Manhattan Gas-light Works, a company that was installing streetlights in that area of the city and digging a network of underground pipes in order to do so. (See *New York As It Is* [1837], 14.)
44. *Longworth's City Directory* (New York, 1821), 315.
45. November 3, 1832, in Pintard, *Letters,* vol. IV, 106. By the end of the 1820s the area that had come to be known as Chelsea Square was home to a substantial population, much of it poor and/or immigrant. By the 1830s Moore was watching Irishmen on St. Patrick's Day marching along the periphery of

his property—down Twenty-third Street, then turning south on Eighth Avenue. (See Patterson, *The Poet of Christmas Eve,* 92–93.) Like most of the men who owned great uptown estates, Clement Clarke Moore erected fences around his property.

46. Hosking, "The Life of Clement Clarke Moore," 28–31.

47. Moore, *A Plain Statement,* 6, 12, 39, 62. Elizabeth Blackmar interprets Moore's complaint as implicitly understanding that New York's urban development actually functioned as a public works program to provide jobs for the poor and unemployed—a program Moore opposed (Blackmar, *Manhattan for Rent,* 162–63). Cartmen, whom Moore singled out for criticism, had developed a reputation for especially rude and surly behavior by 1820, breaking speed limits and running down pedestrians—much like the modern taxi drivers who partly replaced them. See Graham Hodges, *New York City Cartmen, 1667–1850* (New York, 1986), 116–17, 127. Hodges indicates that many wealthy New Yorkers chose to move out of downtown New York after being awakened regularly by the sound of "hundreds of cartmen racing their vehicles at dawn" (Hodges, 121). In the late 1820s Moore was actually planning to move out of Chelsea to a still-rural area of Manhattan several miles to the north; he changed his mind only when his wife died in 1830. In 1839 Moore purchased an estate up the Hudson River at Sing Sing, and in 1850 he rented a house in Newport, R.I., where he spent his remaining summers. (Patterson, *The Poet of Christmas Eve,* 93–94, 149–50.)

48. "[T]he great and good St. Nicholas . . . took . . . New Amsterdam under his peculiar patronage, and has ever since been . . . the titular saint of this excellent city." Irving, *A History of New York,* vol. I, 120 (book 2, ch. 7); see also 454, 639, 655.

49. Ibid. (1812 ed.), vol. I, 253 (book 4, ch. 6: "ease, tranquility"); vol. I, 246 (book 4, ch. 5: "meddlesome and fractious"); vol. I, 254 (book 4, ch. 6: "long pipes . . . short pipes"). Irving introduced the story of the "pipe plot" only in the 1812 edition.

50. Lauren J. Cook, "Snow White Little Instruments of Comfort: Clay Pipes and Class Consciousness at the Boott Mills Boarding Houses," a paper delivered at a meeting of the New England Historical Association, Lowell, Mass., April 21, 1989. There was a practical reason that workers used short pipes: it was possible to smoke while working. But what may have begun as a practical necessity became, by the nineteenth century, a political gesture. (E.P. Thompson might call it "theatre.") Similarly, smoking a long pipe became an *assertion* as well as a sign of gentility and leisure. See, for example, Irving's use of long pipes in "Rip Van Winkle."

51. Patterson, *The Poet of Christmas Eve,* 99–101.

52. Blackmar, *Manhattan for Rent,* 195–96. See also Lockwood, *Manhattan Moves Uptown,* 205. John Pintard made the same point in 1832; see letter of November 3, 1832, in Pintard, *Letters,* vol. IV, 106.

53. Blackmar, *Manhattan for Rent.*

Edgar Allan Poe Detecting the City

Amy Gilman

EDGAR ALLAN POE IS AN UNLIKELY URBANIST. HIS TALES AND POEMS USUALLY conjure up visions of decaying mansions covered with dense green foliage; interiors with secret vaults and dungeons; dark, moldy rooms wrapped in cobwebs; and far-off, almost magical places, all of which harken back to some earlier premodern era and sensibility. Indeed, the hectic world of an urban metropolis with its busy streets, crowded houses, and noisy entertainments seems remarkably far away from what we usually think of as Poe's imaginary landscape. Yet several of Poe's most important tales, notably "The Man of the Crowd" and the Dupin trilogy, which consists of "The Murders in the Rue Morgue," "The Mystery of Marie Roget," and "The Purloined Letter," are all located in the major western cities of the nineteenth century—London, Paris, and New York, respectively. All of them were written in the 1840s—years that were crucial in the development of the modern city—and, with the exception of "The

Purloined Letter," which takes place indoors, all make use of city spaces to develop their narratives.[1] These stories draw upon specifically urban events and situations: a man frantically moving through a dark urban crowd; the mysterious and exceptionally brutal killing of an elderly woman and her daughter in a residential Parisian neighborhood; the discovery of the murdered and abused body of a beautiful young woman in the Hudson River. These are by now sensational and familiar events that titillate with their explicit themes of violence and bodily destruction and with their implicitly sexual overtones. In fashioning them Poe at once confirms our sense of the modern city as a dangerous place where random violence, desolating loneliness, and sexually motivated murder take place. But he also establishes the city as a place teeming with activity, discovery, and possibility—a place not only of death but also of life and pleasure.

In these tales Poe creates cityscapes filled with rich detail and precise descriptions. Crucial to the narrative rather than mere backdrops to the tales, these descriptions locate us quite definitively in a specific time and space. The depictions of Paris, London, and New York are visual as well as kinetic and move us to experience quite viscerally the recreated street scenes. Ironically, these urban settings are more imaginary and metaphoric than real. For although Poe lived and worked in several important American cities (Baltimore, Philadelphia, and New York), he usually placed his urban tales in cities he hardly knew at all. He had lived in London only as a child and had never even seen Paris (indeed his faulty and fanciful reconstruction of the Paris streets led Baudelaire to comment that it was unnecessary "to point out that Edgar Poe never came to Paris").[2] And, perverse as usual, when he did choose to tell a story associated with a particular city he knew well (New York in "The Mystery of Marie Roget"), he chose to "set" the story in Paris. Nevertheless, Poe thought seriously about the city both as a site of metropolitan culture and as a place in which to explore the modern psyche.[3] Indeed, Poe's city tales are filled with the rich detail, nuances, and fearsome turmoil of urban life. Through them Poe insinuates us into the streets and neighborhoods of fictionalized but surprisingly recognizable metropolises and then uses the fictional recreations to explore the questions and dilemmas posed by the rise of the actual city and modern urban culture.

In his "city stories" Poe also developed the genre of the detective story, a form generally associated with urbanization and the development of mass culture. Here the older form of the gothic tale (usually set in the countryside) was replaced by the ratiocinative technique and the classic form of the modern mystery, complete with a horrible crime (often associated with sex and death), a brilliant and intellectual (if emotionally detached) detective, and a murder victim of relative insignificance.[4] It was a form that drew much from the Victorian street literature and melodrama that Poe knew so well: the pamphleteers of Grub Street, *The Newgate Calender*, and the Penny Dreadfuls.[5] But in Poe's works murder and mystery moved from the street to a conscious aesthetic form that was consonant with the deeper psychological themes created by the tensions of a new urban culture. And in these works the tensions and dynamics are large: the chaos of daily life and the imposition of social order; the irrational intensity of emotional life and the logic of the intellect; the battle between love and death.

In grappling with these themes Poe proved himself a man of his time. The need to order and control the urban scene was characteristic of nineteenth-century city culture, and Poe lived in and wrote about metropolitan cities at a crucial moment. These were years of social and economic transformation characterized by unprecedented rates of demographic and geographic expansion, emerging industrialization, increased stratification of class and gender lines, and increased fissures within the culture itself as a new mass popular culture arose and distinguished itself from a belles lettres tradition. That the city, whether New York, London, or Paris, was disordered and apparently chaotic seemed clear to most contemporary observers, and many besides Poe looked for ways of making it comprehensible and orderly, of bringing it literally under control. But what differentiated him from other writers and journalists (for he was both) was his belief that the chaos expressed natural and real phenomena and that the imposition of order of any kind was at best a temporary form of control over forces that were essentially uncontrollable.

Writing of Charles Baudelaire (whom he identifies as the quintessential early urban modernist), the critic Walter Benjamin noted the strong affinity Baudelaire found with Poe, an affinity linked to Poe's "images of big-city crowds." Poe, Benjamin tells us, captured for Baudelaire the classic example of the crowd, and that crowd, in turn, came to represent what Benjamin called "the agitated veil" through which Baudelaire saw his own Paris.[6] Poe's relationship to the city and to modern city culture is complex and ambivalent. Yet, taken as a group, Poe's city tales raise important literary and cultural issues ranging from questions about his contribution to the development of narrative structure and authorial point of view to such related issues as the development of the mystery as a genre, the significance of the detective as a modern hero, the use of melodrama and conundrums, and, perhaps most strikingly and graphically, the depiction of the atomized female body in modern fiction.

Closely tied to these issues are questions about the relationship between Poe's art and the development of American mass culture, and the ways in which Poe's conception of the city introduces us to a whole range of modern literary themes. These tales, moreover, locate Poe at the beginning of a particularly urban and modern literary tradition at a critical point in the development of American culture. In focusing on Poe's uses of the city and city culture, this essay will, I hope, raise more questions than it answers in arguing that Poe's urban tales are themselves extraordinary "clues" to the development of modern urban culture and consciousness.

❧

Let us begin by looking at "The Murders in the Rue Morgue," a tale set in mid-nineteenth-century Paris. This story introduces us to the character Monsieur C. Auguste Dupin (the prototype for private detectives like Sherlock Holmes, Maigret, or Hercule Poirot) as well as to the unnamed narrator of the ratiocinative tales, an American gentleman who has recently arrived in Paris. Dupin, we are told, is a highly intellectual and literate gentleman of "an illustrious family [who] had been reduced to . . . poverty" but was able, nonetheless, "by means of a rigorous economy, to procure the necessities of life without troubling himself about its superfluities. Books, indeed, were his sole luxuries." At length, the narrator and Dupin "arranged to live together" during the former's stay in Paris, and they took up residence "in a time eaten and grotesque mansion" in a "retired and desolate portion of the Faubourg St.

Germaine."[7] Dupin and his new companion ("we should have been regarded as madmen," says the narrator) lived in "seclusion" and "existed within ourselves alone." "Enamored of the night," they hid behind the closed shutters during the daylight hours, "admitted no visitors," and "sallied forth" for lengthy nocturnal walks through the streets of Parisian neighborhoods "arm and arm, continuing the topics of the day or roaming far and wide until a late hour seeking amid the lights and shadows of the populous city, that infinity of mental excitement which quiet observation can afford."[8]

Dupin and his companion are soon confronted with the newspaper account of the barbaric murder of two other withdrawn and nocturnal characters, Madame L'Espanayer and her daughter. Their bodies, brutalized and dismembered, are found in or near their top-floor apartment house residence. Although the apartment is in total disarray, the door has remained locked, no sign of possible entry or exit is revealed, and no clues are found. Witnesses however, have all heard two voices in the middle of the night: one in French (uttering the phrase "Mon Dieu"), but the other in some unidentified foreign tongue (perhaps English, Spanish, Italian, etc.). The murder scene itself is grotesque: "The apartment was in the wildest disorder—the furniture broken and thrown about in all directions. . . . On a chair lay a razor, besmeared with blood. On the hearth were two or three long and thick tresses of grey human hair, also dabbed with blood." The corpse of the daughter was found head downward and forced up the chimney, and that of the mother was outside "with her throat so entirely cut that, upon attempt to raise her, the head fell off."[9] The police are dumbfounded and Dupin alone is able to solve the murder. His solution is bizarre and funny, for the murderer proves to be an orangutan —a beast owned and brought to Paris by a Malaysian sailor. Only such a beast, Dupin rapidly concludes, could have the physical characteristics that matched the available clues (an enormous reach and a harsh voice without language), could have negotiated the system of windows and alleys, and could have been able to exert the sheer physical force necessary for the brutality of this crime.

But what is important initially is the relationship Dupin establishes early in the tale between himself, his city, and his intellectual discoveries. For Dupin's insights are consistently and intimately related to his ability to use his immediate landscape to solve the crime. Toward the beginning of the story Dupin's brilliance is revealed to us as we proceed through the nighttime streets of Paris with him and his companion. He displays an uncanny ability to read his friend's mind—to "fathom" his "soul," an exercise he engages in by deconstructing the Parisian street scene before him. The particulars of this everyday scene—the horses, the local characters, even the patterning of the cobblestones on the street—form for him a series of logical associations that, he infers, occurred within the mind of his companion.[10] As they walk down a "long dirty street in the vicinity of the Palais Royal," Dupin lays out his deductive method, explaining the process by which he moved back and forth between his companion's expressions and the visual images created by the street scene to understand the associational links that formed the content of his friend's mind:

> You kept your eyes upon the ground—glancing, with a petulant expression, at the holes and ruts in the pavement (so that I saw you were still thinking of the stones), until we reached the little alley called Lamartine which has been paved, by way of experiment, with the overlapping and riveted blocks. Here your countenance brightened up, and, perceiving your lips move, I could not doubt that you murmured the word "stereotomy," a term very affectedly applied to this species of pavement.[11]

These details allow Dupin to move from the exterior and visually specific world of Paris to the interior of his companion's mind. The particulars of the street have become not only clues to the workings of the mind but also the contextual framework for the inner life itself. This movement from the labyrinthine streets of Paris to the labyrinthine mind of Dupin and his companion is rapidly juxtaposed with another set of external and internal worlds: that of the street with its relative or at least habitual order, and the total chaos of the apartment where the two murder victims lie in total disarray. With an eye toward similar detail, this time from the daily newspaper that contained an elaborate record of the testimony elicited from all the witnesses and neighbors, Dupin proceeds to solve the crime. The paper tells him that among the witnesses were a mix of artisans and foreigners typical of a metropolitan city: a French laundress, a French silversmith, a Dutch restaurateur, an English tailor, a Spanish undertaker, and an Italian confectioner. Their identity and testimony provide Dupin with the crucial information he needs: namely, that each believed the voice heard in the night to be foreign, yet it was familiar to no one. From this he concludes that the voice was in fact not of human origin, confirming his opinion that the murderer was not human at all. And finally, it is the class and ethnic diversity of this distinctly urban group, and especially their diverse languages, that leads him to reconstruct the crime. In "The Mystery of Marie Roget," we meet an equally diverse, if somewhat different, city group.

Poe begins "The Mystery of Marie Roget" by disclaiming that there is any similarity between his tale and the events surrounding the real murder of the 21-year-old Mary Rogers in New York in the summer of 1841. Actually, Poe has no intention of disclaiming at all. In this story he instead attempts to solve a real and unresolved case by applying his own ratiocinative technique to the publicly available clues with an eye toward "an analysis of the true principles which should direct inquiry in similar cases."[12] And while Poe sets the story in nineteenth-century Paris (changing Mary the cigar seller to "Marie," the perfumerie girl and *grisette*), his references and footnotes transpose all of the French sites to their real locales in New York in 1841. Indeed, Poe's strange cross-referencing of these two cities seems to suggest the extent to which early nineteenth-century cities were already international in character, as well as the fact that he perceived this narrative to be somehow "French" in both mood and tone.

Nonetheless, Poe's "real" setting is New York, a city he had lived in and knew quite well. The streets and locales are New York, not Paris (they are individually identified as such in the 1845 edition of the story), and his characters are the gangs, ruffians, and nouveaux riches of that unique city rather than French confectioners or restaurateurs. Once again Poe moves us directly into the familiar arena of life in an urban setting, drawing (as in "The Murders in the Rue Morgue") upon the city's daily press for his information and clues. But here he goes several steps beyond his initial effort: He states quite clearly that *all* of his information is drawn from the penny press (the New York *Mercury*, the New York *Journal of Commerce*, the New York *Commercial Advertiser*, the New York *Evening Post*, the New York *Standard*, the New York *Express*, the New York *Courier and Inquirer*, etc.) and that all of it is based on the real and not the imagined. Here quite literally the texts of the city provide the material for the tale: The real story of Mary Rogers, her life, romantic ties, and work relationships become the essential clues to the murder's ultimate solution. Thus reading the murder through urban texts, Dupin and the narrator read the city and in the process reconstruct their own version of a woman's life. This method makes Poe's portrait of Mary/Marie truly compelling, so much so that the fictive Marie has superseded the real or historical Mary, just as Poe's recreation of the events (if not his solution to the crime) has infused all subsequent accounts. This is so because Poe, more than any other writer or commentator, understood and expressed the "mystery" of this woman's life and the symbolic meaning she held within New York City life at that particular moment in time.[13]

The events take place in lower Manhattan, specifically the area around city hall, close to the docks, the newspaper trade, and the commercial center of the city. The story places us in touch with the darker side of the metropolis, with its sleaziness, its free-floating men and women, and its implicit violence. It is primarily a male-centered world composed of sailors, tradesmen, and street characters, and it is a world where sexuality is always close to the surface and often closely connected with violence. In depicting the murder of Mary Rogers, then, Poe moves us directly into the dark, complex web of a particular set of characteristically urban relationships.

In choosing to write about the legendary Mary Rogers, Poe draws us definitively into a city event, one that engaged the popular imagination of its own time precisely because it tapped so many familiar and sensitive issues in the city of New York in the 1840s. At the time of her death in the summer of 1841 the real Mary Rogers was young, beautiful, and a well-known figure in her neighborhood. She lived with her mother, an elderly boardinghouse keeper, on Nassau Street and had been romantically involved with two of its residents, a clerk or lawyer and a corkcutter, both of whom were prime suspects in the murder. Rogers had apparently worked as a milliner, and several years prior to her death she had worked behind the counter of Anderson's Tobacco Shop (a store owned by the aggressive merchant of the same name who would later become an important figure in New York City real estate and politics).[14] The store was a local hangout for politicians, writers, and journalists and was frequented by well-known literary figures including James Fenimore Cooper, Washington Irving, and probably Poe. Here the young and pretty Miss Rogers came to be known, in the words of the penny press, as the "Beautiful Cigar Girl." Rogers had disappeared before—probably for an abortion—but this time she did not return; the discovery of her murdered body floating in the Hudson River filled newspaper copy in the young and highly sensational penny press for years to come.[15]

In order to "solve" this "real" murder, Poe presents us with a series of possible solutions to the crime, all of which correspond to those ascribed to by nineteenth-century commentators: that the murder was committed by a gang, by one of several lovers (each of a different social class), or even by Mary herself in an act of suicide. This pursuit of verisimilitude causes Poe to lose some of his usual sense of play and gamesmanship, but the reader gains some valuable insight into the texture of the early nineteenth-century city.[16] For this is a story not only of murder but also of sexual violence in an urban setting, and Poe has constructed a tale that artfully combines the popular nineteenth-century love of melodrama and romance within a distinctly modern framework of detachment and rational analysis. In order to solve the murder Poe has his detective-hero Dupin reenact not the murder scene (as in "The Murders in the Rue Morgue") but Mary's own mysterious and romantic life. Mary thus becomes a vision of the modern city woman who, like the city itself, is both dangerous and seductive and fits Poe's classic version of a beautiful, dying woman. In this narrative of Mary's life, Poe's New York on a hot summer morning in July 1841 is a city fixed in time and space, a place as still and eerie as Mary's waterlogged corpse; a city where danger comes not from strangers but from people whom one presumes to know. In this context violence, particularly violence against women, is horrific, but it is almost anticipated, as Poe's city becomes a kind of urban frontier, its inhabitants all newcomers who form a heterogeneous mix without ever bonding into communities. Alone, acting out their passions without the force of reason, they commit amoral acts of death and destruction. Poe artfully combines death and eros, and through seemingly unending descriptions of the female body (most of them quoted directly from the penny press) he thoroughly indulges his audience's thirst for lurid and graphic detail while anticipating both the voyeurism and narrative detachment of later urban texts.[17]

A similar aura of desperate loneliness characterizes Poe's earlier story, "The Man of the Crowd." Set in nineteenth-century London, it is told to us by a narrator who has just ventured out into the city after a long and presumably debilitating illness, who now watches the London crowd through the window of a coffeehouse. From here he observes the street scene and becomes fascinated with the frantic journey of an elderly and disheveled man whom he soon follows for two nights and a day to nowhere through the London streets. Unlike "The Murders in the Rue Morgue" or "The Mystery of Marie Roget," this story presents no particular mystery to be solved and has essentially no plot. Nonetheless, through it Poe moves us directly into the cityscape and uses the crowd and the city as central characters in the narrative. Translated by Baudelaire, the story is seen by Walter Benjamin and others as an important link in the development of an urban modernist tradition.[18] Poe's portrayal of the crowd in this story is indeed extraordinary. It takes on a life of its own, ominous and secretive, ebbing, flowing, and moving with an irrepressible force and mysterious erotic power. The crowd here is controlled by no one but instead becomes a medium through which we see the city, its varied inhabitants, and ultimately ourselves. Looking through the window, the narrator introduces us to the crowd:

> This latter is one of the principal thoroughfares of the city, and had been very much crowded during the whole day. But, as the darkness came on, the throng momently increased; and by the time the lamps were well lighted, two dense and continuous tides of population were rushing past the door. At this particular period of the evening I had never before been in a similar situation, and the tumultuous sea of human heads filled me therefore with a delicious novelty of emotion. I gave up, at length, all care of things within the hotel, and became absorbed in contemplation of the scene without.[19]

Our observer begins by looking at the "passengers in masses," thinking of them "in their aggregate relations." Soon, however, he "descended to details, and regarded with minute interest the innumerable varieties of figure, dress, air, gait, visage, and expression of countenance." The crowd becomes complex, a mixture of all urban types ranging from those "who were undoubtedly noblemen, merchants, attorneys, tradesmen, stock-jobbers" to "the tribe of clerks" to those who provided "darker and deeper themes for speculation." Among these were "sturdy professional street beggars," "modest young girls returning from long and late labor," "women of the town of all kinds and of all ages," and "piemen, porters, coal-heavers, sweeps; organ-grinders, monkey-exhibitors, and ballad-mongers, those who vended with those who sang; ragged artisans and exhausted laborers . . . and all full of a noisy and inordinate vivacity which jarred discordantly upon the ear, and gave an aching sensation to the eye."[20]

In the course of the story the narrator is taken by a particular "countenance which at once arrested and absorbed [his] whole attention," that of the decrepit old man who begins to move furtively through the nighttime crowd. As the narrator pursues the stranger through the night, he traverses a variety of London neighborhoods until, as the "shades of the second evening came on" and he was "wearied unto death," he stopped in front of the wanderer and "gazed at him steadfastly in the face." The old man does not notice him, and the narrator comes to understand that the man of the crowd is the one "who refuses to be alone," the man who like the city itself cannot be read.[21]

❧

For Poe the modern city allowed individuals a freedom of movement and possibility that would have been unknown to them in more provincial or traditional settings. With its complex web of streets, its patterned and varied landscapes, and its endless array of characters, the city conveyed excitement, energy, and activity. (This activity is liberating and sexual and dangerous for Marie; it infuses the man of the crowd with a strange, albeit temporary, source of kinetic energy.) In these urban tales Poe plunges us into the realm of ordinary city scenes (the streets, the neighborhood, the crowd) and lives and extracts from them extraordinary events—experiences that are uniquely important and symbolic and that are at once possible within the context of everyday life while they also transcend it. Here the ordinary flows into art and reemerges as the source of mystery, horror, and death. (Here Poe anticipates Baudelaire's conversion of the mundane into the artistic and the beautiful.)[22] The city, the locus of ordinary lives and events, becomes a space that permits both freedom and unfreedom, interconnectedness and fragmentation, energy and excitement as well as loneliness and death.

Poe viewed the city as a place fraught with meaning but one that was essentially morally neutral. Thus Poe's city is potentially dangerous not just because it is the city but because of the particular way in which it facilitates the ordering of human relationships and releases the controls of traditional society. In Poe's world the city becomes a public space in which modern men and women, operating essentially alone, create the artifacts and characteristics of modern culture only to become the arbitrary victims of their own creations. This space becomes an urban wilderness, analogous in its understated and charged eroticism to the natural wilderness of the sea or the frontier. And within this urban wilderness Poe explores a set of distinctly modern themes: alienation, identity, sexuality, and the atomization of contemporary life.

Poe's characters all operate within this city space as social isolates; they are individuals without traditional families or even meaningful kin relationships (when these do exist they are odd or eccentric as in "The Murders in the Rue Morgue," or fraught with generational discontinuity as in "The Mystery of Marie Roget") and even without significant friendships. What happens to these urban characters happens to them alone, and largely *because* of the extent to which estrangement is a characteristic of city life. Thus Marie Roget proceeds towards her death through familiar streets. A known neighborhood figure, Poe tells us that she nevertheless "might have proceeded, at any given period, by any one of the many routes between her residence and that of her aunt without meeting a single individual whom she knew or by whom she was known."[23] Within the city all of these characters live within their private worlds. The city has become the space where men and women are simultaneously alone and members of the crowd: They are a public composed of private and isolated souls.

In exploring the alienation and loneliness that he believed characterized modern city culture, Poe also points us to the larger problem of identity, a problem that was always central to his work. "Nothing," Poe informs us in pursuing the killer of Marie Roget, "is more vague than impressions of individual identity."[24] And indeed in "Marie Roget" this subject is paramount, not only because we seek the identity of the killer but also because the real "mystery" of the story has to do with the identity of Mary/Marie herself. A major portion of "Marie Roget" is devoted to fixing the identity of Marie, a subject that allows Poe not only an extended discourse on Marie's body but also on the seemingly unrelated topics of knowledge and probability. Even her physical identity is dubious: Was her body the one that was found? If so how do we know, and what characteristics (garters, gloves, a delicate frame) make possible physical identification? More importantly: Who was Marie and how did her distinctly urban life (as a shopgirl? a *grisette*? a new urban woman?) lead her toward death?

In "The Murders in the Rue Morgue" we are similarly concerned with the identity of the killer: Who was he, was he human or not, and *how* do we know what we know? But once again we move quickly to the problem of psychological identity and identification: Who were these two strange and lonely women and what about their quirky lives led them to such an end, deaths in which their physical identities are so largely obliterated by the violence of the crime itself? How do their identities reflect on the even more mysterious identities of Dupin and his companion? And finally, in "The Man of the Crowd": Who is the narrator? Who is the man of the crowd? What is the relationship between the individual and the mass within the darkened streets of the nineteenth-century metropolis? Does the narrator ultimately confront his own self when he meets face to face with the old man, and what do these confrontations tell us about our own selves and identities?

In both "Marie Roget" and "Rue Morgue" the themes of identity and self-knowledge are closely connected to the way Poe explores the nineteenth-century preoccupation with the relationship between nature and the urban environment.[25] The identity of Marie, *grisette*, represents that which is young, beautiful, and natural, and her death thus suggests the fate of nature and natural beauty within the hard city spaces. In "The Murders in the Rue Morgue" the murderer is an ape, a precivilized (or is it more civilized?) version of man who, like the human murderer of Marie Roget, has gone amuck within the city. Like a slave, this ape had been captured and brought by ship to France where a sailor "at length succeeded in lodging it safely at his own residence in Paris." Wounded, the beast was kept in seclusion, but it learned quickly the habits of its master, who found it one night "razor in hand, and fully lathered . . . sitting before a looking glass attempting the operation of shaving."[26] A manlike creature without language, this ape nevertheless exhibits human characteristics. But in creating an ape murderer Poe apes us; he plays with our thirst for violence and makes fun of our gullibility. And in the end the ape is no more than an animal brought from the wild into an artificial landscape where it proceeds to adapt, literally aping men until he commits the ultimate human/antihuman act—murder.

In both these tales the bodies of women are quite literally torn apart or otherwise physically destroyed, almost beyond recognition. The murdered body of the mother in "Rue Morgue" has been decapitated and "the body, as well as the head, was fearfully mutilated—the former so much as scarcely to retain any semblance of humanity."[27] In "Marie Roget" the descriptions of Marie's corpse are similarly macabre and grotesque—all the more chilling because they are told from the point of view of a thoroughly detached observer. Here the narrator, reading from the texts of the penny press, describes Marie's corpse for us: "Her face was suffused with dark blood, some of which issued from the mouth. . . . About the throat were bruised impressions of fingers. . . . The arms were bent over the chest and were rigid. . . . The flesh of the neck was much swollen. . . . A piece of lace was found tied so tightly around the neck as to be hidden from sight. . . . She had been subjected . . . to brutal violence."[28]

Drawn from popular melodrama and, in the case of "Marie Roget," directly from the penny press, these descriptions catered to the popular taste that Poe at once disdained and cultivated. They "aped" the content of the dailies and went one better, providing titillating visions of torn limbs, detailed renderings of the female body, and implicitly sexual and obsessive depictions of petticoats, garters, and the like. But ultimately not even James Gordon Bennett, the scandalous editor of the New York *Herald*, could compose copy as lurid and visually specific as Poe's. On the one hand, it is hard to take these passages of Poe's seriously; surely we are not expected to when, for example, he accuses the investigating officer in "Rue Morgue" of "busy-bodyism." Both the images and the descriptions in the commentary are intended as sendups of popular fiction—in the manner of Poe's own critique in "How to Write a Blackwood's Article." On the other hand, these descriptions do fill Poe's stories, and, whether satirical or not, they matter in light of Poe's own clear fascination with the pornographic and the grotesque. More importantly, such images were rapidly becoming mainstays of popular commercial culture, which was increasingly drawn to lurid descriptions of the female body. They mark the beginnings of this sort of representation in modern culture; in light of contemporary feminist criticism, they are early examples of an emerging discourse that was at once sensational, voyeuristic, and sadistic and that focused on the body as a point of integration for what seemed to be a culture disintegrating at every point.[29] Poe thus becomes a crucial link in understanding how such images became integrated in the American cultural vocabulary, and especially the vocabulary of modern popular fictions. Moreover, these narrative descriptions and situations locate Poe as a forerunner to this modern urban discourse rather than as an anomalous figure within the American literary tradition.[30]

These sensational aspects of Poe's work also betray the writer's own preoccupation with playing for the marketplace. As Michael Allen has suggested, one of Poe's central literary tasks, one that to a large extent "dictated the form of his work" and one that he never adequately resolved, was to cater to the tastes of two audiences—the literary "elite" and the emerging new mass audience of the nineteenth-century city.[31] But in contending with this problem of creating forms that were both aesthetically and commercially viable, Poe also expressed the dilemma inherent in nineteenth-century city culture. In the final analysis, he came closer than most to meeting the complex requirements of a world that was itself dividing at every point and establishing sharp distinctions between highbrow and lowbrow culture, between the literary fictions of women and men, and between the entertainments of the urban crowd and the refined tastes of a burgeoning Victorianism.[32]

Indeed, Poe's fascination with the grotesque, the macabre, the violent, and the sensational was both highly idiosyncratic and culturally relevant and provides an important view of the underside of

American Victorian culture. More importantly, his preoccupation with these aspects and issues provides a symbolic representation of the chaos and disjointedness of modern urban culture. For his images of bodily destruction (including the literal separation of head and body) raise, once again, questions about identity, unity, and psychic and physical integration. The destruction of the body, especially the female body, becomes in fact a metaphor for extreme social discontinuity and for the potential upheaval and breakup of all interpersonal life within the modern city. This is particularly true if, as Christine Buci-Glucksmann suggests in her discussion of Walter Benjamin, the female body can be seen as an extended metaphor for the modern city. The body thus becomes splintered into parts as fractured as city social life itself.[33]

Even in his construction of the character Dupin, Poe contended with the psychic and spiritual fragmentation of things urban. Indeed Dupin, who meets Poe's own conception of a "bi-part" soul with both a creative and a "resolvent" aspect, is a supreme example of a fragmented personality, split between reason and emotion, a man who lives in a world dominated by his own private reveries. Dupin is riddled with contradictions and mirrors the fragmented aspects of Poe's urban spaces while he simultaneously helps us as readers to resolve their inherent chaos. Dupin, genius, madman, and perennial observer, who lives within the context of his own bizarre imagination, becomes our guide to the modern city. And here Poe's sense of irony, humor, and hoax is at its most brilliant and beguiling. This gentleman who initially led us on our journey through the city streets, using city clues to solve city crimes and then retreating once again behind the closed doors of his own domestic interior, is the maddest of any urban character we encounter, a man who cannot confront the daylight but who "sees" through the shadows. As our urban escort and "detective" he is an urban sociologist, a man who observes the city, its people, and its happenings from the perspective of a detached observer. A true reader of the city, Dupin uses urban texts for evidence, plays with problems of knowing and understanding, and solves the most "outré" of urban events. The ultimate modern man, he watches and waits, using reason and patience to outwit a given situation. Using clues from the material world he proceeds to solve the crime and in so doing transforms the chaotic and incomprehensible city into a mapped-out terrain, one that in the end is reordered and reassembled for us by an *apparently* rational observer.[34]

Like any true "modern man," Dupin maintains a detached stance, but his detachment helps to mask what is an essentially amoral sensibility. Able to explore the most horrific events without betraying any emotion or moral judgment, he is the ultimate voyeur, watching without participating and without engaging in the emotional or physical aspects of life itself. While others react with horror and repulsion at the murder scene and corpses in "Rue Morgue" and "Marie Roget," Dupin remains steadfastly unmoved, his passivity placing in relief the more emotional, and presumably more human, responses of others. It is in the final analysis Dupin who detects the city for us, using both scientific rationalism and romantic intuition as the tools of his trade. Thus detecting the city, Dupin seems to make sense out of chaos, solve the mysteries, piece the bodies back together, and bring things under control. He appears to make understandable bizarre and inexplicable events. But although Dupin may solve the crime, he merely gives the illusion of solving the more complex puzzle of city life by applying what is only an orderly veneer to a disorderly and distinctly urban world.

Notes

1. "The Man of the Crowd" was originally published in *Gentleman's Magazine* 7 (December 1840), 267–70, and in Poe's own edition of *Tales* (New York, 1845), 219–28; "The Murders in the Rue Morgue" was originally published in *Graham's Magazine* 18 (April 1841), 166–79, and in *Tales,* 116–50; "The Mystery of Marie Roget" was originally published in Snowden's *Ladies' Companion* 18 (November, December 1842 and February 1843), 15–20, 93–99, 162–67, and in *Tales,* 151–99; "The Purloined Letter" was originally published in *The Gift: A Christmas, New Year, and Birthday Present* MDCCCXLV (September 1844), 41–61, and in *Tales,* 200–18. All references to these stories in this essay are taken from Thomas Ollive Mabbott, ed., *The Collected Works of Edgar Allan Poe* (Cambridge, Mass., 1978), 3 vols. Hereafter referred to as *Works.*
2. Poe was more than arbitrary in fashioning the geography of Paris. See the comments of French critic E.F. Forgues reviewing Poe's *Tales* in the *Revue des Deux Mondes,* October 1846, in Mabbott, *Works,* 777, f.n. 17.
3. Poe was cofounder (with Charles F. Briggs and Henry Watson), coeditor, and eventually sole editor and owner of *The Broadway Journal,* from its initial publication in January 1845 until it ceased publication in February 1846. The journal was intended to be a high-quality literary review dedicated to publishing

original American work. It also had a distinctly urban character, paying attention to a wide range of city events and subjects ranging from architecture to theatre to "city amusements."

4. For a discussion of the genre, see John G. Cawelti, *Adventure, Mystery and Romance: Formula Stories as Art and Popular Culture* (Chicago, 1976), 81.

5. For a good discussion of this literature in England, see Richard Altick, *Victorian Studies in Scarlet* (New York, 1970). Poe's satirical treatment of this literature is found in much of his writing and is specifically addressed in his "How to Write a Blackwood Article," in Edmund Clarence Stedman and George Edward Woodbury, eds., *The Works of Edgar Allan Poe,* vol. IV (New York, 1927), 198–211. For a more recent treatment of Poe's rather ambivalent relationship to the new sensational literature and his uses of the mid-century irrational impulse, see David Reynolds, *Beneath the American Renaissance: The Subversive Imagination in the Age of Emerson and Melville* (New York, 1988), 225–48.

6. Walter Benjamin, "On Some Motifs in Baudelaire," in Hannah Arendt, ed., *Illuminations* (New York, 1969), 72, 168.

7. *Works,* 531–32.

8. *Works,* 533.

9. *Works,* 537–38.

10. Poe was fascinated by the process of street paving as well as by the way in which ancient methods of road construction still prevailed, establishing remarkable continuity between the streets of the modern city and those of ancient Rome. See his essay "Street Paving" in *The Broadway Journal* I:16 (April 19, 1845), 1.

11. *Works,* 535–36. Nancy Horrowitz uses this key passage as an example of Peirce's abductive method. For her semiotic approach to Peirce and Poe, see "The Body of the Detective Novel: Charles Peirce and Edgar Allan Poe," in Umberto Eco and Thomas Sebeok, eds., *The Sign of the Three: Dupin, Holmes, Peirce* (Bloomington, Ind., 1983), 179–97.

12. Poe details his intentions in a letter to his friend George Roberts on June 4, 1842. See James A. Harrison, ed., *The Complete Works of Edgar Allan Poe,* vol. XVII (New York, 1902), 112–13.

13. Poe lived in Philadelphia when he wrote the tale but was clearly familiar with the circle of New York journalists and writers who covered the Mary Rogers story. And while Poe may have "solved" the crime by fixing on a theory of a lone assassin in the original version of the tale, he was quickly confounded by the convergence of what he called "real" and "ideal" events. In the fall of 1842 a deathbed confession by an innkeeper seemed to confirm the already widely held belief that Rogers's death was the result of a botched abortion. This accounts for the changes Poe made in his revised text of the story, which appeared in 1845. The Mabbott edition annotates all the variations in the text and includes extensive notes on the original event.

14. Rogers worked in many of the trades typical for young women of her day: boardinghouse keeper, milliner, salesgirl. Following English custom, young, attractive women were often hired as cigar-store clerks specifically to attract the trade. The extent to which Rogers was representative in some way of working-class women of her day was crucial in making her story into myth. Actually truth was stranger than even Poe's fiction and the "real" circumstances of the case still remain wrapped in mystery and subject to a myriad of interpretations. The case remains a classic unsolved mystery, although the likelihood is that Rogers died as the result of an abortion.
15. The most complete accounts are in the New York *Tribune*, the *Commercial Advertiser*, the New York *Herald*, and the New York *Evening Post*. Modern accounts of the murder include: Raymond Paul, *Who Murdered Mary Rogers?* (Englewood Cliffs, N.J., 1971) and John Walsh, *Poe the Detective: The Curious Circumstances Behind "The Mystery of Marie Roget"* (New Brunswick, N.J., 1968), both of which focus on Poe's reading of the events and contain the text of the 1842–43 and 1845 versions of the story. For a study of the cultural meaning of the case as urban melodrama, see Amy Gilman, "L'Assassinat de Mary Rogers: Sexualite, crime et culture au milieu de dix-neuvieme siecle dans la ville de New York," in Robert Muchembled, ed., *Mentalities: Histoire des Cultures et des Societies* 3 (October 1989).
16. David Ketterer argues that since "The Mystery of Marie Roget" depends so heavily on ratiocination and so little on imagination, the story ironically becomes the best demonstration of Poe's own belief that the reasoning and imaginative faculties work most effectively in conjunction. See *The Rationale of Deception in Poe* (Baton Rouge, La., 1979), 245.
17. For a good discussion of death and eros in Poe's work, see Edward Davidson, *Poe: A Critical Study* (Cambridge, Mass., 1964), 105–35. A more recent treatment of the same theme is J. Gerald Kennedy, *Poe, Death, and the Life of Writing* (New Haven, Conn., 1987).
18. Benjamin takes issue with Baudelaire's presentation of the man of the crowd as a *flaneur*, arguing instead that he is "what had to become of the *flaneur* once deprived of the milieu to which he belonged." "This urban setting, depicted by Poe," Benjamin writes, has for Poe "something barbaric: discipline just barely manages to tame it" (*Illuminations*, 172–74, 170–80). Robert Byers's excellent essay, "Mysteries of the City: A Reading of Poe's 'The Man of the Crowd'" draws upon many of these same themes placing Poe within a Marxist framework, emphasizing his place in the modernist tradition. In Sacvan Bercovitch and Myra Jehlen, eds., *Ideology and Classic American Literature* (New York, 1987), 221–46.
19. *Works*, 507.
20. *Works*, 508–10.
21. *Works*, 511, 515.
22. Marshall Berman, *All That Is Solid Melts into Air* (New York, 1982), 159–60.

23. *Works,* 749–50.
24. *Works,* 748.
25. See Stuart Blumin, "Explaining the New Metropolis: Perception, Depiction and Analysis in Mid-Nineteenth Century New York City," *Journal of Urban History* 2 (November 1984), 12–13.
26. *Works,* 564, 565.
27. *Works,* 538.
28. *Works,* 730.
29. The parallels between the work of Poe and the development of the modern cinema (especially Hitchcock and Sternberg) abound. See Laura Mulvey's classic essay "Film and Visual Pleasure" and Christine Gledhill, "Recent Developments in Feminist Criticism," both in Gerald Mast and Marshall Cohen, eds., *Film Theory and Criticism* (New York, 1985), 803–16, 817–45. For a feminist reader–response-oriented interpretation of Dupin's ability to "read" this crime, see Judith Fetterley, "Reading about Reading: 'A Jury of Her Peers,' 'Murders in the Rue Morgue,' and 'The Yellow Wallpaper,'" in Elizabeth A. Flynn and Patrocinio P. Schweickart, eds., *Gender and Reading: Essays on Readers, Texts and Contexts* (Baltimore, 1988), 155–58.
30. For a discussion of Poe's "place" in the modern literary tradition, see Edmund Wilson's 1926 essay "Poe at Home and Abroad," in Wilson's *A Literary Chronicle: 1920–1950* (New York, 1956), 65–76.
31. Allen also notes that in attempting to resolve this dilemma and cater successfully to the marketplace, Poe was hindered most of all by his own elitism. Michael Allen, *Poe and the British Magazine Tradition* (New York, 1969), 38, 182.
32. See Larry Levine's *Highbrow/Lowbrow* (Cambridge, Mass., 1988), on the bifurcation of American culture in the nineteenth century.
33. Christine Buci-Glucksmann, "Catastrophic Utopia: The Feminine as Allegory of the Modern," in *Representations* 14 (Spring 1986), 220–29.
34. Davidson, especially 214–22.

❧

Knowledge and the Marketplace

Donald M. Scott

IN OCTOBER OF 1855, HENRY WARD BEECHER TRAVELED TO OHIO ON A lecture tour. A major "intellectual sovereign of the day," Beecher was among the most luminous of the stars of the public lecture system that flourished during the middle decades of the century, commanding the best fees and attracting the largest audiences. When, for example, he lectured in Springfield, Massachusetts, in 1856, a special train was put on to enable people from all over the Connecticut River Valley to hear him. Beecher's 1855 Ohio tour, however, was not nearly such a triumph. From the outset it was engulfed in a fierce controversy that followed Beecher every step of the way and continued well after he had left the state. The source of all the fuss was the particular way in which the tour was arranged. Beecher did not follow the usual course of booking his engagements through local lecture associations, even though the leading lecture societies in Cincinnati, Columbus, and Cleveland had "made strenuous efforts" for two years to secure him. Beecher had initially entered into negotiations about a set of lectures "at the West" with one Samuel Ward, secretary of the Chicago Young Men's Lecture Association, who had agreed with the Cleveland and other associations to go East to "make a joint effort to secure certain Lecturers, among them Mr. Beecher." But instead of working through Ward, Beecher signed a contract with one E.S. Wells, an "agent" from Chicago, who agreed to pay Beecher $1500 for 12 lectures. Wells selected the places, booked the halls, and arranged a set of lectures that were "independent" of any of the "courses" sponsored by the local lecture societies that had tried to secure Beecher. In addition, Wells doubled the 25-cent admission that the associations ordinarily charged for lectures. Moreover, because they were independent lectures, the proceeds that were left after Beecher's fee and other expenses had been paid went to Wells and not, as was customary, to the sponsoring associations.[1]

When Beecher's arrangements for an independent tour under Wells's "agency" became known, the response was immediate and vehement. He was charged with breaking his promises to various associations to lecture for them should he ever visit their cities and with "making positive engagements with one association and then breaking them for a higher offer." He was also condemned for such sharp haggling for an excessively high fee that, in the words of the *Cleveland Herald*, the association had to reject Beecher's final demand out of "respect for themselves and the interests of the association." And, most of all, he was condemned for "letting" himself to a "speculator who [charged] unusual prices" solely to "enhance his profits," for, in effect, turning himself into a "curiosity" under the "management" of a needy "showman."[2] The mock advertisement in the *Daily Clevelander* made the point with devastating effect:

GRAND LITERARY CIRCUS
Mr. Wells of Chicago . . . . Manager
The Manager announces that, at an expense of $125 per night, he has effected an engagement with that distinguished individual, the
REV. HENRY WARD BEECHER
who will make his **only appearance** in Cleveland, on Wednesday Evening, October 24th. The public are requested to contribute fifty cents each towards paying the celebrated performer more money for an hour's talking than an intelligent mechanic can make by nine hundred hours' labour, in three months.[3]

The response did not stop at mere condemnation: newspapers in all the cities urged the public to boycott Beecher's lectures. The *Cleveland Herald* "advised" its readers "to effectively put a damper upon all such gouging designs of showmen, by staying away, and thus leaving this clerical imitator of the example set by traveling curiosities to discourse to bare walls, and the exhibitor, Mr. Wells, to pay expenses out of his own pocket."[4] In spite of Beecher's attempts at explanation and apology during the tour, the boycott was successful: the *Columbus Journal* gleefully reported that receipts "in this city amounted to less than twenty-five dollars,"[5] and the *Cleveland Herald* declared that in the three largest Ohio cities—Cincinnati, Columbus, and Cleveland—Beecher addressed a grand total of "449 men, women, and children."[6]

The controversy continued even after the tour was over and Beecher had left the state. While in the midst of the tour, Beecher (as well as a few surrogates or "friends") had responded to the charges, asserting that he had broken no promises and that the whole thing was the result of a series of "misunderstandings" and "misconceptions."[7] In a letter to the *Cleveland Plain Dealer* on October 25, 1855, he admitted that "fifty cents (except for lectures devoted to some charitable end in the community, and where the fee may be regarded as a contribution to some public end) is too much [and] that it would be better to charge less than twenty-five cents," but argued that because of his contractual agreement with Wells he had no control over the price charged for his lectures. He even argued that it "would answer the ends of popular education better were lectures to be afforded for a shilling [12½ cents] and this could be done with profit to managers if Halls were large enough."[8]

After Beecher had returned East, he sent a much longer and far less apologetic response to his critics. Adopting a tone of judicious calm (while not masking the offense he took at the slander that had been leveled against a man of his stature and reputation by "angry men in an excited community"), he patiently laid out the facts of the case to prove that he had violated no promises and that he had not engaged in unseemly haggling and had, indeed, turned down an earlier offer by Ward of $250 for a single lecture. Rejecting the characterization of Wells as an "agent" and "speculator," he portrayed him as a "Chicago merchant," "an upright Christian gentleman, a member of the Presbyterian Church" whose "interest" in the whole affair was less profit than a desire to use his hall for lectures that were "creditable and useful to the community." Moreover, he insisted that the arrangement he had made with Wells was "just such as every lecturer makes who agrees with a committee to perform an honorable service for a stipulated reward." But Beecher did not stop there. He went on to reject the grounds for questioning "the remuneration which I receive per lecture." "The public," he insisted, "had no more to do with that than they have with a surgeon's fees, a lawyer's charges, an engineer's agreement, or an author's copyright." Such things, he argued, "are regulated by a necessary law," the law, as another lecturer put it, of the "money-market."[9]

The *Cincinnati Gazette* (which printed Beecher's response) rejected his argument. To the editors, the "mainly objectionable feature" had been the whole arrangement with Wells. They agreed that "as a man" Beecher "had a right to make money in any honest way which suits his taste and talents" but insisted that under "our lecture system" a lecture was a public act governed by rules different from those governing people who entered "the [lecturing] business on their own responsibility." In bypassing the committees, "Messers Beecher and Wells," the *Gazette* concluded, "attempted to introduce a new system, and they have deservedly failed. One has lost reputation, and the other has lost money."[10] The final published comment on the affair was not Beecher's but an editorial entitled "The Rights of Intellect" by Horace Greeley in the *New York Tribune* on November 24. The editorial was a full embrace of the principles of the market that went well beyond Beecher's own position. Agreeing that Beecher had gone "in his own time and manner—not in obedience to the calls of lecture associations," and that Wells's "speculation" didn't pay, Greeley defended the actions of the Ohio public: "If those who stayed away did so because they did not think the lectures worth the price charged, it was all right; and if they did it as testimony, it was also well." However, Greeley argued, "there is an assumption underlying the concerted effort to put down those Lectures which is not well, . . . the assumption that while every man owns his own legs and arms, whatever brains there may at any time be in the community are common stock, to be at the public beck and call, and to be used for the public good,—without regard to their possessor's good."[11] Whereas the *Tribune* article appears to have been the last salvo in the public controversy, a certain kind of closure to the drama itself was achieved in the next lecture season when Beecher returned to Cincinnati. This time he lectured under the auspices of the local lecture society with a very different result: a standing-room-only crowd of 2300 people jammed into the largest hall in town to hear his lecture on patriotism (the lecture he had been slated to deliver the year before), for which he received only enthusiastic accolades from the Cincinnati press as well as $150, $25 more than the "usual" price he had sought the year before.[12]

❧

The imbroglio over Beecher can be seen as a kind of flashpoint that exposes the cultural issues and tensions that accompanied some of the changes taking place in the organization of American intellectual life in the middle decades of the nineteenth century. Perhaps the most immediately obvious change over the eighteenth century was the dramatic expansion of the audience for knowledge. At least until the end of the eighteenth century, formal knowledge—learning gained through reading and study rather than skill acquired through practice or lore transmitted through tradition and custom—was essentially the possession and province of genteel elites. Indeed, the display of learning in ordinary speech as well as in oratorical performances on public occasions, through writing, and by the possession of libraries was one of the essential badges of gentility that set the "better sort" clearly above their "inferiors" and reinforced the deference through which they exerted intellectual leadership and public dominance. By the 1840s, however, the ever-broadening audience for what was usually referred to as "useful knowledge" was thought to have expanded to encompass the entire "public." Moreover, a vast array of new institutions and new forms of printed and oral discourse had been devised to satisfy the public's seemingly limitless search for useful knowledge.

Not only had the public seeking knowledge changed and expanded, so too had the social character of the producers of knowledge. Earlier, for the most part, formal knowledge had not been created and disseminated as an essential part of the means by which its producers sustained themselves materially. Printers and booksellers, to be sure, were tradesmen who supported themselves by the production and sale of books and other printed goods, but most producers of knowledge itself had been gentlemen whose engagement in the life of the mind was product and sign of the leisure that identified them as gentlemen.[13] By the 1840s, however, public demand for useful knowledge was increasingly met by people who had devised new kinds of intellectual careers in which the production and dissemination of knowledge were an essential part of how they earned their livelihood; by people, in short, who had made knowledge their "profession." As William Charvat has pointed out, it was the 1830s and 1840s that saw the rise of the "profession of authorship" in America. Though Charvat's analysis was confined largely to poets and writers of fiction, the "profession of authorship" was one that included those for whom publication—quite literally the placing of knowledge or information before "the public"—was a central activity from which they derived their vocational identity. The boundaries subsequently placed between "creative" and other forms of literature or between "men of letters" and "men of science," or between writers for the public and scholars, were far less distinct. These various practitioners, moreover, were alike comprehended under a series of generic labels, such as "literary men," "public men," and "public teachers." Finally, the relationship between such figures differed markedly from the structures of hierarchy and deference within which intellectual leadership had traditionally been exercised. It was more open and voluntary, in nineteenth-century terms, more "democratic": anyone who would be an "intellectual sovereign" had to persuade the public that he or she possessed knowledge that was "worth" the expenditure of their time and money.[14]

Not surprisingly, the Beecher affair revolved around what was referred to as the "public lecture system," the institution that perhaps more than any other embodied all changes that had taken place in the organization of American intellectual life.[15] In the first place, it exemplified the changing nature of men of letters and learning as "public men" and, accordingly, the transformed character of the relationship between the thinker and the public. It was also a central institution by which to construct and sustain an intellectual career. Lecturing was not only an effective way to earn a livelihood (more remunerative and reliable, for example, than royalties or many ministerial posts) or to secure an often much-needed supplement to a professorial, clerical, or journalistic salary or modest private income. Ralph Waldo Emerson, for example, depended upon lecturing for almost half his income;[16] Lewis Agassiz's lecture earnings amounted to a substantial supplement to his Harvard salary;[17] and Park Benjamin, one-time poet, editor, and literary agent, was unabashed about making lecturing his "profession" because it was more lucrative than any other form of authorship he had tried.[18] Public lecturing was also an essential and effective medium for establishing and maintaining the idea "in the public mind" that one possessed a form of useful knowledge it desired. Combining print, publicity, and performance, the "public lecture system" enabled persons occupying a wide range of positions—editorships, pastorates, agencies in voluntary associations, professorships—as well as freelance pundits, reformers, and men of letters and learning to secure a public for the particular kind of knowledge they championed as well as the specific audiences they needed to make lecturing "pay." Indeed, few thinkers of the period who wished to establish a public role for themselves failed to avail themselves of the mechanism of public learning.[19]

What is most revealing about the Beecher incident is the extent to which the procedures and values of the "money market" had penetrated the production and dissemination of knowledge. In a fundamental way, knowledge had become almost wholly fungible, an essentially inexhaustible kind of intellectual raw material to be mined and shaped into a constantly expanding panoply of intellectual goods and products. Indeed, in the almost infinitely expansive range of subjects written or lectured about, almost anything and everything had been turned into a matter of formal knowledge, something that could be packaged in oral or printed form and then quite often literally peddled or purchased. For the purchasers, knowledge was sought as an essential "resource" or good by which to attain "success" and "position." In a certain sense, it had become the cognitive equivalent of the frontier—boundless, continually expanding, open ended and open to all, to be used in what Abraham Lincoln called "the race of life" in whatever ways one's will, desires, talent, and effort seemed to dictate. As Joseph Kett has pointed out, in the dominant (though not only) vision, the quintessential democrat was the "self-made" person of humble origins who used will and effort rather than privilege or preferment "to rise above his circumstances."[20] Such strivers often were forced to turn to useful knowledge in the absence of land or a patrimony to expand their life chances. Not only did the possession of it give them access to a proliferating range of jobs that involved the dissemination of knowledge, but it could also be turned into a commodity that they often quite literally peddled and sold. Elias Naison, for example, tried to turn knowledge to account in a number of ways as he forged a career for himself away from the textile mills that had seemed his destiny once his father had had to surrender the family farm. At one point he hit upon the scheme of writing subscription histories first of famous women and then of his hometown of Hopkinton, Massachusetts. But neither of these projects found enough takers to come to fruition. A bit later he secured a position in an academy in Waynesboro, Georgia, and then turned to newspaper work, followed by attempts to earn money as a lecturer, first on botany (he charged five dollars for his course) and then on phrenology, a form of knowledge that also enabled him to earn money "reading heads" at 25 cents apiece.[21]

Not only had knowledge itself become a commodity: in many though not all instances the dissemination of knowledge had become a commercial exchange. Earlier, of course, the transmission of knowledge had relatively rarely involved an exchange of money between the possessors of knowledge and the recipients of it. Knowledge was often bestowed or exchanged among gentlemen as a gift or token of mutual esteem and respect, or in the case of gentlemen lending books from their libraries to "deserving" young men, as a form of patronage. But in the American context, at least, the essential model for the bestowal of knowledge upon "the public"—deriving from the transmission of sacred knowledge—had been that between clergy and congregation.[22] Similarly, the traditional structuring of church and religion, clergy and community provided the essential template for the early knowledge societies. In the case of the clergy, the congregation or parish provided a minister with the "living" that enabled him to fulfill his essential office as a "teacher": in none of these instances did the dissemination of knowledge involve a direct monetary exchange for the knowledge received.[23] By the 1840s, however, the dissemination of knowledge was increasingly accompanied by just such an exchange. In addition, of course, the producers and disseminators of knowledge increasingly depended in part for their livelihood upon the sale of their works, either directly to the public as in a popular lecture or through publishers and periodicals, which paid them fees or royalties. Though such "offerings" might be construed or justified as serving social ends greater than the material well-being of those engaged in the profession of authorship, they were nonetheless undertaken as essential acts in earning a livelihood and in the construction and maintenance of a career as a literary person or public teacher.

The monetary exchange involved in the dissemination of knowledge, moreover, did not simply indicate the cost of a particular intellectual good. It symbolized value or worth in a larger sense as well. What was of importance—on one level at least—was not so much the amount of pay but the *fact* of payment. One commentator, referring to lectures, put it in terms that applied equally to print products: "People will not go to a lecture if they think a lecturer has 'given' his service. The public think that if it is not worth pay it is not worth hearing."[24] It was not the pay that *bestowed* value—it was knowledge itself that possessed value. (Though obviously related, the "right" to payment for a knowledge product was a different and perhaps even more complex issue.) Rather, pay *certified* that the exchange was one of value and legitimated it as such: pay signified the acceptance of a knowledge claim, that one possessed and the other had received knowledge that had worth and value.

The implication of the market into intellectual life went even further. For those pursuing intellectual professions, success increasingly involved their not only selling their products or services but also "marketing" themselves as purveyors of some desired form of useful knowledge. The intellectual itinerants and peddlers, of course, provide the most obvious and dramatic examples of the process. Representative of the type, perhaps, is one Dr. Darling who can be found in Worcester, Massachusetts, in 1825 lecturing on "the elements of chemistry," in Greenfield, Massachusetts, in 1844 giving a course on "phrenology," and in 1848 back again in Worcester lecturing on "physiology." (His arrest in Newfame, Vermont, in 1844 as a suspect in a bank robbery suggests the possibility that he may have entertained the thought of a rather different career.)[25] Most successful of the species, however, were those impresarios of "applied phrenology," the Fowler brothers, who built a lucrative lecturing and publishing business out of what might be thought of as a kind of "patent idea," grounded on far-reaching and comprehensive theory but also applicable as a guide to the decisions or remedy for the problems of daily life—career choice, marital happiness, financial success, resistance to temptation, and control of base desires.

Such figures relied upon vigorous advertising to attract the attention and patronage of the public. Usually depending upon the take at the door rather than set fees for their earnings, they would "hire a hall" and announce themselves and their wares (often they used their lectures to sell publications or attract clients for private "consultations") with posters and newspaper ads that were usually far larger, more lavish in design, and more extravagant in their claims than the handbills by more decorous and "reputable" intellectual sovereigns. (Invariably they would give their first lecture free, hoping to attract an audience eager to come back and pay for the rest of the lectures in the course.) The itinerants' ads, moreover, made a number of claims. They connected their particular subject to the grandest possible themes—democracy, the glories of the creation, the secrets of the universe, the "laws" that governed the body or the emotions, etc. They also stressed the effort and exertion—the "originality"—of their lectures, pointing to the expense and hardship they had endured to bless the public with their particular brand of knowledge. A great deal was also made of the expense and uniqueness of the props—of the experimental apparatus if it was a science lecture, of the paintings and tableaux if it was an historical or biblical lecture, of the brilliance and authenticity of the costumes and artifacts if it was a travel lecture. The ads also usually listed endorsements purportedly from clergymen, educators, and leading citizens, all of whom seemed to vouch for the importance of the subject, the character and ability of the lecturer, and the good taste and "chasteness" of the performance. Finally, the ads stressed popularity, endorsement by "the people," by pointing out the size and enthusiasm of the audiences that had responded to them, especially in the larger, cosmopolitan centers to which smaller, more provincial towns increasingly looked for their cultural cues.[26]

Although such intellectual sovereigns as Benjamin Silliman, Bayard Taylor, and Ralph Waldo Emerson might try to distance themselves from such hawkers as Dr. Darling and Professor

Bushbee, the market imperatives upon them were not so different. The claims in the lavish ads mirrored the very same values and claims by which the more respectable and established figures sought to establish themselves with the public. (A principal difference, especially in the 1840s and early 1850s, is that they were able to work through forms of local endorsement and did not need to shout quite so loudly to get the public's attention. By the late 1850s, however, their posters were almost as large and insistent as those of the hawkers.) For they too depended upon techniques of promotion and publicity to keep both them and their works "before the public" and to maintain the idea that they were pursuing the "profession of authorship" and thereby could at least earn a livelihood, if not achieve the standing of intellectual sovereignty.

Finally, this increasingly marketlike world of knowledge was essentially a "free-market." It seemed to operate according to the logic of the market itself or market forces. The increasing demand for useful knowledge not only brought an ever-larger supply of producers into the market and into competition with each other but also kept pushing up the price of a number of products. When Elisha Kane, for example, returned from his Arctic expedition, which he and others reported on in the weekly press, he was beseiged by more than 100 invitations to lecture, and his subsequent book was advertised and sold very widely.[27] And from 1848 to 1860 the top lecture fees rose from 50 to 200 dollars.[28] This market, moreover, was not a privileged or regulated one but was open to "free" entry by producers or consumers. As the phenomenon of intellectual itinerancy suggests, it seemed that anyone who had the will and willingness to expend the labor could come before the public as the purveyor of some form or other of useful knowledge (whether one "succeeded" or not was another question). And the consumers were equally free to participate as they would—to shop, select, and purchase or not. On at least one level, then, the relationship between thinker and the public at large had become an exchange between free and equal agents. (There were, to be sure, such domains as churches, schools, and learned societies in which the relation between the possessor and the recipients of knowledge remained outside the *immediate* logic of a market transaction. But these were confined, essentially private associations: It was when knowledge—and thinkers—entered the public arena that it and they entered a marketlike intellectual domain. The relationships, for example, between Beecher and his Plymouth Church congregation, and between Benjamin Silliman and his Yale classes or the American Academy of Arts and Sciences, was very different from their relationship to their lecture-going, book-buying public.) In fact, the penetration of the procedures of the free market into the production and dissemination of knowledge not only dissolved the structures of hierarchy and deference through which learned gentlemen had bestowed their knowledge upon the general public, but it also seemed to have reversed the direction of the flow of power. In many ways the "market," as Americans came to envision and enthrone it, was homologous to the "democratic" principles and procedures they simultaneously developed and enshrined. Intellectual "success," the ability to "rise" through effort and talent to a position of intellectual "sovereignty," depended not only upon talent and effort rather than privilege or station but also upon the ability to win the support of "the public." Not surprisingly, the apologists for the public lecture system made the homology explicit. The system was described as one in which "the money-market" served as an "infallible test" and "a ready standard by which to try all prominent men," and it was also extolled as a kind of election.[29] *Harper's Weekly* pointed out that "the score or two" among the "hundreds" who had risen to "universal popularity" had done so because they had "passed the severe test of repeated delivery before lyceum audiences in different parts of the country."[30] And Josiah Holland, who dubbed the public lecture system "the most democratic of our democratic institutions," asserted that "there is no literary tribunal in this country that can more readily and justly decide whether a man has anything to say and can say it well, than a lecture audience."[31]

❧

This penetration of the market into the procedures for disseminating knowledge to the public framed the Beecher episode, which essentially composed itself as a public contest and campaign. It was enacted before "the public" and addressed to it. Though the controversy was conducted as a set of exchanges between Beecher and his defenders on the one hand and the local lecture committees and editors on the other, what they were contending for was public opinion and support, support that in the end was to be expressed through the public's market power. Both money and public influence were at stake. Beecher stood to lose not only his fees (and Wells his apparently hoped-for profit) but also possibly some of his future earning power. The committees stood to lose both the income they often depended upon to finance their libraries and rooms and their power to define local intellectual life. (The societies were not so worried about competition from "itinerant" lecturers like the Fowler brothers who lectured "on their own hook" and operated essentially outside the more formalized "public lecture system." But the results could be disastrous if the very "stars" the societies used to headline their courses—the Beechers, the Ormsby Mitchells, the Bayard Taylors, the Ralph Waldo Emersons—were lured into their communities as "independent" lecturers by "agents" who could offer ever higher fees.) Here, local intellectual leaders had perhaps the most to lose—namely, their role in elevating public knowledge and taste by selecting the leading figures of the day to present to their local constituencies. If such stars could come into the local community "independently," both the editor's and committee's prestige and ability to shape public taste would be undermined. On this level, the episode pitted Beecher's drawing power as a national intellectual star against the power of the committees and editors as local arbiters of culture.

These, then, were the stakes. But the contest was waged on a field of meaning. In the competition for support of the public, both sides invoked ideas and values about "knowledge," "the market," and "democracy" that they assumed the public to hold. This contest, however, was not simply between older values and new practices and did not simply array "the market" as represented by Beecher against "custom" and traditional values as championed by the committees. On the contrary, both Beecher and his antagonists stationed themselves—differently to be sure—upon a common but shifting field of ideas and values. Both embraced and rejected dimensions of the market and both embraced and rejected older ways of viewing the place of knowledge in society as they tried to develop the most persuasive argument possible. Both sides, in Beecher's words, sought not only to put themselves "in the right" but also to define the right of the whole complex situation.

Both parties invoked a conception of knowledge itself as a "higher thing" that could provide American society with "the common ground" that would serve both as the antidote to the conflict and turmoil of democracy and as the foundation for continued "progress." This idea of knowledge as a kind of surrogate for earlier forms of religious and political orthodoxy was first articulated most fully in the arguments justifying the foundation of various learned societies set up in the early decades of the republic. But it was also fully embodied in both the general lyceums of the 1820s and 1830s and in the public lecture system. This was a conception of knowledge that placed it in a realm outside and above politics and religion as well as outside the marketplace. It was believed that for knowledge to provide society with a "common ground," it had to be protected as knowledge, to be immunized against contamination by partisanship, sectarianism, or self-interest.[32] This did not require the kinds of certification that later came to be associated with disciplines. Instead it required procedures to monitor motives and character and thus ensure that those who claimed to possess knowledge acted out of disinterestedness rather than from partisanship, sectarianship, or self-interest. Indeed, knowledge societies of all kinds—learned societies as well as lyceums and lecture societies—carefully excluded from the discourses they accepted as constituting knowledge anything that smacked of partisan or sectarian advocacy. Moreover, a principal criterion for selection into a "learned" society was not only demonstrated "devotion" to knowledge but also "character," defined as dedication not to self-interest but to the public good. Another corollary to this conception of knowledge was the definition of the act of disseminating knowledge essentially as a "service" or an "office" that one undertook for the public good. In the early learned societies and lyceums people donated their services out of a sense of public duty. When such offerings were subsequently published, the act of publication was proclaimed to be undertaken as a gesture of public benevolence by the sponsoring society rather than at the initiative of or for the benefit of the author. Even in the case of the clergy, remuneration was construed, not as an exchange for the service but as a way of exempting them from the day-to-day necessities of making a living and thereby freeing them to devote themselves to the "higher things" that formed the substance of their essential office.[33]

Both sides situated their arguments clearly within this framework. In its final response to Beecher's long defense, the *Cincinnati Gazette* (after rhetorically conceding that, technically at least, Beecher had not broken any promises) rested its case against his lecturing in Cincinnati "upon the conditions of the Wells contract" on a crucial distinction between Beecher "as a man" and "as a minister." The *Gazette* conceded that "as a man" Beecher had "a right to make money in any honest way which suits his taste and talents" but insisted that "as a minister" Beecher had not only acted illegitimately but also violated the essential boundaries by which knowledge was protected as a public good.[34] (Had the incident involved a nonclerical figure such as Silliman or Bayard Taylor, the *Gazette* would probably have used the generic term "public teacher.") The distinction embodied the notion that a public lecture was a public service, undertaken not for gain but as part of the "great work" of "popular improvement" to which the "public teachers" who were called as lecturers, and the lecture societies alike, were devoted. (It was, of course, partly Beecher's reputation as "one identified so closely with so many good causes" that had made him such an attractive candidate for sponsorship by local lecture committees.) Conversely, the attack on Beecher portrayed him as having forfeited his "public character." This image of Beecher as transgressor was constructed out of a vision of the market as the embodiment of precisely the kind of contamination that knowledge as a public good needed to be immunized against. His bargaining was portrayed as stemming from self-interested motives rather than public character, an attempt to enlist the forces of the market purely to "gouge" the public and make more money for himself. The charge that Beecher had "hired himself out to some Barnum" pushed the trope even further. By doing that, the *Gazette* insisted, Beecher had become "the property of a speculator" (and his lectures purely commodities) whose sole purpose was profit.[35]

Beecher's answer to the charges against him (issued as a "statement of fact") tried to occupy the same ground. He went into great detail recounting exactly how the sequence of negotiations and arrangements had developed. Beecher addressed from two directions the charge that his motives had been those of a mere man seeking to make money as his taste and talent allowed. He denied that he had engaged in market practices by showing that he had not broken any promises or tried to "gouge" higher prices out of the committees. He also argued that the arrangements he had made were the standard ones "every lecturer makes who agrees with a committee to perform an honorable service for a stipulated reward." He portrayed such arrangements as ways of exempting lecturers from direct, sullying involvement in the market. More positively, he portrayed his actions as thoroughly grounded in a sense of public service and responsibility. He, too, invoked his clerical position, expressly disassociating himself from lecturing as something he did for the sake of remuneration. (Beecher insisted he was not a "professional lecturer" who depended upon lecture income for his livelihood.) He pointed out that he had turned down more lucrative invitations from both Ward and Wells out of a sense of duty to his "home charge" at Plymouth Church. The same sense of public service, he suggested, lay behind his insistence that if he were to come to the West, it would only be worthwhile if he did not confine himself to Chicago but also "visited many of the places to which I had been urgently and repeatedly invited, accomplishing the greatest amount of [good] work possible in one absence from home."[36] (One of Beecher's defenders put a rather different construction on Beecher's insistence: "sufficient remuneration to make it pay.")[37]

In addition, Beecher tried to turn the rhetorical tables on some of his critics. He implied that the committees might not have been nearly so disinterested as they professed to be, that their calumny against him and Wells might have a bit of the profit motive lurking behind it. He again asserted his "judgement that the greatest benefit to the community" would be had if prices were lower and lecture halls larger so that persons of "slender means" could attend, and he wondered if the community's failure to object to high prices for events (often of a "low" character) whose proceeds would not enter their coffers did not suggest "some deeper feeling behind this pretence for so sudden and violent an indignation." And he charged that the committees' insistence that Wells get no recompense for his "time, trouble and responsibility" was the "arrogant . . . avarice of societies which propose to themselves public ends."[38]

The idea of knowledge as a public good was only part of the ground on which the contest between Beecher and his antagonists took place. Equally at play was the underlying acceptance by both sides of knowledge as a product and commodity. Here, it was Beecher who most firmly announced the terms. His maneuvering around the charges that he had violated the canons of service reads as a largely defensive attempt to make his way through an ideological minefield. But when it came to defending his "reward" for his lectures, he confidently claimed the market as his strongest ground:

> As to the remuneration which I receive per lecture, I humbly think that the public have no more to do with that than they have with a surgeon's fee, a lawyer's charges, an engineer's agreement, or an author's copyright. These things are regulated by necessary law. No committee will offer a man more than they think his services are worth. It is not extortion or avarice for a man to accept remuneration which is in proportion to the ascertained worth of his services.[39]

This argument contained a conception of the value embedded within a public lecture that was very different from the value it possessed as a public good. It rested upon the idea that it was the lecturer's labor and talent—in Greeley's terms the "intellect"—that imparted value to his production, that transmuted the inchoate stuff of knowledge into a product that had ascertainable "worth" for others. And this operation of intellect as a form of labor gave lecturers the right of property in their product, the "right" to demand "remuneration" for giving it to others. Finally, the ideological move of assigning responsibility to the "necessary law" of the market removed Beecher from complicity in "ascertaining" the worth of his lecture. That was not the result of his motives and actions but of the operation of natural law. And what gave Beecher's invocation of this "necessary law" added rhetorical power was the fact that the competition of committees all over the country to secure his services kept jacking up the price. Beecher suggested that the attempts by the Ohio committees to interfere with the "law" of the market violated broader, democratic values. He closed his "statement of facts" by pointing to the danger "that such associations will gradually . . . usurp authority and demand that all lecturers shall come to the community by their 'course,' making independent lectures an offense, to be visited with punishment through the organized interference of the local associations between a lecturer and the citizens." And, he asked, did not such usurpation amount to "censorship," the power of the associations to determine who might or might not lecture in their community and abridge the freedom of "the citizens" to hear whom they pleased, a freedom, he implied, that could best be guaranteed by "law" of the market?[40]

No less than Beecher, the lecture societies and editors arrayed against him fully embraced knowledge as a market product and commodity. The central difference in how their acceptance of the market figured in the moral position they tried to establish was that they did not, indeed *could* not, directly avow it. In effect, the market exerted a "silent" but nonetheless powerful presence in the construction of the ground upon which they made their stand. Their use of the market to represent the illegitimacy of Beecher's actions—making it the rhetorical opposite that established the morality of their own position—left them little room to grant it the legitimating force of natural law. To do so, of course, would have been to surrender the ground entirely to Beecher. But their silence—they talk about market motives, but never name the market—had a deeper dimension: what in the end it "suppressed" was the fact that from the very beginning they were as deeply implicated in the market as Beecher was. As the committees' efforts (loudly proclaimed in the ads for their "courses") to secure the "best" lecturers demonstrate, it was precisely the value established in the market that "ascertained" for them Beecher's "worth." Moreover, this unacknowledged acceptance of the market as conveying value extended beyond acceptance of the fact of pay as the symbol of the value that a knowledge product itself possessed knowledge. The "worth" of a lecture for the committees also lay in its market-determined value as an exchange commodity that they in turn could sell for a "profit." Significantly, in its attack on Beecher, the Columbus newspaper charged that in giving Wells the exclusive right to "sell" his lectures, Beecher had given Wells a "monopoly" that cut them out of the market. In the end, if Beecher's embrace of the "necessary law of the market" enabled him to separate how worth was ascertained from the question of motives, the committee's suppression of their implication in the market enabled them to extract value from it without surrendering to that law their "right" and power to bring "knowledge" as a "higher thing" to their communities.[41]

❧

What, then, does this little tempest suggest about the relationship between knowledge and the marketplace in mid-nineteenth-century America? It does not, I think, indicate a process by which the new (knowledge as product) was coming to replace the old (knowledge as public good). Rather, it suggests how knowledge had become simultaneously and so confusedly both a "higher thing" and a commodity in the marketplace. The problem lay precisely in how the two modes of knowledge had become at once entwined and placed in tension with each other. The two conceptions of knowledge embodied cherished and largely unquestioned values and ways of establishing value that not only conflicted but that also were in fact defined in contrast with each other.

The idea of knowledge as a public good derived from the conception of knowledge as a "higher thing" beyond the reach of self-interest. Its social force depended upon public confidence that those who proclaimed knowledge had not appropriated it for partial or selfish ends. But the market not only introduced a notion of a property right in knowledge into the procedures for disseminating it; it also introduced a mechanism for establishing and signifying the value of knowledge that operated without reference to knowledge itself. These mechanisms were grounded in a conception of the free play of precisely that "self-interest" against which knowledge as a public good was thought to provide a necessary ballast. In addition, the implication of knowledge into the market as product seemed to turn invocations of the idea of the public good of knowledge into market ploys, statements that served to enhance its value as pure commodity. (Both sides in the Beecher incident, for example, suggest that the other side's profession of concern for the good of the public masked what were really self-aggrandizing motives.)[42] In the end, perhaps, the penetration of the market into the dissemination of knowledge created the cultural conundrum Herman Melville (who tried but essentially failed to make his way on the lecture circuit) identified so bitterly in *The Confidence Man*. In the novel it is impossible to figure out whether the central figure in his many guises as a purveyor of knowledge is a man of disinterested character in whom the public can place its trust or whether he is nothing more than a diabolically clever confidence man, pretending to offer the public knowledge of great value and all the while duping them.[43]

The extrication of knowledge from Melville's conundrum is a further story that cannot be delivered here. Suffice it to say that it required remapping the social location of knowledge, a remapping that involved constructing both institutional and cognitive barriers that would protect knowledge as a "higher thing" from the influences of both the market and a domestic public. This remapping in turn involved the delineation of clearly bounded academic disciplines and the construction of professions around them as well as the creation of the scholar and scientist as expert, a social type very different from the general "man of letters" as a public man.[44]

Notes

1. This incident is described in David Mead, *Yankee Eloquence in the Middle West, 1850–1870* (East Lansing, Mich., 1951), 133–41.
2. See "The Beecher and Wells Matter," *Cleveland Evening Herald*, October 27, 1855, and "Statement of Facts," *Cincinnati Daily Gazette*, November 15, 1855, for the fullest contemporary accounts of the affair.
3. *Sandusky Daily Commercial Register*, October 14, 1855, quoted in Mead, *Yankee Eloquence*, 139.
4. *Cleveland Evening Herald*, October 22, 1855.
5. *Columbus Journal* reprinted in *Cleveland Evening Herald*, October 26, 1855.
6. *Cleveland Evening Herald*, October 25, 1855.
7. *Cincinnati Daily Gazette*, October 25, 1855.
8. *Cleveland Plain Dealer*, October 25, 1855.
9. *Cincinnati Daily Gazette*, November 15, 1855.
10. Ibid.
11. *New York Tribune*, November 24, 1855.
12. *Cincinnati Daily Gazette*, November 17, 1856.
13. See, generally, Alexandra Oleson and Sanborn C. Brown, *The Pursuit of Knowledge in the Early American Republic: American, Scientific and Learned Societies from Colonial Times to the Civil War* (Baltimore, 1976); William J. Gilmore, *Reading Becomes a Necessity of Life* (Charlottesville, N.C., 1987); and Richard D.

Brown, *Knowledge Is Power: The Diffusion of Information in Early America, 1700–1865* (New York, 1989).

14. See William Charvat, *The Profession of Authorship in America* (Columbus, Ohio, 1976) and R. Jackson Wilson, *Figures of Speech: American Writers and the Literary Marketplace from Benjamin Franklin to Emily Dickinson* (New York, 1989).

15. For lecturing and the lecture system see Robert J. Greef, "Public Lectures in New York, 1851–1878: A Cultural Index of the Times" (Ph.D. diss., University of Chicago, 1941); Carl Bode, *The American Lyceum: Town Meeting of the Mind* (New York, 1956); and Donald M. Scott, "The Popular Lecture and the Creation of a Public in Mid-nineteenth Century America," *The Journal of American History* 66 (March 1980), 781–809.

16. See Ralph J. Rusk, *The Life of Ralph Waldo Emerson* (New York, 1949).

17. See Edward Lurie, *Louis Agassiz: A Life in Science* (Chicago, 1960).

18. Park Benjamin to the president of the New Bedford Lyceum, October 18, 1850, Park Benjamin Papers, Butler Library, Columbia University. See also Merle M. Hoover, *Park Benjamin, Poet and Editor* (New York, 1948).

19. See Donald M. Scott, "Print and the Public Lecture System, 1840–1860," in William L. Joyce et al., eds., *Printing and Society in Early America* (Worcester, Mass., 1983).

20. See Joseph Kett, *Rites of Passage: Adolescence in America, 1790 to the Present* (New York, 1977) and David F. Allmendinger, Jr., *Paupers and Scholars: The Transformation of Student Life in Nineteenth-Century New England* (New York, 1975).

21. Elias Naison diary, Elias Naison Papers, American Antiquarian Society, Worcester, Mass.

22. See Rhys Isaac, "Books and the Social Authority of Learning," in Joyce et al., *Print and Society in Early America*, 278–99.

23. See Daniel Calhoun, *Professional Lives in America* (Cambridge, Mass., 1965) and Donald M. Scott, *From Office to Profession: The New England Ministry, 1750–1850* (Philadelphia, 1978).

24. Edward Everett Hale, *James Russell Lowell and His Friends* (Boston, 1899), 110.

25. Edward Jenner Carpenter diary, September 17, 1844; February 2, 1845; May 12, 1845, Carpenter Papers, American Antiquarian Society, Worcester, Mass.

26. This analysis is based on the superb collection of posters and broadsides in the Graphics Collection of the American Antiquarian Society, Worcester, Mass. See also Donald M. Scott, "Itinerant Lecturers and Lecturing in New England, 1800–1850," in Peter Benes, ed., *Itinerancy in New England and New York* (Boston, 1986), 65–75.

27. *Hampshire Gazette*, January 22, 1856.

28. The ways in which the "market" kept forcing the fees for the lecture "stars" ever upward can be seen in the papers of the Northampton Young Men's Institute, Forbes Library, Northampton, Mass.; the papers of the Albany Young Men's Society, Albany Public Library, Albany, New York; the Minutes of the Worcester Lyceum, 1829–1856; and the Record Book of the

Petersham, Massachusetts, Lyceum, American Antiquarian Society, Worcester, Mass.

29. Thomas Wentworth Higginson, "The American Lecture-System," *MacMillan's Magazine* XVIII (May 1868), 53.
30. "Reviews and Literary Notices," *Atlantic Monthly* (July 1860), 120.
31. Josiah G. Holland, "The Popular Lecture," *Atlantic Monthly* 15 (March 1865), 365.
32. See, for example, *Address to the Members of the American Antiquarian Society: Together with the Laws and Regulations of the Institution* (Worcester, Mass., 1819) and Daniel Drake, *An Anniversary Discourse on the State and Prospects of the Western Museum Society* (Cincinnati, 1820). See also Arnold Thackery, "Natural Knowledge in Cultural Context: The Manchester Model," *American Historical Review* 79 (June 1974), 672–709.
33. See Scott, *Office to Profession*, 1–18.
34. *Cincinnati Daily Gazette*, November 15, 1855.
35. *Cincinnati Daily Gazette*, October 23, 1855. See also the *Cleveland Evening Herald*, October 27, 1855.
36. "Statement of Facts," *Cincinnati Daily Gazette*, November 15, 1855.
37. *Cincinnati Daily Gazette*, October 25, 1855.
38. "Statement of Facts," *Cincinnati Daily Gazette*, November 15, 1855.
39. Ibid.
40. Ibid.
41. *Daily Capital City Fact*, October 18, 1855, quoted in Mead, *Yankee Eloquence*, 137.
42. *Cincinnati Daily Gazette*, October 23, 1855, and November 15, 1855; *Cleveland Evening Herald*, October 27, 1855.
43. See the discussion of Melville's *Confidence Man* in Neil Harris, *Humbug: The Art of P.T. Barnum* (Boston, 1973).
44. See, generally, Thomas Haskell, *The Emergence of Professional Social Science* (Urbana, Ill., 1977); Alexandra Oleson and John Voss, eds., *The Organization of Knowledge in Modern America, 1860–1920* (Baltimore, 1979); and Thomas Haskell, ed., *The Authority of Experts* (Bloomington, Ind., 1984).

❧

The Culture of "Leg-Work": The Transformation of Burlesque after the Civil War

Peter G. Buckley

IN 1867 MARK TWAIN TRAVELED TO NEW YORK CITY ACCOMPANIED BY HIS splenetic and imaginary companion, Mr. Brown. Over the next six months Twain completed his journalistic tour of duty by surveying the "sunshine and shadow" of the metropolis, from the Five Points to Fifth Avenue, and the sundry charitable and religious institutions between such extremes. Many of the sights, and the comments he made upon them, were predictable, having been selected by most literary visitors to the city since Dickens; yet the most novel aspect to Twain's panorama is the attention he paid to an expanding range of commercial institutions that lined Broadway above Bleeker Street: the dry-goods houses, hotels, theatres, and restaurants. Though he complained frequently about the luxury and velocity of this commercial zone, one feature—the presence of young, fashionably dressed women—disturbed him in a different manner:

> Charming, fascinating, seductive, bewitching! To see a lovely girl of seventeen, with her saddle on her head, and her muzzle on behind, and her veil just covering the end of her nose, come tripping along in her hoopless, red-bottomed dress, like a churn on fire, is enough to set a man wild. I must drop this subject—I can't stand it.[1]

Twain could not drop the subject, if for no other reason than that such women appeared to link the commercial sites of the city into one desirable whole. Of course, his sighting of such "clipper built girls" on the living stream of Broadway might have been his personal way of seasoning the regular fare served up to readers of the *Alta California;* yet, given his facility with literary types, it is more likely that he was consciously exporting to the West a newly arrived figure in the journals, if not streets, of New York and London—the so-called "Girl of the Period."

This girl achieved formal shape in a series of articles written by Elizabeth Lynn Linton for *The Saturday Review.* For Linton

> The Girl of the Period is a creature who dyes her hair and paints her face, as the first articles of her personal religion—creature whose sole idea of life is fun; whose sole aim is unbounded luxury.[2]

This girl's adoption of fashion is, according to Linton, only one mark of the wholesale breakdown in parental authority. The rest of her essay catalogs the sins the girl encounters as she steps ever closer to the borders of the *demi-monde:* "It leads to slang, bold talk and general fastness; to the love of pleasure and indifference to duty; to the desire of money before either love or happiness; to uselessness at home, dissatisfaction with the monotony of ordinary life."[3] In sum, the advent of this new women threatened to alter the basis of marriage and thereby to wreck the very foundations of society. Henry James, reviewing Linton's work, considered such talk standard sensationalism, another instance of "an immense pressure of unleavened literary matter" crushing critical thought; nevertheless he noted that the young urban woman had indeed "compromised her natural freedom of movement" with the recent extension of fashion.

> She has, moreover, great composure and impenetrability of aspect. She practices a sort of half-cynical indifference to the beholder (we speak of the extreme cases). Accustomed to walk alone in the streets of a great city,

> and to be looked at by all sorts of people, she has acquired an unshrinking directness of gaze. She is the least bit hard."[4]

Again, James might have been speaking from personal experience. No doubt increasing numbers of young women were promenading on Broadway, and perhaps they refused to return the young author's glances. Yet the novel character of the commercial street does not determine how the new representations of women brought in their train a string of other anxieties: about the uncertainties of marriage, the perils of fashion, and the drift into luxury. Nor does it explain why the girl of the period is handled, in literature, as a species of ritual inversion. Not only does her presence challenge the established cultural hierarchies of class and gender but also often reverses them: directness of gaze replaces demure submission, the parading of feminine charm in an aggressive manner points to her being "masculine in mind," and where we once might have read her true character in the face, we now are provoked by the sensuality of legs. She herself is theatrical in manner, and so is the writing about her.

To a historian of theatrical forms the Girl of the Period seems strangely familiar. Her gaze, her aggression, her theatricality, and indeed her yellow hair were mirrored and perhaps preempted by her "nude" burlesque sister on stage. Between 1866 and 1872, New York's "legitimate" theatres housed a mania for female spectacle drama. In melodramatic ballet, opéra bouffe, and, most importantly, blonde burlesque, women in short skirts pushed Shakespeare, realistic melodrama, and the opera to the wings. Even before Twain spied the bewitching young women of Broadway, linking together a city of commercial abundance and possibility, he had taken in a performance of a balletic troupe in *The Black Crook:*

> Beautiful bare-legged girls hanging in flower baskets; others stretched in groups on great sea shells; others clustered around flutted columns; others in all possible attitudes; girls—nothing but a wilderness of girls—stacked up, pile on pile, away aloft to the dome of the theatre, diminishing in size and clothing, till the last row, mere children, dangle high up from invisible ropes, arrayed only in camisa.[5]

Though one cannot argue that this simply presents a case of reverse cultural mimesis, of Twain reading life through art, it does appear that the vogue for female spectaculars, and the discussion about their social effects, served to frame the characterization of fashionable women in public urban environments. This essay examines some features of a very circular discourse that brought within its orbit social feminism, "nude" actresses and dancers, and the Girl of the Period in the streets. Its primary focus is on the burlesque itself, and it assesses, in Olive Logan's words, "a record of a period in the history of drama which will long be remembered as an extraordinary one."[6] The essay offers a broader context for understanding the "nude woman question": that of a burgeoning commercial culture that appropriated plebeian forms in its search for the novel, the spectacular, and the sensual. In this context, "nudity" became a metaphor for a more general transgression of the boundaries of class and gender in Second Empire New York.[7]

The most persistent and celebrated critic of "leg-work" in America was the actress Olive Logan. Though she had been moderately successful herself, especially playing tragic roles during the Civil War, she nevertheless decided in 1864 that she would henceforth "live by the pen." This appears to have been a vocational strategy worked out with some care. In becoming an author by profession she would at last have equal status with men and share in the serious readership of polite monthly magazines. Most importantly, she would no longer be employed by theatrical managers increasingly interested, to her mind, in profit rather than "drama." Rather than be trapped on the commercial stage, she might ascend above it as "critic" and then remove the glaring faults from an otherwise worthy career: "I am . . . going to continue a defender of the drama, with voice and pen, always and everywhere."[8]

Thus began a remarkable series of critiques of "the show business" that included every style of public performance from Henry Ward Beecher's theatricalized sermons to exhibitions of Learned Pigs.[9] Logan first tackled the "Drunken Drama," claiming that depictions of inebriation on stage were more likely to encourage emulation by "the Bowery Boys" than a reformation of their habits. Indeed, compared to the so-called moral drama presented in working-class theatres, the social effects of "the leg business is trivial," she wrote in 1867. But what she then detected was the growing tendency, even by managers of refined houses, to make money by displaying the "private vices" of actors. New York, she claimed, demanded a drama that represented "real life" in all "its refined and agreeable phases."

In one way the refrain sounded familiar. Logan was simply adding her voice to the general chorus that lamented the unremitting decline of the legitimate stage. This lament can be heard in New York as early as the 1820s with the advent of popular melodrama, the rise of the star system, and the arrival of the vigorous plebeian audiences of the Bowery. Through the 1830s, respectable patrons of the theatre had, in Philip Hone's words, "first retreated to the boxes, and then left the houses altogether." The construction of the Astor Place Opera House in 1847, however, signalled that some kind of renaissance had been effected. A number of genres, notably Italian opera, William Mitchell's comic burlesque, and the debowdlerized Shakespeare offered by Kean, witnessed, according to the *Times*, "signs that the stage has been reformed." Moreover, a whole range of theatres had been built on upper Broadway stretching to Union Square, in close proximity to the residential refinement of the 15th and 21st wards. These theatres all included a family circle, replacing the guilty third tier of prostitutes, and extensive, ornamental salons in which patrons could socialize away from "the din and craft" of the street. By the close of the Civil War, 16 houses offered entertainments that were then considered legitimate, and receipts from this stratum alone totalled three million dollars annually.

Though there were many gradations of refinement by audience and cultural form, and much commerce between the Bowery and upper Broadway stages, it is still possible to claim that at the end of the Civil War New York's theatrical life was highly divided by both genre and social geography. And it was these divisions that the "leg business" first called into question.

Logan provided a telescoped history of "leg-work," running from "brunettes" to "blondes," that overlooked a local tradition of stage nudity and that narrowed existing distinctions between spectacle and burlesque. The brunettes in question were the scantily clad balletic chorus of *The Black Crook*, seen by Twain and first staged at Niblo's Garden in September 1866. Nominally, *The Black Crook* was a melodrama loosely based on the Faust legend. It contained the usual stock characters of the wicked count, an innocent rural youth, and the alchemist. This drama, however, occupied only a small part of over four hours of magical transformations, light displays, and musical and balletic chorus work. The central attraction was the *premières danseuses,* Marie Bonfanti, Rita Sangalli, and Betty Rigl, European dancers who had been trained at La Scala, Milan, and Porte St. Martin, Paris. Directed and choreographed by David Costa, these dancers portrayed pastoral, demonic, and fairy scenes that fleshed out the skeleton of the play.[10] Critics judged the final fairy transformation as the most "fabulous," "beautiful," or "luxurious" spectacle ever witnessed on a New York stage. "All that gold," enthused the *Tribune* reporter:

> and silver, and gems, and light, and women's beauty can contribute to fascinate the eye and charm the senses is gathered up in the gorgeous spectacle. Its luster grows as we gaze, and deepens and widens, till the effect is almost painful. One by one, curtains of mist ascend and drift away. Silver couches, on which the fairies loll in negligent grace, ascend and descend amid a silver whirl.[11]

With continuous changes in scenic design and ballet composition, including the introduction of the cancan in 1867, *The Black Crook* ran for 16 months, grossing one million dollars.

Jarret and Palmer's success with *The Black Crook* (which had appeared in a rather different form on the London stage) encouraged other managers to search for similar blends of scenic effect, music, and dance. The most available import was opéra bouffe, and the 1867 season witnessed five productions of Offenbach's work, all including mild "leg-work" drills and dances.

Finally, in Logan's schema, came the blondes of Lydia Thompson's troupe, in all four British troupes that performed elaborately staged variety entertainments composed of topical sketches, songs, and dances. They were called "burlesques" of pantomime, classical myth, and opéra bouffe though, unlike satire, they required no exacting familiarity with the original work for their effect.

Despite these differences in formal genres, Logan lumped balletic melodrama, opéra bouffe, and burlesque into the single category of "leg-work," assuming that nude limbs formed the main strategy of enticement. Her analysis was shared by the clergy—notably Rev. Charles B. Smyth, who hired the Great Hall of Cooper

Union to reveal "The Nuisances of New York, Particularly the Naked Truth"[12]—by polite monthlies, such as *Harpers,* and by roughly one-third of the daily press. Initially, the theatrical, sporting, and fashion presses did not make "nudity" the focus of their critique; after all, equal displays of nakedness had been seen from "principal boys" in pantomime for two decades. The nudity was new, however, in being particularly kinetic. The costumes were designed to accentuate the limbs rather than the torso; they suggested action, not merely show. Apart from Richard Grant White's remark that Pauline Markham (of Lydia Thompson's troupe) had found the long-lost arms of Venus de Milo, the performers did not possess classical proportions. Lydia's legs were, to the eyes of one critic, "elephantine and licentious." They were made for movement and aggressive gesture. Together with knowing winks and double entendres, they broke through, so to speak, the sanctified space between performance and audience that two decades of management and critical taste had sought to construct.[13]

In addition to the presumed sexual commerce between the audience and stage, concern was also expressed about the intermingling—or "the promiscuous nature," in the *Tribune*'s words—of genres. Logan was correct in denying that the new pieces held to conventional theatrical forms. *The Black Crook, White Faun,* and *Ixion* were variety entertainment in which any "piece of business" could be exchanged for another. Any unity to these performances was acquired by the innovative use of spectacle and machinery, the gorgeous backcloths and lighting, and the dancing, pageantry, and processions of women. The plays were called burlesques only because they juxtaposed the classical or fabulous event with contemporary enthusiasm or blended high life with the commonplace like the existing "extravaganza." Yet unlike the earlier forms of extravaganza, which frequently had pointed social satire at its core, "legwork burlesque" seldom possessed much by way of plot, moving instead through a series of protean changes in character, location, and style owing more to the tradition of pantomime.

Moreover, previous to *The Black Crook* the term *burlesque* in America usually denoted men's work. At William Mitchell's Olympic theatre, famous for introducing extravaganza and travesty to New York after 1840, almost all of the cross-dressing was undertaken by the male leads. It was one thing to recognize the "unsexed" nature of Lady Macbeth by the presence of stubble on her chin, quite another to see, in Lydia Thompson's troupe, a group of women dressed in top hats and frock coats displaying the appetites of men about town, smoking cigarettes and exchanging information about the track and gaming table. Thompson had achieved remarkable effects by combining the standard inversions of traditional extravaganza and by superimposing the transgressions of gender.[14]

Unfortunately, we will never know how the sexual aspects of burlesque performances "worked" to achieve comic effects for the majority of the audience. Yet critics were in broad agreement that when women assumed male roles, both gender and theatrical conventions were exploded. The female impersonations by men in pantomime and travesty resulted in delineations of strange-looking women; with Lydia Thompson's legs in view the audience was never in doubt that she was advancing herself as a *female* performer, even though acting male roles. As the *Times* remarked, she became "a prometheus in ardor and ambition," and Logan thought her "peculiarly and emphatically herself." For Logan, this lack of disguise made the "nude" actress the very antithesis and the most active challenge to developing feminist notions of "self-support." The leg artiste gained employment not because of her talent and knowledge but merely because of her sexual attractiveness. Rather than becoming an independent economic actor, she became a performing slave before the male gaze.[15]

Logan was no doubt particularly concerned with the problem of the male gaze because she had been praised by Elizabeth Cady Stanton, among others, as a new advocate of feminist causes after her exposure of the "leg-business." Though the two women were from very different backgrounds, Stanton's selection of Logan made sense for a movement that wished to make some accommodation with New York's fashionable set. As Logan ascended the feminist lecture platform as "author" she also appeared in rich black satin panniers. Lucretia Mott found Logan's speech and appearance both "overdressed" and lamented that her remarks, at times "of so coarse a nature," had followed closely upon evening prayer.[16] For Mott, then, Logan's brash style, her fashionable appearance, and her self-promotion amounted to a female performance itself, undercutting the moral imperatives of feminism gained during its earlier abolitionist phase. This public confrontation between Mott and Logan over the appropriate style for the lecture stage produced ever-converging discourses about feminism, "leg-work," and fashion. The very theatrical season (1868/69) that witnessed Lydia in *Ixion, Ernani, The Forty Thieves,* and *Sinbad the Sailor* also saw the appearance of a reenergized social and political feminism with the publication of *The Revolution* and the formation of Sorosis (one of the first women's clubs) and The National Woman's Suffrage Association.

Though no acting scripts exist that might detail the depth of topical allusion in Thompson's work, it does appear from reviews that burlesque artistes began to incorporate impersonations of their female critics and to lampoon feminist platforms. Olive Logan became a favorite target. In *Sinbad the Sailor; or; the Ungenial Genii and the Cabin Boy,* Thompson made a remark about Logan that even the broad-minded *Clipper* considered "objectionable"[17]; *Lurline,* staged at Woods Theatre in 1870, ended with a "grand moral ballet" "of strong minded women, which might much better have been spared, inasmuch as it is neither humorous nor tasteful, and which presents personalities of all the better-known champions of women's rights in unseemly and uncouth gyrations."[18]

It was this brashness, her steady return of the gaze from all parties (together with some impolitic remarks from her manager Henderson about the character of American audiences), that led to increasing press concern about the social effects of burlesque. In her last vehicle of 1869, *Sinbad,* Thompson collapsed whatever distinctions remained between the creature James observed in the street and her own stage presence. The "matrimonial market" scene (which burlesqued the slave market in Boucicault's *The Octoroon* and Gerome's painting "L'Almée") disclosed Thompson as "the Girl of the Period" replete with a huge blonde wig and wearing the latest "Grecian Bend" fashion from Paris. "She straddles well a velocipede," chaunted Lydia, and is very much aware of her "own awarishness."[19]

Again, we do not know what the large audiences for burlesque made of such comedy. Burlesque never works if it seeks to elicit a committed response from the audience. It specializes in inconsequentiality, puncturing through absurd juxtapositions the pretensions and enthusiasms of the day. There is little evidence that the majority were shocked or offended or undertook a revolution in domestic arrangements. Nevertheless, the increasing outcry by Logan and the reformist press, and perhaps Thompson's militant topicality, made the jokes and juxtapositions have a "life" beyond the moment of their performance. For William Dean Howells, who entered the debate in May 1869, what was intended to be frivolous ended up as subversive and permanently disturbing.

> The members of these burlesque troupes, though they were not like men, were in most things as unlike women, and seemed creatures of a kind of alien sex, parodying both. It was certainly a shocking thing to look at them with their horrible prettiness, their archness in which was no charm, their grace which put to shame.[20]

This subversion of women's nature began to be handled discursively as a disease, and like most social diseases it was presumed to come from "below" or "abroad." There was then a general attempt, in writing, to reestablish the boundaries of respectability and the thresholds of class, a critical effort to distance the comic life of "leg-work" from the society that was obviously supporting it. Logan recognized that the blondes played with the referents and ambiguities of class in a fashion normally associated with minstrelsy and music hall. She especially despised Lydia Thompson's version of F.C. Burnand's *Ixion, or the Man at the Wheel*, "whose chief piquancy was derived from the fact that the women who performed it talked slang and sang coarse songs with a very good imitation of that English accent which had hitherto been associated in our minds with ideas of culture and refinement."[21]

This triple promiscuity of form, gender, and class concerned moral journalists like Logan, the clergy, and established theatre critics, but they did not deter an audience in search of lavish visual, vocal, and choreographic entertainment. Indeed it is difficult to overestimate the popularity of "leg-work" pieces between 1866 and 1873. Including opéra bouffe such as *La Belle Helene* and *Orphée aux enfers*, nude drama accounted for 30 percent of the performance offerings in those years. Twenty-three different productions of Offenbach, or burlesques thereof, took place on nine different stages. Lydia Thompson's troupe alone presented 425 nights of variety entertainment. The *Clipper* recalled that "the regular theatregoers commenced to give the legitimate a cold shoulder, and gave their patronage to the music halls, where they could witness a variety of performances, something that was spicy and highly flavored at that." Edwin Booth's Shakespearian comedies suffered declining attendance, leading Mark Twain to suggest that the famous tragedian would have to "make a little change and peel some women" if he wished to go along with the current taste.[22]

"Leg-work" burlesque also passed back down Broadway to the popular sites of amusement. Tammany Hall's "salon de concert" featured a native-born corps de ballet by 1869, their most popular piece being *The March Of The Horse Marines.*[23] Tony Pastor's vaudeville house first featured a female minstrel troupe in the same year. The Third Avenue skating rink introduced a "stripped" feature in their velocipede exhibitions.[24] The Bowery Theatre presented its own version of *The Black Crook* in October 1868, leading the *Times* to suggest that a fissure now cut through all strata of performance spaces:

> Not very long ago the Bowery was the only place in New York where ballet and spectacle could find an audience. Of late, however, Broadway has quite shamed the Bowery with the warmth of welcome it has extended to these and many other feverish entertainments peculiar to the "East Side."[25]

"A culture of leg-work"—the *Tribune*'s phrase—overwhelmed public spaces. *Cartes de visites* appeared in store windows. "Our very streets," stated the *Clipper,* "are infected with a strange theatrical disease just now, and no man can look at the many-colored bills posted on our dead walls without getting a 'caste' in his eye, which makes all around 'red hot.'"

Where had this rage for "leg-work" come from? Because many of the performers were foreign it was easy to give this disease an external etiology. However, nude women had been resident on the New York stage for at least 25 years. They first appeared in prurient tableaux vivants, or model artist exhibitions, in the "free-and-easies" within the Bowery and Chatham Street axis after the panic of 1837. We know little about these exhibitions beyond the suggestive advertisements in the popular press that wonderful likenesses were to be offered of Susanna and the Elders and later, Hiram Power's Greek Slave. Nude tableaux vivants gained a more legitimate, or more organized, form in Dr. Colyer's troupe of artistes that wandered around the popular stages. In 1848, the extension of this craze to side-street stages attracted the attention of the magistracy that was itself extending its police powers governing the stage—a movement that was instrumental in producing the Astor Place riots of 1849. In that year three houses were raided, and the managers received insubstantial fines. By 1850, theatrical criticism and geographical location safely assigned such presentations to the plebeian world of popular amusement.[26]

The 1850s and early 1860s witnessed a proliferation and geographical extension of the concert saloon, offering a variety of female companionship both on and beyond the stage. As in the case of the London music hall, these places of amusement emerged from the tradition of the free-and-easy, though now with the manager gaining formal control over the presentations. Infamous largely because of their use of "pretty waiter girls," concert saloon managers appear to have recruited the female staff to perform travesties or simply imitations of balletic dancing, breakdowns, jigs, and clog work. In 1862, a further tightening of licensing laws (usually termed the Concert Hall Act) attempted to differentiate the rough from the respectable by banning the sale of liquor in places of amusement that possessed a curtain dividing the stage from the audience. But as the *Times* remarked, this law only served to increase the traffic between a rowdy clientele and performers of equally dubious character. From prosecutions undertaken by the Society for the Reformation of Juvenile Delinquents, to whom all city licensing fees were still given, we know that in 1866 at least three concert saloons presented the "moving" tableaux of the female chorus: the Pavilion on upper Broadway, the Dew Drop Inn at 13th Street, and the Tammany Free and Easy on West Houston.[27]

At a number of points throughout this quarter-century of demimonde nudity, "leg shows" made their appearance on more established stages without causing a sensation of the order of 1868 or indeed gaining a permanent place in the repertoire. In 1857 Laura Keene took over the Broadway theatre for a season of spectaculars that featured a female chorus of singers and dancers dressed in flesh-colored tights. In 1860 Adah Issacs Menken appeared in the male role of Mazeppa, long a favorite melodrama of the Bowery stage. The grand hippodramatic sensation of the play, which once represented the flight of a republican hero from the Tartar hordes, now disclosed Adah seemingly nude in flesh-colored leggings and shirt, strapped to the back of a galloping horse. One year later another nude female appropriation of a previously staged drama occurred with *The Naiad Queen.* Here a chorus of water nymphs, led by the "fascinating dancing of Rosa Wood," transformed into "forty beautiful young ladies in 'the Abode of the Fairies.'" A display of military Amazon marching rounded out the bill (a scene that *The Black Crook* would later popularize).[28] This chronology may disclose the surfacing of the local plebeian and popular forms or the gradual increase in the genteel audience's taste for the exotic and the sensual. There had indeed been a gradual geographical incursion of minstrelsy and protean farces up Broadway toward the known respectability of Union Square.[29] However, in most of the accounts of the origins of late-sixties "leg-work" so far examined (with the exception of the *Times* article) *The Black Crook, Ixion,* and other such pieces were billed or criticized as foreign importations, having little connection with the native tradition of vaudeville or the free-and-easy. In Logan's case, overlooking local nudity allowed her to advance the claim of native republican virtue, to stir nationalistic feelings, and to maintain the moral and geographical distance between the Bowery and upper Broadway.

But even here the differentiation of forms by origin proves an illusion or a convenience. London extravaganza was indeed more advanced in its eclecticism and showiness—but not, as Logan and Booth both thought, because of its supposedly continental tastes. The first overtly popular form to be incorporated into London's legitimate burlesque was American blackface minstrelsy, after Thomas "Jim Crow" Rice's tour of Britain in 1836. Topical satires such as *The Enchanted Isle* (1841) had Prospero playing the bones. The famous soubrette star Marie Wilton had introduced a "regular cellar-flap" breakdown into H.J. Byron's *The Maid and the Magpie* in 1858. Incorporation of American popular idioms, including Yankee acts, was followed by music-hall appropriations of nonsense refrains and traditional and topical airs. As Michael Booth notes, 1860s London burlesque became a "compound of musical hall, minstrel show, extravaganza, legs and limelight, puns, topical songs, and gaudy irreverence." The popular culture of the Bowery and Chatham Street had arrived at Union Square by way of London's Gaiety and Strand theatres.

Confusion over the form, the extent of the nakedness, and the ellipsis of origins was matched by contradictory assessments of the character of the audience. The long runs of *The Black Crook* and

Ixion must have been sustained in part by the presence of a fashionable audience of both men and women. Certainly the houses staging these spectacles, Niblo's Garden and Wood's Theatre and Museum, were eminently respectable, liquor-free, spacious, and (by the standards of the time) expensive. George Temptleton Strong allowed his wife to attend *The Black Crook,* and the elite Union League Club, of which he was a member, reserved one of the boxes for a whole month. Logan singled out Lydia Thompson's troupe, however, for attracting men who were, so to speak, at the margins of the domestic hearth. Along with older "bald heads," "young noodles of New York fast life began to shower them with bouquets, and to take them to drive in Central Park, and give them late suppers at fashionable hotels." Again, seeking to preserve some hope for the return of the legitimate, Logan elaborated a reformer's model of contagion, in which "vicious" sites of amusement attracted centripetally the unsuspecting and the weak-willed.

Press reports on the audience attending the nude drama are disappointing if one expects to find detailed descriptions of the social compositions of the crowd. There are no direct revelations of a *nouvelles couches sociale* such as appeared in the café concerts of T.J. Clarke's Paris. Both respectable and sporting press alike comment on the heterogeneity of the crowd, resorting to the usual late eighteenth-century genre of the parade of "types." Richard Grant White attended a matinée performance of Lydia Thompson's *The Forty Thieves* expecting to find

> coarse and flashy people but on the contrary, it was notable in the main for simple and almost homely people. Comfortable, middle aged women from the suburbs, and from the remoter country their daughters, groups of children, a few professional men, bearing quality in their faces, some somber farmer-looking folk, a clergyman or two, apparently, the usual proportion of nondescripts, among which were not very young men.[30]

The popular press used such census to make a different point. An article in the *Clipper* entitled "Legs and Busts" reversed the class origins of the declension in public morality. Looking at the popularity of "leg-work" it saw no reason to indict managers and performers for what was a general desire of a supposedly refined audience for spectacle and titillation; indeed, according to the sporting press (which no doubt counted bald heads among their readership), it was middle-class women who formed a luxurious display in and of themselves. The "busts of *grandes dames*" in theatre boxes and private ballrooms, suggested the *Clipper*, were no less enticing than the legs of "their humbler and scarcely more offending sisters" on the stage. Liberal application of "Madame Jumie's Mammarial balm" was more depraving to society than flesh-colored tights. "Have the great cities suddenly been turned into exaggerations of the slave markets of Constantinople and Trebizond, where human flesh goes by the pound, and the goods need to be freely exposed for the sake of finding a purchaser?" asked the *Clipper* rhetorically. Though the answer was in the affirmative, there was little point in harping on an irreversible change. If the clergy and representatives of "the moral journalism" wished to do anything practical they should subscribe to a new statue of immodesty to be erected in Union Square: "Bust by Mrs. A., or Miss B. of Fifth Avenue or Murray Hill; legs by M'lle Kitty Wriggle of the Theatre Unmentionable."[31]

Lois Banner has described the ways that lower bustlines and fuller figures were incorporated into American notions of beauty after 1860, in part because of the stage fashion. However, the change in fashionable figure is not so important for the purposes of this argument as the proliferation of public spaces in which they were displayed. After the Civil War, a new circuitry of commercial institutions in the city—hotels, dry-goods houses, restaurants, and theatres—had created public arenas for self-presentation and the exercise of fashion at some remove from the street. By 1866, in Walt Whitman's estimation, the Central Park equestrian drive had taken the place of the Broadway promenade of the 1830s, and the new Delmonico's, opened in 1862, was the first to remove partitions so that diners could view the rest of the assembly. Though it is difficult to establish the norms of behavior and attitude through random benchmarks, it does appear that luxury, once the greatest of evils in a republic, had ceased to operate as a negative moral category. As early as 1857, Richard Grant White, the father of architect Stanford White, had claimed for the fashionable set that "we reject spartan values in our recreations and our public life, we are only too pleased to be amused."

New York, unfortunately, had no equivalent of Paris's Goncourt brothers, who consciously celebrated in great detail the escape from the parlor into a new world of social and commercial pleasure. White probably comes closest, yet he worried (during the time he was having an affair with Pauline Markham) what the passage into a larger theatricalized world meant for the maintenance of moral character and shared aesthetic feeling. In the "age of burlesque" he examined the outbreak of "absurdity" sweeping over three continents. On the surface, White thought, nude drama and "leg-work" appeared "gross outrages of decorum," but only in terms of standards of feeling that no one held to any more. Romantic presentations of sentiment had given way to "a critical temper of caricature": "we seem not equal to a grand scene; our nervous system will not bear the strain; we are under a tempest of feeling; and seek refuge in scorn and ridicule."

Unable to determine the true dimensions of character, theatre audiences turned their attention to spectacle and arts of staging. In this regard, Lydia Thompson's *The Forty Thieves* is no different in kind from the historical pageantry of Edwin Booth's *Othello*. As in life, claimed White, only ridicule and the ridiculous on the stage allow us to repress our self-doubts and uncertainties:

> The drama, as an intellectual diversion of the mind from one channel of thought to another, has passed away, I think, forever. The public, even the cultivated public, in all countries, prefers that kind of theatrical entertainment at which it is not required to think. It asks, not diversion, a *turning* of the mind from one object to another, but the pleasure of the senses while the mind lies dormant. It seeks only to be amused. Of this mood, burlesque as "spectacular extravaganza" is the natural and inevitable product. We of the Anglo-Saxon race at least, have probably seen the last of our legitimate drama.[32]

Only two years after White's statement, however, Logan declared formally her victory over "leg-work" and prurient spectacle. Drama had been kept alive as literature and had now returned to the stage. Her claim, if one is content with personalistic explanations, may have its foundations more in her own return as a playwright for Augustine Daly's new Fifth Avenue house than in any statistical assessment of performance offerings. Certainly there had been a modest rejection of the vogue for French opéra bouffe, with only one house regularly staging Offenbach's work after 1871. This led the *Herald*, in a nationalistic vein, to celebrate that "the power of taste" had returned:

> Opera Bouffe may well be said to have seen its palmiest days. Manifestly the product of the lower empire and its loose ways, this deification of the demi-monde has almost passed with the other false gods of Napoleonism.[33]

Yet the vogue for spectacle, for lavish use of color and mechanicals, and for elaborately staged burlesque only slightly abated, mostly due to the termination of local contracts for the seven troupes of foreign performers, who then moved on to other cities. The most decisive check on the fashion for "leg-work" occurred during the deep Depression of 1873, which not only closed three variety theatres but also forced Booth into temporary bankruptcy. The Depression also allowed for a more aggressive policing of the plebeian appetite for "leg-work" at the cheaper downtown houses, and the political recoil from the collapse of the Tweed Ring produced a favorable climate for the introduction of sundry Comstockian initiatives for the suppression of vice. After February 1875, a municipal regulation and a state law banned suggestive dancing, especially the cancan, in places without a formal stage and tightened the enforcement of the excise law. The Society for the Reformation of Juvenile Delinquents prosecuted four concert saloons for evading the licensing requirements in that year, and two Chatham Street booksellers, Joseph Hall and Peter Jacobson, were indicted for selling obscene pictures of "ballet girls."[34]

This flurry of reform appears to have done nothing to halt the spread of female variety entertainment, even though burlesque itself gained its more modern designation as a girlie show for an exclusively male clientele. Ironically, the "leg-business" effected a feminization of the American stage at every level. Women gained a more active role in olio entertainment such as minstrelsy, and male/female comedy teams became a standard in variety and vaudeville after 1870. The ballet, having once fallen into the Bowery stratum, was raised again in spectacle and in entr'actes into refined performance spaces. The nude drama then was not banished from the stage by Logan, Comstock, or the depression of the early 1870s; rather, it was naturalized by managers and performers, especially in the use of a female chorus, into the mainstream of commercial and fashionable entertainment, where it remains today.

Some modification of burlesque's aggressive features had, of course, taken place. In pantomime and new genres of native musical drama, an effort was made to restore the plot or establish variety as entertainment fit for the whole family. The term *musical comedy* arose as a way of describing a new, distinctively American form of family entertainment. The first play to be branded as such was E.E. Rice's *Evangeline* (performed at Niblo's in July 1874). This spectacular incorporated many of the features of burlesque travesty—topical skits and puns, clog dances, transvestite roles, and so forth, though short skirts were noticeably absent. As Rice underscored in his playbills, performers were "carefully selected and specially engaged for the production of REFINED EXTRAVAGANZA embracing all the beauties of Opera Bouffe and Burlesque, without the objectionable features of the English and French productions."[35] Sensuality, color, and spectacle overcame the stronger travesty and rough-and-tumble forms of the traditional pantomime and burlesque. In the case of England, this naturalization of the female chorus into native musical comedy was completed by Gilbert and Sullivan, whose first collaboration, *Thespis* (1871), had originally been censured for its use of silver tights. By 1883, however, William Archer could see this complex shift, like Logan, in terms of a victory:

> No doubt there is still, and will always be while the present constitution of society maintains itself, a special public for mere "leg-pieces," but the general public seems, for the moment at any rate, to have turned its back upon the flesh pots of Egypt . . . , there has been a fall in the demand owing to powerful native competition in the shape of those most popular entertainments of the day, the Gilbert-Sullivan operettas. Here, at least, is a matter for almost unmixed rejoicing. The victory of Gilbertian extravaganza over opera-bouffe as adapted for the London market, is the victory of literary and musical grace and humour over rampant vulgarity and meretricious jingle.[36]

From 1873 until the arrival of Ibsenite naturalism there existed a period of relative equanimity and self-satisfaction in stage representations of middle-class life. The raw transgressions of the blonde burlesque were contained in the Gilbertian taste for the mildly eccentric. There remains the problem of accounting for the sudden popularity of "leg-work," without invoking a disembodied "spirit of the age." Howells, after making a characteristically brave attempt to understand the social meaning of burlesque, threw up his hands, stating that only "an historical gossiper" in the future would demand clarity.

Why might large sections of the respectable theatre-going public have embraced cultural forms that before the war they repudiated? Theatre historians have suggested some kind of psychic release from the war years, and postwar environments may indeed be unusually "fluid" in admitting into the commercial mainstream forms that had once been tagged as bohemian, avant-garde or merely "popular." Yet what appears central in the case of 1860s burlesque is the novel nature of the urban commercial environment and women's place within it. How were women, especially the young and unmarried, going to stand, ideologically speaking, in the new spaces of urban consumption—in theatres, lecture platforms, open restaurants, dry-goods houses, and the street itself? How was a class that had devoted so much energy to broadcasting domestic piety in the previous half-century going to accommodate feminists' demands for self-support or the increasing availability and power of fashion?

The furor over burlesque registered such questions. The explosive form of the performances themselves aired such tensions, and also produced laughter and profits, and perhaps fell prey to their resolution. Representations of women's bodies and behavior absorbed and masked larger changes in the nature of the social body. The young Henry James quite consciously saw the literary possibilities in such a metaphorical maneuver, though he thought that Linton had for a time destroyed a subject to which he himself was later to return.

> It is impossible to discuss and condemn the follies of "modern women" apart from those of modern men. They are all part and parcel of the follies of modern civilization, which is working itself out through innumerable blunders. It seems to us supremely absurd to stand up in high places and endeavor, with a long lash and a good deal of bad language, to drive women back into the ancient fold. . . . We are all of us extravagant, superficial, and luxurious together."[37]

Notes

1. Samuel Clemens, *Mark Twain's Travels With Mr. Brown,* ed. Franklin Walker (New York, 1940), 88.
2. Elizabeth Lynn Linton, *Essays Upon Social Subjects* (London, 1883), 2. The "Girl of the Period" article first appeared in the *Saturday Review,* March 14, 1868. The essay provoked a remarkable controversy, which has been nicely discussed in *The Women Question: Society and Literature in Britain and America, 1837–1883,* vol. II, ed. Elizabeth K. Helsinger et al. (Chicago, 1989). Linton's essay appeared as a pamphlet that sold 40,000 copies for one printer alone.
3. Linton, *Essays Upon Social Subjects,* 4–5.
4. Henry James, "Modern Women," *The Nation,* October 22, 1868, 332–34.
5. Clemens, *Travels with Mr. Brown,* 85.
6. Olive Logan, "The Nude Woman Question," *Packard's Monthly* (July 1869), 198; reprinted as a chapter in *Apropos of Women and Theatres* (New York, 1869).
7. Lois Banner has already suggested some links between feminist activity and the appearance of the burlesque in *American Beauty* (Chicago, 1983), 319. For a sensitive exploration of the connections between fashion and feminism in the period see William Leach, *True Love and Perfect Union* (New York, 1980). I thank Leach for reading an earlier draft of this paper, and also Barbara Balliet, whose essay on "Olive Logan and the Stages of American Feminism" formed a tandem with this piece at the American Historical Association conference in 1986. I have also benefited greatly from reading Robert C. Allen's extensive treatment of burlesque in his *Horrible Prettiness: Burlesque and American Culture* (Chapel Hill, 1991).
8. "The Drunken Drama," *The Galaxy* 4 (May–December, 1867), 934–41.
9. The full range of Olive Logan's criticism and some biographical material are included in *Before the Footlights and Behind the Scenes* (Philadelphia, 1870).
10. Kristina Gintautiene, in her unpublished dissertation *The Black Crook; Ballet in the Gilded Age* (New York University, 1984) provides a listing of the 8 secondes, 20 coryphees, and 40 native-born members of the corps de ballet who were involved in the initial production. The premières mainly danced on pointe, but most of the others helped with drills, waltzes, and more popular forms of dance.
11. *New York Tribune,* September 17, 1866.
12. Some of Smyth's thoughts were reprinted in the *New York Herald* for November 19, 1866. The *Herald*'s lead in lambasting "leg-work" was in part due to the managerial ban on placing advertisements in the paper.
13. *The Galaxy,* April 1869, 605.
14. An exception to Mitchell's standard for cross-dressing was his utopian farce *The Mirror of Truth,* in which "women assume the prerogatives of men, and the males are degraded into ridiculous specimens of effeminacy." See *The Albion,* January 25, 1845.

15. In reply to the critics who suggested that she wrote from feelings of jealousy, Logan insisted that she was motivated by sympathy for "the numerous modest and virtuous actresses who are crowded from a sphere which they could honor and adorn" (Olive Logan, "The Nude Women Question," 169).

16. *New York Times,* May 19, 1869.

17. *New York Clipper,* June 5, 1869.

18. *New York Clipper,* May 18, 1870.

19. *New York Clipper,* June 7 and June 19, 1869.

20. William Dean Howells, "The New Taste in Theatricals," *Atlantic Monthly* (May 1869), 643.

21. In *Ixion* all male roles were played by women, with the only male in the troupe being cast as Minerva. In the history of the theatre such a preponderance of actresses over actors had never been achieved before the 1860s and is still rare today.

22. Booth blamed his bankruptcy in 1874 on the success of the "leg-drama," making the inevitable pun that he was interested only in the "*leg*itimate." See Daniel Watermeier, ed., *Between Actor and Critic: Selected Letters of Edwin Booth and William Winter* (Princeton, N.J., 1971), 49

23. This was at the newly constructed hall on 14th Street, a full description of which is given in the *New York Times,* January 3, 1869. The variety theatre was on the third floor. This troupe went on to give an extravaganza called *The Glorious Seven:* "The Remarks of the boys in the gallery ought to have been sufficient to have any lady with the slightest pretensions to modesty retire, but boldly did they face it out" (*New York Clipper,* February 12, 1870.)

24. *New York Clipper,* August 17, 1869.

25. *New York Times,* October 9, 1869. The Bowery version of *The Black Crook* was entitled *The Crimson Shield, or, Nymphs of the Rainbow.* It contained the Demon Dance and the new cancan number ("The latter is amusing here as elsewhere; but, as a Florentine critic said, 'it ought to be performed with closed doors,'" stated the *Times*). However, the peasant and baron were replaced by a group of knights in order to include the required sword-fight scene. See George Odell, *The Annals of the New York Stage,* vol. 8 (New York, 1921), 465.

26. The best survey of living statuary, and its passage from genteel to plebeian stages, is Jack McCullough's *Living Pictures in New York* (Ann Arbor, Mich., 1986).

27. Parker Zellars, "The Cradle of Variety: The Concert Saloon," *Educational Theatre Journal* 20 (December 1968), 578–85.

28. Amazon marching appears to antedate the Civil War. *The Albion* (May 29, 1858) refers to a group of "Salt Lake Amazons—a company of pretty waiter girls dressed in the old and ever agreeable burlesque style" in *Deseret Deserted* at Wallack's. For more on Amazon marching see Leland Croghan, *New York Burlesque, 1840–1870: A Study in Theatrical Self-Criticism* (Ph.D. diss., New York University, 1974), 153.

29. Mary Henderson, in *The City and the Theatre,* makes the observation that between 1850 and 1870 the various forms of staged commercial culture were more differentiated in geographic space than before or since.
30. Richard Grant White, "The Age of Burlesque," *The Galaxy,* August 1869, 260.
31. "Busts and Legs: or, The Farewell of the Fig-Leaves," *New York Clipper,* March 7, 1868.
32. Richard Grant White, "The Age of Burlesque," *The Galaxy,* August 1869, 266.
33. *New York Herald,* September 12, 1871. This comment was passed on the failure of Offenbach's *The Princess of Trebizonde.*
34. *New York Times,* January 28, March 25, April 15, 1875. For a general article on the New York City "Vice and Obscene Literature Bill," see April 21, 1875.
35. Quoted in Deane L. Root, *American Popular Stage Music, 1860–1880* (Ann Arbor, Mich., 1981), 151, 152. A new production of *Aladdin,* also in 1874, was described as "a favorable specimen of the new school of burlesque, in which artistic dancing is substituted for the cellar-flap breakdown, in which the music is carefully selected, and executed in a way worthy of the comic opera, and in which gracefully designed costumes take the place of the old red, green, and blue abominations."
36. William Archer, *About the Theatre* (New York, 1886), 20–21. See also Jane W. Stedman, "From Dame to Woman: W.S. Gilbert and Theatrical Transvestism," *Victorian Studies* 14 (September 1970).
37. Henry James, "Modern Women," *The Nation,* October 22, 1868.

❧

Imagining the City

James Gilbert

IN THE EARLY 1890S IT MIGHT BE SAID WITH SOME TRUTH THAT CHICAGO could imagine itself as a prototype for the emerging urban culture of modern America*. These were the years of the great World's Columbian Exposition, or Chicago World's Fair, when new skyscrapers pierced the sky; they extended through the days of the disastrous Pullman strike, the founding of cultural institutions such as the University of Chicago, and the beginning of the City Beautiful movement. Chicago doubled in size between 1880 and 1890 to become one of the largest cities in the world, with a history that scarcely stretched back a single generation to a swampy village with a score of settlers in 1833. By the 1890s, what was happening nationally to cities had its extreme version on the shores of Lake

*Some of this material appeared previously in James Gilbert, *Perfect Cities: Chicago's Utopia of 1893*. University of Chicago Press, 1991.

Michigan. For good or ill, the city encompassed the emerging future. Thus, despite the hyperbole, there is something true in the words of Chicago writer George Ade:

> The World's greatest achievement of the departing century was pulled off in Chicago. The Columbian Exposition was the most stupendous, interesting, and significant show ever spread out for the public. As a demonstration of civic pride, community enterprise and nation-wide cooperation—revealing the progress and culture and creative impulses of the whole world—it has not been matched.[1]

Of course, as almost everyone quickly recognized, this time of achievement and innovation had a precarious life. Edgar Lee Masters intimated as much in his poem "White City":

> And lo! How white, how glorious
> These fanes and Temples now appear;
> How pure a mood is now o'er us.
> The evening bell is sweet and clear.
> And there by Dian's brow, how near,
> A star shines singly and alone;
> Right o'er the dome's symmetric sphere!
> The flags against the sky are blown—
> And all we cherished once is quickly gone.[2]

If this special vision of Chicago's moment flashed through a narrow aperture of time in the 1890s, in the years of the fair construction and the Pullman strike and the dreadful Depression of 1894, its meaning, nonetheless, has a rather broader significance, particularly in the development of orientations toward the emerging urban world. This sense of the presentation of the city did not die quickly because it embodied the hopes and anticipations of many of Chicago's most important boosters. By exploring these ideas about what the city could be, we can suggest something about what Helen Rosenau calls the "ideal city"—the culturally and aesthetically unified notion of an urban environment.[3]

The question is: Whose perspective? Whose culture? Whose city? One answer centers on the middle class and its place in this emerging urban world. By no means was Chicago an easily defined or comfortable place for such people. I say this despite common wisdom to the contrary. There is a familiar picture of cultural struggles in the late nineteenth century of working-class, women's, and ethnic groups against established middle-class culture—resolved in favor of the middle class. Possibly the 1890s did attest to the triumph of corporatism summed up in the pristine, white city of the fair.[4] This was, after all, the intended effect of the exposition.

Such impressions are problematic, or at least they require significant modification. The "late Victorian silent majority" of middle-class Americans (and the social and economic elite whom they emulated) experienced as much disorientation in the cities as immigrants and the working class. They too lived in a burgeoning corporate, bureaucratic, organizational capitalism, but the effects of this emerging system were experienced differently. Confronting a huge foreign population (Chicago had only 29 percent two-generation American-born citizens in 1892) and consequently aware of the growing divergence of cultural expressions, diversity, and choice in the city, middle-class Americans were strangers—tourists if you will—in the new city as much as any other newcomers. Unlike other groups, however, they ventured into this wilderness of cultural multiplicity carrying with them the assurance that they understood and bore the traditional hopes of a regenerate American culture. If nothing else, these hopes created the demand for imaginary space in which they could establish their own interests and institutions.

To be more specific about their endeavor, their task of coming to terms with the city was made enormously difficult by the emergence of commercial culture as much as it was by the fear of working-class strikes or socialism. Commercial culture was not new to the 1890s, but it was rapidly changing and taking on many of its modern characteristics. Most noticeable (and threatening to some observers) was the flourishing alliance of commercial culture with immigrant subcultures. The resulting development of modern popular culture appealed to a commonality fabricated out of diverse urban expressions. Like a vaudeville performance with many acts, this modern mass culture appealed to different audiences simultaneously because it quoted so extensively from among American ethnic and class cultures. Perhaps in sanitizing these expressions or placing them in a traditional moral landscape, the new urban cultural impresarios succeeded in removing the modernist sting to their presentations in theatre and, later, film. But they did not disguise the challenge nor ultimately deflect some of the opposition of middle-class and elite groups to commercial urban popular culture, an opposition that has resurfaced frequently throughout the twentieth century in controversy after controversy.[5] The most serious challenge, of course, was the seductiveness of this culture and its appeal to middle-class patrons.

Whereas one response to this threat was to censor culture, a possibility explored at the time and afterward, a more interesting and important effort was to construct an urban environment that would be hospitable to middle-class residents and tourists. An essential aspect of that construction was imaginative—the creation of an impression, a stereotype of the city as a safe, inviting, exciting place, yet overall a sober environment.

During the 1890s, when impressions of the city were hardening into clichés, Chicago seemed to redefine the urban experience in this fashion. This redefinition promised (at least in a general, perhaps even abstract way) to stifle a growing problem of cultural alienation and establish a sanctuary of culture and stability for middle-class families disoriented by the incredible diversity of the urban environment. As Daniel Burnham, architectural master of the World's Fair, wrote somewhat later of this vision: "The cream of our own earnings should be spent here, while the city should become a magnet, drawing to us those who wish to enjoy life. . . . Then our own people will become home-keepers, and the stranger will seek our gates."[6]

This great midwestern metropolis appeared poised to shape the urban encounter into something new, inviting, fanciful. For a few years, writers, city planners, tourists, businessmen, and middle-class citizens thought of Chicago as the city of the possible, which, despite its remarkable cultural variety, could be made a place of comfort and familiarity. This optimism, of course, was decanted with the opening of the World's Fair in 1893. As one of the city's earlier historians put it, "during the six months when the Exposition flourished before people's eyes, it roused Chicago to an exalted idea of what a city could be like."[7] But optimism also reflected the reasons Chicago won the contest to host the Columbian celebration in the first place. Thus the city itself, as well as the exhibit at Jackson Park, counted as one of the great tourist attractions of the late nineteenth century.[8] The fair was to be an exalted metaphor for the commonplace reality of Chicago.

Yet Chicago's redefining moment was also brief, cut short by the whiplash of the 1893 Depression, extinguished by the terrible Pullman strike of 1894, and spoiled by the rediscovery of scandal and misery. In the period that followed, other middle-class visions of the city emerged to challenge the optimism of the earlier period and to urge a sober, more engaged encounter with urban reality.

This essay will explore the fascinating collective effort in the early 1890s to establish a visual image, a gridwork of ideas that would universalize a particular attitude toward the city of Chicago. Internalized by the viewer, these notions would structure experience, divert sensations into established perspectives, and provide a focus of attention that would enhance some impressions and obscure others. In the production of this urban cliché, this stereotyped reaction to the city, the guidebook played a crucial role in designating the space where middle-class tourists—and residents—could feel comfortable.

Given the enormous interest in the Columbian Exposition of 1893 and the anticipated profits, Chicago publishers produced a large number of guidebooks and souvenir photograph books. Taken together, these books provide a fascinating source that is closely linked to contemporary newspaper journalism and histories of the city. This guidebook journalism is constructed of equal parts enthusiasm and boosterism; it frames a comprehensive vision of the city, not as experienced but as it was intended to be seen. This Chicago was a city whose visual and physical character was defined in advance. The result was a literature written to the expectations of millions of tourists and visitors traveling into the city during this decade.

A number of peculiarities in this literature merit discussion, and I shall just list them here: (1) Most guidebooks to Chicago present very little if any history of the city; (2) most begin with either this truncated background or a description of the arrival at the train station; (3) almost all emphasize the remarkable cosmopolitanism of the city—indeed, they exaggerate it; (4) yet none of the books steers the visitor to parts of the city where cosmopolitanism is anything but accidental; (5) very few of the books present a serviceable walking tour of the city; (6) instead, Chicago is presented as a series of disconnected points and places to be visited with no sense of the city in between; (7) there are frequent references to confusion; (8) in the guidebooks and souvenir photography books, buildings and monuments are routinely pictured in isolation from their surroundings and empty of people; (9) souvenir photograph books during this era do not picture the city with a skyline; (10) instead, tall buildings are represented as freestanding, without any discernible urban context.

Before addressing some of these curiosities, I want to emphasize the fact that tourists were only a part of the huge stream of travelers pouring into Chicago in the mid-1890s. In fact, a principal function of the guidebook was to differentiate the tourist from these other voyagers, to provide an itinerary and urban vision to differentiate him or her from the inevitable crowds encountered along the way. This confrontation could not be avoided; indeed, the initial entry into the city at the railway station was likely to be the most confusing and crowded moment—a deep but brief baptism into Chicago's cosmopolitanism.

Who were these other travelers streaming into the city railroad depots? One large group included foreign immigrants. Between 1890 and 1900 their population in the city increased by about 140,000 permanent residents. This total passes over the thousands of others who moved in and out of the city or passed through in transit, so the impression upon a tourist would be substantially greater. The same may be said of American-born immigrants to the city: workers, families, young men and women who came in search of work, and numbering in the hundreds of thousands. There were also legions of businessmen and salesmen from other cities and towns—part of the peripatetic commercial economy of the late nineteenth century. There was a special, small group of foreign travelers like Rudyard Kipling, William Stead, and H. G. Wells, who gained individual notoriety for their stinging criticisms of the city. There were founders of utopias like John Alexander Dowie, who built his storefront church in 1893 next to the World's Fair grounds and later removed to a real-estate venture he called Zion that manufactured much of the lace sold by Marshall Field. And there were American tourists numbering perhaps in the millions who came to see Chicago—that quintessential modern city—and the fair's White City-within-a-city—the future nested inside the present like a Russian doll.

The guidebooks and souvenir photograph books, with their "memories waiting to happen," were intended for tourists, but they assumed the presence of this other, ubiquitous crowd of travelers in public places and in unguarded encounters. Of course the crowds and confusion, the prodigious choices of urban life, and the myriad possible perspectives on the city were all the more justification to purchase guidebooks and souvenir photograph books. Their purpose, after all, was to separate the light of pleasure, entertainment, and instruction from the shadow of industry, routine, and poverty.

Who were the tourists of the late nineteenth century, and what might they expect from a visit to the city? Most obviously, they had two possessions in enough abundance to differentiate them from many other venturers to Chicago: They had sufficient funds to take the train and live in the peculiar and expensive suspended animation of hotel or boardinghouse life; they also had ample time for a visit. Most of the guidebooks to the city and the fair assumed an extended visit of around two weeks with expenses running around $55 per person, excluding travel.[9] This outlay of time and expense certainly excluded most working-class men and women. So middle- and upper-class tourists were the expected audience of these books that ranged in price from around a few cents to about two dollars.

By the 1890s tourism in the United States had become a thriving business aimed at just such an audience. Much of it was promoted by railroads, steamship companies, and touring companies like Cooks. While a European tour or the exploration of exotic places had been possible for the very wealthy in the early- and mid-nineteenth century, leisure travel by the last decade of the century was changing rapidly. After the Civil War a stream of tourists poured into newly built watering places, exclusive resorts, and grand hotels. Agencies like Cooks and several American travel businesses offered extended excursions through the United States or abroad to Egypt, Mexico, and Cuba.[10] Travel advertising and columns in newspapers and journals became common (for example, *Travelers Magazine*, begun in 1901, and *Tourists' Monthly Magazine*, begun in 1906). By the turn of the century railroads began to publish their own travel magazines.

Initially much of the travel inside the United States sought out romantic or exotic sites—"sacred places," as John Sears calls them. These places of natural wonder—Mammoth Cave, Niagara Falls, Old Faithful—were often imagined and described in sacred terms, as sublime spots of nature combining religious awe and pastoral aesthetics.[11] Less attention, however, was paid to urban tourism up to the time of the Chicago World's Fair, except to such uncommon cities as Washington, D.C., and New Orleans.[12] A typical excursion of this period was the Pennsylvania Railroad Tour to Mexico, "Affording Four Weeks in the Land of the Aztecs." The advertising brochure is noteworthy for its very strong sense of novelty:

> The Pennsylvania Company is not unmindful of the fact that pleasure travel is increasing year by year. The American people are awakening to the realization that there is something to be seen on this continent and it is the purpose of these tours to provide the ways and means of gratifying their patriotic inclination.[13]

Stay home; don't go to Europe, the company advised. Still the railroad company was keen to reassure the traveler, particularly the single woman, who could depend upon the presence of an experienced matron-chaperon. Travel plus accommodations and meals brought this tour to $445; surely this was an exoticism at first-class prices.

Despite a growing travel industry and an expanding clientele, tourism to the city as a city remained a relatively new experience, and the guidebooks written in the 1880s and 1890s addressed this novelty. Certainly guidebooks had been published well before this time, particularly for places like New York City. A good example is Appleton's series *New York Illustrated*. Yet there are shifts and developments in the genre that suggest a new audience and purpose in the late nineteenth century. For example, an address to the reader in Rand McNally's *A Week in New York* of 1891 disclaimed for the book any ulterior motive such as advertising for hotels, theatres, or stores—as if to confirm that many of the earlier books did, indeed, have the unacknowledged purpose of leading the unwitting tourist to some commercial establishment.[14]

Many of these new guidebooks were sold around or in train stations, and a number of them opened with a discussion of the arrival in one of Chicago's rail depots. In late nineteenth-century Chicago, a number of new railway stations were built to accommodate the huge numbers of travelers as well as the expanding population of the city. In part these depots represented the fruits of consolidating lines; in part they were larger terminals built to handle increased traffic. Embellished in eclectic styles such as Gothic and

Romanesque, they had huge, cathedral-like waiting rooms. Some, like Central Station, installed stained-glass windows to make the religious quotation explicit.[15]

The purpose of these enormous common rooms was, in fact, dispersal and triage, either into trains or the city streets or to a number of special places reserved for travelers. These included men's barbershops, smoking- and waiting rooms (some designed to recall men's clubs), and bath- and toilet rooms; women's waiting rooms, toilets, and baths; and restaurants. Some of the newest stations set aside special immigrant shelters.[16] Because stations were easily accessible to the interior of the city, they also furnished easy entrance to those who wished to greet passengers—for whatever purpose.

For those among the estimated 175,000 daily travelers into Chicago who knew their destination, passage through this confusion of choices and crowds was easy and familiar. But for newcomers—tourists and immigrants of all sorts—there were imagined and real perils. An early "guidebook" to Chicago and New York written in 1873, *The Spider and the Fly, or Tricks, Traps, and Pitfalls of City Life* by "One Who Knows," presents a fascinating and vivid picture of the Chicago train station that frequently recurs in later books. Trains into the city were greeted by all manner of shady sorts: "runners," "baggage-smashers," "hack-drivers," "scalpers," "hotel-runners," and "immigrant runners," each with a specialized dodge. Additionally, according to this book, representatives of dubious employment agencies that had advertised for young female workers met the trains and then whisked newcomers off to some low or degraded work in saloons and restaurants, or worse.[17]

The situation became so critical that in 1888 the Chicago YWCA founded the Travelers Aid Society to greet trains and established a residence for transient women seeking employment in the city.[18] Although the society focused primarily on protecting young women from prostitution or misleading promises of employment, it also served a wide variety of travelers: immigrants, those who were lost or confused or penniless. As an annual report of the New York Society remarked: "The Society counteracts at the outset of city life the evil influences which meet confused and inexperienced travelers upon their arrival."[19] Travelers Aid even sent volunteers into State Street department store waiting rooms to assist women who took refuge there. But by far their greatest clientele fell under the category of those with a "lack of knowledge of the city."[20] During the Columbian Exposition, the agency was both active at train stations and on the fairgrounds, where it had an exhibit in the Woman's Building. At the St. Louis World's Fair in 1904, the national organization, based upon its experience in Chicago, mounted a much greater effort.[21]

What the Travelers Aid Society accomplished for immigrants, single women, and lost or confused travelers and what the special services of the station offered to the familiar traveler, the guidebooks promised to the tourist who arrived with little knowledge of the city and armed only with the pages before him or her. For many tourists the initial confrontation with the city was likely to be the most perilous. As Rand McNally (probably the leading guidebook publisher of this period) noted in a paragraph lifted from its 1891 guide to New York: "An arrival in Chicago or any other large city, alone and for the first time, is an ordeal to which many persons look forward with justifiable dread."[22]

Whether accurately or in self-service, many of the guidebooks featured this ordeal of confusion and offered knowledge that would enable the tourist to escape it. The Pennsylvania Railroad World's Fair guidebook of 1893 featured a typical short dramatic sketch that illustrates this point:

> A jumble of vehicles, a murmur of many sounds swelling into a roar, an all-pervading odor of bituminous smoke, a street corner with an iron canopy stretching high above your head across the sidewalk and a row of picturesque buildings opposite.[23]

Just as this situation begins to overpower the reader, out of the confusion appears a porter to rush the traveler safely into a cab.

Many of the guidebooks exploit this dramatic mechanism either as a rhetorical strategy to convince buyers of the necessity of the guidebook or as an example of how to avoid the pitfalls of the city. One noteworthy exception is a book with a very different purpose, *Mysteries of Chicago* by George W. James. It more properly belongs to a long tradition of "gaslight" guides to urban underworlds. As such it caricatures the ordinary guide in an astute fashion. "The visitor to Chicago who comes for pleasure and recreation," the author writes, "is taken by his friends in an elegant carriage down Grand Boulevard, Drexel Boulevard . . . past palatial residences. . . . He views its massive, Babel-like, public buildings and its great hotels." But James contends this is not the reality of Chicago, which he then proceeds to describe in vivid detail.[24]

Sometimes guidebooks also addressed people other than travelers for the purpose, once again, of fixing a particular sense of the city onto experience. The widely advertised guide by Thomas E. Hill, *Hill's Souvenir Guide to Chicago and the World's Fair*, published in 1892, spoke to "Americans and People in all Parts of the World . . . and to Those Inhabitants of Chicago Not Yet Fully Acquainted with Their Own City."[25]

Aside from the physical confusion of entering the polyglot city that was emphasized in the reiteration of the concept of cosmopolitanism by a number of guidebooks, there was the confusion of choices. If the city was defined by a cacophony of ethnic groups and languages spoken, all apparent in the train station, it was also a place where the scale and intensity of life occasioned vast numbers of choices: among hotels, eateries, places to visit, clubs, churches, organizations, theatres and other amusement centers, newspapers, and so on. Without a guide to these places, the visitor would be overwhelmed by the offerings of urban institutions.

The structure of the guidebooks often emphasized this point by promoting anxiety about choice and then offering simple remedies. For example, Edwin Stine's *What Everybody Wants to Know about Chicago* opens with extravagant descriptions of space and intimidating lists of public and private cultural and civic institutions. Everything is described by cost, size, number, and multiplicity. The author lists institutions, places of amusement, societies, clubs, and businesses. He enumerates, among other things, 497 churches, 301 newspapers and publications, 3569 saloons, 31 theatres, 62 societies, and many art galleries, hotels, music teachers, and photographic studios.

Clearly the intent is to convince tourists to rely upon the guidebook for direction through this daunting list of possibilities. Initially presenting an inventory of cultural choices available to visitors, Stine proceeds to sort them out, to validate special places and institutions. He recommends hotels (even proper ways to bestow charity); how to shop; how to recognize gamblers; how to take public transportation.[26]

If exaggerating the confusion of cultures and the hurly-burly of the train station provided compelling opening strategies for guidebooks, another tactic, equally as disorienting, was to begin with

Chicago's strange history—or, more correctly, its absence. In fact, it would be most accurate to describe the historical sections of most guidebooks as anti-historical. Few, if any, considered more than a few events in the city's past, and indeed they turned this inattention to history into a virtue and a comment on the meaning of the present. The point made almost unanimously by these guides was that Chicago's future revealed its essence; its lack of a past only emphasized this contention. The one event, universally mentioned, was the great fire of 1871, from which the city had arisen, Phoenix-like, to rebuild. In effect, the fire obliterated history by reducing the physically old city to ashes. Secondarily, the Haymarket affair of 1886 was often treated in the same fashion: a challenge, a conflagration of tempers and violence surmounted and obliterated by the future. With this transformation, Haymarket became a tourist spot, a monument to the past denied.

This vision of future transformation could take a number of forms. John Flinn, in *Chicago: The Marvelous City*, begins with a frontispiece of a female figure reviving and the caption "Chicago has Arisen—Solace in Tribulation." Not even in the Arabian Nights with its glorious colors of "Oriental fancy," he boasts, "is there a tale which surpasses in wonder the plain, unvarnished history of Chicago."[27]

In Hubert Bancroft's *Book of the Fair*, the history of Chicago is described as incomparable. Search history, he challenged, and the reader would never find a city of "such phenomenal development." Thus the city's past renewals reach into and define the present and future. As Robert Musket put it in *Chicago, Yesterday and To-day*: "This is an age of wonders and this is a city of wonders." The time was not distant when Chicago would be "the metropolis of America."[28] Chicago, according to Carroll Ryan in *Chicago the Magnificent*, "in its particularities is a city of the future. A twentieth century city it should be called, when compared with other cities of Europe and America."[29]

As a city of the future, Chicago's reality did not dwell in dark and corrupt places or in poverty and confusion but in the bright glimpses of progress seen in public monuments, tall buildings, its transportation system, and, of course, the World's Fair.[30] The lack of history, although initially disorienting to the tourist who might think of him- or herself as rooted in tradition, could deny the present, even the existence of those elements of the city that blemished its impression. The association of the city with the future and the black, smoky, urban world with the past stressed excitement and change while it repudiated the city in between.

One final, brief comment on the guidebooks: Few if any of them provided dependable itineraries through the city. Many advised a slow drive along the avenues with wealthy residences; many suggested a stroll in Chicago's parks. Certainly, monuments, tall buildings, department stores, civic buildings, and cultural spots were listed and located. But compared to contemporary guidebooks to New York, there was little if any attention given to a continuous, unfolding perspective of the city in which these places were situated. Unlike the stroll or drive up Broadway (with selected deviations) in New York, the trip to Chicago navigated from point to point, as if the city were disconnected from itself.[31] Also by contrast, in some books such as the *Sun Guide to New York*, published in 1892, there is a strong suggestion of the sophistication of Manhattan—that is, the celebration of diversity. Consequently, this guidebook suggests a visit to the slums and the better-off immigrant neighborhoods.[32]

The somewhat different perspective of Chicago guidebooks emphasizes, in defining a vision of the city, its revolutionary character and the possibility that despite its urban qualities—its confusion, slums, and edgy violence—the city will emerge as a safe, middle-class environment. They offer a way to see, imagine, and experience the city in compartmentalized fashion. They offer the tourist a sense of urban life that although strange and unexpected, perhaps, defines cultural possibilities that match the expectations of a future metropolis as utopian as Edward Bellamy's Boston of the year 2000 or William Dean Howells's Altruirian cities.

This imaginary imposition is graphically evident and reinforced in many of the souvenir photograph books sold during the 1890s. There are two general types of books depicting the city. The first, for example, A. Wittemann's *Views of Chicago: Photographs in Black*, features realistic views of crowded, busy streets and industrial sites in addition to idealized pictures of public buildings and homes of the wealthy.[33] (Even Wittemann, however, alternated realistic pictures with placid, monumental views.) Later versions of this subgenre, like *Pictorial Chicago*, published in 1930, devoted most of their attention to distinctly urban scenes: baseball games, crowds, industry, and "the ghetto" as well as a number of skyline perspectives.[34]

The other common format was especially favored by Rand McNally, which, beginning in 1893, published a large number of picture books of the city (often merely shorter or longer versions of prior editions). The repetitive format of these picture books opens generally with one picture of a confusing and crowded downtown street. Packed with shoppers and vehicles, dust, signs, and tall buildings, these shopping canyons give the initial impression—much like the train station—of disorientation and of the much boasted-about cosmopolitanism of the city. This opening, however, is frequently the only such photograph in the book, or one of only a few, as example follows example of tall Chicago buildings, monuments, parks, houses of the wealthy, civic buildings, and perhaps the stockyards. Some books also include "birds-eye views"—taken from tall buildings or artistically rendered—to represent the ensemble of the city. These resemble nothing so much as contemporary Currier and Ives renditions of the city stressing its bucolic setting and exaggerating the prominence of its religious venues. There are occasional pictures of bridges, beaches, racetracks, and railroad stations. Haymarket Square, filled with vendors, wagons, and customers is often included. But there are few churches and fewer if any pictures of ordinary people on ordinary streets. Typically, in the 1900 edition of its *Views of Chicago,* the publishing house promised something it never thought to deliver: "The photo-sketches describe the tumultuous life of the most cosmopolitan city in the world."[35]

In fact, the photo-sketches were specially designed pictures that denied the cosmopolitan character of the city as much as the guidebooks led the tourist away from such impressions. Rand McNally and other publishers created this idealized urban representation with frequent use of photo-sketches. These clearly doctored photographs are partly erased, etched over, and then reproduced. Two particular elements are frequently removed: Either the architectural context is missing (that is, the attached buildings on either side of the subject are missing or blurred), or vehicles and crowds have been brushed away from the streets and sidewalks around the building. Usually, the perspective of the camera or the artist is from a corner, showing the building centered in the middle of the picture. This angle extends the foreground and allows the camera or sketch to frame the entire building while it obscures the context on either side. Finally, the camera angle is generally at street level looking upward. Of course, there are exceptions to each of these generalizations, but many photographs follow this format. Street scenes are devoid of crowds. Instead, a sketch of a lady, gentleman, and perhaps a lamppost provide perspective to the setting. Sometimes the same figures reappear in several photographs. In each case they seem to be spectators, not participants in urban life. This presentation of the city through photo-sketches, with annual revisions of the Rand McNally books, continued well into the 1920s. Eventually, however, the rugged skyline and streets and industrial scenes supplanted the faked, empty grandeur of earlier depictions.

There are some interesting parallels in this format to the developing aesthetics of amateur urban photography in this period. Influenced by Impressionist art, the blurred elegance of this photography, associated with New York photographer Alfred Stieglitz and his theory of "pictorialism," created picturesque examples of cityscape in the mid- and late 1890s.[36] Yet one can see striking differences. Whatever the embellishments, cutting, and atmospheric effects, to Stieglitz the camera and what it could capture were sacrosanct. To the souvenir book publishers, the agenda was neither art nor beauty but a technique put to the service of monumentality and boosterism—or "grand-style," as Peter Hales calls it.[37]

Several things might be said about this odd manipulation of the building's image. The late nineteenth-century tolerance for mixed media, for confusing drawing and photography, was clearly stronger or at least different from our own age. The obviously counterfeit pictures are offensive to a modern eye that sees hundreds of photographic images each day. What we see today is changed and enhanced a hundred ways, but the artist's touchup is rarely explicit.

The merger of photography and artistic rendering in the Chicago souvenir book has a purpose that can be suggested when these photographs are compared to landscape paintings, for they intentionally have some of the same features. There are two interesting similarities: The first is the placement of the monumental natural object (a tree, a mountain, a waterfall, a cloud)—or the building—at the center of the canvas. Second, there is often an ancillary focus on figures such as a man and a woman, a shepherd—the well-dressed lady and gentleman—who are also witnesses to the natural phenomenon being celebrated and who serve to lend perspective

FIGURE 1. The Insurance Exchange Building, La Salle and Adams Streets. This photo-sketch from Rand McNally's 1893 *Pictorial Chicago* has been significantly altered. All street activity has been wiped away, but to give perspective to the depiction, four figures and a fire hydrant have been added. This artifice makes the picture into a sort of urban landscape and lends serenity to what was, in reality, a bustling corner. (Reproduced by the Library of Congress from *Pictorial Chicago*.)

FIGURE 2. Ashland Building, Clark and Randolph Streets. This second portrait of Chicago from Rand McNally in 1893 is entirely redrawn and highly stylized. The artist's pen makes a gesture toward the existence of urban crowds but divides them into small, discrete groups. The effect is to underscore visual order where there probably was none and to tame the motion that an untouched photograph would inevitably capture. (Reproduced by the Library of Congress from *Pictorial Chicago.*)

and size. In such landscapes, the force of the sublime is conveyed by these conventions.

The photo-sketches of Chicago buildings suggest a similar pastoral sublimity, a transformation of skyscrapers into monumental, almost natural objects, existing not as part of a skyline or a continuous grid of the city but standing apart from the urban environment. Even a skyline would emphasize the unity and spatial coherence of the city that these photographs seem to deny. The nullification of their actual environment—that is, other buildings as well as the confusion and bustle of the real city—recontextualizes them in terms of the other photographs in the souvenir books. These include avenues of splendid townhouses, city parks, monuments, and other similarly pictured buildings. This photographic Chicago becomes an idealized city, a perfect visual counterpart to the highly selective guidebook presentation.

The purpose of both sorts of books is the presentation of a city of monuments, of spaciousness and openness, of convenience and lack of congestion. This sanitary view, contrasted to the inevitable experiences of the tourist in the train station or in the city streets, demands an act of imagination, an artistic, even ideological view, to see Chicago as it is becoming, a Chicago of the future, an exemplary city of the twentieth century, a utopia. This occlusive style also typified the World's Fair guidebooks that universally detailed the buildings and exhibits of the White City and rarely, if ever, even mentioned the popular midway (or if they did consigned it to a small section in the back of the book).[38] In photographs and prose this presentation was meant to appeal to the middle-class tourists who were its obvious audience and who were probably content to see the real city of Chicago in terms of an unfolding future that had their safety, comfort, and imagination at its heart. It was a vision that denied, for a precarious moment, the very existence of the remarkable popular culture that was developing at the same time and in the same urban space, as well as the multitudes who were its creators.

Notes

1. Quoted in Fred C. Kelly, *George Ade: Warmhearted Satirist* (Indianapolis, 1947), 106.
2. Edgar Lee Masters, "The White City," in *A Book of Verse* (Upper Saddle River, N.J., 1970), 125–126.

3. Helen Rosenau, *The Ideal City, Its Architectural Evolution in Europe,* 3d ed. (London, 1983), 2, 162.
4. For an example of the triumph of middle-class culture, see Elliott Gorn, *The Manly Art, Bare-Knuckle Prize Fighting in America* (Ithaca, N.Y., 1986). See also Robert W. Rydell, *All the World's a Fair: Visions of Empire at American International Expositions, 1876–1916* (Chicago, 1894) and Alan Trachtenberg, *The Incorporation of America: Culture and Society in the Gilded Age* (New York, 1982). Trachtenberg's splendid essay depicts the triumph of the corporate mode of production and culture, achieving its apex in the White City of the 1893 fair. His interest, in this book, is in the larger questions of hegemonic forces in America expressed at the turn of the century. My approach asks some rather different questions, specifically about the middle class as it operated inside this new world. The problem for the people I discuss was not so much the threat of labor unrest or even monopoly control, although these were important, but the emergence of a popular urban culture that threatened to overwhelm (and eventually did overwhelm) the inherited notions and beliefs of the middle classes coming to occupy parts of such cities as Chicago.
5. In the course of writing a previous book, I explored middle-class attacks on mass culture during the 1950s as, in part, a dissatisfaction with what was perceived to be the working-class and black content of youth culture. See James Gilbert, *A Cycle of Outrage: America's Reaction to the Juvenile Delinquent in the 1950s* (New York, 1986).
6. Daniel H. Burnham and Edward H. Bennett, *Plan of Chicago,* ed. Charles Moore (Chicago, 1909), 124. Burnham made statements like this for several years.
7. Henry Justin Smith, *Chicago's Great Century, 1833–1933* (Chicago, 1933), 114.
8. Louise Wade notes that over one million tourists visited the Chicago Stockyards in 1893. Louise Carroll Wade, *Chicago's Pride: The Stockyards, Packingtown, and Environs in the Nineteenth Century* (Urbana, Ill., 1987), xiv.
9. Albert W. Fulton, *What Will It Cost Me to See the World's Fair?* (Chicago, 1893), 31.
10. Hugh DeSantis, "The Democratization of Travel: The Travel Agent in America," *Journal of American Culture* 1 (Spring 1978), 3–7.
11. John Sears, *Sacred Places* (New York, 1989), 5–10; 209–10.
12. Donna Braden, *Leisure and Entertainment in America* (Dearborn, Mich., 1988), 294.
13. Pennsylvania Tour to Mexico (Philadelphia?, 1891), 5–6.
14. Rand, McNally & Co., *A Week in New York* (New York, 1891).
15. C. H. Mottier, "Central Station Group," *Western Society of Engineers Journal* 42 (October 1937), 255; see also Jeffrey Richards and John M. MacKenzie, *The Railway Station, A Social History* (New York, 1986), 3, 41–42.
16. Richards and MacKenzie, 45, 287.

17. One Who Knows [Henry William Herbert], *The Spider and the Fly* (New York, 1873). Herbert was a popular historian and an expert, under another pseudonym, on hunting and fishing and horse raising.
18. Travelers Aid Society of Chicago, *Centennial History* (Chicago, 1988), no pagination.
19. Traveler's Aid Society, *Seventh Annual Report, 1912* (New York, 1913), 4.
20. Travelers Aid Society of Chicago, *Centennial History*.
21. "A History of Travelers Aid Society of Boston," Richard Soricelli, typescript, in Travelers Aid Society papers, Washington, D.C., passim.
22. Rand, McNally & Co., *Pictorial Guide to Chicago, the World's Fair* (Chicago, 1893), 69.
23. Pennsylvania Railroad, *Guide to the Columbian Exposition with Descriptive Notes of the Cities of New York, Philadelphia, Baltimore, Washington, and Chicago* (Philadelphia, 1893), 17.
24. George W. James, *Mysteries of Chicago* (Chicago, 1891), 13.
25. Thomas E. Hill, *Hill's Souvenir Guide to Chicago and the World's Fair* (Chicago, 1892).
26. Edwin Stine, *What Everyone Wants to Know About Chicago, the World's Fair City* (Chicago, 1891), passim.
27. John J. Flinn, *Chicago: The Marvelous City of the West*, 2d ed. (Chicago, 1892), frontispiece, 17–18.
28. Hubert H. Bancroft, *Book of the Fair*, 2 vols. (Chicago, 1895), vol. 1, 35; Robert Musket, *Chicago, Yesterday and To-day* (Chicago, 1893), 4–8.
29. Carroll Ryan, *Chicago the Magnificent* (New York, 1893), 3, 11.
30. Peter Hales makes much the same point about "grand-style" photography in his fine book *Silver Cities: The Photography of American Urbanization, 1839–1915* (Philadelphia, 1984), ch. 2–3.
31. See Taintor's *City of New York* (New York, 1895).
32. *The Sun Guide to New York* (New York, 1892), 2–3.
33. A. Wittemann, *Views of Chicago: Photographs in Black* (New York, 1892).
34. *Pictorial Chicago* (Chicago, 1930).
35. *One Hundred Photographic Views of Chicago* (Chicago, 1900), no pagination.
36. Alan Trachtenberg, *Reading American Photographs: Images as History* (New York, 1989), 169–87.
37. Hales, *Silver Cities*, passim.
38. A striking contrast to this view can be seen in Baedeker's *The United States*. This book, filled with information for the foreign visitor, is more reminiscent of de Tocqueville than the booster visions of Chicago journalists. Karl Baedeker, *The United States with an Excursion into Mexico: Handbook for Travellers* (New York, 1893), 280ff.

❧

"The Smile that Pays": The Culture of Traveling Salesmen, 1880–1920

Susan Strasser

"There was a time when a good share of the drummers used to hie themselves away to one of their rooms to play a quiet game of poker," traveling salesman Wilbur Castelow recalled in *Only a Drummer,* a small book of reminiscences that he published privately in 1903. "You cannot get but a very few of them to do it to-day: it is on account of the reputation they wish to carry with the house they represent."[1] Castelow was one of many writers who commented on the transformation of the hard-drinking, hard-living drummer (so called because he "drummed up" business) into the modern commercial traveler, a company man and a family man. "Drummer," the San Francisco tea merchant A. Schilling & Co. had advised its

The author wishes to thank Laura Anker, Tim Spears, and Matthew Smith for their comments on a written draft of this essay and the participants in the Columbia University Seminar on American Civilization, who heard and discussed an earlier version.

salesmen in 1884, "conjures up a vision of volubility and brass . . . of pertinacity and impudence."[2] By the turn of the century, salesmen's magazines shunned the term, usually preceding it with "old-fashioned," and almost always associating "drummers" with alcohol, womanizing, and flashy dressing. Writers in these magazines preferred "commercial traveler" or "traveling salesman" and frequently tried out such nomenclature as "ambassador of commerce" or "knight of the grip." Unlike the "drummer," the modern, more carefully trained and supervised "commercial traveler" was a model of self-discipline; corporate sales management techniques and a large self-help literature taught him to manage himself in creating a restrained, genial personality.

The transformation of the drummer was part of a larger set of changes in a distribution system adjusting to mass production and the creation of markets for nationally advertised goods.[3] The wholesalers who employed most of the early drummers had dominated nineteenth-century distribution, taking bids on white soap or tenpenny nails from manufacturers, then promoting the goods to retailers. As the customers of neighborhood grocers and druggists began to request not soap but Ivory, the wholesale merchants' position deteriorated, for they could obtain that product only from Procter and Gamble, on Procter and Gamble's terms and at Procter and Gamble's price. The salesman was a pivotal figure in the ensuing power struggle. Both manufacturers and wholesalers recognized that advertising did not in fact displace the essential personal contact that the drummer had provided. Wholesalers continued to depend on salesmen to promote privately labeled products to retailers, now in competition with nationally advertised brands. Manufacturers organized their own sales forces, not so much to sell products as to enlist retail support in marketing campaigns that entailed store displays, samples, coupons, demonstrations, and other promotional efforts as well as print advertising. The modern sales force became part of the modern company image.

In a rapidly expanding economy, commercial travelers were in great demand. The field offered an avenue of mobility for white men, requiring no skills except the ability to speak English and maintain a pleasant demeanor. The small town boy or the immigrant's son who dreamed of money, larger worlds, and independence from bosses and wives could earn more than other workers and operate with a degree of freedom quite substantial in comparison with factory employment, if he could adjust to life on the road. According to census figures, the number of commercial travelers increased nearly sixfold between 1880 and 1920, whereas total gainful workers slightly more than doubled.[4] Naturally, census figures were low for a population on the move. "The census is incorrect," the president of the Commercial Travelers' National League stated flatly, testifying before the U.S. Industrial Commission in 1899. Suggesting that many travelers were enumerated under the headings for clerks and salesmen, he estimated 350,000 travelers for 1890, a year the census showed fewer than 60,000.[5]

Most of the early drummers worked for wholesalers, whose sales forces had expanded with the railroads.[6] Wholesalers took the major responsibility for opening up territory to manufactured goods; to the extent that there was a national market before national marketing, it was created through sales, not advertising. Regional wholesale houses needed field representatives to offer personalized service to retailers spread out over hundreds or thousands of miles. Their traveling salesmen crisscrossed America on trains to investigate and handle loss and damage claims, assist in credit checks and collections, and sell goods to distant customers. They unpacked their trunks and sample cases in small cities so that local merchants could see the goods without having to travel to Chicago or New York. To drum up business in more remote places, they rode horses and stagecoaches; salesmen operating out of Denver for Marshall Field's substantial wholesale business even took bobsleds through open country.[7]

Because the nineteenth-century salesman worked far from his employer's direct supervision, he was free to behave as he chose. "As long as he was a pioneer, covering new territory, opening up new business, he was allowed to do pretty much as he pleased, provided he delivered the goods," one writer reminisced in *The Commercial Travelers' Magazine* in 1910. The oldtime drummer was a "live wire," a fashion leader who knew "the latest slang, the latest song, the latest joke, and often the latest dance. . . . Many a good man went down the road of booze or cards or girls."[8] An earlier celebration of the drummer concurred:

> He is known as a missionary, sent out to convert the untutored trader; the drummer to rattle up trade, and make a noise for the house. He is of romantic turn, is fond of cheerful company, loves a congenial spirit, and regards a sprightly maiden's chatter as better than lost time.[9]

Many writers—and jokes about farmers' daughters—portrayed salesmen as womanizers, emphasizing the allure of the apparently sophisticated traveling man to lonely innocents like Theodore Dreiser's Sister Carrie, whose first lover, the drummer Drouet, typified the "masher." Women who worked in retail trade were said to be especially susceptible, like the milliner in George Ade's 1903 play *The County Chairman* who yearns to see Chicago: "I've had so many traveling gentlemen tell me about it. Do you know, I love drummers! They're so much more refined than most of the men around here."[10] But Wilbur Castelow claimed that the womanizing image was overdrawn. Salesmen did understand sexual matters, he acknowledged; living in hotels, they witnessed much illicit sexual behavior, especially apparently solid citizens enjoying extramarital liaisons. But few drummers really had sweethearts in every town, and experienced ones discouraged the women most easily available to them, who paraded past hotel lobbies; "drummers can read them just like a newspaper, no matter how they may dress."[11] Successful drummers used willpower, Castelow maintained, to keep these tempting women from wrecking their lives.

Whatever their sexual habits and preferences, traveling appealed to men who liked male companionship and were at least ambivalent about family life. "It is a positive fact," Castelow asserted, "that when a drummer is at home, he wishes he was away again; then, when he is away, he wishes he was back home again." Even those with comfortable homes and adorable wives became "very nervous and irritable" at home, yearning to be on the move every time they heard or saw a train.[12] On the road, they lived in a fundamentally male milieu. Women had always been acceptable in retail trade and some did work as drummers,[13] but they were excluded from the culture that assisted adaptation to life on the road and provided keys to commercial success. An adventurous woman might travel on trains and engage hotel rooms for herself, but even with the best knowledge of the trade she could never be one of "the boys," as commercial travelers were almost universally called.

In railroad diners and smoking cars, in restaurants and hotel lobbies, and at organizational banquets recorded in photographs that show scores of men dressed in suits, white shirts, and ties,[14] "the boys" formed networks that operated independently of employers and that cut across industries. Partaking in what one writer called in 1919 the "freemasonry which prevails among the tribe of traveling men,"[15] they took trolleys to city parks on summer evenings, shared the hotel sample rooms where their wares were on display, did favors for one another, passed on tips and gossip, and above all talked business in the dining car and the smoker, the "road club room."[16] A leading self-help book for salesmen stressed the importance of this camaraderie. "When you meet other salesmen, swap experiences with them," wrote Nathaniel Fowler, one of the era's most popular business writers, in *Practical Salesmanship* (1914). "You are a member of a great traveling school of business, from which there is no graduation, for you study on forever." A man on the road had time to himself, Fowler continued, but he ought not "to become a hermit on the road, to go to his room and stay there between his selling efforts. . . . Contact with other salesmen is necessary for social enjoyment and is a profitable proposition. Without effort one can in conversation swap experiences of great selling value."[17]

The informal networks and social clubs led to formal organizations that promoted salesmen's interests. In 1869, the New York-based Society of Commercial Travellers published a defense of the commercial traveling system aimed at abolishing the many local license laws that failed to distinguish people selling by sample from peddlers.[18] By 1872, another New York organization, the Commercial Travelers National Association, had obtained discounts for members and their baggage from railroad and steamboat lines covering over thirty thousand miles of travel, from about a thousand hotels, and from Western Union. This organization also promised to work against the license laws—most of which were ultimately declared illegal under the 1887 Interstate Commerce Act—and to establish accident insurance and aid for the unemployed.[19]

In 1910, the *Commercial Travelers Magazine*, a quarterly publication of the Springfield, Massachusetts, Commercial Travelers Club, listed 28 traveling salesmen's associations, including fraternal groups, insurance companies, burial societies, and the Christian

Commercial Traveling Men's Association, the "Gideons" of Bible fame.[20] These groups held social events, built club houses, lobbied for laws requiring hotel fire escapes, and above all, in huge organizations, sold insurance. The Travelers Protective Association of America held a 7000-member convention in Milwaukee in 1892.[21] The Order of United Commercial Travelers of America (UCT), a fraternal order that sold accident insurance, received more than 14,000 applications for new members in 1908 and 1909.[22] In 1914, the International Federation of Commercial Travelers of the United States, composed of 16 insurance associations, was reported to have a combined membership of 400,000.[23]

Not everybody who bought insurance from such an organization was even a full-time commercial traveler, much less an active member, but both the *Commercial Travelers Magazine* and *The Sample Case,* the monthly official organ of the UCT, reported good turnouts at conventions, banquets, clambakes, and other public rituals. At many such meetings, members wore the ceremonial robes and headgear typical of the secret fraternities.[24] Although Temperance was a tenet of the UCT (along with Unity and Charity) and a feature of its gatherings, they were acclaimed for good times.

The fraternal culture of the railroad smoker and the organizational banquet found rivals in the corporate-sponsored cultures that manufacturing companies created as they began to take responsibility for their own marketing.[25] Organizing their new sales forces using methods that were to prevail throughout the twentieth century, corporations provided instruction and motivation to their traveling men at training sessions and conventions and in publications, circular letters, and daily personal correspondence. Sales-management techniques were focused on fostering company loyalty in order to keep good salesmen and enhance their abilities to promote new products. These efforts complemented the many samples, premiums, display racks, trade-journal advertisements, and company house organs: materials designed to prepare storekeepers for salesmen's visits that would profit the manufacturers.

The new management techniques were intended to establish trained, salaried sales forces capable of mounting modern merchandising campaigns. The drummers who worked for wholesalers might push a competitor's products or their own private labels; they could not be expected to hold product demonstrations in stores, convince retailers to incorporate manufacturers' logos in local newspaper advertising, or fill display windows with pyramids of the manufacturer's product. Manufacturing companies therefore sent out their own salesmen who acted as the personal agents of marketing campaigns that coordinated consumer advertising with other forms of promotion. Some manufacturers continued to rely on wholesale merchants for the physical aspects of distribution but organized sales forces to do promotional work; salesmen attended workshops to learn how to make attractive window displays and were responsible for holding store demonstrations and handing out samples. Other companies eliminated the middleman entirely: handling their own wholesaling, they hired salesmen to introduce products into new territories, check retailers' credit, and supervise shipments. Armour & Co. employed 4000 salesmen worldwide in 1913, "the most wonderful merchandising machine in the world," according to the company's advertising manager.[26] Although this was almost certainly the largest, sales forces in the hundreds were not uncommon.[27]

Most companies followed sales-management methods introduced by the National Cash Register company, which organized the first sales conference in 1886 and inaugurated formal training eight years later.[28] Its founder, John H. Patterson, instituted innovations in all areas of corporate life and held ideas that parallel corporate-culture concepts fashionable among managers a century later. By 1900, the company was considered "the model industrial institution of America, if not the world."[29] NCR factory workers were among the first to be provided with free showers, lockers, a library and reading room, a cafeteria, and good lighting; the company conducted kindergartens and home-economics classes, held gardening contests with cash prizes, and sponsored sports competitions. These policies undercut but did not prevent union organizing efforts.[30]

NCR corporate culture was particularly strong among its salesmen and sales managers. Within two years of the company's first sales training school in 1894, every salesman had either been to the training or left the company. At the school and at conventions, NCR men studied standardized presentations and participated in role-playing sessions that went on as long as two hours, performing merchants' parts as well as their own. In 1900, Patterson set standards that made possible comparisons among the different territories, assigning each agency and each salesman a quota that depended on the nature of the territory. A one-hundred-dollar register contributed four points to the quota, a one-thousand-dollar machine, forty points. Salesmen who exceeded their quotas were eligible for prizes and lionized at sales conventions; such rewards were in part intended, as even a laudatory history of Patterson's sales policies put it, "to form habits and tastes that only more money could satisfy."[31]

At most companies, the new sales forces were paid salaries instead of commissions. Commissioned salesmen tended to call only on regular buyers and sure prospects; they would neglect non-saleswork like writing reports, holding store demonstrations, and trimming dealers' windows.[32] They were prone to shirking collection work because it did not pay, and they might overstock retailers who would then fail to meet financial obligations. Employers preferred, therefore, to pay salaries instead of commissions and to motivate sales forces by other means. Similarly, sales managers were advised—and most understood—that salesmen would serve the company better if they reimbursed actual expenses than if they provided a fixed allowance. Reimbursement created clerical labor and the potential for friction between salesmen making reports and managers checking them, but salesmen with fixed expense accounts would economize by staying in cheap hotels, tarnishing the company images that their employers had begun to build. They would also avoid work that required extraordinary expenditures, such as visits to out-of-the-way towns that could only be reached by horse, stagecoach, or later, automobile.[33]

Like expense accounts and good clothes, autos served to distinguish salesmen from other workers; like conventions and contests, they distinguished progressive companies from other firms. According to *The Sample Case*, many firms furnished cars for their salesmen by 1911. National Cash Register was again among the first, but the practice was especially widespread among farm-machinery manufacturers, whose salesmen had to tour the countryside.[34] These companies made the salesman's job more attractive to married men, who might now spend Sundays with their families thanks to more flexible transportation. Most important for company loyalty, they put salesmen on the road by themselves, taking them off the trains and away from the "road club room."

Whether in automobiles or on trains, salesmen were never entirely free of their employers, who improved methods for keeping track of them. Surveillance was hardly new. "Many a drummer has been asked when he returned home from a trip about certain things that happened in cities where he had been that he was concerned in, and he never dreamed his house would find them out, but it did," Castelow wrote in 1903; some men discovered that they had been shadowed for an entire trip.[35] With large sales forces more carefully organized, managers were employed specifically to keep track. Manuals—some explicitly adopting the jargon of scientific management—suggested map and tack systems for following salesmen's movements as well as a variety of daily, weekly, and monthly reports.[36] By the early 1920s, companies were explicit about their plans to keep track of sales employees. "Watch your step," the Parker Pen Company advised its salesmen on the first page of its 1923 sales manual. The makers of Pet milk warned that daily reports were analyzed on Hollerith machines. "Any errors are immediately detected and recorded . . . This system of checking quickly brings to our attention men who are chronic offenders and enables us promptly to take steps to insure correct reports."[37]

Most companies' sales-management policies, however, emphasized carrots, not sticks. Following the NCR lead, sales contests and conventions—company-sponsored rituals—were common in large manufacturing and wholesaling companies by 1910. Manuals for sales managers routinely included guidance for holding effective meetings and instructions for establishing quotas and sales competitions. Conventions were to be carefully planned, from the roll call at the start to the rousing finish.[38] More than 300 salesmen came to the fourteenth Heinz convention in Pittsburgh in 1902 on specially hired trains from both east and west. For seven working days, usually well into the evening, they heard about 20 talks a day: "Our Seed and Vegetable Farms and Salting Houses," "Pickling Vinegar—The Most Effective Way of Selling to the Merchant," "Broader Salesmanship," and others. On the final afternoon, according to the company magazine *Pickles,* "there was more enthusiasm than could be seen at most political conventions and almost continually there was cheering and singing." The closing banquet featured pickle-shaped ice cream, leatherbound souvenir books, and speakers including the president of the National Association of Manufacturers, the head of the nation's largest outdoor advertising firm, and H.J. Heinz.[39]

Such methods, one 1914 manual acknowledged, cost a great deal of money, but it cost more "to operate a lot of poorly trained men with little or no enthusiasm." At conventions, salesmen could make friends within the company; managers from sales and advertising departments could cooperate in launching marketing campaigns. Conventions and contests would produce salesmen who "refer to the house as 'ours'—who consider themselves not distinct selling units but members of a big, growing family."[40]

The many salesmen who worked for smaller companies, however, did operate as "distinct selling units." Their opportunities to learn the lessons of modern salesmanship came in the form of the countless books, magazine articles, and correspondence courses that taught the cultivation of a new type of selling personality, distinct from that of the drummer.[41] Most of this literature insisted that salesmen were made, not born, almost always in that language; the born salesman presumably did not need to buy books on salesmanship. And because they worked alone, with little supervision from bosses, they had to make themselves.

For the new modern salesman, working alone was to provide a justification for discipline, not the license of the drummer; above all, the advice literature asserted, salesmen needed self-control. "The danger of being your own 'boss,'" one 1918 manual explained, "is that you will not apply yourself as assiduously as you would if you had to punch a clock, . . . but development of the success qualities . . . will give you the power of self-control, and you will be your own master—not the slave of your negative qualities."[42] Temptations abounded on the road, but as Nathaniel Fowler pointed out in *Practical Salesmanship*, they beset people everywhere:

> Temptation was put into this world for a purpose—to be overcome and mastered. The bad man on the road would probably have been a bad man at home. . . .
>
> No one should refuse to go on the road because of the temptations which will surround him. If he has the right stuff in him, he will come out ahead.[43]

The "right stuff" could be cultivated, with self-discipline and good habits.

Most books on salesmanship stressed the appropriate use of time, a primary issue for workers who had to supervise themselves. "A loss of two hours a day means before the end of the year two whole months crossed off the calendar," wrote Worthington C. Holman, a former NCR employee and editor of *Salesmanship: The Magazine for Business Getters,* in *Ginger Talks,* a 1905 book that sold more than 150,000 copies in its first edition. "There is not an hour of life," he continued, quoting Ruskin, "but is trembling with destinies—not a moment of which, once past, the appointed work can ever be done again, or the neglected blow struck on the cold iron."[44] Fowler offered advice on leisure time as well: chapters on "What to do Outside of Business" (have a hobby) and "What to Read" (newspapers and magazines—"do not be a book-worm"). He approved of rest, but not of wasting time: "loafing is not resting."[45]

Exercise was one worthwhile way of using time on the road. Fowler urged against becoming an athlete, but recommended walking, playing ball, and joining a gymnasium.[46] (In 1909 *The Sample Case* reported that at least one hotel, the Plankington House in Milwaukee, had installed an exercise room for guests, fitted with punching bags and other equipment.)[47] Salesmen's advice books were nearly unanimous on the necessity of fitness and vitality. The *Salesmanship and Sales Management* volume of the popular Alexander Hamilton Institute "Modern Business" series cited Emerson: "In the last analysis, great human achievements rest on perfect physical health."[48] Holman's *Ginger Talks* began with a famous epigraph preaching "the doctrine of the strenuous life," from the president of the United States. "The average salesman," Holman wrote, advising against alcohol and indigestible food, "would be ashamed to treat a second-hand lawn mower with as little consideration as he extends to the delicate mechanism of his own body."[49]

The body should be cultivated for appearance as well as health; in essence, writers instructed salesmen to package themselves, always appearing in public with shiny shoes, clean fingernails, and smooth shaves. Fowler admitted that outside appearances bore no relation to intrinsic qualities but maintained that in business, "what we wear, and all parts of us which can be seen, are of commercial consequence."[50] Most advice books stressed that clothes should be pressed and spotless, then went on at greater length about avoiding the exaggerated costumes of the flashy drummer. "Just as the finest French plate-glass is the kind that is entirely unobtrusive to the eye, so the best dressed man is he whose apparel attracts no attention to itself," the Alexander Hamilton book maintained.[51] "Over-dressing," Fowler wrote, "is against good taste, good morals, good breeding, self-respect, and good business."[52] *The Salesman's Handbook*, from the best-selling series of the Scranton, Pennsylvania, International Correspondence Schools, quoted Pope:

> Be not the first by whom the new are tried
> Nor yet the last to lay the old aside.

It was possible, the ICS handbook admitted, to err on the conservative side, dressing "in a demure style that is hardly adapted to the forceful business man." But the book suggested that more salesmen erred in the other, more "conspicuous" direction, reinforcing the older image of the drummer.[53]

Although carefully pressed clothes and well-tended bodies required discipline and self-control, the most fundamental object for the salesman's self-restraint was his ever-genial personality.[54] Salesmen must hide their real feelings, never betraying frustration or discouragement about difficult customers or despondency over private afflictions. Customers would respond positively—that is, with orders—to men they liked to have around and looked forward to seeing. "Cheerfulness," wrote Holman, "is God's medicine."[55] In *How to Sell* (1915), which provided sample dialogues that put greater emphasis on a salesman's actual interactions with customers than his earlier *Practical Salesmanship*, Fowler devoted a short chapter to "Selling Sunshine."[56]

During the course of a sale, the essential character traits were enthusiasm and confidence, which fostered courage. As Holman put it:

> A salesman without nerve is like a jelly fish. The jelly fish is an inoffensive sort of animal, with no disagreeable qualities to excite prejudice; but he has no spine. Consequently his only possible method of progression is to drift. He washes along with the slow tide and never arrives anywhere. When there is anything worth while doing in the fish world, Bro. Jelly fish is never among those present.[57]

Elsewhere Holman offered an illustration entitled "Enthusiasm Breaks All Bonds." A "modern Gulliver" lay on the ground, bound by Lilliputians labeled "Blue Days," "I Can't," "Wasted Time," "Low Aim," "Laziness," "Downcast," and "Tomorrow." The caption urged the reader not to let "the devils of indifference" get the best of him. Text on the facing page declared, "The salesman's personal force is an influence that emanates directly from his own unlimited belief in his proposition. It is the magnetic power of sheer earnestness."[58] A "catechism" published in another manual, to be repeated daily as "mental and moral discipline," provided a litany that built confidence in the goods, the belief that customers needed them and that the price was fair, and the conviction that the salesman was "justified in asking a 'prospect's' time and attention." "Am I going to sell every man I call on to-day?" it ended. "Most decidedly."[59]

But even with the most positive attitudes, salesmen sometimes lost sales and confronted difficult customers. "The traveling man must digest disappointments as he does a plate of blue points, for he swallows them about as often," one writer declared in a collection of reminiscences entitled *Tales of the Road.*[60] The International Correspondence Schools handbook claimed that some customers purposely tried to make salesmen angry. This was just another form of temptation, and the effective salesman would count to 10 to slow down his response.

> This advice is easier to give than to carry out, but the man who controls himself once has started on the control habit and thereafter finds it easier to hold the reins on himself. Self-control relates not merely to the temper but to every other weakness: loose or profane talking, idling, drinking, immorality, discouragement, etc.[61]

Poems published in *The Sample Case* suggest that salesmen did attempt to cultivate sunny personalities. "A Toast to the UCT" (to be drunk, in this temperance organization, without "the red nectar") described members as "princes of laughter and mirth" with big smiles and big hearts, who "carry the sunshine wherever they go."[62] "Always Be Happy" implied that real happiness was possible for those who would stop grumbling and remember that things could be worse. "Then see if it really won't honestly pay/To be happy," it ended.[63] Another piece of *Sample Case* doggerel, "The Smile That Pays," likewise linked sunshine and sales:

. . . I smile because I know it pays.
It means dollars and cents in many ways.

To me, life has not been 'One long song.'
There's many a thing that has gone wrong.
But I don't peddle troubles where're I go.
For who wants to hear my tale of woe?

You have your troubles and so have I,
I show my samples and ask you to buy.
Do you think if I was a hard luck cryer
That I would find you an easy buyer? . . .

I can't sell goods with a hard luck tale,
So I smile, keep happy, and make my sale.[64]

Skillful salesmen controlled customers' dispositions as well as their own. Talking to a customer, according to Holman's *Ginger Talks,* was "like walking around in a dynamite factory." The customer was "made up of combustibles—pride, prejudices, vanity, sensitiveness, conceit. Be careful not to touch a match to any of these; avoid friction—it throws out sparks."[65] One phrenologically inspired selling manual described the customer's anger in physiological terms involving nerves and blood vessels, suggesting that anger stimulated and exhausted the heart. "Tiring out a buyer," the manual explained, "is the worst way of selling goods that there is, for the buyer knows that he has been forced into buying, and will avoid the salesman thereafter."[66] To avert the possibilities for anger, salesmen were advised to avoid controversial subjects, especially politics.

Despite recommendations that amounted to nearly constant dissimulation, many of the advice books also preached honesty. Most books glanced over the question of honesty with customers, maintaining simply that salesmen who hoped to establish repeat customers had little option but to tell the truth about the fundamental qualities of the goods and the policies of the house. Holman stressed another kind of honesty, crucial to self-discipline. "Be honest with yourself at least," he wrote. "Never lie to your own soul. Seek out the truth. Look for the actual fact and stare it in the face. See things as they are."[67] Such scrutiny had its time and place, however; those who practiced it in the presence of customers risked self-consciousness, never an effective way to make a good impression.[68]

The Alexander Hamilton Institute text linked honesty with an issue almost as central to the advice literature as to the manufacturers' training programs: company loyalty. Everybody knew that padding an expense account was dishonest, but so was the man

> who fails to get a sample room when he knows that his negligence will hurt the interests of his house; who waits over a train or two to have the company of a fellow salesman to the next stop—or so as not to break up a congenial card party; who carries a side line; or who spends his spare time in such a manner as to give his house below-par service.[69]

The daily catechism began with company loyalty. "Am I working for a good house?" the salesman was to ask himself. "Yes," he should affirm.[70] Both the commercial advice literature and the salesmen's magazines suggest that loyalty was stressed because many salesmen believed that their steady customers would continue to patronize them even if they changed jobs. A 1911 article in *The Sample Case,* "Who 'Owns' the House's Trade?" maintained that a good salesman could more easily make another good connection than his firm could replace him; "the demand for first-class salesmen far exceeds the supply," it stated clearly. Still, it answered the question in the title by siding with the employer.[71] The Alexander Hamilton Institute's textbook proclaimed firmly that "the salesman should realize that the territory is an asset of the house."[72]

A salesman making less money than he wanted to make would leave for another job "as soon as he becomes fully aware of the market value of his grade of ability," wrote leading business writer J. George Frederick in *Modern Salesmanagement* (1919). The way to keep them was to pay well; money was both the most effective reward for company loyalty and the best way to produce it. Salesmen, Frederick claimed, calling on the image of the drummer, "live to a large extent on the exterior."

> In other words, food, clothing, comfort and appearances in life are especially close to their hearts and spirits. . . . Salesmen meet each other and compare notes in hotels and trains, and latterly in clubs and associations, and whether they are over-aggressive or silent with regard to asking for more compensation, they feel deeply on the subject.

High pay cost employers less in the long run, Frederick told them, than continual turnover.[73]

"Who 'Owns' the House's Trade?" addressed the loyalty question using both the rhetoric of selling sunshine, with its concern for the daily trials of the salesman, and the era's class-conscious rhetoric. It described "the man with samples, . . . out in all sorts of weather night and day, enduring untold discomforts, with nerves keyed up to the highest point, and at times so despondent that he almost prays for the train on which he is traveling to run off the track and end his miserable existence." In contrast, the boss "gets out of a warm bed and after a good breakfast goes down to business about 8 o'clock, sits around enjoying genuine Havanas until the sun is getting low, when his chauffeur appears at the door waiting to take him home for the day."[74] Even so, the writer urged salesmen to recognize the risks that bosses took in the market, their difficult decision-making, the problems of financial panics and dull trade, and the "exquisite anguish" of the sales manager who could not find good men to sell his products.

In the midst of the recession of 1914, when stocks were low and "everybody bought from hand to mouth, if at all," the *Commercial Travelers Magazine* was less charitable, denouncing bosses as inconsiderate. "He was never on the road a day," one (possibly fictional) salesman was quoted, speaking about his young sales manager, son of the firm's largest stockholder. "Has no more conception of how hard it is to get business than a blind fool." Traveling salesmen needed to make sales to feel satisfied, the article stated. "It is one long hard struggle to keep up courage and act cheerful when they cannot feel so."[75]

In the next issue, the magazine published a long editorial, "A Word to the Bosses," peppered with adjectives like "arrogant" and "bumptious." Bosses thought they knew everything; they treated drummers like order-taking automatons. Experienced salesmen smiled when the boss kicked; they "know their own worth also, know their own grip and pull with their customers, now old-time friends many of them. Know also that competing firms stand ready to hire them without a question." Younger, newer salesmen could not be so brave. Buying and making things was easy enough for people with money, tools, and workers.

> But go out and sell it to those who are stocked plum full of someone else's goods and satisfied. Go and convince men who believe in the other fellow's make, that yours is best. . . . To land him, in short, is quite another

> matter. And so we say to you, *Mr. Boss*, put your bump of conceit in your waste basket, or swap it for a dog and shoot the dog. Go out and call on a few of your own customers.[76]

Bosses should praise their salesmen in encouraging letters, not write critical ones that concentrated on employees' faults. "Ask their advice in some minor point," the article told the boss. "You need not follow it; probably won't." Such treatment would, however, make salesmen want to serve and give them courage. The boss who discouraged his salesmen weakened his sales force.[77]

In a chapter devoted to "Employer and Employee," Fowler attacked such thinking. The boss had to be respected because he *was* the boss; the discipline of rank and station was as critical as self-discipline. "While you are in the forecastle of salesmanship, and have not become a ward-room officer, take off your hat to the man on the bridge if you would do your work better and gain promotion quicker," he wrote. Some employers might treat employees like machines, but too many salesmen expected too much personal attention from bosses who had numerous people to supervise. Employees should seek promotions, not new jobs. A good salesman would leave his job "only after deep and long consideration. He realizes that his employer has troubles and annoyances which no employee has to bear."[78]

Probably the greatest source of friction between salesmen and bosses was the matter of credit and collections. Organized salesmen discussed collections at their meetings and in their magazines, generally as another arena for self-discipline, a job that had to be done.[79] At the same time, they perceived collection work as inimical to their sales personalities: it was difficult to sell sunshine and demand payment at the same time. The salesman's decision-making about the sale necessitated a balancing act, according to a parody in *The Sample Case:*

> *To Sell or Not to Sell*
> *(Hamlet's Soliloquy Commercially Applied.)*
>
> To sell or not to sell?
> That is the question.
> Whether 'tis better to send the goods
> And take the risk of doubtful payment,
> Or to make sure of what is in possession,

And declining, hold them.
To sell, to ship, perchance to lose—
Aye, there's the rub!
For when the goods are gone
What charm can win them back
From slippery debtors? . . .[80]

Bosses too rarely appreciated the problem, treating salesmen as field agents of the credit department but expecting them also to make quotas. Moreover, credit departments corresponded with customers behind salesmen's backs, operating, as one *Sample Case* writer put it, on "a cold mathematical basis," as opposed to the "flesh and blood factor that counts between the salesman and the customer."[81]

That "flesh and blood factor" was the central object of all of the salesman's self-discipline. The distribution system depended on it. Manufacturers and wholesalers needed men in the field who would perform the functions of the old drummer, representing the firm in credit disputes with retailers, dealing with damaged shipments, and bringing new products and commercial news from the world beyond the store, the neighborhood, and the small town. But they also needed men who would carry out the new promotional techniques that constituted modern marketing campaigns. Branded, advertised products were altering personal relationships between storekeepers and their customers. Although some observers believed that advertising would eliminate sales, consumers bought mass-produced goods at stores run by merchants whose purchasing decisions were still made in consultation with salesmen.

Unlike the drummer, the new salesman was less marked by his independence than by his participation in a system that merged his personality with the image of the company he worked for. Companies paid for that allegiance, spending great sums on salaries and bonuses, good dinners and hotel rooms, training programs and lavish conventions, and in the process creating loyalties that might compete with those established in the railroad smoking car. Like the drummer's job, the new salesman's offered good pay and relative freedom without requiring extensive academic work or manual training. But the controlled geniality of the modern commercial traveler took discipline. At the sales meeting or alone in his hotel room with the self-help literature, the salesman learned to keep his courage up, control his temper, and wear the smile that made sales.

Notes

1. Wilbur Elijah Castelow, *Only a Drummer: A Short History of the Commercial Travelling Salesman's Life* (N.p., 1903), 19.
2. A. Schilling & Co., *Advice to Traveling Salesmen Introducing Perfection Canned Teas* (San Francisco, 1884), 3.
3. This larger transformation is the subject of my book, *Satisfaction Guaranteed: The Making of the American Mass Market* (New York, 1989).
4. Calculated from Alba M. Edwards, *Comparative Occupation Statistics for the United States, 1870 to 1940,* U.S. Department of Commerce, Sixteenth Census of the United States: 1940 (Washington, D.C., 1943), 100, 110.
5. Testimony of P.E. Dowe, U.S. Industrial Commission, *Preliminary Report on Trusts and Industrial Combinations* (Washington, D.C., 1900), 27.
6. On nineteenth-century wholesaling, see Glenn Porter and Harold C. Livesay, *Merchants and Manufacturers: Studies in the Changing Structure of Nineteenth-Century Marketing* (Baltimore, 1971) and Alfred D. Chandler, Jr., *The Visible Hand: The Managerial Revolution in American Business* (Cambridge, Mass., 1977), 209–23.
7. On the use of bobsleds, see Robert W. Twyman, *History of Marshall Field and Co., 1852–1906* (Philadelphia, 1954), 94.
8. Rev. Henry H. Morrill, "Drummers Old and New," *The Commercial Travelers' Magazine,* September 1910, 321.
9. George L. Marshall, *O'er Rail and Cross-Ties with Gripsack. A Compilation on the Commercial Traveler* (New York, 1892), 13.
10. Quoted in Truman E. Moore, *The Traveling Man: The Story of the American Traveling Salesman* (Garden City, N.Y., 1972), 37.
11. Castelow, *Only a Drummer,* 14; see also 12, 31–34.
12. Ibid., 15.
13. Castelow suggested that his readers might be surprised at the number of female drummers (ibid., 8). In 1914, popular business writer Nathaniel Fowler introduced his *Practical Salesmanship* with a note explaining that every word in it was addressed to women as well as men; the masculine noun and pronoun would be used "only for convenience" and because "constant mention of both sexes would be confusing and require unnecessary repetition." Nathaniel C. Fowler, Jr., *Practical Salesmanship, A Treatise on the Art of Selling Goods* (Boston, 1914), vii. Still, only about 1.6 percent of the commercial travelers listed in the 1910 census were women (Edwards, *Comparative Occupation Statistics,* 69).
14. See, among many other examples, the photograph of the Annual Banquet of United Commercial Travelers in Wheeling, West Virginia, on November 28, 1908, published in *The Sample Case,* February 1909, frontispiece.
15. Archer Wall Douglas, *Traveling Salesmanship* (New York, 1919), 143.
16. See Castelow, *Only a Drummer,* 19; Charles N. Crewdson, *Tales of the Road* (Chicago, 1905), 145–46; "road club room," 161.

17. Fowler, *Practical Salesmanship,* 67–68.
18. Society of Commercial Travellers, *The System of Commercial Travelling in Europe and the United States: Its History, Customs and Laws* (New York, 1869).
19. Commercial Travelers National Association, *Hand-Book* (New York, 1872), 4. On licenses, see Cyrus H. Smithdeal, "Commercial Travelers and the Law," in T.H. Pace, *The American Commercial Traveler: A Bright, Sparkling, Up-to-Date Book Worth Its Weight in Gold to the Young Commercial Salesman* (Richmond, Va., 1905), 80–81.
20. "Register of Commercial Travelers' Associations," *The Commercial Travelers Magazine,* June 1910, 195–97.
21. Moore, *Traveling Man,* 34.
22. "Editorial Ideas: Four Assessments This Year," *The Sample Case,* December 1909, 385.
23. "The Commercial Traveler at the San Francisco Exposition," *The Commercial Travelers Magazine,* April 1914, 45, 47–48.
24. See, among many examples, the photographs of the Degree Team of Superior Council, no. 333, Superior, Wisconsin, *The Sample Case,* July 1915, 16, and of the Worcester Council, Worcester, Mass., *The Sample Case,* September 1915, 224. For a discussion of fraternal organizations, see Mary Ann Clawsen, *Constructing Brotherhood* (Princeton, N.J., 1989).
25. On the concept of corporate culture in historical work, see Charles Dellheim, "Business in Time: The Historian and Corporate Culture," *The Public Historian* 8 (Spring 1986), 9–22.
26. E.B. Merritt, "How Armour & Co. Are Solving Their Vast Selling Problem," *Printers' Ink,* January 23, 1913, 4; "Reasons Back of Armour's Selling Policies," February 27, 1913, 6.
27. On sales force sizes, "Should the Credit Man Travel—A Reply," *The Sample Case,* December 1909, 383–84.
28. See Roy W. Johnson and Russell W. Lynch, *The Sales Strategy of John H. Patterson, Founder of the National Cash Register Company* (Chicago, 1932), 142, 230–33.
29. "The National Cash Register Company," *Printers' Ink,* February 14, 1900, 3.
30. See Samuel Crowther, *John H. Patterson: Pioneer in Industrial Welfare* (Garden City, N.Y., 1926), 205.
31. See "The National Cash Register Company," *Printers' Ink,* February 14, 1900, 3–4; Crowther, *John H. Patterson,* 196–204, 234–35 and passim; Johnson and Lynch, *Sales Strategy of John H. Patterson,* 230–35, 257; T.C. Henry, *Tricks of the Cash Register Trust* (Winchester, Ky., 1913), 8. "To form habits . . .": Johnson and Lynch, *Sales Strategy,* 69–70.
32. J. George Frederick, *Modern Salesmanagement, A Practical Handbook and Guide* (New York, 1919), 141–42; Herbert F. DeBower and John G. Jones, "Sales Management," part III of *Marketing Methods and Salesmanship,* Modern Business Volume III (New York, 1914), 466–69.

33. See Charles Wilson Hoyt, *Scientific Sales Management* (New York, 1912), 157–62; W.A. Waterbury, "Points to Watch in the Expense Account," in A.W. Shaw Company, *Salesmanship and Sales Management,* Library of Sales and Advertising vol. 1 (Chicago, 1914), 109–15. See also Castelow, 24–25.
34. "Selling By Automobile," *The Sample Case,* November 1911, 1–2.
35. Castelow, *Only a Drummer,* 17.
36. See W.A. Waterbury, "Guiding Salesmen by Map and Tack," in A.W. Shaw Company, *Selling Methods,* Library of Sales and Advertising vol. 4 (Chicago, 1914), 137–46; B.C. Bean, "What Your Salesmen Should Report," ibid., 153–59; DeBower and Jones, "Sales Management," 473–79.
37. Parker Pen Company, "Here's the Big News" (n.p., 1923), [1]; The Helvetia Company, "Sales Manual" (St. Louis, Mo., June 5, 1923), 12. Both in Baker Library, Graduate School of Business Administration, Harvard University.
38. On contests, see Walter H. Cottingham, "Using Contests to Spur on Salesmen," in Shaw, *Salesmanship and Sales Management,* 93–108; DeBower and Jones, "Sales Management," 492–99; Hoyt, *Scientific Sales Management,* 115–30. On conventions, see DeBower and Jones, 502–8; Hoyt, 89–94; W.C. Holman, "Making a Sales Convention Pay," in Shaw, *Salesmanship and Sales Management,* 116–27.
39. *Pickles,* International Convention Number (February 1902), in Smithsonian Collection of Business Americana Foods Box 16, Heinz. "There was more enthusiasm": p. 7.
40. DeBower and Jones, "Sales Management," 509.
41. See, among many others, Fowler, *Practical Salesmanship;* The System Company, *How to Increase Your Sales,* 3d ed. (Chicago, 1909); Arthur Frederick Sheldon, *The Art of Selling, For Business Colleges, High Schools of Commerce, Y.M.C.A. Classes and Private Students* (Chicago, 1911); International Correspondence Schools, *The Salesman's Handbook* (Scranton, Pa., 1912); Nathaniel C. Fowler, Jr., *How to Sell* (Chicago, 1915); John G. Jones, *Salesmanship and Sales Management* (New York, 1917); Simon Robert Hoover, *The Science and Art of Salesmanship* (New York, 1917); National Salesmen's Training Association, *The Art and Science of Selling,* 8 vols. (Chicago, 1918); YMCA, *Salesmanship, The Standard Course of the United YMCA Schools,* 4 vols. (New York, 1920).
42. NSTA, *Art and Science of Selling,* 26.
43. Fowler, *Practical Salesmanship,* "What to Do . . ." and "What to Read," 206–19; "temptation was put . . . ," 69.
44. Worthington C. Holman, *Ginger Talks: I—The Talks of a Sales Manager to His Men* (Chicago, 1908), 52–53. The circulation claims for the first edition may be found on the back of Holman's pamphlet "Sales Ginger, No. 1" (Chicago, 1905), in the Smithsonian Collection of Business Americana (Salesbooks-Patent Models).
45. Fowler, *Practical Salesmanship,* 221.
46. Fowler, *Practical Salesmanship,* 223.

47. *The Sample Case,* December 1909, 382.
48. Jones, *Salesmanship and Sales Management,* 149. See also Hoover, *Science and Art of Salesmanship,* 16–22; YMCA, *Salesmanship,* Book I: *The Salesman and His Job,* 87–106.
49. Holman, *Ginger Talks,* 90.
50. Fowler, *Practical Salesmanship,* 108.
51. Jones, *Salesmanship and Sales Management,* 169.
52. Fowler, *Practical Salesmanship,* 108.
53. International Correspondence Schools, *Salesman's Handbook,* 38.
54. For a modern discussion of these issues, see Arlie Hochschild, *The Managed Heart: The Commercialization of Human Feeling* (Berkeley, Calif., 1983).
55. Holman, *Ginger Talks,* 77.
56. Fowler, *How to Sell,* 304–5.
57. Holman, "Sales Ginger" pamphlet no. 4, 2–3.
58. Holman, *Ginger Talks,* 20–21.
59. Sheldon, *Art of Selling,* 93–94.
60. Crewdson, *Tales of the Road,* 55.
61. ICS, *Salesman's Handbook,* 30–31.
62. L. Inez Eden, "A Toast to the UCT," *The Sample Case,* December 1909, 372.
63. C.I. Talles, "Always Be Happy," *The Sample Case,* December 1909, 384.
64. W.E. Hooker, "The Smile That Pays," *The Sample Case,* August 1911, 82.
65. Holman, *Ginger Talks,* 76.
66. Chas. Lindgren, *The New Salesmanship and How to Do Business by Mail* (Chicago, 1909), 20.
67. Holman, *Ginger Talks,* 147.
68. See Sheldon, *Art of Selling,* 86.
69. Jones, *Salesmanship . . . ,* 160.
70. Sheldon, *Art of Selling,* 93.
71. W.T. Du Bose, "Who 'Owns' the House's Trade?" *The Sample Case,* August 1911, 96.
72. Jones, *Salesmanship . . . ,* 187.
73. J. George Frederick, *Modern Salesmanagement, A Practical Handbook and Guide* (New York, 1919), 138–40.
74. Ibid., 95–96.
75. "Our Sample Case: Business Conditions," *The Commercial Travelers Magazine,* April 1914, 5–6.
76. "A Word to the Bosses," *Commercial Travelers Magazine,* July 1914, 151.

77. See also Wilfred Pearce, "Spoiling Good Salesmen by Constant Nagging," *The Sample Case,* January 1909, 29.

78. Fowler, *Practical Salesmanship,* 89–91.

79. See, for example, John Allen Sweet, "Credits and the Firm," *The Sample Case,* April 1909, 218–20; "Should the Credit Man Travel—A Reply," *The Sample Case,* December 1909, 383–84; "Credit Man or Traveling Salesman, Which?" *The Sample Case,* July 1915, 17–20; J.O. Goodpasture, "Selling and Collecting," *The Sample Case,* September 1915, 225–26; A.M. Grigg, "Some Observations on Credits," November 1915, 381–83.

80. *The Sample Case,* July 1911, 22.

81. W.B. Reynolds, "Make the Credit Man Travel," *The Sample Case,* September 1909, 178.

❧

Organization as Artifact: A Study of Technical Innovation and Management Reform, 1893–1906

Peter Dobkin Hall

ORGANIZATIONS ARE FREQUENTLY STUDIED AS PRODUCERS OF ARTIFACTS BUT are seldom themselves considered artifacts. This fact is due to the conventional assumption that the forms and functions of organizations are determined by natural selection in the marketplace (efficiency/effectiveness), whereas the form and function of ceramics or furniture are more idiosyncratically shaped by craftsmen or industrial laborers. Both organizations and material artifacts are, in

I wish to thank the American Council of Learned Societies and the General Electric Foundation, whose generous support underwrote the research on which this paper is based. I am also grateful to Richard McHugh and Marshall Chiaraluce of the South Central Connecticut Regional Water Authority, who permitted me unrestricted access to the New Haven Water Company archives. Earlier versions of this paper were presented to the Complex Organizations Seminar (COSI) at the Institution for Social & Policy Studies, Yale University, and to the 1987 annual meeting of the Association for the Study of Connecticut History.

fact, the outcomes of market relationships. But to say this is not to concede that the market relationships are simple. Viewing organizations from the same analytical perspective as objects enables us to appreciate their complexity.

The form of an organization, like that of an armchair or a platter, is the outcome of a complex set of transactions between producers and consumers: the producers and their "tradition" (colleagues, competitors, and other players in their field of activity), and the consumers and the "public" of which they are a part (their families, friends, and others who share in the activity of consumption). In fact, artifacts are no more clearly bounded or physically discrete than organizations because both are produced and consumed by individuals who also participate in social, economic, and political activities that may or may not be related to their object/organizational roles. Furthermore, just as the same object can be perceived and used by different individuals in different ways, so the purposes and goals of organizations can be unclear, since they frequently bring together individuals whose motives for working together may not only vary but may also, in certain cases, be significantly opposed. Organizations and artifacts are only outcomes of behavioral systems. The systems themselves are elusive and intangible.

It is useful at this point to ask what we really mean when we use the term *organization*. Clearly we are not referring to the infinitely complex totality of actions and affects that comprise it. We are, in fact, referring to some aspect of the behavioral system at a particular point or series of points in time. When we do this we are dealing with the realm of artifacts. A measurement or series of measurements, a set of interviews, accounting statements, letters, or photographs are, like chairs, houses, and ceramics, no more than outputs of behavioral systems at particular points in time. They are, as such, no more than starting points for the interpretation of the systems that produced them.

Within any advanced culture there is a range of ways to organize productive activity. The utilitarian function of production can be fulfilled by duly observing the constraints imposed by available resources, technology, and demand. Beyond utility, however, is a broad realm of choice. Firms can be sole proprietorships; partnerships; unincorporated associations; for-profit, non-profit, or government corporations; or government bureaus and departments.

Within firms, production can be organized in a variety of ways: labor can be specialized or generalized; components of production can be performed by family members, apprentices, employees, inside contractors, or outside contractors; control of the work process can be centralized and bureaucratic or decentralized and democratic.

The creation and transformation of organizations embody behavioral processes identical to those associated with the production of more tangible artifacts. Choices of organizational type and of operational characteristics, though constrained by utilitarian considerations, are determined by the socialization of producers (which delimits goals and the range of behavioral and mechanical technologies available to them), negotiations between producers and consumers, and the values of the society in which these transactions take place. This context of choice does not differ significantly from that associated with, say, seating furniture. Though constrained by physical forces and the strength of materials (seating furniture must, after all, be able to support the person seated on it), the choice of stool, bench, side chair, armchair, throne, or whatever, the settings in which they are used—and their styles of appearance, materials, and manner of construction—present a range of possibilities in which efficiency and effectiveness may or may not be important.

Viewing organizations as artifacts makes it possible to apply to them the same kinds of functional analysis long used by cultural anthropologists and archaeologists. Organizations, like objects, can be seen as having *technomic functions*, through which they solve problems directly imposed by the environment; *socio-technic functions*, which impose structure and/or reflect the social relations of involved individuals; and *ideo-technic functions*, ritualistic and ceremonial features that embody and express the values of participants.[1]

This multilayered approach, through which organizational data are analyzed as artifacts, may help to clarify—and depolarize—the debate over organizational change. Using this approach, scholars will be encouraged to reconstruct the systems that created those examples rather than opportunistically selecting historical examples that buttress pet theories. When they do reconstruct they will find themselves using past data to generate theory rather than using theory as a pretext for looting the past for appealing baubles.

Organizational Artifacts

Business corporations are great recordkeepers. Annual reports, board-meeting minutes, correspondence files, ledgers, and receipts, once created, tend to be saved. The very extensiveness and density of corporate archives often obscure rather than reveal a firm's activities, goals, and organizational culture. This obscurity is compounded by corporate recordkeeping procedures. Because technical, administrative, and fiscal information tends to be filed in separate locations, reflecting the specialization of activities within the firm, we often fail to appreciate the need to look at this information as a whole. (To do this does not impose an artificial unity of purpose on the firm; rather, it provides a basis for evaluating conflict and consensus within it.)

In spite of their apparently straightforward language and intent, corporate records must be treated like any other body of written documents. They inevitably say more than they appear to say—or reveal their real meaning in what they omit. The nuances of words and the implications of accounting categories tend to get lost in the passage of time. Recovering their meaning requires reconstruction of their setting. Who compiled the information? To whom was it directed? What purposes, internal or external, might it have served? Only by recreating the context can we begin to deal with content. Unless we do so, we find ourselves merely "playing tricks on the bones of the dead."

This essay is an effort to interpret a particular corporate artifact: the New Haven Water Company's first treatment plant, built at Whitneyville between 1902 and 1906. This facility served more than a utilitarian purpose. It was constructed at the same time as the firm's first administrative headquarters. Its erection coincided with fundamental changes in the company's recordkeeping practices: its first use of photographs to document its activities; the inception of written monthly reports from supervisors of major facilities; and the establishment of systematically kept newspaper clipping books and files of technical and political information relating to public utilities. Taken together, these suggested that the construction of the filter plant was symptomatic of a deeper and more significant shift in managerial technique.

When the Whitneyville Filter was built, the New Haven Water Company was already one of Connecticut's largest and most profit-

FIGURE 1. Exterior of New Haven Water Company's slow sand filter on completion in 1906. (Courtesy of South Central Connecticut Regional Water Authority.)

able corporations. At a time when most industries were making products for other industries to consume, the water company was one of the few putting out a product for a mass of private consumers. By 1912, when it made its first annual report to the Connecticut Public Utilities Commission, the company was serving more than 150,000 people in seven towns. Its operating system comprised more than 800 miles of mains, 1000 fire hydrants, and 11 reservoirs with a combined storage capacity of 5.3 billion gallons. Capitalized at 5 million dollars, the company's 60,000 shares were owned by

FIGURE 2. Funereal interior of filter plant, 1906. (Courtesy of South Central Connecticut Regional Water Authority.)

1052 stockholders, 844 of whom lived in Connecticut. Its bonded debt amounted to a little over 1 million dollars against assets valued at 5.5 million dollars. The company earned 1.3 million dollars during the fiscal year ending June 30, 1912, and paid out 8 percent dividends.[2] Where did the company's capacity to engage its managerial and technical tasks originate? Did it gradually evolve as a rational response to growing demand for the company's product? Or was it a managerial doctrine like Taylorism, imposed on the firm from without, which merely used high technology, expertise, and bureaucracy as a means of acquiring and legitimating power?

FIGURE 3. Self-portrait of photographer looking down into pipe gallery, c. 1904. (Courtesy of South Central Connecticut Regional Water Authority.)

Management by Force of Personality

Until the end of the nineteenth century, business corporations—even very large ones—were indistinguishable from the personalities of their proprietors. This was not a coincidence. The great industries of the years after the Civil War were usually the personal creations of vivid personalities like Andrew Carnegie, who had clawed his way up from textile-mill bobbin boy to the world's greatest steelmaker, and Cornelius Vanderbilt, who became involved in transportation rowing passengers across New York Harbor in a small boat, then invested his savings in steam ferries and finally ended up in control of the great New York Central Railroad empire.

FIGURE 4. Multiple exposure of construction worker immured in concrete, c. 1906. (Courtesy of South Central Connecticut Regional Water Authority.)

It hardly mattered that Carnegie, Vanderbilt, and Rockefeller—or New Haven's magnates, Oliver Winchester, Eli Whitney, Jr., and James Brewster—used other people's money to create industrial baronies. People entrusted their fortunes to these men not because they had good credit ratings but because, in the highly personalized world of nineteenth-century finance, their word (usually) was their bond. Investors of the Gilded Age bet on personalities, not on managerial methods; on friendship and kinship, not on balance sheets and projections of anticipated earnings.

This way of doing business had both its assets and its liabilities. On the positive side, this highly personal approach to industrial management permitted risk-taking that, by modern standards, would be unacceptable. Entrusting the construction of the New Haven Waterworks to Eli Whitney, Jr. (1820–1894), was, from this perspective, no more than a statement of trust in Whitney as a person. He had neither knowledge nor experience in public water-supply systems. His use of his own water rights during the two decades in which he ran the Whitney Armory was, if anything, a testament to incompetence.[3] His motives for being involved in the water project had more to do with his desire to consolidate his manufacturing operations than to supply the public with water.[4] Nevertheless New Haveners, doubtless looking back to old Eli Whitney's (1765–1825) complete ignorance of gunmaking and his subsequent creation of a revolution in manufacturing technique, hoped that the son would follow in his father's footsteps.

Their faith was not entirely misplaced. Whitney *did* create a working public water system. He overcame the ignorance and vacillation of the electorate by sheer force of will, by legal strategy, and, most of all, by his willingness to subscribe one-third of the capital of the company.

But the liabilities of proprietary management soon became evident—and grew more evident over time. The idea of moving water from the impounding reservoir at Lake Whitney to the distributing reservoir on Prospect Hill using the power of the Mill River was a wonderful example of Yankee ingenuity. It was very much in line with Whitney's decision to salvage the old Town Truss bridge, which had carried the Hartford Turnpike across the old Armory mill pond by putting it on rollers and pulling it by oxen to Davis Street (where it stood until the 1930s).[5]

On the face of it, the water-powered pumps were a marvel of frugality. They cost nothing to run. No one need be hired to tend them. But they were phenomenally wasteful of the limited flow of the Mill River—requiring four gallons of the river's flow to move one gallon from Lake Whitney to the Prospect Hill Reservoir. The shortcomings of the arrangement became increasingly evident by the end of its first decade of operations, when the company was forced to install auxiliary steam-powered pumps at Lake Whitney in 1870.[6] From an engineering standpoint, it was an absurd makeshift—a technological solution worthy of a talented amateur, which is what Whitney was. In fact, as events would show, even the choice of Prospect Hill as the location of the distribution reservoir, with an elevation of only 125 feet, was woefully inadequate to the needs of the growing city.

Though clearly the central figure, Eli Whitney, Jr., stayed in the background as vice president. He evidently perceived the inherent conflict of interest between his proprietorship of the armory, the major consumer of Lake Whitney's power, and his role in the water company, which drew on Lake Whitney as its major source of supply.[7] Only after the armory closed in 1888 did the family take full control of its management.

Four decades of personal domination left a legacy of successful mismanagement. Though the quality of its product was questionable, the regularity of its dividends was not. The New Haven Water Company had conquered more competent rivals like the Fair Haven Water Company, whose engineering competence was not matched by its personal connections to the suppliers of capital essential to corporate survival.[8] It had successfully defeated efforts by the city to buy it out in 1881 and 1891. But, as the press comment of the 1890s makes clear, it faltered in supplying safe water reliably to homeowners, businesses, and industries. The rising tide of complaints was capped by the disastrous typhoid epidemic of 1901, the cause of which proved to be the waters of the New Haven Water Company.

In fact, it would be stretching the term *management* to apply it to the New Haven Water Company as it was run before 1894. President Henry Dawson ran the company with an iron hand between 1867 and 1893. He was a cunning politician and competent financier. But neither he nor his mentor, Eli Whitney, Jr., really understood the complexities of the managerial task. The company owned extensive properties—a slew of reservoirs, miles of mains—but they were not a system in any operational sense. They were kept running by makeshift expedients, not by planning and expertise.

Changing the Guard: The Rise of Modern Management, 1893–1906

The fact that there are no photographs documenting the water company's growth during the first 40 years of its existence reveals its primitive conception of itself as a corporate entity. The absence of photographs is as revealing as the absence of a corporate headquarters until 1903. The company was literally run out of the back pockets of Whitney and Dawson, and its corporate affairs were indistinguishable from their personal interests. The company only began to move away from a proprietary management style in 1894, when Eli Whitney III (1847–1924) became its president.

The educational ethos that shaped the younger Whitney and his generation was boldly stated by Harvard's President Charles W. Eliot in his 1869 inaugural address:

> As a people, we do not apply to mental activities the principle of division of labor; we have but a halting faith in special training for high professional employments. The vulgar conceit that a Yankee can turn his hand to anything we insensibly carry into high places where it is preposterous and criminal. We are accustomed to seeing men leap from farm or shop to courtroom or pulpit, and we half believe that common men can safely use the seven-league boots of genius. . . . Only after years of the bitterest experience did we come to believe the professional training of a soldier to be of value in war.[9]

The younger Whitney was very much a man of his times. Like many others whose outlooks were formed by the Civil War, he absorbed beliefs in both the importance of specialized training and the value of bureaucratic organization. Though not an engineer, he evidently understood what engineering involved. He supplemented his classical education at Yale (B.A., 1869) with two years of postgraduate study, one at the Sheffield Scientific School and another at MIT. When Whitney III joined the water company's board in 1893, he quickly learned that he was the odd man out. For even after his father's death and Dawson's retirement the following year, the board remained under the control of men whose viewpoint was narrowly parochial.

Whitney III took over the presidency of the water company at a particularly difficult time. After years of acquiescence, citizens were beginning to question the competence of the "Christian gentlemen to whom God in his infinite wisdom had entrusted the property interests of the country."[10] Nationally, a variety of movements were forming to reduce the power of private capital. Locally, Democratic politicians like Mayor J.B. Sargent were forging alliances with organized labor and socialist groups to challenge major corporations.

The increasing radicalism of the electorate had made the 1891 renegotiation of the water company's franchise and service contract with the city an unusually bitter one. Though himself a businessman, Mayor Sargent railed at the company, accusing it of having bribed the board of aldermen, the legislature, and the press to get its way. Though the company won out over its opponents, it was clear that its performance would be critically scrutinized in the coming decade, when the contract would again be considered for renewal.[11]

In running the company, Whitney III thus faced two problems. On the one hand, he had to establish his authority over his own board of directors; on the other, he had to save the company, in which he had a substantial personal stake, from the advocates of municipal ownership. The rhetoric of technology and professionalism would prove the keys to accomplishing both ends.

Through the 1890s, the tide of public complaint about the quality of water service rose steadily. In retrospect, it is difficult to say whether service was actually deteriorating or whether the complaint level was merely a measure of political unrest. Perhaps the most serious charges were leveled by the secretary of the Connecticut State Board of Health, who in February of 1893 asserted that the Mill River watershed was contaminated by runoff from water closets, barnyards, and factories and that the city was, as a result, in danger of a cholera epidemic during the coming summer.[12] Subsequent investigations by the press affirmed the truth of the board's claims. Dawson, who was serving out his last months as NHWC president, responded with characteristic brusqueness:

> There is not any purer water which enters any city in the Union than that which comes from Lake Whitney. It is to the interest of the Water Company to keep a careful watch that impurities shall not exist in the water and we do so. This hue and cry about impure water is all bosh and it is doing great injury to the city of New Haven.[13]

Dawson was probably right in asserting that Lake Whitney's water was no worse than it ever had been. Farms, factories, and residences had lined the banks of the Mill River for decades. New Haven had not suffered a major epidemic since the 1830s—indeed, annual mortality and morbidity rates from water-borne diseases were considerably lower than those in most American cities.[14]

Whereas Dawson had been willing to brush off public alarm about the condition of the city's water, Whitney was not. He had been carefully monitoring the company's deteriorating public image since the mid-1880s by collecting press comment on its activities.[15] The core of his concern was not water quality, but political economy. This is suggested by an undated fragment of an interview with Social Darwinist Herbert Spencer included in Whitney's *Clipping Book I:*

> Since I began to write there has been a clear reaction against individual liberty. We are certainly tending toward State Socialism, which will be a worse form of tyranny than that of any government now recognized in civilization.
>
> And after State Socialism, what?
>
> Military despotism. At present the State is absorbing the individual activity of men. It is intermeddling in all manner of ways in what should be private enterprise to such an extent that the people will one day awake to it; but it will be long before they make an effective resistance. I cannot but think that the struggle will be severe.

Under this Whitney wrote, in the only annotation contained in the book, "to contemplate."

It seems clear that, as Whitney contemplated Spencer's dire forecast, he must have had his own problems in mind. Every 10 years, the independence of the company had become more tenuous. In 1881 its enemies had merely been angry supporters of the Fair Haven Water Company; by 1891 it had faced a broad political spectrum of opposition that had only been defeated by the most desperate measures. Who knew what it would have to confront in 1901? The signs were hardly reassuring with populist radicals in firm control of the Democratic Party and increasing numbers of respectable people taking positions against corporate business. Viewed from this perspective, the issue at stake was not merely the survival of the New Haven Water Company but of civilization itself.

The challenge was not only ideological—it was practical as well. The company would have to respond to public concerns. Unless it did so, its position would continue to deteriorate. Eventually investors would lose confidence in the firm, unwilling to trust their funds to an enterprise whose future was uncertain. Without willing investors, the company would be unable even to maintain its current levels of service—and expansion into the growing suburbs would be impossible. And this would make municipal takeover a certainty.

The time had clearly passed when political action could help. Saving the company and, at the same time, pushing back the tide of socialism could only be accomplished by working within the company. Even to do this required that Whitney first gain control of the company, which remained dominated by an inflexible and backward-looking board of directors. The atmosphere of crisis in the mid-1890s, though it had little basis in fact, presented him with an opportunity to assert his authority. Rather than dismissing public criticism, he began to respond to it.

The first phase of Whitney's plans, while expensive, was not really innovative in a managerial sense. The company began purchasing land surrounding its reservoirs—the nucleus of the vast watershed holdings of today.[16] And, with the construction of the Chamberlain and Bethany dams, it secured larger and safer alternatives to its existing source of supply. This action had important managerial implications. Creating a far-flung supply system made it impossible for any single manager to oversee the whole operation, as had been possible when the company's plant was concentrated at Whitneyville. Responsibilities would have to be delegated to competent individuals, each capable of taking charge of a component of the system. And methods would have to be devised to coordinate their actions as well as to facilitate the flow of information within the system.

Furthermore, the acquisition of the watershed created a demand for new kinds of expertise.[17] Forest management, especially in conjunction with public water supplies, was a specialty. Because no one in the company had experience in this field, the task was contracted out to Yale's new School of Forestry—a practice in line with the company's earlier contracting of engineering, construction, and water-testing work. But unlike earlier contracting activities, this one was undertaken with the ultimate goal of generating the expertise that would permit the company to manage its own forests. The relationship with the Yale School of Forestry legitimated the use of professional expertise by the corporation and thus helped to justify the managerial revolution within the firm.

Management, Technology, and Politics, 1898–1902

Whitney had begun pressing for a filter plant in 1895, when he formed a filtration subcommittee of his board of directors. His efforts got nowhere. The members of the subcommittee were the two staunchest reactionaries in the company. Although they went through the motions of investigating filtration—writing letters to companies selling patented processes—they never took the issue seriously, and the filter proposal was voted down in 1897. Whitney, however, persisted. He began subscribing to the *Transactions of the American Society of Civil Engineers*, which was addressing itself with increasing frequency to issues of water treatment. And he initiated a correspondence with George W. Fuller, former Massachusetts state biologist and an expert on water filtration. Finally, as the opportunity arose through death and resignation, he began replacing the Dawson men on his board with directors more sympathetic to his viewpoint. By 1898, he had gained a working majority. Even with a more sympathetic board, however, persuading the directors to invest one million dollars in the still-experimental technology of water filtration would take some doing.[18]

The difference made by the new board was subtle but important. Although the structure of subcommittees created under Dawson remained in place, their role changed. As Whitney devoted his efforts full-time to the affairs of the company, he gradually took control of the flow of information. He established internal accounting systems that monitored the activity of each component of the system. His clipping books kept track not only of local press coverage but also of technical and political matters affecting public utilities throughout the country. Most important, gathering information on such matters as filtration was left not in the inexpert hands of the directors but was taken over by Whitney and his hand-picked secretary, David Daggett. Controlling information gave Whitney the ability to become a true manager, shaping the agenda of board meetings and selectively channeling to the directors information that would largely determine their decisions. As he did so, the board became a ratifier of his policies rather than an active participant in policy-making.

Though by 1898 the board had essentially withdrawn from areas requiring technical expertise, it had the final say in matters affecting the financial stability of the firm. Filtration, though a technological issue, was a fiscal one as well because of the enormous expense involved. In spite of Whitney's best efforts, the board remained dubious about making such an investment. But Whitney was not discouraged. With an eye to the upcoming renegotiation of the franchise and service contract, he began making public statements that portrayed him as a champion of technological innovation and a friend of public health:

> President Eli Whitney of the water company said this morning that the citizens of the city seem to be very satisfied with the water supplied to them, and that they were justly satisfied. "We are doing all we can," he said, "to make the water as pure as possible, and are making changes toward this all the time. . . . We are also keeping abreast of the times in regard to systems of filtration which have been invented but which are not yet in practical operation anywhere.[19]

This was the opening shot in a barrage of orchestrated publicity. On May 25, 1899, the *Palladium* reported that the directors of the company were "on a tour of the lakes." On June 7, Professor E.L. Bissell was reported to have pronounced New Haven's water "free from all disease" and urged citizens to drink plenty of it. On June 27, the *Palladium* noted that the banks of Lake Whitney had been denuded of shade trees and long rows of wire fences had been erected in order to give the city "the purest water possible." These favorable reports were juxtaposed against the growing threat of municipal takeover. In May of 1899, a minority report of New Haven's Board of Aldermen called for municipal ownership of all public utilities. Colonel Seth Ullman, the city's Republican boss, was said to be ominously silent on the subject.[20]

Whitney's artful and self-conscious portrayal of himself as a champion of innovation would serve him well. It enabled him to seize the high moral ground, providing him with a public constituency that conservative board members could not easily ignore, for to stand in Whitney's way would be viewed as standing against progress and against the public interest. Whitney's stance also facilitated his dealing with the proponents of municipal ownership, for by portraying the company as innovative and himself as the champion of innovation, he made it difficult for the company to justify municipal ownership on any but ideological grounds.

Events also worked in Whitney's favor. The fall of 1899 was exceptionally dry. The situation was so serious that by November Bridgeport, Connecticut's third-largest city, had run out of water. But while towns and cities all over the state were running dry, the New Haven newspapers, undoubtedly prompted by the water company, were trumpeting that the city had suffered "very little trouble from the drought." Because of the way he had structured public perception, even the great typhoid epidemic, which began in April of 1901, worked to Whitney's advantage.[21] Although the epidemic was traced to the waters of the company's Lake Dawson reservoir, state health officials absolved it of responsibility—blaming instead the Woodbridge physician who had instructed the family with whom the outbreak had originated to bury excreta and other infected materials without first disinfecting it. By the time the epidemic had run its course, more than 400 citizens had been stricken, of whom 10 died. Thanks to Whitney's skillful leadership, the company not only emerged free of blame, but his advocacy of filtration had finally become irresistible. In May of 1901, one month after the epidemic began, the board gave Whitney permission to retain G.W. Fuller to advise the company on its proposed filtration plant.

Though Fuller had only begun to study the condition of the company's reservoirs in June of 1901, Whitney, with his eye on the contract negotiation, was already issuing confident statements about the company's plans. "It is gratifying to know," stated the *Leader* on its editorial page,

> that the New Haven Water Company proposes to spare neither expense nor trouble in making the water supply the best that the most expensive means of filtration can provide. The company has spent a great many thousand dollars in bettering sanitary conditions about its reservoir properties and now it has employed the best expert in the United States to formulate plans for still further improving the water supply and making it possible to deliver this all-important necessity for human use of safety and purity.
>
> An expenditure of about one million dollars is contemplated and we are informed that this enormous sum will be exceeded if there should be necessity.
>
> We commend the policy of President Whitney and his associates who are thus demonstrating that they are wise businessmen and good citizens.

> The purity of the water supply is a matter of grave consequence to every human being in this city. The water company realizes this fact and proposes to leave nothing undone that will guarantee absolute safety.[22]

But as Whitney worked to portray the company in the best possible light through the summer and fall of 1901, he found himself preoccupied on two fronts. First, his political opposition was grinding up its propaganda machine and, as in 1891, putting together a coalition of organized labor and middle-class progressives who favored municipal ownership. Second, Fuller was leaning in the direction of recommending two filters, one at Lake Dawson, the other at Lake Whitney.

Whitney was not keen on the prospect of having to build two filters. With a capitalization of only three million dollars, for the company to expend two million dollars on filtration was out of the question. Furthermore, he had particular reasons to want to locate the filter at Lake Whitney. The first was purely personal: He had been trying to negotiate the sale of his father's estate near Lake Whitney to the company.[23] Locating the filter there would provide the company with a good reason to take his father's Armory Street properties off Whitney's hands. The second was strategic: Lake Whitney and its watershed had been the target of concerns about pollution for decades; to place the plant there would be a very tangible way of answering these concerns. In addition, placing the filter at Whitney, by the side of New Haven's major roadway to Hartford, was a very visible way of demonstrating the company's commitment to public health.

In September of 1901, Fuller inadvertently leaked his recommendations to the Connecticut State Health Commissioner, who in turn leaked them to the press.[24] Whitney was able to suppress publication and obtain pledges of silence from both Fuller and State Health Commissioner Lindsley. He then used Fuller's embarrassment over the incident—and, no doubt, the threat of losing his lucrative fee for completing the filtration report—to persuade the biologist to recommend that the filter be located at Lake Whitney and, in passing, to come out against public ownership of the company.[25]

Completed in November of 1901, Fuller's report placed Whitney in an advantageous position to pursue his two main objectives:

consolidating his authority within the company and keeping the company in private hands. The achievement of the first goal was already well in hand even before Fuller's report was delivered. Annotations of correspondence and minutes of board meetings suggest that the directors were completely excluded from considering the relative merits of filtration methods. Whitney, Secretary Daggett, and Engineer A.B. Hill handled all of the company's dealings with Fuller, and as a result the board learned only what Whitney wanted it to learn. Obviously they knew nothing of Fuller's suggestions for a two-filter system or his preference for filtering Lake Dawson over Lake Whitney.

The construction of the filter and the continuing acquisition of watershed lands promised to further strengthen Whitney's hand. Both would reinforce management's monopoly of operating information because both required specialists whose decisions, by their technical nature, would have to be mediated through management. Furthermore, both filtration and watershed operations required considerable increases in the number of people employed by the company. This too would strengthen the position of management because only it could monitor and control extensive operations involving large numbers of employees. Although no figures exist on the number of people the company employed during this period, it appears that operating expenses rose from $7000 in 1863 to $148,000 in 1901.[26]

Resolution of the filter question permitted Whitney to approach the service-contract debate in the most favorable possible public position. Not only had Fuller's report vindicated Whitney's policies but it also permitted Whitney to present himself as the city's leading advocate of scientific approaches to water quality. Also, by committing the company to constructing the filter, Whitney could argue that NHWC was making a significant—and very expensive—concession to public demands for pure water. This concession, Whitney would argue, required a more favorable contract, since the company could hardly expect investors to back a firm that might, at the whim of the electorate, be taken over by public authorities. At the same time, building and operating the filter would raise the value of the company's assets beyond the ability of the city to buy it out.

Public hearings on the water contract began in December of 1901.[27] As they ran their course, the company kept a very low profile—in sharp contrast to Dawson's 1891 blusterings. Company officials attending the hearings dispassionately provided facts but refrained from expressing opinions that might inflame the opposition against the company. Whitney knew that the coalition favoring municipal control was unstable and that, by depriving them of ammunition, they would inevitably turn on one another. This is exactly what happened. While the moderates favoring municipal control concentrated on the financial advantages of public ownership, the radicals broadened their attacks on the company to an all-out assault on "cultured pietists," "plutocratic plunderers," "sophistical lawyers"—the city's respectable element.[28] As the cause of reform splintered itself, Whitney and the water committee of the board of aldermen hammered out a contract.

As finally drafted in February of 1902, the contract did not give Whitney everything he wanted—but it came close. Though he would have preferred a perpetual franchise, which would have permanently freed the company of municipal oversight, he did manage to extend the contract period from 10 to 25 years. He also obtained a pledge from the city not to impose a tax on the company's franchise. In exchange, the city would receive free water for municipal purposes, lower meter rates for private consumers (a meaningless concession, since less than 10 percent of consumers were metered), and a commitment by the company to build a filter plant.

Structures and Symbols of Modern Management

The NHWC initiated two major construction projects in 1902, the slow sand filter at Whitneyville and an office building at 100 Crown Street in the heart of downtown New Haven. As specialized technological and administrative centers, these structures served as both symbol and substance of the triumph of scientific management.

The symbolism of the filter was embodied in its design. The laboratory was to be the only above-ground part of the structure. Presided over by a professional chemist employed by the company, he would not only supervise the operation of the filter but would also provide continuous monitoring of all the reservoirs. In its layout, the plant both forcefully asserted the preeminence of scientific expertise and articulated the conception of the water company as a *system* rather than a patchwork of facilities.

The Crown Street headquarters echoed the filter as statement of operational integration. In building separate centers for its technical and administrative units, the company concretely articulated its understanding of two basic principles of modern management, on the one hand the functional differentiation of units (the distinction between staff and line activity), on the other hand their consolidation into an integrated and centrally controlled enterprise. Technical decisions became the arena of specialists, but their decisions were bounded by the objectives formulated by financial and administrative specialists at 100 Crown Street.

The symbolic function of the filter was most forcefully asserted in its unorthodox design and method of construction. It was to be a purely engineered structure, utterly functional, with no concessions to conventional notions of beauty. This was a departure from the company's normal practice as well as from the aesthetic norms of the New Haven business community. The 1862 structure housing the water-driven pumps at Lake Whitney Dam was constructed in the Renaissance Revival style. The 1870 Armory Street Pump House, though boasting a 70-foot smokestack, was replete with Greek Revival references, including a pediment and antepilasters. Even the Crown Street headquarters accented its plain brick facade with decorative gestures to the Italian Renaissance. This adaptation of old styles to incongruous uses was characteristic of New Haven's business architecture well into the twentieth century. This tendency found its most extreme expression in the 1927 Union and New Haven Trust Company Building, a 13-story office building that its architects called "a tower of pure colonial design."[29]

But the filter's rhetoric of innovation would be more than skin deep. Though it could have been built using traditional methods and materials, Whitney decided to follow the suggestions of engineer A.B. Hill, one of whose associates, Charles Ferry, had been advocating the use of reinforced concrete. We do not know where Ferry learned about reinforced-concrete building techniques. The earliest engineering discussion of the subject appeared in the *Transactions of the American Society of Civil Engineers* in December of 1901 under the title "Steel Concrete Construction: An Informal Discussion."[30] Discussants on the panel included William B. Fuller, brother of sanitary engineer and water company consultant George W. Fuller, as well as Henry S. Jacoby, an architect and engineer from Pennsylvania. Jacoby was deeply involved with men who were organizing large-scale portland cement production in the Lehigh Valley and who were, as part of that effort, eager to launch major construction projects in order to demonstrate the possibilities of portland cement as a structural material. It seems likely that Fuller himself urged the use of reinforced concrete, since he attended the ASCE meeting. Whether he infected Ferry with his enthusiasm or brought Ferry to Hill's attention is not known. (Ferry's interest in concrete would, however, not be temporary. He is best known for his design of the 1914 Yale Bowl, a structure that, because it is largely underground and makes extensive use of reinforced concrete, is a structural analog to the filter.)[31]

Although reinforced-concrete construction served the symbolic purpose of emphasizing the company's commitment to innovation, it also served the more tangible purpose of articulating the new forms of labor relations integral to scientific management. As David Brody's work on the iron and steel industry has shown, the craft unions were viewed as a major obstacle to the implementation of new management techniques.[32] Though the power of the skilled craftsmen in the steel industry was broken by the early 1890s, they remained strong in the construction industry. While other crafts lost their prerogatives with the rise of industry, the construction unions actually became stronger. The rise of the great mills and factories, most of them multistory masonry-pier structures, required the labor of countless craftsmen.

Reinforced-concrete construction brought industrialization out of the factory and onto the construction site. The technique imposed on workers hierarchical discipline and reduction in skills. The boss of a reinforced-concrete job was the structural engineer, a manager who directed the specialized work of the carpenters in setting up forms, of the metalworkers in shaping reinforcing elements, and of the concrete mixing crew. It mattered little that the carpenters, metalworkers, and concrete mixers possessed the general body of skills to carry out their tasks, since assembling the structure required technically informed guidance. The construction task—once under the supervision of contractors who hired masonry and carpentry crews, each of whom controlled their part of the job—came under the supervision of the engineering firm, which assumed complete responsibility for the activities of all the workers, regardless of skill.

The radical implications of reinforced-concrete construction, rather than its novelty, probably accounts for the slowness with which it was adopted in Connecticut, where the Irish-dominated craft unions had considerable political clout. Though construction of the Lake Whitney filter began in 1902, another reinforced-concrete structure would not be undertaken until five years later, when the New Haven Railroad built its Cos Cob power plant. The technique only began to be commonly used in the state on the eve of the First World War, when the urgency of war production permitted employers to introduce many managerial and technical innovations, many of which would have been successfully resisted under other circumstances.

The Whitney filter was intended to serve not only as a demonstration of a new construction technique but also as a model of the labor process in the setting of the modern corporation. Until the turn of the century, virtually all specialized and labor-intensive tasks, from water testing through pipe laying, were contracted out. Under this system, each contractor took responsibility for his job, setting wages, hours, and conditions of work. As its scope and scale of operations expanded after 1900, the company began internalizing many basic functions. Working under a centralized administrative hierarchy, specialists directed the activities of increasing numbers of unskilled workers under conditions controlled by the company. Needless to say, such a regime took a dim view of organized labor.

Reinforced-concrete construction, because it segmented the labor process into components requiring little skill from the mass of workers, brought with it a number of dividends. It would not be necessary to employ union labor, since the largely Irish construction unions were both ignorant of the new technique and actively resistant to learning it. Hiring unskilled Italians promised not only to diminish the power of the labor movement, which had been in the forefront of efforts to municipalize the company, but also to aggravate rivalries within New Haven's ethnic community, thus reducing its political power.

The strategy was partially successful. Such policies undoubtedly intensified the already bitter conflict between the Irish and Italians—a conflict evident not only in the development of national congregations in the Roman Catholic Church but also in the tendency of Italians to become Republicans, Irish to become Democrats. But the Italians did not remain unskilled. Working on projects like the Whitneyville filter gave them an edge over the Irish in knowing how to use the new technique—an edge that assumed considerable importance when, on the eve of the World War, defense-industry demand created a market for the new technology and those who knew how to use it. The rise of such construction dynasties as the Arrigonis of Middletown and the D'Addarios of Bridgeport was intimately tied to the increasing use of reinforced-concrete construction for factory buildings and, later, for roads and bridges.[33]

That these labor policies turned out to be empowering rather than exploitative was not completely accidental. While it is true that such prophets of scientific management as Frederick W. Taylor were opposed to organized labor, their opposition stemmed less from a desire to be exploitative than their belief that unions created disincentives to productivity and, as a result, impeded the economic empowerment of workers.[34] They expected the new system to encourage workers to think of themselves as capitalists who, by increasing their productivity and being rewarded for doing so, would move rapidly into the middle class. There is reason to believe that Whitney shared this viewpoint, for, though the size and diversity of the company's workforce grew steadily, labor-management relations were remarkably personalized and concerned with employee welfare. Because of this, NHWC workers remained outside the union movement until 1942.

Finally, the symbolic and substantive significance of the filter is embodied not only in the structure and its method of construction but also in the evident desire of the company to document the process. Boxes of glass slides enabled managers to dramatically demonstrate their mastery of innovation both to such internal constituencies as directors, stockholders, and investors and to the public through lectures and lantern shows for schools and civic groups. They also became an important instrument for "selling" both the company and the new management style with which it had identified itself.

The filter plant as a structure serves to focus our attention on the central trends in the development of the water company. For it is this revolution in management—the differentiation of administrative, financial, and technical activities—and their integration within a unified bureaucratic structure, accomplished at the turn of the century, that made possible the company's great initiatives during the 1920s. Without such symbols of progressive management, the company would not have gained public confidence and freedom from political interference. Without these, it could not have undertaken the great initiatives of the 1920s that transformed an urban utility into a regional one. The political, administrative, and technical skills learned in the years 1898–1906 laid the groundwork for achievements on an even grander scale.

Conclusion

Profitability and efficiency were not central concerns for the NHWC, since they were virtually guaranteed by the firm's monopoly. Its core concerns centered on noneconomic issues, particularly Whitney's desire to differentiate himself from his father (always a problem in family businesses), to assert managerial authority, and to enhance the firm's political autonomy. Although the solutions to these problems inevitably had economic implications, their outcomes were not necessarily determined by their economic consequences. Had the company's actions been governed by public health concerns, it would have located the filter at Lake Dawson, which not only supplied half the city's water but also most of its cases of typhoid. But a facility at Lake Whitney would be more visible and hence would better serve the company's political purposes.

The sheer bulk of the water company's records, together with their highly technical character, tempts a historian to simplify the task of interpretation by assuming the firm's rationality. While it is true that the company's growth and survival depended an its successful adaptation to a changing environment, the foregoing suggests that this adaptation, even though it resulted in greater productive efficiency, was not undertaken for narrowly economic reasons and that the economic outcome may well have been incidental. Treating this organization as an artifact avoided such overly simple rationalism. The reconstruction of context permitted a prospective view of the choices faced by historical actors, which in turn served as a basis for understanding their goals, motives, and underlying values.

One of the greatest gaps in American studies has been its inattention to economic life. The study of business and economic life has been isolated from the mainstream of historical scholarship. Perhaps approaching organizations as artifacts is the key to bridging this gap. As an alternative to sterile rationalism, this perspective permits us to see business corporations and the people within them as more than economic actors, as full participants in society, politics, and culture, with economic factors as only part of the continuum of influences on their actions.

Notes

1. James Deetz, *In Small Things Forgotten: The Archaeology of Early American Life* (Garden City, N.Y., 1977).
2. New Haven Water Company, "Report to the Connecticut Public Utilities Commission, 1912," South Central Connecticut Regional Water Authority Archives, New Haven, Conn.
3. Although inventive mechanically, the younger Whitney evidently made little effort to upgrade the armory he had inherited from his father. Whitney Arms were produced at three separate factory sites spread along the Mill River until 1860. Karyl Lee Hall and Carolyn Cooper, *Industry on the Eli Whitney Site, 1798–1979* (Hamden, Conn., 1984).
4. His efforts to consolidate his operations did not begin until the mid-1850s, 15 years after he had taken charge of the armory. Eli Whitney, Jr., "Business Diary, 1852–1860," Eli Whitney Papers, box 11, folder 173.
5. The story of the moving of the Town Truss bridge is related in Rachel Hartly, *The History of Hamden* (Hamden, Conn., 1959), 279.
6. A critic of the New Haven Water Company, John Osborn called Whitney's water-powered pumping system an example of "boy engineering." Osborn's 1881 attack on the company provides a rare and detailed view of the facilities and finances of both the NHWC and of its rival, the Fair Haven Water Company, of which Osborn had been superintendent. John Osborn, "The New Haven Water Company. A Letter to its Stockholders Showing Its Mismanagement in the Past and Its Imperative Needs in the Future. An Inside History Which It Behooves the Stockholders to Read, Consider, and Digest," South Central Connecticut Regional Water Authority Archives, Fair Haven Water Company Folder.
7. John Osborn was particularly vocal on the subject of Whitney's and the company's conflicts of interest. They again became a matter of public

comment during the city's 1891 effort to take over the company. In an acrimonious public exchange of letters, NHWC President Henry Dawson and J.B. Sargent, New Haven's mayor and former Fair Haven Water Company president, were still quarreling over the company's "sweetheart" power-supply contracts with Whitney. "Mr. J.B. Sargent Gives His Version of the Strife between the Water Companies" and "H.S. Dawson's Caustic Reply," *New Haven Palladium,* undated items in New Haven Water Company *Clipping Book I,* 1890–1896, South Central Connecticut Regional Water Authority Archives, 8.

8. The Fair Haven Water Company, in locating its reservoirs at high elevations, was able to operate its system without pumps. Its sources of supply were more numerous, abundant, and pure than the New Haven's single reservoir at Lake Whitney. The Fair Haven's directors, however, were mostly small businessmen and manufacturers, few of whom sat on the boards of the city's banks. Virtually all of the New Haven's men were directors or officers of banks. The ledgers and directors' books of the Fair Haven Water Company detail the firm's shaky methods of financing and increasingly desperate and unsuccessful attempts to meet its obligations after the Panic of 1873. The Fair Haven's records are in the archives of the South Central Connecticut Regional Water Authority.

9. Charles W. Eliot, "Inaugural Address," in Richard Hofstadter and Wilson Smith, eds., *American Higher Education: A Documentary History* (Chicago, 1961), 608–9. On the outlook of Whitney's generation, see Robert Weibe, *The Search for Order* (New York, 1967) and Burton Bledstein, *The Culture of Professionalism* (New York, 1976). Whitney III's career is best summarized in the obituaries published in the New Haven papers when he died in June of 1924. (*New Haven Leader,* June 12, 1924; *New Haven Union,* June 13, 1924; *Evening Register,* June 13, 1924.)

10. This famous letter of Philadelphia & Reading Railroad President George F. Baer on the subject of the 1902 coal strike is quoted in William Cahn, *A Pictorial History of American Labor* (New York, 1972), 188.

11. On Sargent's 1891 campaign against the NHWC, see "Mr. J.B. Sargent Gives His Version of the Strife between the Water Companies," undated clipping, NHWC *Clipping Book I;* "H.S. Dawson's Reply," undated clipping, NHWC *Clipping Book I;* "Mayor Sargent's Theories," *Register,* March 24, 1891; "The Water Company's Contract," *Register,* March 20, 1891; "Postponed Indefinitely—Scheme to Buy Waterworks," *Register,* March 17, 1891; "The Water Question—Shall the City or a Monopoly Supply Adam's Favorite Beverage?" *New Haven News,* April 1901; "Water Company Tactics," *News,* May 19, 1891; "The Water Company and Its Official Friends," *News,* May 20, 1891; "The Water Question: The Views of Mayor Sargent and President Dawson on the Subject," *Palladium,* October 5, 1891.

12. See "Vegetable, Not Animal Matter," *Register,* May 18, 1891; "Water is Healthy, but Its Terribly Offensive," *Register,* May 21, 1894; "Offensiveness at the Lakes," *Register,* June 10, 1891; "Impure Lake Whitney Water," *Palladium,*

March 6, 1892; "New Haven's Grave Danger," *Palladium*, March 8, 1893; "Is Lake Whitney Water Bad?," *Register*, March 6, 1893; "Water of Lake Whitney Drained into by Many Closets," *Register*, June 9, 1893; "Dr. Lindsley's Warning," *New Haven News*, February 15, 1893; "The Fishy Water Supply," *Register*, June 19, 1896; "The Water Tastes Bad," *New Haven Leader*, May 12, 1894; "Cannot Drink City Water," *News*, May 16, 1894. These, together with other undated clippings, are contained in *Clipping Book I*, 1890–1896, South Central Connecticut Regional Water Authority Archives.

13. H.S. Dawson quoted in "The Water is Pure," *Leader*, March 6, 1893.

14. George W. Fuller, one of the country's leading experts on water quality, made a retrospective study of typhoid in New Haven in the eight years preceding 1901. According to his report, "the permissible annual typhoid fever death rate per 100,000 population" was considered by sanitarians to be 20 to 25. Typhoid deaths from the NHWC's two most polluted sources of supply, Lake Whitney and Lake Dawson, were 16 and 24, well within the limits of acceptability. George W. Fuller to David Daggett, September 3, 1901.

15. Whitney III evidently began clipping articles on the company a decade before he joined its board. The earliest book, *Clipping Book I*, contains scattered items dating back to the mid-1880s. After 1894, when he became president, the clipping books took on a regular and systematic form and a standardized format. The contents of later volumes were not restricted to articles relating to the NHWC but include brochures, court decisions, and correspondence relating to public-utilities law, government regulation, and technology in other cities. The clipping books are in the water authority archives.

16. The purchases of watershed lands began in 1894, after Dawson's resignation and his replacement by Whitney III. They were undertaken in direct response to State Health Commissioner Lindsley's criticism of the condition of the Lake Whitney watershed (*Register*, June 9, 1893). On Whitney's cleanup of areas surrounding Lakes Whitney and Saltonstall, see "City's Water Supply . . . Men Kept Busy Patrolling the Banks and Officials Watchful to Abate Nuisances," *Leader*, May 2, 1899; "Test of the Waters," *Palladium*, May 10, 1899; "Changes at Whitney—Banks Entirely Denuded of Trees," *Palladium*, June 27, 1899; "Water Company Prohibits Fishing in All of Their Reservoirs," *Leader*, July 25, 1901.

17. See Ralph C. Hawley and William Maughan, *The Eli Whitney Forest—A Demonstration of Forestry Practice* (New Haven, Conn., 1930). In 1901, Whitney contracted with the newly established forestry school to manage its watershed lands. Not coincidentally, Whitney was a Yale trustee.

18. Fuller himself testified to the uncertainty of filtration as a method of water treatment in a letter about the NHWC in 1897: "With regard to the New Haven water case, I do not know very accurately the conditions which you have to face or the merits of the methods of handling the case. I am puzzled to know of anyone who knows both sides of the question, namely: odors and filters. Since a failure to meet the demands of this particular case would be a very serious matter on a large scale both to you and the Water Company, I

believe as a business venture it is safest to actually try it on a small scale for that period. You could have your representatives there if you wished, to improve your procedure, if possible, and the merits of the method on a practical scale could be passed upon by some competent professional man acceptable to you and the Water Company." Quoted in Morison-Jewell Filtration Company to Ellsworth I. Foote, NHWC secretary, March 18, 1897. Filtration file, water authority archives.

19. "Company Aiming to Improve Service All the Time," *Palladium,* May 25, 1899.

20. "New Haven Thinking Seriously of Ownership of Municipal Corporations," *New York Herald,* May 23, 1899.

21. On the typhoid epidemic of 1901, see "New Fever Outbreak," *Palladium,* April 11, 1901; "Typhoid Fever Scourge Is Growing More Serious," *Leader,* April 10, 1901; "Fewer Typhoid Cases—14 Reported Today," *Register,* April 11, 1901; "Yale Warns Students; Typhoid Precautions," *Register,* April 10, 1901; "Blame Bethany Officials," *Leader,* April 12, 1901; "Forty More Fever Cases," *Leader,* April 6, 1901; "The Fever Epidemic," *Journal-Courier,* April 11, 1901; "293 Cases Reported—15 Since Yesterday," *Register,* April 12, 1901; "The Fever Outbreak," *Leader,* August 8, 1901; "The Typhoid Fever Scourge Still Threatens the City," *Leader,* August 8, 1901; "How a Nest of Typhoid Germs on a Farm Nine Miles Away Crept down the Hill into a Brook, Then into a River, into a Reservoir, Then Through the Water Pipes and Gave Typhoid Fever to a Thousand People in New Haven, Conn.," *Leader,* January 1, 1902.

22. "For the Best There Is," *Journal-Courier,* June 6, 1901.

23. The company's board meeting for August 9, 1900, contains the report of arbitrators who were ironing out the details of the purchase of the "Gun Factory Property." NHWC Directors Books, South Central Connecticut Regional Water Authority Archives.

24. George W. Fuller to David Daggett, October 18, 1901, in which Fuller apologizes to the company for his indiscretion; George W. Fuller to Charles A. Lindsley, October 18, 1901, in which Fuller denies that his "informal views" were the substance of his forthcoming recommendations and takes Lindsley to task for doing "a serious injustice to me and a still greater one to the Water Company"; George W. Fuller to David Daggett, October 19, 1901, in which Fuller again apologizes for his indiscretion and expresses delight that his comments "will be kept out of the papers."

25. Fuller to Daggett, October 29, 1901, in which Fuller promises to express his views on municipal ownership and inquires about other points in his report "which might be modified, perhaps, or elaborated on." Fuller's mistake and his subsequent willingness to bend his recommendations to suit the company were doubtless due to his failure to understand the difference between his role as a sanitary consultant paid for his professional competence and as a consulting engineer who was marketing a product. Fuller had only moved

into the latter activity in the spring of 1901, when he became a member of the firm of Rudolph Hering and George W. Fuller, Hydraulic Engineers and Sanitary Experts. The NHWC job was his first in his new role.

26. It is difficult to obtain authoritative figures on the NHWC's operating costs during this period, because it published no annual reports between 1879 and 1927. The rise in operating costs was provided by Eli Whitney III in a letter to the water committee of the board of aldermen. Quoted in "General S.E. Merwin's Proposal," *Leader*, December 28, 1901.

27. The 1901/02 contract renegotiation was a microcosm of the larger political struggles of the 1890s. Wealth, represented by the water company, was arrayed against commonwealth, as represented by a coalition of middle-class urban reformers, the trade unions, and socialists. This coalition broke up in the months between December 1901 and February 1902 as the extreme antiplutocratic rhetoric alienated more moderate supporters of municipal ownership of public utilities. For all of its sound and fury, public agitation had little bearing on the real issues, for New Haven could not afford to buy out the company.

    The filtration issue played a key though ironic role in the negotiations. Opponents of the company had been pressing for a filtration plant. Because its cost was estimated at one million dollars—20 percent of the company's capitalization—its construction made municipal ownership even more expensive and hence less likely. Whitney used the filtration issue cleverly. Though he intended to build one anyway, in his dealings with the city he treated it as a concession to public demand and argued that without a lengthened contract period or, better yet, a perpetual contract, the company would be unable to attract investors in the project.

    On the 1901/02 renegotiation, see "New Haven Thinking Seriously of Ownership of Municipal Corporations," *New York Herald*, May 22, 1899; "For City Gas Plant," *Palladium*, May 10, 1899; "Offer of the Water Company," *Register*, December 21, 1901; "Water and the People," *Leader*, December 26, 1901; "General S.E. Merwin's Proposal," *Leader*, December 28, 1901; "The Water Contract," *Leader*, January 14, 1902; "Mass Meeting at Music Hall," *Leader*, January 17, 1902; "The Water Contract Fight," *Leader*, January 21, 1902; "Has New Haven Been Betrayed?" *Leader*, January 27, 1902. The most extreme proponents of municipal ownership published their own newspaper, *Our Plain Duty*, edited by Henry W. Vail.

28. W. Trueman, "The Passing of the Penniless Plute," *Our Plain Duty*, February 13, 1902.

29. Architectural modernism did not come to New Haven until the mid-1930s, with the construction of Carina Mortimer's "Regency design with a dash of the International Style" residence at 268 Bradley Street, built in 1936, and the Southern New England Telephone Company headquarters at 227 Church Street, constructed in 1937. Elizabeth Mills Brown, *New Haven: A Guide to Urban Architecture and Design* (New Haven, Conn., 1976), 114.

30. American Society of Civil Engineers, *Transactions* XLVI, 93–128.

31. On the design of the filter, see Charles A. Ferry, "New Haven Filtration Plant," Connecticut Society of Civil Engineers, *Transactions*, XXI, 305ff.

32. David Brody, *The Steelworkers: The Nonunion Era* (New York, 1960).

33. Matthew Roth, *Connecticut: An Inventory of Historic Engineering and Industrial Sites* (Washington, 1981). The earliest reinforced-concrete structure listed in the inventory is the Cos Cob Power Plant of the New York, New Haven & Hartford Railroad, built in 1907. The construction technique does not appear to have been used with any frequency in industrial buildings before 1915.

    The earliest reinforced-concrete structure built by an Italian-American firm that I have been able to identify is the Merriam Manufacturing Company factory in Durham, built by the Arrigoni brothers in 1919. During the 1920s the Arrigonis became leaders in concrete construction, receiving the contract to build the first concrete road in the state, a section of Route 9. Frances E. Korn, Robert Munhall, and Milton Whited, "Town Industries," in *Durham, Connecticut, 1866–1980: A Century of Change* (Durham, 1980), 49–50; Peter D. Hall, *Durham: History and Architecture* (Middletown, Conn., forthcoming).

34. From its beginning the promoters of scientific management made much of their philanthropic intentions. Henry Towne's pioneering paper, "The Engineer as Economist," delivered at the 1886 annual meeting of the American Society of Mechanical Engineers, viewed industrial efficiency as the key to solving the war between labor and capital. Towne himself was both a major technological innovator and a leading welfare capitalist. Frederick W. Taylor, "the Father of Scientific Management," expanded on this point in *Principles of Scientific Management* (New York, 1911).

    Taylor recognized that his management techniques were particularly applicable to reinforced-concrete construction. The year *Principles of Scientific Management* appeared, he also published *A Treatise on Concrete, Plain and Reinforced* (New York, 1911), which included a chapter by William B. Fuller, brother of the engineer who designed the Whitneyville Slow Sand Filter. The following year he authored (with Sanford E. Thompson) *Concrete Costs: Tables and Recommendations for Estimating the Time and Cost of Labor Operations in Concrete Construction and for Introducing Economical Methods of Management* (New York, 1912).

❧

Child-World in the Promised Land

William Leach

"THE VAST UNFOLDING OF THE MODERN CHILD-WORLD," ANNOUNCED A Marshall Field's business editorial in 1912, "is important to this mercantile institution. Not every person realizes that there is a children's demand for merchandise and service. Yet there is naturally. Little people's interests, their desires, their preferences, and rights to merchandise are as strong and as definite as those of any adult portion of the community. An ever-growing attention is being given children and their requirements at Marshall Field and Co." Twenty years later an important trade journal repeated the same theme but with less fanfare: "Many stores have found that children form the pivotal point around which to build promotions designed to increase business." In the 1920s a Federal Government report confirmed that "usually the parents decide upon purchases, but in America a growing influence of children is noted. This has led to an appeal to the children in an attempt, through them, to direct purchasing power."[1]

These are remarkable statements, indicating a major redefining of childhood as not something beneath but equal to adulthood and as a powerful mediating influence over adults. For much of the nineteenth century, most children were enclosed within adult society and economy. They worked alongside their parents or with other adults, and they were nurtured or exploited within the context of these relationships. After 1890, in the wake of major changes in economic and social relations, children were generally segregated from adults, signifying major changes in economic and social relations. New educational demands, which followed the shift in adult work toward professional and corporate labor, required that children be sent to school for long periods of time. The rise in wages, increased economic prosperity, the improved status of women, and the decline in the birthrate also made it possible for parents to devote more time and money to the educational well-being of their children. Increasingly, children spent a great deal of time with their peers and were treated by adults as a group apart, with special needs and desires.

Through no effort of their own, children acquired preferences and rights equal in importance and scope to those of adults. Yet, through no fault of their own and at the same time that their parents were becoming intimately involved in their welfare, children also found themselves cut off from adults in new ways and exploitable in new ways. They also became vulnerable to the stress and exhilaration of new needs and expectations that children of former times barely had the opportunity to imagine much less experience or articulate.

In this essay I address some of the ways Americans redefined childhood in the midst of these substantial transformations. Marshall Field's editorial notwithstanding, children do not have the capacity to define clearly their own rights and desires. Only adults have this power. Only adults can articulate the meaning of childhood and make it good or intolerable. Two approaches to childhood in particular are of interest to me: the marketing strategies of American merchants and the complex institutional forces that came into play after 1890 to reinforce the prerogatives of the merchants. Although sometimes in conflict with one another, both groups—the merchants and the institutional collaborators—attempted together to redefine the meaning of childhood within the context of a pervasive money economy and a new urban consumer age.

As a result of the great outpouring of manufactured goods after 1890, American merchants worked tirelessly to open up all domestic channels for the transmission of money and commodities. The focus was nearly obsessively domestic, with merchants staying clear of most foreign markets for the next 30 years. The outcome was the densest domestic consumer market in history. By 1925 merchants had constructed a sophisticated publicity structure (the term comes into vogue in the twenties) for children that dwarfed anything to be found elsewhere in the world. It was inside the large retail establishments that many Americans saw, in the most concrete and visible way, the new division between children and adults. At the same time, however, institutional structures emerged to support this new culture of commodities and money. Without such structures, American merchants could not have been able to fashion the kind of child-world or market that they did. By the 1920s, a new institutional network was operating, consisting of officials at all levels of government, social scientists, psychologists, and reformers. The network contained social workers, doctors and public-health officials, consumer advocates, educators, artists, and writers, many of whom made special contributions to the formation of a separate children's consumer world.

Children's Goods and Everyday Merchandising Strategies

"Grandfather would rub his eyes," wrote one retailer in 1920, "could he but see today" the toys and other children's goods being sold. Before 1890 a limited supply and variety of manufactured children's goods were on the market. There were no store departments for children, simply children's areas carved into adult sections. What appeals were made to children to buy goods were made through adults. Then, in the next 20 years, a veritable explosion took place in the production of children's commodities. The baby-clothing business, one of the smallest industries in the country before 1890 with only one factory to its name, billowed into one of the largest national industries, with 75 factories in New York City alone. Comparable growth occurred in sportwear for children, in pets and candies for children, and in furnishings of all kinds.[2]

Of all the children's commodities marketed in these days that found secure harbor in the burgeoning departments, none outstripped in importance toys, dolls, and playthings. Before 1900 American sale of these goods was dependent largely on German craftsmanship, which dominated and controlled the toymaking business. Moreover, such stores as Macy's in New York and Wanamaker's in Philadelphia, both of which had domestic reputations as toy dealers, displayed what toys they had en masse only on a seasonal basis, breaking up the toy sections once holiday festivities had run their course. In 1908, Siegel-Cooper's department store in Chicago opened its "Toytown" on the sixth floor, laid out in graded streets and avenues and covering an entire block. A few years later, Namm's in Brooklyn and The Fair in Chicago were among many department stores to open year-round toy departments, "to create a desire for ownership at all seasons of the year." In 1912 Marshall Field's systematized its toy display, segregating the toys according to children's ages and by outdoor and indoor categories.[3]

This growth was vastly expanded during and after World War I, a symptom of which was the appearance of the great toy fairs in New York, Chicago, and on the Pacific coast as well as similar fairs given by such department stores as Field's and by Meier and Frank in Portland, Oregon, where manufacturers showed off their toys and buyers made their purchases. Four factors in particular supported this movement: the development of American technology, the swelling demand for children's toys, the imposition of a heavy tariff on imported toys in 1922, and, above all, the wartime collapse of Germany as the main creator of playthings. The last two factors combined decisively to liberate American toy production. Between 1913 and 1917 the United States tripled its toy-producing capacity. It was because of this growth, with its attendant construction of American toy factories, that American businessmen fought aggressively to get a stiff hike in tariff rates. American toy dealers exploited German belligerency to the hilt by continuing after the war to vilify German toymakers as "butchers" and their toys as "blood toys." But Americans had nothing to brag about with their first mass-marketed toy "success," a laughing, prancing mechanical toy, the "Alabama Coon Jigger," first marketed around the world in 1917.[4]

Americans pioneered "cuddle" toys, talking dolls, and soft-bodied, rubber dolls endowed with lifelike features, real hair, and eyelashes. They produced authentic doll clothing, authentic doll carriages, and elaborate doll houses in great quantities. By 1920 doll-carriage production reached 2.8 million dollars, nearly equalling the 3 million dollars spent annually to make real baby carriages. Wheel goods such as bicycles, tricycles, toy cars, express wagons, and scooters multiplied, as did mechanical toys (electric trains, power stations, signal towers) and educational toys (blocks, erector sets, spelling boards, painting kits). Between 1905 and 1925 American production of toys increased 1300 percent. An extraordinary array of toys precisely mimicking on a miniature scale those commodities sold to adults came into existence. And, as Americans expanded their leisure interests and took up the backyard as a playground in the late twenties, manufacturers turned out basketballs, croquet kits, sliding boards, sandboxes, swings, see-saws, portable fabric swimming pools, floating beach toys, rubber balls, joy balls, and swim tubes.[5]

By 1926 the United States was the greatest manufacturer of toys and playthings in the world, a revolution in status completed in only two decades. And, as in the case of so many other goods, practically all the United States produced was for domestic consumption, with only 5 to 8 percent of total output for sale in other countries.[6] This domestic market was crucial, for relative to the world's population, the population of the United States was small, yet its industries churned out goods only for this market. Most of these goods, however, could not sell themselves. They demanded the intervention of such selling techniques as would "open" people up (in this case, children) to desire and appropriation. The sale of these goods required the imposition of temporal and spatial pressures on children as potent as any experienced by adults, pressures capable of changing their imaginative lives. It entailed the forging of an everyday merchandising structure directed entirely at children.

By an everyday merchandising structure retailers meant a system of overlapping media and devices used to appeal to the consumer. This system contained newspaper and magazine advertising, direct-mail advertising, exterior and interior display and decoration, spectacle shows and spaces, and institutional promotions, all often linked together into a system of "tie-ups" to project powerful merchandising messages. Such a structure might have emanated from a single institution or from several similar institutions—restaurants, hotels, stores, theatres—working together to produce the "buying atmosphere." The structure's distinguishing trait was its "theatricality," the way it tended to transform consumer and entertainment spaces into theatrical and fantasy spaces to encourage dreaming, play-acting, and consumption.[7]

Before 1900 such a merchandising structure did not exist for adults or for children, except in the most primitive form. By 1912, however, the year of Field's remarkable editorial, these conditions were being altered. Like other large stores, Field's was developing a complicated set of enticements for adults, and it was lifting appeals to children out of their adult confines. The intention of retailers was to manipulate adult consumption by weighing it down with artificial pressures: "Every attention shown the child binds the mother to the store." At the same time, the stores sought to locate themselves at the center of children's lives and thus to insure future consumption. Get people as children, the stores reasoned, and you will have them for a lifetime. "Let us remember," Harry Selfridge, manager of Marshall Field's, told his staff in 1902, soon after the inauguration of Field's Children's Day, "that these children are the future customers of this store, and that impressions made now will be lasting."[8]

Everyday merchandising strategies to attract children reproduced the adult structure in nearly all ways. Children's goods were separated into distinct sections, then into departments, then arranged in a coordinated fashion with other departments in a tie-up formation. Public-relations people like Edward Bernays conducted market research into the "psychological needs" of children in the mid-twenties to see what kinds of colors they preferred in their clothing. Special posters were constructed for children as well as special catalogs and souvenirs and, increasingly, special newspaper and magazine advertising.[9]

In 1919 Field's published a full-scale children's advertising column, "Juvenile World," in the Chicago dailies, with special announcements in "children's language"; it was so successful that the store later converted it into a full-fledged 16-page magazine for children, profusely illustrated on coated paper and filled with juvenile poetry and fiction. Hudson's of Detroit soon followed with its *Children's Magazine* and bimonthly *Boys' News*, as did New York's

Lord and Taylor with its *Jolly Times* and Wanamaker's in Philadelphia and New York with its *Jolly Book For Boys and Girls,* all distributed free of cost. Some adults never forgot these magazines. In the 1970s one Philadelphia woman, who had regularly received Wanamaker's *Jolly Book* as a child in the 1920s, asked the store to please mail her a photocopy of that "great little magazine" as a keepsake.[10]

From the early twenties into the thirties, both large- and medium-size department stores either operated their own radio stations or plugged into established ones to appeal to children. In 1923, Gimbel's in Philadelphia, which owned one of the most powerful stations in the country, inaugurated a "Kiddies Show" emceed by Uncle WIP, whose name derived from the station's signal call. On the air every night from 7 to 7:30, 52 weeks in the year, Uncle WIP told stories and answered children's letters. He read roll calls of children's birthdays and invited youngsters from around Philadelphia to join the store's "Kiddies' Club" by sending in postcards addressed to WIP. WIP's first invitation to join drew responses from 25,000 children.[11]

The appearance of special places for children in department stores, similar to those supplied for adults, followed closely upon the growth of this relatively fixed merchandising agenda and reflected the spatial and temporal allocations ("children's hours") being made for children in libraries, theatres, city playgrounds, and schools. Of such spaces in the stores, store playgrounds were the most significant, set aside for the special needs of children and prefigured by the baby-carriage checking facilities of the 1880s and the nurseries of the 1890s. In 1911 Marshall Field's had the largest playground in America, a "permanent" spot to entertain 300 to 400 children a day throughout the year. In the same year, Chicago's Boston Store decorated its playground to look like an "immense forest." Display men dressed the store walls with vines and branches and covered the store columns with bark. Small boats sailed across an indoor lake stocked with fish. By transforming this artificial space into a natural haven, this store tried to make children feel relaxed, content, at home.[12]

Women brought their children to these places in droves, impressing health "experts" who visited the playgrounds to study their effects on children. Many women left their children for hours in the playgrounds (often violating the two-hour limit) while they shopped about in the stores. Others did no shopping at all, but still deposited their children with the nurses. What impact this behavior had on children is debatable, although one Arnold Constable buyer in New York reported that "once the children play" in the store's playground (which was closely "tied-in" to a nursery, a toy room, a doll house, and a children's shoe store), "they never forget it. In fact we always have a hard time getting the youngsters out. They never want to go."[13]

By 1920, children could get haircuts, hair treatments, shampoos, and manicures in barbershops that resembled adult beauty parlors and often served as adjuncts to playgrounds. Just as the nurseries metamorphosed into playgrounds, so the drab barbershops evolved into "Happy Lands," tiny echoes of the new urban amusement parks, where children had their hair cut on hobby horses, tigers, or elephants. Children could look at themselves in distorting mirrors, read comic books, or watch puppet shows in the small barbershop theatres. At Mandel's in Chicago, children in the barbershop could observe other children through glass-framed partitions in the nearby toy room, climbing towers or swarming over the toboggan slides. These shops doubled as nurseries, with women dropping their children off in them once the allotted time in the playrooms had expired. Boys and girls sometimes spent hours in these de facto day-care centers without their mothers.[14]

Besides these special spaces for children there were also entertainments offered at almost any time of the year to "remind children constantly that the store thinks of them and is interested in them." Children feasted on the celebrated expertise of demonstrators who came to the stores: Eugene Sandow, the famous muscle-bound weightlifter, in purple tights at Wanamaker's to demonstrate sporting equipment; Max Fleischer, the cartoonist, at Stern's to paint pictures; Marlin the Magician to do tricks at McCreery's; and Chicago baseball stars to pitch and catch before the very eyes of boys and girls in Field's toy department. Hundreds of children joined the clubs in aviation, biking, embroidery, and camping organized for them by the stores and often accompanied by free instruction.[15]

Theatrical productions for children in all seasons, usually fairytale playlets performed in or near the toy departments in little store theatres or in the main-store auditorium theatres, made children readily aware of the "treasures" surrounding them if they only dared look. At performances of *The Wonderful Wizard of Oz* in Field's, children were given free green spectacles to observe the "delights" of Field's own Emerald City. In lieu of theatricals, children might get to hear fairy tales delivered by professional storytellers in settings overflowing with toys or overrun by live chicks and rabbits.[16]

The impression of the department store as an institution dedicated to the interests of children was amplified by the philanthropic activities of the merchants. As "distributors of Happiness" to poor children, merchants gave away toys and dolls, overcoats and underwear. They made substantial contributions to children's charities. They invited the poor to attend holiday benefits in honor of the poor themselves. Even more important, the stores established their caring image by paying attention to individual boys and girls and by inviting children as individuals to participate in, and even to provide, the store entertainments and decorations. At matinee Saturday performances in store theatres or on holiday occasions, and often on radio, children recited, sang, played instruments, danced, and performed stunts before other children. Over 600 "pictures done by the young people of Philadelphia and the county nearby" were exhibited at Wanamaker's in Philadelphia in 1916. In the fall of 1928 Macy's permitted over 50 children to paint the panels in the store's toy department. Carson, Pirie, Scott in Chicago made little girls and boys "hostesses" and "hosts" at the store playroom, where each child welcomed guests of its own choosing and commanded the store's amply stocked cookie jar.[17]

The stores compiled mailing lists of children's names, addresses, and city locations, usually obtained from school records, at store contests, at Christmastime by the store Santa Claus, or from the thousands of letters received over the course of the year. These lists not only made it simpler for children to get their own promotional literature but also allowed merchants to acknowledge the children's birthdays and remind parents that their children should be celebrated. "We keep an up-to-date card file on all the boys in the town," wrote one friendly California merchant. "You can break into a boy's heart by getting over on his side of the fence. . . . We send him letters on his birthday. We tell him we have a little present waiting for him at the store. You can imagine how much the average youngster is pleased with this attention."[18]

Toys, Parade Spectacles, and the Cult of Santa Claus

The most sensational and crucial component of the children's merchandising structure was not everyday but special and holiday related—the theatrical and spectacular activities that grew up around the toy departments after 1905. Today, department-store toy sections have virtually shriveled into nonentities. But in the early twentieth century they were the pivots of the children's market and the center of holiday merchandising. By the twenties the toy departments reflected the theatricality that had swept through adult consumer-entertainment institutions. They were not simply selling places but fantasy spaces, juvenile dreamworlds, the embodiments of the "Spirit of Play," as retailers like to argue. It was through them that merchants successfully achieved the age segmentation of the market and raised the "child-world" above the adult in strategic importance. Nourished in part by the modern adult need for fantasy and magic, for imaginative freedom, for an alternative world free from anxiety and "full of wonder," the merchandising treatment of toy departments cemented the alliance of children, stores, and consumer desire. It helped create a culture that imposed extraordinary market pressures on adults, creating another important channel for the free flow of commodities and money.

"What a change there has been," said one retailer in the year of Field's innovative editorial, "in the method of making toy displays, and what a revelation to children. . . . Now we have a horde of attractions that were not even dreamed of ten years ago." From the moment this shift gained speed, merchants transformed the interiors of toy departments, focusing on color and light as the major materials of theatrical enticement for children. Display managers radiated display areas with diffused colored light. They hung lights in globes of color and decorated with incandescent "starlight," facilitated by great strides in lighting technology after 1905. Toy departments soon emerged as the most visually pleasing and fantastical spaces in the stores. They expressed the "real romance of the fairyland of toys." "Give your toy store a name," urged one proponent of color, "preferably with color attached." How about "At the Sign of the Red Rabbitt," or "Pink Pig," or "Purple Cow"? the man suggested. In the 1920s, when such aesthetic movements as futurism and cubism struck the fancy of merchandisers, decorators showed remarkable "invention in their color planning." They decorated display areas with "eye-filling color," with cobalt blues, bright oranges, "gorgeous purples," "color upon color," an "orgy of color."[19]

From the 1910s far into the 1920s, many merchants installed circuses and menageries into their toy departments at Christmastime. They employed professional performers and "real live" animals rented from vacationing circuses. The menageries, small miniature zoos indicative of the profligate influx of imported animals and birds into this country after 1900, complemented the year-round pet departments in the stores, where people could buy anything from lion cubs to birds of paradise. Sometimes merchants lined their holiday toy departments with cages filled with rare birds or with reindeers, tigers, leopards, panthers, and hyenas. Where real circuses and menageries were impracticable, merchants created giant mechanical panoramas or make-believe carnivals with stuffed animals and big papier maché figures.[20]

By the 1920s practical and literal-minded merchants, who had at one time rejected the necessity of employing theatrical devices in selling, were now thinking in color and in theatrical metaphors. They were turning their stores (or parts of them) into "carnivals," "fairy tales," "pink elephants" if you will and, of course, into homes for Santa Claus and his Christmas brood. Throughout most of the nineteenth century, Santa Claus was an ambiguous figure, a floating icon not yet securely anchored to any one institution. Nor did he occupy any specific place in any institution. By the mid-nineties, when the large department stores first began to dominate the retail districts, the floating status of Santa changed, with merchants laying the most irresistible and powerful claim to him and to the imagery of the Christmas holidays. It was in this decade that urban consumer capitalism first gave shape and substance to American Christmas rituals. And it was also the time when "live" Santas first took up residence in the children's Christmas toy sections and became central to the strategies of consumer enticement. Ingenious parade rituals were devised around the cult of Santa Claus.[21]

At first, in the nineties, retailers groped for ways to exploit Santa for commercial purposes, situating him in small, out-of-the-way sections of the store. Then in leaps and bounds and in city after city, the world of the department-store Santa Claus unfolded in all its glory. Stores competed everywhere for ways of bringing him to town. Santa was brought from afar on railroad trains, flown in, dropped from balloons, met by thousands of people, paraded through towns and cities, and then deposited with great fanfare in the main stores, which had become the major community centers for the urban middle classes. Escorted into the toy departments, Santa sat on his lavishly decorated throne and worked busily away during the day in his workshop attended by gaily dressed drones. He had his own radio shows (by 1925, nearly every city in America had its own "radio Santa Claus"). It was standard practice by World War I for children to sit on Santa's knee and for him to promise them their heart's desire, give them souvenirs, and request that they write him directly about their wishes. By the mid-twenties, stores like Gimbel's in New York were getting thousands of letters weekly, all of which were apparently answered by staff writers, signed by "Santa," and indexed for future use. Wanamaker's and Bloomingdale's, among other stores, made extravagant motion pictures of these holiday activities, which were shown as advertising shorts in theatres around the country.[22]

Among the most impressive interior Christmas spectacles were those at the New York and Philadelphia stores of John Wanamaker, the greatest of American merchants. Wanamaker developed an interior holiday parade so sophisticated and expensive that few retailers could even come close to matching it. A devout Presbyterian, the founder of the Bethany Sunday School Movement who time and again expressed his loathing for the theatre, Wanamaker did more than any other American businessman to theatricalize merchandising in the grand style. He thought and wrote in metaphors about his stores. In his old age, when he took up the pleasure of writing his own business editorials for Philadelphia newspapers, he described his stores as "beehives," "Easter Eggs," "Rainbows," "Five Miles of Golden Chain," "Autumn Festivals." When a minister challenged him with the notion that homage to Santa Claus drew into question the validity of a Christian Christmas, Wanamaker reassured him that "young people very early grow to understand that (Santa Claus) is a mere pleasantry and tradition. I do not believe that it detracts from the story of the coming of Christ."[23]

In the late 1890s Wanamaker already had a large children's business but a rather plain and small toy department. During the next 15 years, however, as theatricality spread throughout urban institutional life, changing the character of hotels, restaurants, amusement spots, and even the theatre itself, Wanamaker became more and more aggressive in his approach to children's merchandising. In November of 1912 he decided to eliminate the "business atmosphere" and redesigned his toy store and the huge rotunda of his New York store at Astor Place and Broadway in lower Manhattan "in a manner really theatrical in appeal." Decorators put up murals and hung semicircles of multicolored lights from ceilings. They planted "terrifying" green dragons and large plaster heads of comic figures all over the first floor. Mirrors sent out flashes of colored light.[24]

From this point on, the toy departments in New York and Philadelphia grew bigger and more fantastical, literally year by year, as Wanamaker struggled to "out-top" himself and all other merchants.[25] In December of 1914 he moved the New York toy department from the basement into primary visibility on the fourth floor and decorated it and the store rotunda with monster Jumping Jacks, giant clowns, circus shadow pictures, gold and silver cubical stars suspended from the ceiling, and "the Largest Rabbit Family in the World." Then, two years later, Wanamaker launched his store parade. Every day at 10:30 in the morning, from November 9 to the day before Christmas, the lights went out in the toy department and thousands of children got to see the store parade announced by trumpets and drums and led by a uniformed brass band of Wanamaker's employees. A myriad of storybook characters from Jack the Giant Killer to Chanticleer and the Funny Clown followed the band. The parade concluded with the appearance of Santa Claus seated on a royal palanquin and carried regally by four Eskimos to his Royal Red Theatre in Santa Town. New features were added in the 1919 New York parade—little girls masquerading as snowflakes, little boys as silver stars and tinkling bells, and a 15-foot locomotive "seemingly self-propelled" and drawing a flat car loaded with a giant packing box marked "Handle With Care." In the midst of the toy department sat Santa on a rainbow-colored balcony with a blue-and-gold rail. A sort of Oriental deity surrounded by elves and gnomes, he passed out three-inch dolls to the children who sat on his lap.[26]

For the Christmas of 1922, the year John Wanamaker died, the New York store's display artists continued to "out-top" themselves. They created the most "gala festivities" in the store's history.

Futuristic Christmas trees, inspired by modern Russian aesthetics and painted in blues, greens, yellows, reds, and touched with gold, filled the rotunda and the toy department. Decorators applied the same colors to the store pillars. Lights, concealed in the decorations, blinked on and off by automatic control. After assembling in the toy department at the usual parade time of 10:30, children and adults heard the sound of a 16-piece jazz band playing "The March of the Wooden Soldiers" from somewhere deep in the store. As the band approached, Santa Claus stepped in view at the entrance of one of the aisles. Then the spectators saw the band, a group of black musicians led "by a gigantic negro resplendent in his bright red and blue costume and using a saber as a baton." "Real show people" and "freaks" came next. A midget pulled a doll carriage with a doll in it much bigger than herself. Ladies-in-waiting wheeled in the parade's king and queen on their throne. Next in line were courtiers dressed as Robin Hoods, Egyptian dancing girls and boys, and a long line of cages filled with stuffed wild animals. Men came through dressed as bears, lions, tigers, and monkeys, followed by a "live" trained bear and his trainer and a grotesque "monster" composed solely of a pair of legs and a big round head. Green earrings dangled from the "monster's" floppy ears. At the end was a famous carnival duo from Ringling Brothers Circus—the dwarf, Joe Short, and "The Cardiff Giant," George Auger, "the hugest of all circus giants." By all reports, the parade attracted thousands of children and adults from every borough and nearby suburb in New York City. It apparently caused so much crowding on the main floor that there was little space left for shopping.[27]

At about the same time Wanamaker's was pouring thousands of dollars into its interior parade, the management of Macy's on 34th Street was thinking of an exterior spectacle as a way of promoting its toy department and the cult of Santa Claus. The early history of Macy's Thanksgiving Day Parade has been obscured by myths and misconceptions, some of which have been peddled by the store management itself. Macy's did not invent the giant store parade but decided in 1924 to emulate the massive parade already being conducted by Eaton's department store in Montreal (Macy's even thought of cooperating with Eaton's "in the preparation of the floats"). Nor did the store pioneer the use of giant toy figures. The fascination with such figures had a long history, extending back to carnival times in the Middle Ages. After 1900, in this country and elsewhere, when new techniques made it possible to employ them on a large scale, the figures were used more and more to create fantasy spaces where adults as well as children could retreat into the "magic" of childhood and masquerade as Peter Pans and Tinker Bells. By the 1920s these figures, mass produced and supplied by such companies as Messmore and Damon in New York City, had become standard features of a new world of artificial things (the store manikins, the little toys, the puppets) that mimicked the "real" world.[28]

The most enduring myth about the Macy's parade, however, concerns the parade's provenance and how it was conducted. According to Macy's public relations legend, the parade was initiated and organized entirely by Macy's employees, especially by recently arrived immigrants from Italy, Poland, and the Slavic countries, who longed to find some public way to celebrate their ethnic backgrounds and, in a climate of "Americanization" fever, to demonstrate their right to participate in American life. These immigrants were still in touch with the vivid carnivalesque traditions of their mostly Catholic pasts, which set them apart from native Protestant Americans who practiced less flamboyant forms of parading.[29]

There is much truth in this "legend." Hundreds of Macy's employees, many dressed in their own homemade ethnic costumes—some masquerading as animals and clowns, others as policemen on stilts—did parade down 145th Street and Convent Avenue. They did march with a jazz band of black Macy's employees, a procession of floats depicting many fairy tales, and Santa Claus and his reindeers. The immigrants did accompany Santa to Macy's entrance door on 34th Street. There is evidence to show, moreover, that Macy's immigrants marched with Santa because they wanted to "redefine" the meaning of Thanksgiving Day parading, which had been for so long tied to immigrant poverty and with begging in the streets. As the novelist William Dean Howells wrote in 1907 of the tradition in New York City, "the poor recognize (Thanksgiving) as a sort of carnival. They go about in masquerade on the eastern avenues, and the children of the foreign races who populate the quarter penetrate the better streets, blowing horns, and begging of the passers." It was perhaps the goal of the Macy's employees to destroy this older association of Thanksgiving Day parading with immigrant poverty and to forge a newer association with plenitude, carnival affirmation, and Americanness.[30]

The fact is, however, Macy's paid many of these immigrants to march in the parade. More important, the parade's conception and the decision to have it came from management, not from the employees, as the 1924 minutes of the store's executive council meeting make abundantly plain and as shown by the leadership of Percy Straus, the Straus brother in the twenties who was determined to push the store in a "sophisticated" theatrical direction. In a paradigm, perhaps, of the kinds of relationships and collaborations necessary to form a new urban American culture of consumer desire, the immigrants got to affirm themselves as "Americans" (as Santa's helpers, as advocates of the child-world, no less), and Macy's got a very powerful promotional boost.[31]

Macy's parades of the early twenties were on a rather small scale, but they were nonetheless important coordinated events meant to showcase the toy department and its Santa Claus. The best theatrical artists were hired by the Strauses to conceive the floats, costumes, and masks. The stage designer Norman Bel Geddes ran the 1926 show, for instance, and the famous puppeteer Tony Sarg played a major role in the history of Macy's parade. By 1927 the parade had become Santa Claus's "official" entry into New York City, with 400 Macy's employees leading the way and wearing the grotesque masks designed by Sarg. Behind them marched a big "smoke-breathing dinosaur" attended by several prehistoric cavemen. A 25-foot dachshund sailed by along with gigantic turkeys, chickens, and roosters and a huge Robinson Crusoe desert island led by a forest of walking trees and wild animals. At the end was Santa Claus in a cockpit of an airplane. After reaching Macy's store, Santa ascended a flight of red-carpeted steps to his throne on top of the store's marquee. With a flourish of trumpets he signaled the unveiling of Sarg's "magnificent marionette window spectacle," thus formally opening New York's Christmas season.[32]

In the 1920s the cult of Santa Claus had become an indispensable aspect of American merchandising, with the result that intense pressures were placed on parents. In one department store after another, Santa assured children that their wishes would be granted. He gave them free gifts and took their names. A direct wire to the stores from children, the department-store Santa Claus was a subversion and an adversary of parental authority, an expression of the alliance between children and the stores. He was as well, in his new inflated role, an alien presence in an otherwise Christian universe. "Can you tell me," wrote a Texas reform woman, who objected to the cult of Santa Claus, to the Children's Bureau of the United States Government, "what is being done about the widespread use of Santa Claus as advertising medium at stores and on street corners? . . . Some of the women's organizations in Houston concerned with this practice have come to me for information, and I am, in turn, coming to you." "I do not know of any groups interested in doing away with the commercialism of Santa Claus" was the answer she got from the assistant to the chief of the bureau. "I am afraid I have no suggestions to make."[33]

Criticism of this kind, however, had little effect on the course of events. Nor did the glut of Christmas merchandising spectacles, the fear that Santa Claus might be "radioed out," as one merchant argued, blunt the merchants' determination to find new ways to "expand the child world." When merchants speculated that perhaps the public might be tiring of the surfeit of Christmas activities, their reaction was not to diminish but to double their energies. In city after city by the end of the decade, merchants brought the cult of Santa Claus to a new degree of spectacularity.

In Los Angeles in 1929 merchants and downtown property owners collaborated to stage a "series of dramatic events" on a "magnificent scale" to "reawaken the Christmas spirit" and to set a standard for all "community celebrations for children." The merchants began in early October by distributing a "proclamation by Santa Claus," illustrated with four-color pictures, that pledged for downtown Los Angeles "the 1929 Wonder Christmas of all joyous, radiant Christmases that have gone before or are yet to be." On November 2, the merchants sent out hundreds of "dwarfs" borrowed from Hollywood studios into all the downtown stores to open the Christmas departments at one time. Five days later, store windows throughout the city were unveiled at once. Interior decorations were simultaneously installed on November 15. And on the 23rd, exterior decorations were erected at the same time—snow castles on light standards, festoons of greenery and tinsel, and arches of colored lights. All of this was preliminary to the climactic November 28 parade with its giant fairy-tale "grotesques," bands, and a glittering Santa and reindeers. In New York City in 1928 Tony Sarg achieved a new sensational level in his work with the first floating, helium-inflated balloons in the parade's history. The 1929 parade was the "biggest toy parade ever staged in New York." Not to be outclassed, Wanamaker's inscribed a nearly complete amusement park into its toy store in Philadelphia. Wanamaker's also ended the year with a cheap but not unrepresentative Christmas ploy. At the New York store, Santa Claus, enthroned in an "enormous igloo," amazed every child who visited him with knowledge of his or her "exact desires." Santa got this information from one of his "helpers" who, seated at the bottom of a ramp the children used to reach Santa, found out the children's wishes and then communicated them to Santa through an invisible dictaphone.[34]

Institutional Collaborators

After 1900 American merchants had established a clear child's world, a highly theatrical world that linked the stores to the children against the parents. No merchant, I believe, would have admitted that such an alliance with children had emerged. But the total effect of all the enticements created for children was to create just such an alliance, just such an independent child-world, that had the potential to subvert the decision-making authority of parents.

This child's world and its merchandising structure, however, developed also because other institutions and groups contributed to their formation. In the first quarter of the twentieth century, department stores were among the most important institutional anchors of downtown city life. Serving not only as the disseminators of commodities but also of ideas and information sometimes crucial to the community, the stores attracted thousands of people and helped generate a vital city culture. Recognizing their importance, other institutions and groups, whose goals often had nothing to do with merchandising, turned to the stores as mediums of transmission. This reliance had the effect of further endorsing the power of merchants to define the character of the child-world. At the same time, however, it also acted to check the abuse of such power. Given this institutional tension between differing approaches to children that sometimes converged, children and parents were often "protected" from the full impact of a theatrical culture of consumer desire.

I am going to deal here with three important national groups—the consumers leagues, the United States Children's Bureau, and a new group of child psychologists and social workers—who both intentionally and unintentionally contributed to the buttressing of this merchandising child-world. Under Florence Kelley's able direction, the National Consumers League labored to ferret out the exploitation of children in department stores, textile and garment factories, and in candy and glass manufacturing, where children worked long hours at extremely low pay. The league urged strict implementation of compulsory school attendance laws as the best way to prevent exploitive employment, and it supported a federal Child Labor Law (twice declared unconstitutional by the Supreme Court), which gave Congress the power to limit, regulate, and prohibit the labor of persons under 18. This law was finally passed in the guise of the Fair Labor Standards Act of 1938.[35]

The United States Children's Bureau, founded in 1912 under the direction of Julia Lathrop, unified opposition to child labor at the highest level. At the turn of the century, the United States was distinguished by one of the lowest nutrition levels and one of the highest mortality rates for children among western nations. In 1915 the bureau inaugurated Baby's Day, followed by Baby's Week a year later, and Children's Year in 1918, all designed to publicize the need for better infant and maternal care, the improvement of medical and nursing facilities, and the adoption of well-balanced diets. These activities triggered the growth of the child-welfare-commission movement, which, with the help of federal monies, generated over 700 prenatal and children's health centers throughout the country. The bureau held national conferences in Washington to establish and set "new standards for the health, education, and work of the American child," for the baby, the preschool child, the school child and adolescent, and the child in need of special care. Conferences were also conducted on the regional level from New York to San Francisco to make the public aware of the need to protect children, to get them into school, and to keep them out of factories and stores.[36]

The achievements of the U.S. Children's Bureau and consumers leagues were undeniable, opening up a new era in the improvement of children's lot in this country. They were undertaken, however, not only because they were in and of themselves good things (although they were) but also because of the country's prosperity, its expanding technological know-how, and the fundamental changes in adult work that had rendered child labor unnecessary. Moreover, these changes occurred because Florence Kelley, Julia Lathrop, and others collaborated with American merchants to make certain a new and better "child-world" emerged.

The National Consumers League worked tirelessly to persuade department stores to abolish child labor. As Florence Kelley put it in 1912—the year that Field's announced children's separate "rights to merchandise" and that Wanamaker's eliminated the "business atmosphere" in the toy store—we plan to "redeem the holiday season for children." In the early 1890s, when girls and boys still labored in stockrooms and as cash personnel, department-store merchants opposed child-labor reforms. Only 10 years later, partly as a result of the boycotts imposed on the stores by the league, this consensus was reversed. We all agree, said Samuel Woodward of Woodward and Lothrop, Washington's biggest store, in 1906, "that child labor is harmful to the mental and physical growth of the child." Leading merchants like Edward Filene made "generous gifts" to state consumers leagues. By 1911, in response to the leagues' protests, practically all the big stores in major cities had eliminated what Kelley called the "holiday cruelties"—the nighttime employment of children during the holiday season. In a reform that lasted until the 1930s, merchants everywhere followed Wanamaker's lead and closed their doors after 6:30 at night during the last 14 days of the Christmas holidays.[37]

As the grounds for conflict slowly disappeared, the consumer leagues and the department stores soon began to share a common agenda in regard to children's welfare. Florence Kelley drew attention to this development when, in a speech at Gimbel's in 1910 honoring the opening of the New York store on Broadway and 34th Street, she praised "the cooperation in this movement extended by the heads of the great retail concerns in many centers."[38]

The U.S. Children's Bureau relied on centrally located merchants to publicize Baby's Day, Baby's Week, Children's Year, and the Back-to-School Movement. In Boston there were "baby-welfare exhibits and talks" at the big department stores. Retailers of every description around the country sold "baby buttons" and displayed "baby clothes." In one Missouri city, a large dry goods house built an auditorium especially designed for "baby-week lectures." In some cities, the children's bureau reported, the link between the retailers and the baby-week campaigners was so close that "the campaign was in danger of being considered a commercial advertising one."[39]

Retailers needed little inducement from government to get the word out about babies and children. They often voluntarily took up the campaign for children's welfare with a fervor equalled only by state- and federal-government officials. As the alleged embodiments of all that was good for the community, the stores served as major centers for child improvement. "Backed by plenty of newspaper publicity and the government's sanction," wrote the editor of a major trade journal, "the baby welfare campaign has been proved a crowdbringer by many stores." Even before the "government's sanction" released a wave of such promotions, some stores were already sponsoring "Baby Week." They were distributing child-care literature to their customers and arranging window displays around Baby Week themes. Stores everywhere held baby-weighing contests, an important public service since a baby's weight indicated the nutrition level of the child and its capacity to survive.[40]

In 1916 Gimbel's in New York organized "A Better Babies Health Exhibit" in the "infants' salon," offering lectures on twilight sleep, eugenics, the Montessori method, and the care and dress of infants. Male and female doctors conducted classes at the J. S. Bailey department-store chain in Brooklyn on the malnutrition of children and on artificial feeding. Across the country in Seattle, The Bon Marché introduced a nutrition clinic for healthy babies, staffed by a full-time nurse and part-time doctors. The clinic advised on feeding and care and examined 3600 babies in a single year, serving an "in-between class of women, people who can budget to meet all ordinary requirements, but who would find it difficult perhaps to include regular consultation fees with a nutrition or pediatritional expert."[41]

As in other instances, these stores supplied women with services that might not have been available to them elsewhere. Women learned ideas and methods of care that must have contributed greatly to the well-being of their children. But this attention to the needs of babies and children obviously served the interests of the stores as well, justifying the introduction and sale of more and more merchandise, the addition of more departments for children and the expansion of older departments, the commodification of childhood at every age and stage of development. "The little child at birth and for several years thereafter," wrote a merchant in 1919, "has to have an entire world of its own, not only special clothes and special foods, but special furniture, special bathing arrangements, special articles of all kinds."[42]

Department stores worked to sustain interest in children's goods by "segregating infants' requisites in special departments" and by continuing to promote Baby Week and Children's Day long after the government had ceased backing them. In the late 1920s and early 1930s, merchants reactivated both events, celebrated respectively in May and June, in an attempt to "fill up the gap between holiday periods," to give youngsters their "own days," and to provide them with special exposure to every conceivable commodity for a "child's world," Together, merchants, manufacturers, and wholesalers forged "tie-ups" to "promote general celebration of Children's Day." "Surely if the day is to be developed into one of real importance, it should be advertised to the fullest extent."[43]

Child psychologists and educators also supported the goals of the mass-market retailers by articulating a new rational ideology of play. New journals on children—*Child Welfare* and *Children, the Magazine for Parents,* for instance—focused attention on children's need for playthings. "Remember," said one well-known child psychologist, "that the plaything is of vital importance in the life of the child; it is the medium through which he interprets the world as he visions it." It was crucial, the experts claimed, that children have the right toys at every stage of their development. In the thrall of its "destructive instincts," wrote one psychologist, "the baby should have hardy, rubber toys"; the older child, experiencing the urge to act out its "imaginative drama," demands trains, fire engines, wagons, or (for girls) playhouses, sewing kits, and dolls. All children need toys to fulfill their "yearning" for "originality," "imaginative" enrichment, and "muscular" freedom. "Educators and manufacturers," said Patty S. Hill, prominent child educator at Columbia University and composer of the famous children's tune "Happy Birthday," should "cooperate to the best advantage by frequent conferences" to make certain that children get "truly inspirational toys."[44]

Other child experts argued that children should have their own individual play spaces—attics, backyards, corners, basements, special rooms—free from adult supervision. "It is tragic," said one expert, when children do not have their own "playrooms" where they can "keep all (their) strange treasures, . . . put on theatricals, wash doll clothes, or do any other delightful thing (their) lively imaginations may dictate." The experts also wrote that "toys are the means by which children live in miniature the daily life of their elders." By having lots of toys set before them that duplicate adult artifacts and experiences—miniature tractors, refrigerators, trains, cars, and so forth—children will learn how to live in the "real world."[45]

Toy trade journals freely exploited these ideas and quoted repeatedly from the writings of well-known child psychologists and educators to justify the toy industry's production of more and more toys. Although some psychologists often argued that the toy quality was far more important than toy quantity, merchants construed the advice to justify the constant production of new toys. "Children need toys," one toy buyer reported, "as much as they need good bread."[46]

The collaboration between child experts and retailers also took place at toy expositions within the stores, where some of the most highly regarded people in the field came to lecture on play and child psychology. Macy's mounted perhaps the most extensive program of this kind in May of 1928, the year Tony Sarg floated the first helium-inflated balloons over New York City at the Macy's parade. It was in May, moreover, that the store established its educational toy advisory service under the supervision of Edith Boehm, member of the American Child-Study Association. In connection with the opening of the service, Macy's featured a "Play-in-Education Week" to acquaint parents with the educational merits of play and the right kind of "rational" toy. Toys were exhibited for practical educational value—physical exercise and outdoor play; imitation of adult activities; construction and creation; and games for socialization. Store buyers and child experts encouraged parents to purchase toys for their children from each one of these groups."[47]

During the event, noted experts lectured on the importance of play for children. On the whole, they espoused a new permissive approach to child rearing that accepted the independent life of the child and its "inherent" need for more expressive and unhampered play activity. Jay Nash, professor of physical education at New York University, argued that "play developed the personality of the child," and it does so best not in the "dangerous" streets but in the "backyard" full of swings, slides, sandboxes or in "spare rooms" furnished with bookcases and various types of games. Clara Littledale, editor of *Children's Magazine,* underscored the attractions of play over work. Ernest Crandall, director of lectures and visual education for the New York Board of Education, insisted that children learn imitation, manipulation, expression, and dramatization, among other things, from play experiences.[48]

The most eminent people to speak at Macy's in 1928 were Joseph Jastrow, lecturer in psychology at the New School for Social Research in New York, and Sidonie Gruenberg, president of the Child Study Association. Jastrow wrote *Character and Temperament* in 1915, a book on progressive psychology that established his reputation. In the 1920s he turned his hand to the popularization of psychological ideas. Spurred on by his friend, the merchant Edward Filene, he wrote one of the first popular books on "everyday psychology," *Keeping Fit Mentally,* published the year of Macy's exposition and dedicated to Filene. The book opens with advice on how to "keep happy" and ends with chapters on "the cult of beauty" and "the psychology of sports." Chapter 2 deals with children and displays an upbeat, reasonably balanced, and generally permissive orientation to child rearing. Jastrow borrowed from this chapter in his Macy's talk. He praised Macy's for its system of "graded toys." "Failure," he said, "is one of the most serious distractions" for children, "hence it is excellent that you have that graded series of toys. You give a child a tricycle before you give it a bicycle, and so on." Jastrow also maintained that play and its tutelary servant, the toy, activated the imaginative life of the child, thus making a "crucial" contribution to the child's development.[49]

In terms of Macy's goals, Sidonie Gruenberg was a more significant figure than Jastrow, as she had long been recognized as one of the country's leading exponents of flexible, permissive child care. Her imprimatur, therefore, carried more weight than Jastrow's did. A Jewish immigrant from Austria whose psychology intermingled the ideas of G. Stanley Hall, Edward Thorndike, John Dewey, and Sigmund Freud, Gruenberg in 1904 was appointed head of the Society for the Study of Child Nature, an organization renamed the American Child Study Association in 1924 with Gruenberg at the helm and with funding from the Rockefeller Foundation. Like Jastrow, Gruenberg was a popularizer, but unlike him she began her writing career with a mass audience in mind.[50]

In *Your Child Today and Tomorrow,* written in 1912 (again, the year of Field's editorial) and the first book of its kind intended for popular consumption, Gruenberg developed ideas widely held by other psychologists that were compatible with the support of an emerging culture of consumer desire and that clearly explain her presence at Macy's. Gruenberg argued on behalf of the separateness of the child-world. Unlike adults, she said, children do nothing of "moral significance"; neither good nor bad, they are governed by instincts that must be channeled and rationalized. Children have a special right to imaginative play and "individual expression," Gruenberg argued, and should not suffer from "repressive penalties imposed by an arbitrary puritanism which suspects every desire and impulse of being Satanic." Moreover, they should have regular access to money in the form of an "allowance" so that they might better understand it by "spending it."[51]

In a book written with her husband in 1933, *Parents, Children, and Money,* Gruenberg continued to pursue these themes, but she seemed much less sure about the value of a culture that placed so much emphasis on play and on the "protection" of children from the "dangers" of the adult world and so little emphasis on the character of work. Over the years, she wrote in this book, we have "glorified all work-avoiding individuals. Instead of insisting that the conditions of labor, industry, and commerce be made similar for adults as well as for children, we tried desperately to shield our children from the inhuman and degrading conditions of 'labor.' . . . Almost everybody has by now learned that 'only saps work.'" This "shielding" has not only turned children away from work, it has shut them "off from daily contact with . . . adults—contacts that are necessary in the process of growing up."[52]

Here Gruenberg attacked the segregation of children from adults that her child-centered psychology had generally defended and that her Macy's talk reflected. She underlined the dangers for children—ignorance of the modern work process and of life itself—posed by the creation of this adult-inspired culture of play and theatricality.

Child psychologists, government agencies, and consumer leagues all tended to legitimize and even hasten the expansion of new departments and the production of more goods. Even as these groups strove sincerely to advance the health and welfare of children and protect them from exploitation, they were encouraging the emergence of a new culture of consumer desire that separated children from adults, threw them into adversarial relationship in new ways, and fostered in children new kinds of desires and expectations that many parents were simply unable to satisfy. These reformers were also supporting a culture that, by placing such distance between adults and children, helped to foster adult indifference to children, thus creating new grounds for children's exploitation.

Today, this child-world, as it took form in the 1920s, has been transformed. It has been expanded and integrated into the structure of consumer capitalism to such a degree that its boundaries are almost invisible. The older institutions of consumption that shaped it, moreover, no longer play the central role in downtown urban community life that they once played. The institutional tension between two different (but often convergent) views of children has disappeared, and with it the sense of "protection" and social obligation that the institutional reformers provided. What remains is the theatrical-consumer vision of the child-world, an unopposed culture of desire propounded by merchants and marketeers and reinforced by a socially irresponsible commercial mass media.

Notes

1. Laurence Hansen, "Measuring a Retail Market," Trade Information Bulletin #272, Domestic Commerce Division, Washington, D.C., October 13, 1924, 4; *Philadelphia Retail Ledger*, vol. 28, April 1933, 9; and *Advertising World*, March 1912.

2. *The Dry Goods Economist*, November 19, 1921, 225; *Playthings*, March 1920, 144.

3. *Playthings*, March 1912, 75; *Toy World*, April 1929, 4; *The Dry Goods Economist*, December 19, 1908, 13; ibid., September 21, 1893; ibid., November 25, 1893; ibid., November 10, 1910; and *The Dry Goods Reporter*, December 12, 1908.

4. *Playthings*, September 1917, 19; *Toy World*, March 1929, 48; "Report on Value of Toy Manufacturers Based on Summary of Questionnaires Issued by War Industries Board," Toys—General—1918–25, file 205.6, RG 151, Bureau of Foreign and Domestic Commerce, National Archives; ibid., Fletcher Dodge, Secretary of Toy Manufacturers of USA, to BFDC, March 5, 1921; *The Dry Goods Economist*, February 21, 1920; ibid., August 29, 1896, 49; ibid., February 9, 1918, 80; and *Toy World*, December 1929, 40.

5. Bureau of Foreign and Domestic Commerce, "International Trade in Toys," Trade Information Bulletin #445, December 1926; *Toy World*, January 1928, 21; *The Dry Goods Economist*, September 13, 1919 (cuddle toys); ibid., March 28, 1918 (dolls); ibid., February 21, 1920 (dolls).
6. Paul Mazur, *American Prosperity, Its Causes and Consequences* (New York, 1928), 77.
7. William R. Leach, "Transformations in a Culture of Consumption: Women and Department Stores, 1880–1925," *Journal of American History* 71 (September 1984), 319–42.
8. Harry Selfridge, "Children's Day," from "Notes Concerning Subjects of Talks Made by H.G.S. to Department Heads . . . , as Compiled by Waldo Warren, 1901–1906," Marshall Field Archives, Chicago, September 25, 1905; *Toys and Novelties*, April 1911, 10.
9. Edward Bernays, *Autobiography of an Idea* (New York, 1962), 308–9.
10. Jean Beauvais to Reeves Wetherill, Wanamaker's vice president for public relations, March 2, 1975, in file "crack-pot mail," Wanamaker Archives, Philadelphia; *The Dry Goods Economist*, January 10, 1920, 67; ibid., April 8, 1922, 23; ibid., July 11, 1921, 10; *Toy World*, November 1928, 55; *Playthings*, August 1919, 78; *Philadelphia Retail Ledger*, second June issue, 1926, 5; and "Wanamaker's Jolly Book," Wanamaker Archives, c. 1925.
11. *Philadelphia Retail Ledger*, January 3, 1923, 1; ibid., April 1933, 9; the National Retail Dry Goods Association, Sales Promotion Division, *Radio Broadcasting Manual;* and other material.
12. *Toys and Novelties*, April 1911, 3; John Wanamaker and Co., *The Guide Book and Information Concerning the Wanamaker Mail Order Service* (Philadelphia, 1910), 17–18; *The Dry Goods Economist*, June 21, 1902; ibid., December 23, 1893, July 31, 1897, August 22, 1896, October 22, 1898, and February 28, 1903.
13. *Advertising World*, January 1914, 245; *Philadelphia Retail Ledger*, second issue, October 1924, 8; and *Toy World*, November 1928, 55.
14. *The Dry Goods Economist*, November 12, 1910; *The Merchants' Record and Show Window*, March 1913; *Playthings*, June 1919, 97; ibid., May 1920, 85; *The Merchants' Record and Show Window*, May 1920, 37–38; *The Dry Goods Economist*, November 18, 1922, 103; ibid., February 7, 1920; and *Toys and Novelties*, January 1928, 323.
15. *Women's Wear Daily*, January 28, 1928, 1; *The Merchants' Record and Show Window*, February 1933, 15; *The Dry Goods Economist*, November 7, 1914, 103; ibid., April 11, 1903; ibid., September 22, 1900; *Toys and Novelties*, July 1928, 61–62; *Playthings*, February 1912, 56; *Washington Post*, February 24, 1906, 10; *Advertising World*, January 1921, 144; *Domestic Commerce*, August 30, 1933, 5; and "WotSat Club," Wanamaker Archives.
16. *The Dry Goods Economist*, June 12, 1920; ibid., May 14, 1921; *Playthings*, March 1912, 3; ibid., February 23, 1923, 118; ibid., December 1924, 245; *Advertising World*, June/July 1919, 20; *Philadelphia Retail Ledger*, January 17, 1923, 9; and ibid., first April issue, 1925, 8.

17. *Philadelphia Retail Ledger,* second November issue, 1928, 1; ibid., March 2, 1924, 2; John Wanamaker, November 15, 1916, "Bound Editorials, October 1, 1912 to December 31, 1917," vol. I, Wanamaker Archives; *Retailing,* January 9, 1933; *The Dry Goods Economist,* November 12, 1904; ibid., December 16, 1911; *The Merchants' Record and Show Window,* December 1907, 23; ibid., January/February 1905, 1.

18. *Advertising World,* April 1924, 12; *Philadelphia Retail Ledger,* first November issue, 1926, 1; and ibid., July 1933, 12.

19. *The Dry Goods Economist,* November 11, 1922, 17; *Women's Wear Daily,* November 28, 1925, 3; *Playthings,* June 1917, 5; and ibid., December 1912, 44.

20. *The Dry Goods Economist,* December 4, 1920, 85; *Playthings,* December 12, 47–48; and ibid., December 1913, 62.

21. *The Show Window,* November 1899, 209; *The Merchants' Record and Show Window,* November 1908; *Fame,* January 1897, 419; *The Dry Goods Economist,* December 22, 1894; *Washington Evening Star,* December 18, 1899, 13; *The Dry Goods Economist,* October 30, 1920, 43; and Siegel-Cooper and Co., *A Bird's-Eye View of Greater New York and Its Most Magnificent Store* (New York, 1898), 136.

22. *The Dry Goods Economist,* December 14, 1920, 87; *Signs of the Times,* December 1912; *Philadelphia Retail Ledger,* December issue, 1924, 87; ibid., December issue, 1925, 9; ibid., first November issue, 1925, 1; NRGDA, *Radio Broadcasting Manual, The Radio as Publicity Medium for Retailers* (1935), 43; *Toy World,* December 1928, 35; *The Dry Goods Economist,* December 4, 1913, 107; *Playthings,* December 1920, 174.

23. John Wanamaker to Reverend S. W. Steckel, December 11, 1907, in Wanamaker Letterbook, "Personal Letters of JW, December 14, 1906 to February 20, 1908," 763, Wanamaker Archives; and Wanamaker bound editorials.

24. *Playthings,* December 1912, 34; ibid., December 1915, 52–54; *The Dry Goods Economist,* December 22, 1894, 15; and Wanamaker advertising card, "Visit Santa Claus and See the Toys in the Basement," c. 1900, Dry Goods Collection, Robert Warshow Collection of Business Americana, National American Museum of History.

25. John Wanamaker to Rodman Wanamaker, August 10, 1914, Wanamaker Letterbook, Wanamaker Archives.

26. *The Dry Goods Economist,* November 29, 1919, 80; *Playthings,* December 19, 1919, 180; and ibid., November 11, 1917, 37–41.

27. *The Dry Goods Economist,* November 11, 1922, 17; *The Merchants' Record and Show Window,* December 1922, 19–20; and *Playthings,* November 1922, 98.

28. "Minutes of the Executive Council," August 7, 1924, 78, Macy Archives, New York; ibid., September 4, 1924, 87; and *Display World,* March 1923, 12.

29. See William Dean Howells, *Through the Eye of the Needle* (New York, 1907), 308; and Peter M. Itak, "Christmas, Macy's, and the Thanksgiving Day Parade" (undergraduate senior paper, New York University, Spring 1981), 22–31.

30. Howells, 308.
31. "Minutes of the Executive Council," June 12, 1924; August 21, 1924; September 7 and 25, 1924; October 9, 1924; and November 6, 1924, Macy Archives; and "Macy's Christmas Parade, Advertising—Special Events, 173," Macy Archives.
32. *Women's Wear Daily,* November 23, 1927, 2; ibid., November 26, 1927, 17; and *Philadelphia Retail Ledger,* first December issue, 1927, 11.
33. Frances E. Fox, director of Drama Division of the Department of Recreation, Houston, to the United States Children's Bureau, October 9, 1930, Children's Bureau Papers, folder 5–8–1, "Holiday Celebrations," RG 102, National Archives.
34. *The Merchants' Record and Show Window,* January 1929, 36–37; "The Great Toystore Tableaux," Howard Kratz, Wanamaker's Philadelphia display manager, photo album, 1927–31, Wanamaker Archives; John Wanamaker and Co., "The Enchanted Forest," (Philadelphia, 1927), Wanamaker Archives; *Toys and Novelties,* January 1930, 197; ibid., November 1930, 88–89; *Philadelphia Retail Ledger,* September issue, 1933, 17; *Toy World,* November 1929, 88–89.
35. National Consumers League, "Fourth Annual Report, Year Ending March 4, 1903"; and "Highlights in the History of the National Consumers League, 1938," film 113, Library of Congress.
36. Children's Bureau, *First Annual Report of the Chief of the Children's Bureau to the Secretary of Labor for the Fiscal Year Ending June 30, 1913,* Washington, D.C., 1913, 5–15; ibid., *Third Annual Report,* 1915, 11–12; ibid., *Fifth Annual Report,* 1917, 22–24; ibid., *Ninth Annual Report,* 1921, 5–6; ibid., *Thirteenth Annual Report,* 1925, 1–6; and the United States Department of Labor, "Fair Labor Standards for Children," folder 6, Washington, D.C., 1939.
37. Consumers League of Massachusetts, "Report of the Work from March 1900–1," Boston, 1901, 13; Philadelphia Consumers League, "Tenth Annual Report," February 15, 1911, 20; National Consumers League, "Thirteenth Annual Report, Year Ending January 19, 1912, 18; *The Dry Goods Economist,* April 6, 1893; ibid., May 4, 1893; and Samuel Woodward, address before the third session of the second annual meeting of the National Child Labor Committee, Washington, D.C., December 9, 1905, Woodward and Lothrop Archives, Washington.
38. *The Dry Goods Economist,* October 12, 1910, 49.
39. United States Department of Labor, Children's Bureau, *Baby Week Campaigns,* miscellaneous series #5, Washington, D.C., 1917, 23, 63–64; and "Pittsburgh Baby and Child Welfare," record group 102, 1914–20, file 8–1–4–2–1, Children's Bureau Papers, National Archives.
40. *The Dry Goods Economist,* November 1, 1913, 47; ibid., June 28, 1919, 35; John Wanamaker and Co., "The Baby, His Care, and Needs" (Philadelphia, 1913), Wanamaker Archives; Mary Rontaahn, director of the Pittsburgh Baby and Welfare Week, to Anna Louise Strong of the children's bureau, June 7, 1915,

file 8–1–4–2–1, "Exhibits," Children's Bureau Records, RG 102, National Archives; and "Child Welfare Exhibit Number," *The Dallas Survey, A Journal of Social Work,* May 1, 1918, 12, file 8–1–4–2, "Exhibits."

41. *Toy World,* March 1929, 54; *The Dry Goods Economist,* November 28, 1914, 39; and ibid., June 28, 1919, 35.
42. *The Dry Goods Economist,* June 14, 1919, 167.
43. *Toy World,* May 1929, 149; *The Dry Goods Economist,* May 20, 1916, 65; *The Confectioner's Journal,* May 1928, 51–52; *Toys and Novelties,* July 1928, 54; *The Merchants' Record and Show Window,* July 1933, 31; ibid., April 1933, 21.
44. *Playthings,* May 1920, 88; ibid., October 1918, 128; ibid., May 1920, 90; *Toy World,* February 1928, 24; and *New York Times,* October 22, 1988, A-1.
45. *Toys and Novelties,* February 1928, 114; *Children, The Magazine for Parents,* November 1928, 45; *Child Welfare,* January 1926, 277–81; and ibid., December 1928, 183–85.
46. *Toys and Novelties,* February 1928, 114.
47. *Women's Wear Daily,* May 28, 1928, 2; *Toy World,* November 1929, 60; and *Toys and Novelties,* June 1928, 64.
48. *Toys and Novelties,* June 1928, 52, 64; ibid., August 1928, 82; ibid., January 1929, 330.
49. *Toys and Novelties,* January 1929, 329; Joseph Jastrow, *Keeping Fit Mentally* (New York, 1928); and Jastrow, *Character and Temperament* (New York, 1915).
50. Sidonie Gruenberg, unpublished autobiography, c. 1962, 44, 93, 16–17, box 64, Sidonie Gruenberg Papers, Library of Congress.
51. Sidonie Gruenberg, *Your Child Today and Tomorrow* (New York, 1910), 32, 43–46, *Sons and Daughters* (New York, 1916), 145, 235, 312, and unpublished autobiography, 121–23.
52. Sidonie Gruenberg, *Parents, Children, and Money* (New York, 1933), 173–75.

❧

"The Making of a New Mind": American Women and Intellectual Life in the 1920s

Joyce Antler

WITH THE ATTAINMENT OF SUFFRAGE IN 1920, AMERICAN WOMEN ENTERED A new era of public activism. Although their participation in the political process was less vigorous than many supporters had hoped—a product of the changing national political climate as well as women's own interests—there is no doubt that the entitlement to vote ushered in a greatly expanded sense of women's possibilities.

But if the twenties marked a symbolic and in many ways an actual triumph of women's political options, the record of their intellectual progress in that decade is less clear. In certain respects the decade witnessed a critical advance in the prospects of educated women. As Patricia Graham points out, in the 1920s women achieved their highest proportion of the undergraduate

I would like to thank Nancy F. Cott, Ellen Fitzpatrick, Ann J. Lane, and Joan W. Scott for their comments on this essay and Lois Rudnick for comments on a related essay on Mary Austin.

population, doctoral recipients, and faculty members, reaching a peak not again equalled until the 1970s.[1] Nevertheless, widespread sex discrimination in academic hiring, promotions, and salary denied educated women economic and occupational security and reduced their opportunities for intellectual productivity.[2]

This factor was only partially considered in a slew of popular and scholarly articles in the 1920s criticizing women's intellectual achievements and raising the question of whether, indeed, women possessed the highest attributes of mind. Although the empirical investigations of social scientists like Helen Thomas Woolley and Leta Hollingworth were thought to have put to rest assertions of the biological basis of women's so-called mental inferiority more than two decades earlier, the debate about women's intellect resurfaced in the 1920s, testifying to the hardiness of social stereotypes about women's minds.[3]

Though the connection was only inchoately made by feminists during the 1920s, the question of women's "genius," as it was often termed, went to the heart of the cultural debate about gender in the postsuffrage period. Following the legal recognition of women's rights to the vote, questions about the meaning of sexual difference increasingly penetrated other battlegrounds—among them education, economic opportunity, sexuality, and family life. Although the controversy over women's intellect in the 1920s has not attracted scholarly interest, the debate indicated that notions of sexual difference remained prominent among intellectuals, including some feminists.[4] Failing to fully challenge the belief that women possessed less creative and intellectual genius than men, these individuals ultimately succumbed to hierarchical views of mental achievement. To demonstrate the myriad potentialities of women as intellectuals, and therefore as human beings, they had first to question in a systematic and sustained fashion the intellectual culture and credentials of their challengers. Not until the development of feminism as a critical theory—encompassing social history, literary criticism, and cultural analysis—did this take place.

❧

The notion that genius appeared more frequently in men than in women had been a staple of scientific discourse in the 1890s, when

Havelock Ellis published his influential *Man and Woman: A Study of Human Secondary Sexual Characteristics.*[5] Ellis's argument, which became known as the variability hypothesis, posited that males were more variable than women in both negatively valued physical and mental defects as well as in positively valued traits, such as genius. Although criticized in England by Karl Pearson for his use of erroneous data as well as by Hollingsworth and Thompson, who emphasized the problematic sexual bias of Ellis's work, the variability hypothesis continued to gather adherents. Scientists like James McKeen Cattell, in his statistical study of eminent men, and Cattell's student, Edward Thorndike, did much to further its acceptance in the early twentieth century.[6]

Though Ellis and his supporters did not significantly alter their views about the impact of sexual variability on genius over the next decades, by the 1920s scientific research on the subject of intelligence focused on specific mental abilities in both sexes rather than the generalized category of mind. More complex testing of larger samples of individuals eroded faith in a simplistic biological model of gender differences in intelligence. Nevertheless, Ellis's work continued to be cited as proof of at least one example of men's superior intellectual capacities even into the early thirties. "The validity of Ellis' main thesis is confirmed by genetics," wrote one scientific interpreter in an essay on "The Woman of Genius" in the 1931 symposium, *Woman's Coming of Age.* "In the matter of reason, logic, the power to connect ideas, to enchain principles of knowledge and perceive their relationships, woman, even the most highly gifted, rarely attains to the height of a man of mediocre capacity."[7]

Such sentiments were regularly presented to popular audiences in the early 1920s. In a representative essay in the *Atlantic Monthly,* Ramsey Traquair observed that women were "inferior to men in imagination, intuition, and the abstract qualities," claiming the greatest artists and scientists had always been men. Though Traquair granted women superior virtues in regard to social and organizational life, he insisted that these very characteristics were responsible for this nation's anti-intellectualism. America had become a "thoroughly feminized society," with disastrous consequences:

> The characteristics of the American world, its love of activity, its desire to do things, its social and gregarious convention habits, its reform habit, its

> scorn for ultimate principles [and] pure knowledge . . . these are the weakest qualities of women. . . . These qualities . . . are rapidly leading to intellectual death.[8]

In addition to the deleterious effect of women's activism on the quality of intellectual life and their failures as thinkers, critics repeated the arguments of many nineteenth-century male observers about the unfortunate "feminization" of literature. A 1921 article in the *Yale Review* by Joseph Hergesheimer typically argued that women had debased cultural life in their role as audience. Hergesheimer asserted that the fact that "women set the standard, determined the tone, of the characteristic American novel" had led to the "cowardly mediocrity" of American literature, a consequence of the erosion of masculine values and subjects in favor of "prejudices feminine in essence" and a "feminine vocabulary." "Literature in the United States is being strangled with a petticoat," Hergesheimer charged; men needed to "brush the sachet powder from their eyes" and reassert control.[9] The denigration of women's achievements as intellectuals—the assertion, especially, of their inferiority in the highest realms of abstract and artistic creativity—was thus often linked to their dominance as readers. The dual criticism of feminine taste in literature and of women's capacity as thinkers sprang from a common core of distrust of the female mind and in some cases envy of women's power as writers and readers. Impugning women's abilities in both realms denied the legitimacy of many best-selling novels written by women implicitly for a female audience.

The regularity and vehemence of the attack on women's intellects in the 1920s was less surprising, perhaps, than the fact that many feminists agreed with the charges, albeit reluctantly. Of the prominent American feminists who addressed the issue of women's creativity in the 1920s, Mary Austin—novelist, literary critic, poet, and essayist—and Mary Beard, historian, and with her husband Charles, coauthor of the best-selling *The Rise of American Civilization*—presented the most thoughtful and disturbing critiques of women's intelligence. Both women acknowledged the absence of women from the recognized ranks of intellectual greatness but suggested that this lack might have had less to do with the quality and originality of women's contributions than with their distance from male cultural traditions. Though neither developed these observations into a full-fledged theory of gender difference, their writings in many ways anticipated the critiques of knowledge constructed by later generations of feminists. At the same time they reveal the difficulty of developing a theoretical understanding of the connections between women's writing and the social conditions of their work in this era. Although Austin and Beard resisted the masculine definition of intellectual work in its entirety, they nonetheless adopted several of the myths of genius defined by men. In so doing they partially obscured their own visions of a female-identified social theory.[10]

Mary Austin: Everyman/woman's Genius

Although best known for her western and nature writings, Mary Austin (1868–1934), the author of 27 books and more than 250 articles, short stories, dramas, and poems, also wrote extensively of women's cultural roles.[11] Austin's analysis of the woman question began with *Lost Borders* (1909), a collection of short stories, and *The Arrow Maker*, a drama produced in New York City in 1911, both of which featured powerful Anglo-American and Native American women whose unconventional activities subjected them to social disapproval. Her novel *A Woman of Genius*, published in 1912 to general critical acclaim, elaborated the theme of the creative woman's personal sacrifices: its heroine, Olivia Lattimore, a small-town woman who struggles against convention to find her own way as an actress, eventually wins artistic acclaim but loses the man she truly loves.

Active in the suffrage and women's peace movements, Austin temporarily abandoned the problems of creative women as a major focus of her work. Disappointed in the aftermath of the suffrage victory, however, and angry at the reception of her own work by the male literary establishment, in the 1920s she returned to this issue. In a series of articles in literary and popular magazines she examined the presumed failure of women as intellectuals.

"In the current periodicals where our American Intellectuals are actively in evidence . . . there are few women's names, and none that stand out as convincingly, femininely original," Austin wrote in a 1921 article on "American Women and Intellectual Life."[12] Austin found women writers partly to blame for this situation, decrying their inattention to style and form. As an example she cited the works of Charlotte Perkins Gilman, whom she duly noted was "one of the most original of women thinkers." From an aesthetic perspective, however, Gilman's writings were flawed. "Mrs. Gilman is not without style," Austin wrote,

> but it is the style of Mrs. Gilman's mind, thin, vivid, and swift as a lightning streak, rather than the carefully finished instrument of communication. Only in her most ambitious and perhaps most deeply felt works, like "Women and Economics," does it produce organic literary form. Undoubtedly this has lead [*sic*] to misappreciation and the neglect of Mrs. Gilman's contribution long before we have ceased to need it.[13]

The neglect of form with which Austin charged Gilman had often been applied to Austin herself. Perhaps that is one reason why she sympathized with the diminution of Gilman's reputation in the 1920s. But Austin also recognized that it was women's "especial point of view" and their "almost contemptuous avoidance of the Pooh-Bah traditions of learning" that prompted their indifference to style.[14] Though she insisted in this article that she was a "feminist not wholly given over to the conviction of the innate superiority of women," nevertheless she asserted that

> there is no inferiority, but a measure of superior feminine discernment in woman's refusal to occupy herself with the irrelevance of the number of angels that could dance on the point of a needle, or the fallacy of the undistributed middle.[15]

Women's indifference to form could be seen as a rejection of "androcentric" scholarship, which Austin believed was elitist and irrelevant, and a response to the growing ascendancy of empirical study. What the world accepted as "logic" and "science," Austin wrote on one occasion, were little more than "ritualizations of the male approach"—"footnotes and cross references and appendices," all "long argumentative chapters," "solid grey pages," and every "academic insistence on a sequence of presentation which has nothing to do with the way in which facts are gleaned from life and experience."[16]

Austin suggested that women's neglect of style was a consequence not only of the canonized "Podsnappery of the [male] intellect" enshrined in universities and literary magazines and societies but also of the fact that in matters of mind, women and men were substantially different.[17] Woman's "scorn of the impersonal and indirect, her deep sense of social applicability as the test of value . . . [her] habit of shortcircuiting all her process in view of her experience as the center of the family group" were useful qualities. If they ever were to be "authenticated . . . in the institutional world," Austin believed that they could become the basis of a "genuine woman culture."[18]

If female intellectuals were to be recognized for their creative contributions, however, Austin believed they would need the support of organized groups of women. In subsequent articles she was critical of both the feminist movement and the women's club movement, which she had formerly championed, for their failures to recognize women of "greatness." In Austin's view, neither feminists nor club women knew how to select, honor, and utilize the best female thinkers; their inexperience in asserting themselves collectively and their use of male rather than female models of "greatness" inhibited women of brilliance. Neglecting the "social significance" of the creative act, which for Austin meant its gender-specific nature, female audiences could thus be "intellectually imposed upon" by men. Thus the failure of female intellectuals as a class to gain recognition was not only a fault of male bias and exclusion. It was a "humiliating admission" for so confirmed a feminist as herself to make, Austin declared, but the women's movement had done little to support its geniuses.[19] No doubt she had herself in mind.

In spite of her interest in the subject, Austin's writings about women's genius remain fragmentary and inconsistent. Sometimes she proclaimed the existence of an intellect or vision specifically given to women, a special kind of creativity aligned with intuition. In other writings, however, she came close to defining genius as an attribute, in the highest instances, of men. Her contradictory views on the subject of women's intelligence reflect the persistence in her thought of a series of unresolved dualities not only between gender opposites but also between heredity and environment, communalism and individualism, science and religion, progress and stasis. Unable to sustain a unified vision, she alternated or uncomfortably blended polar explanations, privileging one or another of her categories while suppressing the importance of its opposite.

"[It] is the woman's habit to *think the next thing* which enables women to keep their opinions in a continuous state of mobilization without any suspicion of inconsistency," Austin wrote on one occasion. "This capacity for intuitive judgment . . . is what women have to stand on squarely; not their ability to see the world in the way men see it, but the importance and validity of their seeing it some other way."[20]

Austin compared such a female intellectual process based on intuition to male-oriented scientific research and theory building and the prevailing ethos of "objectivity." While writing her book *The American Rhythm*, published in 1923, she admitted to a friend that "what I am really interested in isn't the theory of rhythm, but being able to experience rhythm in all its varieties." Nor did she care about "scientific confirmation. I am going through the paces of that merely out of consideration for the number of people who won't be able to discover what I am talking about unless I drag them over the rocky road of laboratory experiment. . . . But I got to that place on wings of pure delight."[21]

In her autobiography, describing herself in the third person, she further elaborated her processes of insight:

> She would be looking at something that all the world could see, had seen, without being stirred by it, and suddenly, from deep down, there would come a fountain jet of recognition. . . . Without apparently having any choice about it, progress has meant for her a series of forward flashes, long spells of concentrated observation, patient, even anguished inquiry, and suddenly thunder, lightning, rainbow, and the sound of wings.[22]

Despite her condemnation of "male-think" and her privileging of women's intuitive powers, Austin was a careful, if naturalistic, scientific observer. Whereas several critics attacked her work as unscientific and suggestive, others praised the detailed research in her books. In some of her writings Austin specifically recognized science as a helpmeet to women's intellectual ambitions.[23]

Moreover, Austin could become deeply offended if her writings were labeled "feminine" or "intuitive." One of the critics who drew her deepest ire was Lewis Mumford, who in his *New Republic* review of *The American Rhythm* focused on the "authentic intuitions" of Austin's thesis, which, however, he judged as "important," "vigorous," and "wise," even if unproved.[24] Furious, Austin dashed off an angry letter to the *New Republic*, which likened Mumford's criticisms to those of other New York intellectuals who believed that her nonfiction was "a series of intuitions, interesting and arresting feminine guesses, which happen amazingly now and then to be right." Angrily, although she did not identify female thought as intuitive, she expressed her conviction that a female (or "feminine," as she called it) intellectual style, however different from those of critics of a "markedly masculine" journal like the *New Republic*, must be respected.

"I have unreservedly committed myself to the feminine approach," Austin wrote. "I express myself as freely and as definitely in my literary medium, as I do in my social life, as a woman," she added.

> I have always believed that there is a distinctly feminine approach to intellectual problems, and its recognition is indispensible [*sic*] to intellectual wholeness. All that I have ever, as a feminist, protested against, is the prevailing notion that the feminine is necessarily an inferior approach. The fact that most intellectuals of today are theoretically deminists [*sic*], blinds them and us to the probability that subconsciously their judgments are affected by the traditional masculine reaction against the method of the feminine mind.[25]

Two years later, however, in her book on the subject of genius, Austin's identification of a peculiarly female approach to creativity had evaporated. The title of the book, *Everyman's Genius*, which Austin intended to express the democratization of talent and creativity she thought possible, also conveyed the loss of the female-identified quality she had written about 13 years earlier in her novel *A Woman of Genius* and in her essays on women's intellectual life in the early twenties.[26]

Everyman's Genius comments only in passing about gender differences in creativity, although it comments in detail about the characteristics of genius. In Austin's view, genius is racial and evolutionary: "It consists solely in the capacity to make use of inherited psychic material."[27] Lying below the immediate consciousness, creative genius was a product of the liberated "deep-self," whose potential derived from ancestral qualities. Thus genius combined both "inheritance" and "instrumentality": though rooted in hereditary material, it flourished only when "self-originating." Austin argued, therefore, that genius could be acquired; it was the "normal possession of all human beings not actually defective."[28]

Though Austin's description of the creative process attempts to meld heredity with self-determining environmental initiatives, she often emphasizes the former rather than the latter. This reliance on the importance of heredity narrowed Austin's analysis of women's potential and illustrates how Austin succumbed to the biological reductionism inherent in her earlier notions of female intellectuality. In *Everyman's Genius,* Austin declares that men had "more exceptionally differentiated" talents than women in such areas as music, sculpture, mathematics, poetry, and art, since talent expressed individual variations, and men varied more than women. But she observed that genius, defined as a racial, subconscious, and "subjective" quality, was more generally the possession of women than of men.[29] Still, she argues that "the greatest genius of them all, and the best endowed, will more than likely be a man," since women, closer to the business of "race continuation," must restrict their activities (which inevitably narrows their variation).[30]

Although Austin has been justly celebrated for her substantial contributions as an environmentalist who played a leading role in promoting Hispanic and Native American cultures of the West and Southwest and as a feminist who helped redefine the male pioneer tradition, her racialism marred her philosophic and programmatic support of cultural and gender diversity.[31] Her fiction and essays refer frequently and bluntly to characters with Semitic and black "bloodstreams," for example, to which inheritance she often attributed their actions, passions, and thought. Austin's view of women's intelligence and genius as consequences of their "racial" (by which she usually means biological) endowment subjects them to similar stereotypical treatment. "Feminine talents follow racial exigencies more than men," she insists.[32]

By the time she published *Everyman's Genius* in 1925, Austin apparently ceased to believe that "woman culture" could be a viable alternative to the hegemony of male thought. After 1924, when she left residences in New York and California to move to Santa Fe, New Mexico, her attacks against the hierarchies of cultural privilege no longer focused on women but on "folkness." In her lectures and essays she celebrated local and regional artistic, social, and political forms, arguing that indigenous culture, springing naturally from the American environment, was far superior to the imported elitism of metropolitan life.[33] Her support for native culture was practical as well as polemical: she played a leading role in preserving the arts and handicrafts of the Southwest and in 1927 served as a representative to the Seven States Conference on questions of water diversion.[34]

Yet Austin's celebration of folk democracy also had its limits. Although she praised Pueblo communities, for example, for a communalism superior to Fabian or American socialism, she argued that the Pueblos' submergence of individuality caused their economic, if not cultural, backwardness. In spite of her enthusiasm for the cultures of everyday life, she could not entirely quell her admiration for the American spirit of enterprise, which she found lacking in the Native American communities she most revered.

As she found herself drawn to the very traditions of science, technology, and material progress she often berated, so too her championship of folk over elite traditions occasionally faltered. Austin's identification with lowbrow rather than highbrow culture highlighted her estrangement from the scions of literary and academic society and provided her with "prophetic" vision, as she put it, allowing her to recognize the true merits of creative efforts ignored by others. She was one of the first critics, for example, to exalt what she called the "home-centric" literature of Harriet Beecher Stowe and other nineteenth-century female writers. Women were the first to feel that Americanism was a "thing of the heart," she claimed, and they were the first to write about the experiences of men and women in daily life. Thus the first real American literature was crafted by women, not by male artists like Cooper and Melville, who, concerned more with mastering the environment than in understanding its influence, applied old, worn-out patterns of the "chase, the hunt and pursuit" in their works.[35]

But sometimes Austin allied herself with the "high-brows" against the common folk she extolled. In 1926 she campaigned vigorously against the establishment of a chautauqua in Sante Fe by the local women's club, arguing that the cultural standards of the community, and the work of its artists and writers, would inevitably be compromised by the low aesthetic tastes of the club women and the speakers they might import into town.[36] Couching her protest in terms of local culture fighting domination from outsiders, Austin nevertheless showed her disapproval of the small-town "woman culture" she had never really liked. Siding with creative artists rather than popularizers, with insiders against outsiders, with men against women, in this instance she repudiated her trust in the "folk," and in women, as cultural innovators and sources of artistic and intellectual integrity.

Mary Beard: Woman's "Latent Genius" and the Rise of a New American Mind

Although a number of Austin's early essays and fiction focused on the problem of the creative or intellectual woman, Mary Beard's first work on women explored their practical achievements. Her book *Women's Work in Municipalities* (1915), an exhaustive compendium of the work of female social reformers and volunteer activists, remains one of the best analyses of women's accomplishments during the Progressive period. Active in the suffrage campaign, Beard was a staunch supporter of the militant Congressional Union (later the Woman's Party), led by Alice Paul. Beard's support for the Woman's Party waned in the 1920s when it promoted the passage of the Equal Rights Amendment, which Beard opposed, advocating protective legislation for women instead. She wrote little about women during the 1920s, accompanying her husband on travels abroad, but worked with him to produce the two-volume *The Rise of American Civilization* (1927), the most acclaimed of their works on American history.[37]

Beard turned her attention to analysis of America's intellectual women in an article for the American Academy of Political and Social Science's 1929 volume, *Women in the Modern World.* Writing on "American Women and the Printing Press," Beard expressed her dismay at the low output of books by women, despite what she claimed was an open press, and at the fact that so few women's works addressed themselves to serious subjects, especially theory. In her view, the greatest modern thinkers continued to be men. This was not because women lacked access to education, experience, a tradition of writing, or publishing outlets. "Precedents for feminine self-expression" ran back through the ages, she claimed, and American women were particularly privileged regarding opportunities for both informal and formal education and for active participation in American life, which was a prelude to social thought. Furthermore, the literary market was

> greedy for material. The field is free and open to the sexes alike. There was never a time when an excellent manuscript was so little in peril of being refused. Publishers were never so eager for artistry, for freshness of view, for originality, for scholarship, for the findings of experience, for wisdom, for speculation of every sort.

If women were underrepresented in the "elaborate series of social, literary and scientific works, prepared by 'experts,' " and in works of theory, it was not, then, because of discrimination.[38]

"Has the printing press forced out fine latent genius?" Beard asked.

> Have [women] looked at their age in the large and tried to project the future? Or are they mainly concerned with the immediate and the transient? . . . Are there professional thinkers in the sex?[39]

Beard's response to these questions about women's genius begins with a catalog of modern American female writers, grouped according to class background. Women of the leisure class generally remain "languorists or motorists instead of becoming thinkers," with such prominent exceptions as Jane Addams and Edith Wharton, she suggests.[40] "Semi-leisured" women have occasionally become professional writers, particularly biographers; Beard cites numerous writing wives who chose as the subject of their biographies men modeled after their own husbands. She also names other "faculty wives" and "wives of professional men" who, though not of the leisure class, wrote "moral and religious tales, juveniles, sketches, novels, translations, hymns and fantasies" for "pin money"; only some of their work is competent.[41] Beard concludes this class analysis of female thinkers, which she links so closely to marital status, by citing the travel accounts of "wives who move the world over with adventuring husbands" and those of other, single women.[42]

Without reference to background, Beard goes on to discuss other characteristic writing by American women. She mentions the "local color" fiction of Sarah Orne Jewett, Willa Cather, Zona Gale,

Ruth Suckow, and Fannie Hurst, the latter two for their glimpses into "lowlier humanity" and "Hebraic kindred"; describes "agitation literature" penned by Frances Willard, Carrie Chapman Catt, Mary Heaton Vorse, and Charlotte Perkins Gilman; the "freedom" songs and poems of Dorothy Parker and Edna St. Vincent Millay; and other important *belles lettres*. The achievements of academic women, however, are ignored.

Concluding the survey, Beard pronounces judgment: with rare exceptions, she finds, "American women think for the masses, about immediate movements, and as a consequence of concepts of democracy."

> A part of the equalitarian, libertarian, modern age, with its mass strivings and aspirations, women have labored with their pens to deliver messages to the wide public, paint warm portraits of their countryfolk and their interests, reveal social realities and suggest reforms, provide students with equipment for the higher literacy, help the Americans make up their cultural lag, and emphasize the function of the female in civilization.

She is ambivalent, however, about the significance of this fact. Though she does not impugn women for anti-intellectualism, as male critics often did, she asserts that the charge of one critic that "idle curiosity and speculation divorced from utility play so scant a role in our Letters" is particularly applicable to women's writings. On the other hand, she acknowledges that the democratic aspect of female literature—the "natural and healthy expression of the people, by the people, for the people"—has been "no mean accomplishment."[43]

Beard tries to visualize this "democracy thinking of itself, and talking to itself" by conjuring up a "modernized Canterbury procession" of American penwomen of the last 300 years, including "women teachers, preachers, doctors, psychoanalysts, actresses, librarians, civil servants, lawyers, missionaries, nurses, social workers, and explorers."[44] Even if Beard herself seemed unconvinced of its enduring critical qualities, her description provides an insightful glimpse into the variety and novelty of the intellectual work of American women.

Female authors tell us, she writes,

> how they have tried to stimulate romanticism among juveniles, hitherto restricted to tales of war and death; enlarge parental culture; prepare the materials for teaching in the departments of history, art, literature, science, religion, music, pedagogy and psychology; guide the masses through the mazes of religious mysticism . . . ; excavate and observe in classical lands, Mexico and the Orient . . . ; bring a knowledge of the races of man up to date by means of contemporary data; depict the stage in its evolving molds; describe the "see-saw" of politics at Washington; . . . inject medical opinions into homes, church and state; advance legal concepts and ethics; work social changes particularly affecting sex and youth; promote enthusiasm for science through treatises on plants and animals, chemistry, microscopy and sanitation; render aid in the process of orientating industrial classes into the art and learning of the masters . . . ; explain insurgency in art and literature; discuss the century of the woman and the child with a new understanding born of modern conditions and recent theory; pass out improved first aides to homemakers; submit to the printed forum matters they have dealt with on the platform, such as art, sex, literature, music, travel, science, man, woman and manners.[45]

In addition to these diverse and rather "solemn reports of social obligation and responsibility," Beard lists some of the "democratic vagaries and transgressions" that also characterize American women's writings:

> Lilts of rhyme as a woman longs for the quiet countryside, when urban public health binds her to city pavements, confessional revelations of how business women look on business men; how it feels to be a woman of fifty after one has toiled so hard to know what eight million working women want.[46]

Ultimately, however, the issue for Beard is not whether American women write solemnly or humorously enough of immediate, practical, everyday "democratic" life but whether they provide "wide-ranging sweeps of philosophical and critical fancy."[47] This question she must answer in the negative: none of women's expressions "resembles or approaches Aristotelian thinking . . . Platonic philosophy . . . German idealism . . . Ruskinian satire . . . Carlylean rage . . . Voltairean analysis . . . or a Buckle synthesis."[48] Beard gingerly assures readers that this is not necessarily because women possess a "second-rate quality of brain" and offers several reasons for women's absence from critical theory. First, perhaps they have been too involved with "making democracy vocal, democratic and intelligent about itself" to have time for the "sweeps of philosophical and critical fancy with views of humanity and life universally considered"; second, the curiosity necessary for philosophical thought may not be "idle" at all but a "professional" pastime (from which she implies women may be excluded); third, even abstract logic in the masculine mode is not "detached" from life but a part of it; indeed, "politics lies at the core of [the] broadest generalizations" of male philosophers. Thus, women, long at the periphery of politics, not at its heart, tended to write of the practical rather than political concerns of philosophy, embroidering their thought not with the "principles and laws of aesthetics—standards of the sublime and the beautiful, differentiations between good and evil, speculations with regard to the transient and the permanent"—but with "romanticism, movement, and personalities."[49]

As Ann J. Lane has pointed out, the elusive quality of Beard's discussion of woman as thinker in this and other essays arises from the contradictory impulses that characterize many of Beard's works about women.[50] Caught between a premise that emphasizes women's agency in history and denies the force of discrimination against them and her erstwhile recognition of women's marginality in society, Beard praises their intellectual achievements while lamenting their deficiencies in comparison with men's. At the outset of the essay she notes, for example, that women had not "that combination of learning and wisdom which makes them authoritative" in "social, literary, and scientific" fields. Even in such areas as the family, where they should be "expert," men had done the "big work" of thinking. Women "may write gracefully," she acknowledges, "but they are apt to think too gracefully as well."[51] By the end of the article, however, having set forth on a pilgrimage to "see" women writers and their work, she is more convinced of their achievements and puts forth the names of four women whose contributions to philosophy seemed worthy of the best male efforts: Elizabeth Kemper Adams, Mary Follet, Ethel Puffer, and Katherine Gilbert. Beard praises Adams's doctoral thesis for relating aesthetic experience to its "functional relation with immediate working experience," and she admires her challenge to traditional male thought.

> Believing, however brashly, that the last words, law and reasoning have not been established, even by masculine minds as yet, Dr. Adams puts fresh queries and helps to launch American feminism on its task of thinking.[52]

"If the heights of reasoning, as heights have hitherto been defined, are to be ultimately attained by American women, they will be reached only through the avenue of experience," she observes. Because the work of Adams and the other women Beard names suggest an experiential focus, they thus represent "an advance from the periphery, to the center of fields deep plowed by men."[53] At the end of her pilgrimage she is thus able to acknowledge that perhaps there need not be a gulf between the experiential, personal, subjective worlds of women's writing and the "composite wholes" that have dominated systems of abstract thought defined by men.

As women increasingly moved into the mainstreams of political and social life, Beard concludes, they would find "more to think and to say."

> Thus the age of the machine, democracy, and feminism promises to call forth something supplementary to or critical of the systems of philosophy hitherto erected, mainly by men.[54]

It is the future rather than the past that gives Beard hope that women as thinkers might redefine "the heights of reasoning" and transcend the "gossip, song, story, and the incident of the hour" that occupied much of their current thought. Her optimism about the progressive outline of women's advance in American society finally convinces her that there will be material enough in women's experiences for "the making of a new mind" in "the very heart of the latest society's novel energies."[55] Thus her essay ends with the promise of joining heart and mind, politics and philosophy, experience and logic in a new feminine construction of knowledge. Beard's writings on women in the 1930s and 1940s—*On Understanding Women* (1931), *America Through Women's Eyes* (1933), *Laughing Their Way* (1934), and *Women as Force in History* (1946)—and her work to establish a World Center of Women's Archives redeemed this promise. In these works women find their voices, and they are not voices of the "composite whole" but of multiplicity, detail, and experience. Although Beard has not fully reconciled thought and experience, literature and history in her essay on "American Women and the Printing Press," the promenade of female literary pilgrims she sketches in this essay apparently helped her to imagine such a possibility.

❧

Like many male critics and other female writers of their generation, Austin and Beard did not fully recognize the significance of the cultural and theoretical contributions of female intellectuals, several of whom had made powerful and visible contributions to social thought. Yet each hinted at a potentially powerful female intellectual style alternative to the dominant impulses of male theorists.

Austin never completely resolved the question of whether there was, or should be, a female intellectual tradition, separate from men's, founded on intuition and subjectivity. While she excoriated male-oriented styles of logic, science, and rationality, she simultaneously envied the masculine world of knowledge and high culture from which she often felt barred. In some of her writings she promoted a real alternative to this tradition, championing women's clubs as a source of brilliant executive organizing and accomplishment and praising women's magazines for their empowerment of female writers and women's point of view.

In her autobiography, written in the 1930s, and several books on religion, Austin went farther, denying objectivity as a desideratum and identifying female thought with a mystical search for self.[56] Along with her self-proclamation as a "female" thinker and her mysticism, Austin's egocentrism pushed her to the periphery of American cultural life, even though a few critics proclaimed her brilliance. As an outsider (she preferred to call herself "prophetess" or "seer"), she was especially prescient in her recognition of the importance of female writers and in her analysis of the ways in which literary and academic marketplaces discriminated against female intellectuals. Ultimately, however, she took up the defense of Native Americans rather than women and did not develop her theoretical understanding of women's intellectual work.[57] Austin also tended to use gender not as a fluid, historical category but one that was mired in an artificial, oppositional framework linked to racial and cultural dichotomies. Her insights about women's talents and genius were freshest when they examined the specific conditions that hindered or promoted women's intellectualism. But when she focused on women as a symbolic group, outside of history, she gave voice to ideological simplifications that linked gender stereotypes to those of race and class. In the end, Austin fell victim to the ritualistic, categorical thinking with which she charged her opponents.

Like Austin's novels and essays, Beard's writings about women seemed to grow increasingly weird, as Nancy Cott once put it, after Beard's own formulation.[58] Cott and Ann J. Lane find greater continuity in Beard's developing views about women in history than does Bonnie G. Smith, who argues that in the 1930s Beard began to write an "unrule-y" kind of history based on multiple points of view and multiple voices, a history that "broke with all that had gone before."[59]

Beard's writings on the female mind in 1929 suggest a midway point between her first writings on women, which emphasized their constructive activities in the social and political spheres, and her later work, which highlighted women's contributions to cultural life and history more broadly. By 1929, Beard had begun to "see" the parade of American female writers and thinkers but not to acknowledge that their "democratic" writing equalled in importance the grand theories of the masters. Yet in her long list of the subjects of female writers—among them studies of other cultures, of women, and of children, practical medical and scientific advice for homemakers, the education of parents, and the preparation of teaching materials in schools—she documents a meaningful, if inchoate, intellectual tradition different from men's. In framing the outlines of this tradition, she set the stage for a series of later works that would place women at the very center of historical change.

It is ironic, however, that one of the four women Beard praises for richness of philosophic thought, Ethel Puffer, had written her philosophical works more than two decades earlier, when she was single. After her marriage to Benjamin Howes and the birth of two children, Ethel Puffer Howes was unable to secure an academic job or to find the time to do philosophy. Throughout the 1920s she spent her energies writing popular articles that eschewed that "vicious alternative—marriage or career" and created the Institute for the Coordination of Women's Interests at Smith College to help wives and mothers balance family responsibilities with continued intellectual growth.[60] Of the other women who received their Ph.D.'s in philosophy from Harvard during the first decades of the twentieth century, none of those who married found teaching positions.[61] We can presume that, like Howes, they found little opportunity to practice their craft and "write" philosophy.

Beard's virtual neglect of the personal and institutional discrimination faced by educated women in the 1920s suggests that she did not fully acknowledge the privileges her own background conferred or the linkages between gender, class, and power that shaped the careers of intellectual women generally.[62] A lecturer, activist, and writer working outside academia, Beard's marriage to a leading intellectual historian gained her the entitlement to write, as Charles's coauthor, the "wide-ranging sweeps of philosophical and critical fancy" that she believed most female thinkers neglected.[63] That Beard's class analysis of female writers in "Women and the Printing Press" so greatly overlapped with her subjects' marital status implicitly reveals this debt. While together the Beards were describing the "Rise of American Civilization"—a favorite topic of male sociologists, political scientists, and philosophers in the 1920s—female scholars generally gave their attention to much less cosmic, more practical subjects. In marked contrast to the theoretical explorations of culture undertaken by leading male theorists in the *American Sociological Review,* for example, articles by female authors in the 1920s emphasize experiential first-person accounts; studies of ethnic, class, racial, and regional phenomena; or other aspects of applied sociology and social work.[64] Beard acknowledged these disparate themes, but she did not fully recognize that women's seeming inability to write grand theory came at least as much from their exclusion from professional, institutional, and personal arenas that privileged such endeavors as from individual predilection. Nor did she challenge the universality of the great systems of logic constructed by men.

Finally, Beard ignored the achievements of many academic women, usually trained by men, who had authored important studies of social, cultural, and political life. For example, she does not mention Edith Abbott, author of the broad historical study *Women in Industry* (1908); nor Helen Lynd, coauthor with her husband

Robert of *Middletown* (1926), the comprehensive and widely read community study of Muncie, Indiana; nor Margaret Mead, whose pioneering first work, *Coming of Age in Samoa* (1928), an exploration of the cultural determinants of adolescence in Samoa, became an immediate popular and critical success. Despite their wide-ranging contexts, Beard might not have considered these studies "big works" of "philosophical . . . fancy" because they were empirically based. Furthermore, as a nonacademic intellectual who wrote for the general public, she like Austin stood outside the major research centers that had trained Abbott, Lynd, Mead, and other scholarly women. At a time when the new research university, with its professionally trained knowledge seekers, had come to dominate social inquiry, Beard and Austin, rooted in an earlier tradition, seemed unable to recognize and credit the academy as a locus for intellectual women's work.

Beard's suggestion that women's philosophical abilities and perceptions might follow the course of their changing social experience nevertheless hints at a deeper understanding of the relationship of knowledge to social reality. As the actual material and political bases of their lives altered, she believed that women might create "something supplementary to or critical of the system of philosophy hitherto erected, mainly by men," Beard observes at the conclusion of her 1929 essay. The making of a new, presumably feminist, mind would be a consequence of changing lives.

As Beard would focus her attention in coming decades on representing the multiple voices of women in history, so in the 1920s many of her compatriots were already bearing witness to the changing role of American women as thinkers and authors. Their writings not only document the multiplicity of women's activities in the world but also illuminate the beginnings of that "new mind" that Beard prophesied. Though Beard's own Canterbury parade of female authors omitted some of the most original of these thinkers, by mid-decade they were making their presence felt in literature, the arts, and the social sciences. Space permits only a few illustrations of their work.

In psychology, for example, analyst Beatrice Hinkle, arguing that Freud's most important concepts "had absolutely nothing to do with women or girl children," offered a full-scale revision of psychoanalysis. Hinkle emphasized the social context of both male and female psychology and substituted bisexuality in all humans for biologically determined masculinity and femininity.[65]

In literature, Gertrude Stein's radical experimentation with subjective narrative challenged the relationship of language to knowledge and to art, providing culturally alternative modes of literary meaning. Although she celebrated the immediate, spontaneous flow of language, Stein was also a "literary theoretician," as one recent critic puts it, combining the "linear as well as pluri-dimensional; 'male,' as well as 'female.'"[66]

In drama, Susan Glaspell, cofounder and director of the experimental Provincetown Theater, rebeled against conventional dramatic form and language in a series of plays (most importantly, *The Inheritors* and *The Verge*, produced in 1921, and *Alison's House*, which won the Pulitzer Prize in 1930). Hailed by critics for her sensitive handling of feelings and her integration of private and public themes, Glaspell was considered to be a playwright of "ideas" and "intellectual prowess"—one called her "the woman of thought"—who pioneered the development of the modern theatre.[67]

Constance Rourke was another pioneer of American culture: the two books she published in the late twenties and her classic *American Humor: A Study of the National Character*, which appeared in 1931, paved the way for the exploration of popular culture as a major aspect of literary and anthropological research. Like Austin, she celebrated folk art, theatre, craftsmanship, and music: her great goal was to reconcile lowbrow and highbrow, region and nation, in a comprehensive reconstruction of the native roots of American culture.[68]

By the mid- and late twenties, under the guidance of Franz Boas at Columbia University, Ruth Benedict and Margaret Mead had begun to publish new kinds of anthropological studies that emphasized cultural differences rather than unities and challenged traditional alignments of gender and social forms. Bringing their own experiences and values as self-consciously independent, female social scientists to their work, each combined subjective and objective modes of research, self, and culture, or what some critics have named "feminine" and "masculine" approaches.[69]

In addition to this group of pioneers and others named by Beard, the work of Emily Greene Balch, Sophinsba Breckinridge,

Crystal Eastman, Alice Duer Miller, Elsie Clew Parsons, Suzanne LaFollette, Alice Beals Parson, Lorinne Pruette, Anna Garlin Spencer, Katherine Fullerton Gerould, Alyse Gregory, and Willistyne Goodsell, among others, suggests the richness of social thought, essays, and criticism crafted by women in the post-suffrage period. In fiction, such writers as Edna Ferber, Anzia Yezierska, Dorothy West, Zora Neale Hurston, and Nella Larsen produced a body of literature marked by major stylistic innovations and differences from men's texts in regard to narrative distance, voice, and plot.[70]

To claim that all these thinking women reflected Beard's "new mind" or what Austin called a "female intellectual style" goes beyond available analyses of women's writing in this period. Yet collectively the works of many female writers—including those of Austin and Beard themselves—do suggest a divergence from increasingly dominant modes of intellectual inquiry gaining ascendancy in the interwar years. Their experiential focus, new ways of thinking about values and action, and breakdown of subject-object dualisms allied them with John Dewey and other "radical" theorists of knowledge, as James Kloppenberg has termed them, who emphasized the importance of subjectivity, the limits of rationality, and the grounding of truth in experience. While these philosophers had wide influence during the Progressive period, increasingly after 1920 objectivism, or scientism—celebrating hard facts and rigorous, value-free, empirical, quantifiable methods—conquered the domains of social sciences, philosophy, and educational research.[71] Dewey's more relativistic, contextural, and experimental approach to knowledge survived only in selected outposts.[72]

In art and literature, similarly, many new female writers did not gain wide cultural acceptance. While Gertrude Stein, Marianne Moore, and others contributed markedly to the modernist revolution, they did not enjoy great popular success and were viewed warily by critics. Writers like Fannie Hurst who gained huge popular audiences for their works also drew hostile reviews from critics. Beginning in the late 1920s, moreover, as American literature became increasingly professionalized through the establishment of professional journals, graduate programs, and the publication of literary histories, a literary canon was codified that systematically overlooked or excluded female writers.[73]

The fact that many (though not all) female intellectuals in the postsuffrage years stood outside the mainstream of academic, social science, and literary culture enhanced their proclivity to develop innovative, nonhegemonic perspectives. Yet their isolation from the centers of cultural power also limited their recognition and influence.

Inconsistencies in the views of both Austin and Beard about the work of female intellectuals suggests that in the absence of a critical theory that consistently acknowledged the link between privilege and creativity, even the most daring feminist minds could sometimes subsume their visions to the standards of male cultural custodians. The perpetuation of male myths of genius and intellectual achievement denied women their full originality and masked the problems faced by the very real female geniuses of the period (including Austin and Beard themselves)—disparities of power, institutional discrimination, irreconcilable conflicts between creativity and family life, the dominance of male-oriented philosophical systems, and the neglect or hostility of the critical establishment.[74] Women had not equalled the performance of men as thinkers and artists, Rebecca West agreed in the symposium *Women's Coming of Age,* but, she continued drolly, "It is obviously difficult to work when one is constantly being bitten by mosquitoes in the form of criticisms of the female sex in general."[75]

Nevertheless, by the end of the 1920s it was clear that despite the massive cultural anxieties of the decade and the empowerment of a new generation of male intellectuals expert in the construction, organization, and communication of knowledge in which many women did not share, the voices of female writers would not be stilled.[76] In tandem with Beard's premonition about the making of a "new" American mind, in England Virginia Woolf and Rebecca West imagined that the emergence of an extraordinary new talent—a female Shakespeare—might not be a too-distant possibility. Yet "if there were ever to be a woman Shakespeare . . . [or] a woman Dante . . . both alike would seem to men, gross, dangerous, hostile to the one and only truth," West predicted.[77] Her response to that eventuality remains salient today: "Women must learn to go on their way without caring overmuch for the judgments passed on their work by men."[78]

Notes

1. Patricia Albjerg Graham, "Expansion and Exclusion: A History of Women in American Higher Education," *Signs* 3 (Summer 1978), 764–65.
2. Marion O. Hawthorne, "Women and College Teachers," and Willystine Goodsell, "The Educational Opportunities of American Women—Theoretical and Actual," in *Women in the Modern World, Annals of the American Academy of Political and Social Science* CXLIII (May 1929), 146–54, 1–13. Also see Institute of Women's Professional Relations, *Women and the Ph.D.* (Greensboro, N.C., 1930).
3. On the role of female social scientists in challenging Victorian assumptions about women's mental capacities, see Rosalind Rosenberg, *Beyond Separate Spheres: Intellectual Roots of Modern Feminism* (New Haven, 1982). For thorough analyses of particular groups of female intellectuals, see Ellen Fitzpatrick, *Endless Crusade: Women Social Scientists and Progressive Reform* (New York, 1990) and Margaret Rossiter, *Women Scientists in America* (Baltimore, 1982).
4. For a provocative interpretation of the paradoxes of feminism in the 1920s, see Nancy Cott, *The Grounding of Modern Feminism* (New Haven, Conn., 1987). Dorothy Brown offers a broad survey of women's cultural experiences in the 1920s in *Setting A Course: American Women in the 1920s* (Boston, 1987).
5. The book was published by Walter Scott (London, 1894).
6. See for example Karl Pearson, *The Chances of Death and Other Studies in Evolution,* vol. 1 (London, 1897); Helen Montague and Leta Hollingworth, "The Comparative Variability of the Sexes at Birth," *American Journal of Sociology* 20 (1914–15), 335–70; and Hollingworth, "Variability as Related to Sex Differences in Achievement," *American Journal of Sociology* 19 (January 1914), 510–30. On the history of the variability controversy, see Stephanie A. Shields, "The Variability Hypothesis: The History of a Biological Model of Sex Differences in Intelligence," in Sandra Harding and Jean F. O'Barr, eds., *Sex and Scientific Inquiry* (Chicago, 1987), 186–215.
7. Huntington Cairns, "The Woman of Genius," in Samuel D. Schmalhausen and V.F. Calverton, eds., *Woman's Coming of Age* (New York, 1931), 395.
8. Ramsey Traquair, "Women and Civilization," *Atlantic Monthly* 132 (September 1923), 291, 296. Also see Alexander Goldenweiser, "Man and Woman as Creators," in Freda Kirchwey, ed., *Our Changing Morality* (New York, 1924), 129–43. Goldenweiser, a psychologist and anthropologist allied with the circle of progressive social scientists at the New School, argued that woman "has failed, in comparison with man, in the highest ranges of abstract creativeness. On the other hand, woman has shown in her psychic disposition affinities for the concrete, the technical, and the human" (p. 141).
9. Joseph Hergesheimer, "The Feminine Nuisance in Literature," *Yale Review* 10 (July 1921), 718, 725. See the response of Frances Noyes Hart, "The Feminine Nuisance Replies," *Bookman* 54 (September 1921), 31–34. Also see

Clemence Dance, "The Feminine of Genius," *Yale Review* 13 (July 1924), 684–89, and in reply, Edna Davis Romig, "Men As Mothers," *Yale Review* 14 (January 1925), 414–16. Popular articles that addressed questions of women's intelligence include Corinne Lowe, "Why Do Good Women Read Bad Books?" *Pictorial Review* 28 (1927), 15–16; "Do Women Lose Power to Think Earlier than Men," *Literary Digest* XCV (December 3, 1927), 8–9, 67–70, 74–75.

10. Among the feminists who disputed the idea that women lacked genius were Sylvia Kopald, "Where Are the Female Geniuses?" in Freda Kirchwey, ed., *Our Changing Morality* (New York, 1924), 107–26; and Alice Beal Parsons, "Sex and Genius," *Yale Review* 14 (July 1925), 739–52.

11. For biographical material on Mary Austin, see Esther Lanigan Stineman, *Mary Austin: Song of a Maverick* (New Haven, Conn., 1989); Augusta Fink, *I-Mary: A Biography of Mary Austin* (Tucson, Ariz., 1983); Thomas Matthews Pearce, *Literary America 1903–1934, the Mary Austin Letters* (Westport, Conn., 1979), *Mary Hunter Austin* (Boston, 1965), and *The Beloved House* (Caldwell, Id., 1940); Thurman Wilkins, "Mary Austin," in Edward James and Janet Wilson James, eds., *Notable American Women* I (Cambridge, Mass., 1971), 67–69; and Helen MacKnight Doyle, *Mary Austin: Woman of Genius* (New York, 1939).

    Critical studies of Austin include Dudley Wynn, "A Critical Study of the Writings of Mary Hunter Austin, 1868–1934" (Ph.D. diss., New York University, 1939) and Rae Galbraith Ballard, "Mary Austin's *Earth Horizon:* The Imperfect Circle" (Ph.D. diss., Claremont Graduate School, 1977). Henry Smith's "The Feel of the Purposeful Earth: Mary Austin's Prophecy," *New Mexico Quarterly* 1 (February 1931), 17–33, is of special interest.

12. Mary Austin, "American Women and Intellectual Life," *Bookman* 53 (August 1921), 481.

13. Ibid., 484.

14. Ibid., 483.

15. Ibid., 482–83.

16. "Woman Sees Steel," *Bookman* 53 (August 1921), 81–82 (review of Mary Heaton Vorse's *Men and Steel*).

17. Ibid.

18. Austin, "American Women and the Intellectual Life," 484–485.

19. Austin, "Women as Audience," *Bookman* 55 (March 1922), 1. Also see Austin, "Greatness in Women," *North American Review* (February 1923), 197–203.

20. Austin, *The Woman Citizen* (New York, 1918), 19.

21. Cited in Fink, *I-Mary,* 202. Austin boasts that she didn't take a single note while journeying 2500 miles to write *The Land of Journey's Ending,* considered one of her finest works. See Austin, *Everyman's Genius* (Indianapolis, 1925), 229–30.

22. Austin, *Earth Horizon* (New York, 1932), 217.

23. Austin's view that a feminine approach written "in terms of the common experience" was more accessible but not necessarily less factual than the accepted scholarly way found unexpected support years later in a discussion of her book *The Man Jesus* (New York, 1915.) According to one specialist, the book managed to convey the exact physiographic qualities of Palestine without Austin's having been there. See remarks of Edgar L. Hewitt, in Houghland, ed., *Mary Austin: A Memorial*, cited in Inez Tingley Thoroughgood, "Mary Hunter Austin: Interpreter of the Western Scene, 1888–1906" (Master's thesis, UCLA, 1950), 123–26.
24. See Mumford's review of *The American Rhythm* in *The New Republic*, May 30, 1923, 23–24.
25. Mary Austin Papers, Huntington Library, San Marino, California.
26. *Everyman's Genius* supplemented Austin's 10 articles on the subject of genius for the *Bookman* with additional essays and interviews with or statements from 14 creative geniuses, including 4 women: novelist Fanny Hurst, poet Marianne Moore, and dancers Bertha Wardell and Dorothy S. Lyndall.
27. Austin, *Everyman's Genius*, 258, 287.
28. Ibid., 266.
29. Ibid., 254, 262.
30. Ibid., 254–55. Leta Hollingworth made a similar argument some years earlier when she noted "the established, obvious, inescapable fact that women bear and rear children" helped to explain women's lesser eminence. See Leta Hollingworth and Helen Montague, "The Comparative Variability of the Sexes at Birth," *American Journal of Sociology* 20 (November 1914), 335–70, 528. Cited in Rosenberg, *Beyond Separate Spheres*, 101–2.
31. On Austin's contributions to the culture of the Southwest, see Vera Norwood, "The Photographer and the Naturalist: Laura Gilpin and Mary Austin in the Southwest," *Journal of American Culture* 5 (Winter 1982), 1–27; Norwood, "Heroines of Nature: Four Women Respond to the American Landscape," in *Environmental Review* 8 (Spring 1984), 34–56; and Lois Rudnick, "Renaming the Land: Anglo Expatriate Women in the Southwest," in Vera Norwood and Janice Monk, eds., *The Desert Is No Lady* (New Haven, Conn., 1987), 10–26.
32. Austin, *Everyman's Genius*, p. 256.
33. See, for example, "What Is A Native Culture?", "On the Need for New Concepts of the Primitive," "Educating Our Ancestors," "Folk Literature in the United States," and "Regionalism in American Literature," Mary Austin Papers, Huntington Library.
34. Karen S. Langlois argues that Austin renewed her identity as a western writer and supporter of western culture after a disappointing decade (1910–20) in the East, marked by increasing conflict with the New York literary establishment. See Langlois, "A Search for Significance, Mary Austin: The New York Years" (Ph.D. diss., Claremont Graduate School, 1987).

35. See "The American Pattern"; "Understanding America Through Her Literature"; and interview in *Tulsa Daily World,* November 30, 1932, Mary Austin Papers, Huntington Library.
36. "The Town That Doesn't Want a Chautauqua," *New Republic,* July 7, 1926, 195–197.
37. For biographical information on Mary Beard, see Ann J. Lane, ed., *Mary Ritter Beard: A Sourcebook* (New York, 1977; rev. ed., 1988); Nancy F. Cott, "Mary Ritter Beard," in Barbara Sicherman and Carol Hurd Green, eds., *Notable American Women: The Modern Period* (Cambridge, Mass., 1980), 71–73, and Cott, *Woman Making History: Mary Ritter Beard Through Her Letters* (New Haven, Conn., 1991).
38. Mary Beard, "American Women and the Printing Press," in *Women in the Modern World,* Annals of the American Academy of Political and Social Science 143 (May 1929), 197.
39. Ibid., 198.
40. Ibid., 199.
41. Ibid., 200.
42. Ibid., 200–201.
43. Ibid., 203–4.
44. Ibid., 204.
45. Ibid.
46. Ibid., 205.
47. Ibid.
48. Ibid.
49. Ibid., 204–5.
50. Lane, *Mary Beard: A Sourcebook,* 132.
51. Beard, "American Women and the Printing Press," 197.
52. Ibid., 206.
53. Ibid.
54. Ibid.
55. Ibid., 197, 206.
56. Among Austin's works on religious subjects are *Christ in Italy* (New York, 1912); *The Man Jesus* (New York, 1915; rev. ed., *A Small-Town Man,* 1915); *Can Prayer Be Answered?* (New York, 1934); *Experiences Facing Death* (Indianapolis, 1931); and such essays as "The Left Hand of God," "Religion and Modern Conduct," "Notes on the Validity of Modern Mysticism," "The Religious Training of Children," "Do We Need A New Religion?", and "What Religion Means to Me," in the Mary Austin Papers, Huntington Library.
57. In her autobiography Austin wrote that "at the same time that my contemporaries were joining labor organizations and aligning themselves with wage-strikes, I took to the defense of Indians because they were the most conspicu-

ously defeated and offended against group at hand" (*Earth Horizons,* 266). Austin was treated like a celebrity in Santa Fe and turned her attention to the support of local and regional culture after she moved to that city in 1924.

58. Nancy F. Cott, "How Weird Was Beard? Mary Ritter Beard and American Feminism," Seventh Berkshire Conference on the History of Women, Wellesley College, June 1987.

59. Bonnie G. Smith, "On Seeing Mary Beard," *Feminist Studies* 10 (Fall 1984), 401, 405, 412. Also see Cott, *Woman Making History,* 30–35, and Lane, *Mary Ritter Beard: A Sourcebook,* 31–33.

60. Ethel Puffer Howes, "Accepting the Universe," *Atlantic Monthly* 129 (April 1922), 444. Also see Howes, *The Progress of the Institute for the Coordination of Women's Interests* (Northampton, Mass., 1928), and her article, "The Meaning of Progress in the Woman Movement," *Annals of the American Academy of Political and Social Science* 148 (May 1929), 14–20.

61. Bruce Kuklick, *The Rise of American Philosophy, Cambridge, Massachusetts, 1860–1930* (New Haven, Conn., 1977) , 590–94.

62. For the difficulties faced by academic women in the 1920s, see the sources cited in note 2. "The field of college teaching holds comparatively little promise for women," Marion O. Hawthorne wrote in the conclusion to her survey of 844 women at 122 colleges. "The rank and file of the respondents seem to have developed a defensive attitude bordering on martyrdom, and complained, waxed bitter, and voiced resentment toward the conditions of which they were victims" ("Women as College Teachers," 153).

63. Thomas Bender points out that in the decade following his resignation from Columbia, Charles Beard remained wary of institutions and addressed himself to the widest possible public audience rather than academic or research colleagues in government and philanthropy. According to Bender, Beard "embraced the whole public as his habitat as Emerson's man thinking" (*New York Intellect: A History of Intellectual Life in New York City, from 1750 to the Beginnings of Our Own Time* [Baltimore, 1988], 307).

64. To give one example, volume 28 of the *American Sociological Review* (1922–23) lists articles by L. L. Bernard on "The Conditions of Social Progress," Fred O. Bouke on "The Limits of Social Science," H.E. Cunningham on "Intelligence and Social Life," Bruno Laker on "What Has Become of Social Reform," and similar subjects of male sociologists. By contrast, the female contributors to the volume, Anna B. Pratt, Annie MacLean, and Florence Mederith, wrote, respectively, on "Social Work in the First Grade of a Public School," "Twenty Years of Sociology by Correspondence, and "Sociology Applied in the Field of Health."

65. Beatrice Hinkle, *The Re-Creating of the Individual: A Study of Psychological Types and Their Relation to Psychoanalysis* (New York, 1923), especially ch. 6, "Masculine and Feminine Psychology."

66. See Catharine R. Stimpson, "The Sonagrams of Gertrude Stein," in Michael J. Hoffman, ed., *Critical Essays on Gertrude Stein* (New York, 1986), 193. Carolyn Burke's article "Getting Spliced: Modernism and Sexual Difference,"

American Quarterly 3 (Spring 1987), 98–121, suggests that the works of Gertrude Stein, Marianne Moore, Mina Loy, Djuna Barnes, Laura Riding, and other female modernists suggest "more flexible, and imaginative ways of reading" than those of Pound and other male modernists. Burke points out that Stein struggled with her own associations of genius with masculinity until her discovery of "female" modes of creativity in her relationships with Alice Toklas and in female artists like Isadora Duncan (p. 100).

67. After years of neglect, contemporary critics are reappraising Glaspell's work; she is now considered to be one of the foremost architects of the modern theatre, equivalent in many respects to Eugene O'Neill, whose career she fostered at the Provincetown Theater. See, for example, C.W.E. Bigsby, *A Critical Introduction to Twentieth-Century American Drama,* vol. 1, 1900–1940 (Cambridge, England, 1982), 25–35.

68. On Rourke, see Joan Shelly Rubin, *Constance Rourke and American Culture* (Chapel Hill, N.C., 1980), and Samuel I. Bellman, *Constance M. Rourke* (Boston, 1981).

69. See, for example, Virginia Yans-McLaughlin, "Inquisition and Appreciation: Two Approaches to the Study of Anthropologists," *American Quarterly* 36 (Summer 1984), 315–21. Also see Rosenberg, *Beyond Separate Spheres;* Judith Schacter Modell, *Ruth Benedict: Patterns of A Life* (Philadelphia, 1983); Margaret M. Caffrey, *Ruth Benedict: Stranger in This Land* (Austin, Tex., 1989); and Jane Howard, *Margaret Mead: A Life* (New York, 1984).

70. Mary Dearborn, in *Pocahontas's Daughters: Gender and Ethnicity in American Culture* (New York, 1986), analyzes these differences as characteristics of ethnic women's literature which is at once outside and within American traditions. The work of Anzia Yezierska illustrates the tendency of ethnic women writers to merge text and context, subject and object, reality and imagination in the fiction of this period. Also see Rose Kamel, "'Anzia Yezierska, Get Out of Your Own Way': Selfhood and Otherness in the Autobiographical Fiction of Anzia Yezierska, *Studies in American Jewish Literature* 3 (1953), 40–50.

71. For recent works on intellectual life in the early twentieth century, see Dorothy Ross, *Origins of American Social Science* (New York, 1991); James Kloppenberg, *Uncertain Victory: Social Democracy and Progressivism in European and American Thought, 1870–1920* (New York, 1986); Robert Bannister, *Sociology and Scientism: The American Quest for Objectivity, 1880–1940* (Chapel Hill, N.C., 1987); and Bender, *New York Intellect.*

72. Ellen Condliffe Lagemann's "The Plural Worlds of Educational Research," *History of Education Quarterly* 29 (Summer 1989), 185–214, discusses the diminution of Dewey's influence and the triumph of positivism in the social sciences after 1920.

73. On the exclusion of women from this canon, see Sharon O'Brien, "Becoming Noncanonical: The Case Against Willa Cather," *American Quarterly* 40 (March 1988), 110–26; and Paul Lauter, "Race and Gender in the Shaping of the American Literary Canon: A Case Study from the Twenties," *Feminist*

Studies 9 (Fall 1983), 435–63. Also see Gaye Tuchman, *Edging Women Out: Victorian Novelists, Publishers, and Social Change* (New Haven, Conn., 1989), and Kermit Vanderbilt, *American Literature and the Academy: The Roots, Growth, and Maturity of a Profession* (Philadelphia, 1986).

74. Austin always felt that critics ignored her. As Nancy Cott points out, critics also ignored Mary Beard's contributions to the works she wrote jointly with her husband. See Cott, *Woman Making History,* 3.

75. Rebecca West, "Woman as Artist and Thinker," in Schmalhausen and Calverton, *Woman's Coming of Age,* 374.

76. See especially Warren I. Susman, *Culture as History: The Transformation of American Society in the Twentieth Century* (New York, 1984), ch. 7, "Culture and Civilization: The Nineteen Twenties."

77. Ibid., 381. Also see Virginia Woolf, *A Room of One's Own* (London, 1929).

78. West, "Woman as Artist and Thinker," 382.

❧

Immigrant Voices from the Federal Writers Project: The Connecticut Ethnic Survey, 1937–1940

Laura Anker

BURIED IN 93 ROUGHLY CATALOGED BOXES OVERFLOWING WITH THE SCATtered remains of the Works Projects Administration Connecticut Ethnic Survey—fieldworkers' manuals; newspaper clippings; questionnaires; lists of ethnic organizations and foreign-language newspapers; statistical data from factories, unions, schools, churches, and synagogues; and unpublished articles in various stages of completion—are the original yellowing manuscript pages of almost 200 immigrant life histories, about half of which are the narratives of women.[1]

Rare first-person accounts, these oral histories exude the immediacy of experience still fresh in the subjects' minds, recalled within the cultural context of ongoing ethnic community life. They are the narratives of immigrants recorded mainly by immigrants: interviews of the working class conducted by unemployed workers, biographies of residents of ethnic neighborhoods collected in those communities by compatriots who shared similar pasts and a common present.[2]

By recounting the stories of individual Hungarian, Slovak, Polish, Southern Italian, and Jewish families in Europe and in the industrial centers of Bridgeport, New Haven, Hartford, and New Britain, the WPA oral histories provide a detailed description of the overlapping worlds of family, community, and work and of the confrontation between ethnic familial cultures and the exigencies of American urban life.[3] These narratives offer more than nuggets of new information. They integrate the experiences and perspectives of women into the broader portrait of immigrant life, raising new questions and suggesting fresh interpretations from the neglected standpoint of ordinary immigrants about what they believed mattered in their lives.

By inviting the historian to employ a comparative framework for analysis, the Connecticut Ethnic Survey redirects the locus of investigation away from the measurement of mobility, ranking of success, or preoccupation with values as the main determinants of behavior to the concrete processes by which immigrants fabricated particular life strategies in response to specific conditions. Whereas studies that focus on one ethnic group have tended to emphasize intergroup differences and intragroup similarities, the WPA narratives highlight commonalities in the experiences of immigrants from different ethnic groups as well as variations in the responses of individuals with similar cultural backgrounds.[4]

Interviews with immigrant women show them to have been active agents, rather than passive victims of the transformation from preindustrial to industrial culture. Women were engaged in every aspect of the migration process, from decisions about whether to emigrate and where to go to considerations of who should work, in what jobs, how to accommodate, when, where, and how to resist. Their actions were conditioned both by the defense of a culture of mutual obligation and by the transformation of that culture by the migration process and their own strategies for adjustment and resistance. From the interaction of customary practices with new economic realities, women forged strategies of adaptation and protest that stressed the goals of family advancement and community welfare over purely individual needs and that defined success through the prism of household responsibility rather than purely personal gain. These strategies, in turn, mediated the transatlantic renegotiation of gender roles and family relationships.

❧

In the last years of the Great Depression, before political repression and World War II put an end to their ambitious efforts, WPA fieldworkers walked the streets of Connecticut neighborhoods, their own communities, knocking on doors and talking to people. Many interviewers spoke Italian, Yiddish, Russian, Polish, or Hungarian and could interview their neighbors in their native tongues. They talked to immigrants in their kitchens and on their doorsteps as well as in small shops, factories, and ethnic halls. Consequently, project workers (many of whom were themselves women) collected close to 100 women's biographies. "We interviewed women," recalled Pearl Russo in a recent discussion, "because we wanted to and because they were at home." "Most people wanted to talk," she explained. "We were part of a whole culture of storytelling. . . . Now people would rather watch television. When we were growing up . . . (Bridgeport) was vibrant. . . . It had all these nationalities . . . and we knew each other. . . . Today we could live together and be strangers."[5]

The Federal Writers Project employed innovative methods for reconstructing the histories of working-class communities and relating the chronologies to the urban industrial institutions that immigrants met in their everyday lives. Their plan was to create a new composite portrait of Connecticut's peoples, taken from the "bottom upward." They hoped that a positive focus on ethnic pluralism might counter the resurgence of racism at home, which they feared would accompany the rise of Nazism in Europe.[6]

WPA investigators collected data from library archives as well as from immigrant communities themselves. They described neighborhoods in rich detail, noting the physical character of housing and systematically interviewing the people who lived on particular blocks. They compiled lists of ethnic organizations and mutual aid societies, describing their histories, organizational structures, and functions. They went to public and parochial schools, prisons, institutions for delinquents, mental hospitals, restaurants, saloons, and unions, collecting statistics and conducting interviews with bureaucrats and proprietors as well as with inmates and customers. They distributed industrial questionnaires at factories and compiled surveys of workers in specific industries, including their ethnic and gender composition. They interviewed men, women, and children individually, as couples, in families, in their neighborhoods, and at their workplaces.

The life histories collected by the Connecticut Ethnic Survey bear the imprint of the historical period from which they emerged, the particular concerns of the Federal Writers Project itself (the institutional home within which the ethnic survey resided), as well as those of its parent organization, the Works Projects Administration.[7] The Federal Writers Project was recalled by a participant as "a governmental adventure in cultural collectivism the likes of which no nation has experienced before or since."[8] Although this idealistic spirit permeated the activities and consciousness of project employees, the FWP was not intended as a subsidized cultural enterprise. It was established to provide work relief for unemployed writers and other white-collar workers (teachers, secretaries, librarians, ministers, and journalists) caught in the trauma of the depression years.

Created by Executive Order on May 6, 1935, the origins of the Federal Writers Project dated back to the onset of the Depression in 1929, when artists, writers, and other unemployed professionals began to form organizations, write proposals, and gather in massive demonstrations to petition the government for jobs. Funding for the project was conceded by government officials largely in response to this clamor from the left. Harry Alsberg, appointed by Harry Hopkins to head the project, symbolized the conflicting political crosscurrents in which the FWP was caught throughout its turbulent history. A seasoned New Dealer who had already edited two magazines for the Federal Employment Relief Agency, Alsberg also served as director of the respectable Jewish refugee agency, the Joint Distribution League. Alsberg moved among pacifists and philosophical anarchists, proclaiming both his disillusionment with the Soviet Union and his goal of "saving the world from reactionaries."[9]

At its peak in 1936, the FWP employed 6686 men and women at salaries of about 20 dollars a week, for a total of approximately 30 million dollars. These figures represented only a minute proportion of the over 2.5 million individuals who worked on the WPA and a similarly small proportion of its 5-billion-dollar budget. Despite this small budget and relatively few employees, the project bequeathed an impressive cultural legacy to the nation and had a dramatic impact on individual lives. Many important writers (some already famous and others whose careers would be launched by this opportunity) found their way onto the various state and regional projects. Conrad Aiken, Ralph Ellison, Arna Bontemps, Saul Bellow, Margaret Walker, Zora Neale Hurston, Richard Yerby, Kenneth Fearin, Nelson Algren, Anzia Yezierska, and Richard Wright were among the illustrious recipients of FWP support. But the majority of those employed, like the first- and second-generation immigrants who worked on the Connecticut Ethnic Survey, remained anonymous. They may have harbored aspirations for literary careers that were nurtured by the project, but most returned to working-class jobs when their employment on the FWP was terminated by United States entry into World War II.[10]

The first and most famous undertaking of the Writers Project was a series of state guidebooks. On the surface simply new and more complete Baedeker's, these guides were infused with a critical spirit, nurtured by the ideologies and activities of Depression politics and mass movements.[11] In addition to the roadways and tourist information found in typical travel guides, they were intended to provide a comprehensive and readable portrait of a region drawn not only from its monuments and acknowledged heroes but also from the mores, anecdotes, lore, and speech of its people.[12] Jerre Mangione recalled the impact of this project ideology on its participants:

> They saw for the first time, that the population did not live solely under the influence of the Protestant ethic, with its inhibiting bourgeois vision, but that it was a mixture of different groups: Negro, Irish, Italian, German, Russian among others; all interacting with one another in the struggle for survival and assertion, and in the process, generating their own special kind of influence. And they began to believe that the detested values of middle class Americans could be counteracted and even cancelled by a class of Americans that commanded their attention as it never had be-

> fore—the steelworkers, bricklayers, sharecroppers, factory workers, the so called common people whose lives were already vividly interwoven into the fabric of the national character.[13]

By the time several books in the American Guide series were completed, Harry Alsberg had decided to supplement them with studies whose specific purpose was to depict the peoples of America.[14] In 1938 he began to direct resources into such projects, appointing Morton Royce as national consultant for social and ethnic studies. Known for his unlimited courage and energy and for being "somewhat outspoken," Royce went to work immediately. "We discarded the old patronizing attitude toward the immigrant," he wrote, "that of judging a group by the number of doctors, lawyers and big businessmen it had produced. We assumed that every individual contributed, whether he slung a pen or a pick axe."[15]

When Benjamin Botkin joined the Writers Project as head of the Folklore Unit, the two men agreed to work in close collaboration to tell the story of how Americans lived, gathering material on a nationwide scale from first-hand sources. They planned to study ethnic groups using "workers who belong to the respective groups that are being studied, who know the language and the traditions and can get ready access to the human information."[16] Royce and Botkin shared Alsberg's confidence that lack of training would be an asset rather than a liability: "They suspected that as amateur sociologists and folklore collectors, Project workers might turn up data that would be far more interesting and revealing than the dry analyses and statistics of conventional scholars."[17] Furthermore, Benjamin Botkin argued that fieldworkers recruited from the working and lower middle class were "in outlook and sympathy, if not actual circumstance, closer to the bottom and the bottom dog."[18]

Both units used the oral-history method; they shared fieldworkers and jointly participated in efforts such as the Connecticut Ethnic Survey. By assembling "ethnically and occupationally diverse life histories," Botkin and Royce sought to change the image of the immigrant experience in America from a melting pot to a pluralistic mosaic.[19] The energy and enthusiasm with which Royce and Botkin approached this endeavor inspired many of their subordinates, including Frank Manuel, the newly appointed regional director for New England. Manuel was particularly enamored with Royce's grand design "to establish nationwide studies dealing with nationalities and occupations and even with entire communities." For Manuel these studies represented the project's "most significant and interesting work."[20] He moved quickly to establish the Connecticut Ethnic Survey, appointing two Yale professors to head the project. He selected sociologist Thomas Koenig as director, to be assisted by anthropologist David Rodnick, who was to supervise the research staff.

The goal of the ethnic survey, according to Koenig's and Rodnick's plan of study, was to "understand the immigrant . . . by gaining an insight into the manifold phases of his life and the processes whereby he adjusts himself to his environment." "Up to several years ago," the plan argued,

> the problems arising out of this process of cultural amalgamation (have been) dealt with in an incredibly naive manner. . . . All that was necessary to Americanize the foreigner and thus solve the immigrant problem was to allure him or, if need be, force him to learn English and to become naturalized. But Americanization or assimilation . . . involves a give and take process which affects both the immigrant and the native.[21]

The intense investigation of immigrant mores and behavior, Koenig and Rodnick believed, would shed important light on the general nature of culture. "An understanding of immigrant life is undoubtedly indispensable to an understanding of the contemporary American scene, especially in a state like Connecticut, where almost two-thirds of the population are of foreign stock."[22] But such an understanding could not be derived from survey data or the observations of academic researchers who inhabited a world separate from their subjects; rather, the project plan insisted, immigrants had to be allowed to speak for themselves. "By analyzing a considerable number of representative and carefully compiled life histories in their proper settings, a definite picture will be obtained of the processes of adaptation and the problems inherent in the adjustment of various immigrant groups to the American culture."[23]

Immersed in these ideas and goals, Connecticut Ethnic Survey fieldworkers began the process of collecting narratives. To create commonality between interviewer and informant, the plan of study urged that whenever possible "each ethnic group . . . will be investigated by workers who are themselves members of the group, as this has proven to be of definite advantage."[24] When such a match was not possible, project workers selected the people they would talk to based upon their own neighborhood, work, and personal networks. Pearl Russo, a Jewish native of Bridgeport whose parents had emigrated from Lithuania in 1904, interviewed Hungarian immigrants (among others) because of close neighborhood ties and because of contacts she had cultivated through community groups like the International Workers Organization. "I started out knowing somebody," she recalled, "perhaps Mrs. C., then I'd ask them if they knew anybody else whom I could interview. One led to another."[25] Since most interviewers were from the working or lower middle classes, their contacts and networks were to immigrant working-class families. A project directive also required interviewers to write their own life history: "This workers will be asked to do before embarking upon their task of getting the life histories of others, as it will, aside from adding to the number of cases, serve as concrete preliminary experience."[26]

In order to draw a portrait of the entire life of the group, not just that of its leaders or industrial workers, the ethnic survey embraced a community orientation, going to neighborhood stores, coffee shops, saloons, churches, synagogues, and ethnic organizations as well as to immigrant homes and workplaces. To gain "insight into the home, church, social gathering, family function, beliefs and practices . . . ," *The Guiding Outline for Obtaining Life Histories* encouraged fieldworkers to look for what "is unique in the life of the group, the characteristic differentiating it from others":

> For although numerous studies have been made of foreign groups, little, if anything, has been done in the way of a systematic description of the cultures of these groups. A study concerned primarily with the ways the different people . . . live their lives should . . . help considerably toward a better understanding of our complex American life.[27]

Most interviewers, unlike directors Koenig and Rodnick, had not written professionally before their employment on the project. They were unemployed teachers, office workers, small businessmen, labor activists, radicals, or political hacks, whose writing experience frequently consisted of nothing more than a few published letters to a community newspaper. Although a few more prosperous individuals were allowed on the project because of their professional accomplishments or for reasons of political patronage, the majority had to pass a means test and demonstrate their need for work.[28]

Vincent Frazzetta, for example, was born just after his parents arrived in Bridgeport from Sicily.[29] He studied violin in New York, hoping to pursue a musical career. But family economic need forced him to abandon his studies. He earned a living at a series of factory jobs until the Depression, when he found it impossible to find work. Unemployment coupled with frequent outspoken contributions to local newspapers qualified him for the Federal Writers Project. In 1938 he joined the Connecticut Ethnic Survey, where he began interviewing and compiling massive community studies of Italians, Poles, and Slovaks from the Bridgeport neighborhoods in which he had grown up and worked.[30]

Pearl Kosby Russo, another interviewer for the Bridgeport project, was the youngest of four daughters, whose Lithuanian Jewish parents ran a small neighborhood grocery.[31] Despite her parents' reservations, a scholarship from the Sisterhood of the Park Avenue Reformed Temple enabled her to enter junior college. After one year she transferred to Wellesley. In 1932 she graduated "into the depths of the Depression." Ms. Russo later recalled:

> I had ten cents in my pocket. My sisters took a bus home, but since I was the graduate they insisted that I take the train. When I got back to the apartment where I was to live with my two older sisters, I opened the door, sat down in the armchair and cried all afternoon because I had ten cents and didn't know what I was going to do. There were no jobs.[32]

Russo found part-time work tutoring that summer, but was supported almost entirely by her sisters, who were employed as bookkeepers. Finally, through family connections, she got a temporary job selling dresses in a department store. When this ended she was able to find only sporadic employment at a variety of jobs, ranging from selling hats on Saturdays for 25 cents an hour to a more substantial position as a substitute French teacher. Briefly she taught English at night to foreign-born adults, one of the first WPA projects in Bridgeport. In 1937 she became an organizer for the United Mine Workers District 50, serving chemical workers at a pharmaceutical plant in Fairfield. In 1939 she got a job on the Federal Writers Project through an acquaintance in New Haven, a railroad worker who recommended her to his friend, the director of the Bridgeport Ethnic Survey. Together with M.G. Sayers she contributed more than one-third of the women's biographies in the archive as well as numerous men's life histories and block surveys.[33]

Rahel Mittelstein, a Jewish interviewer for the Connecticut Ethnic Survey in New Haven, emigrated to the United States from Moscow in 1923. She was 10 years old when she arrived at Ellis Island with her mother and sister, leaving her estranged ne'er-do-well father behind.[34] The family moved directly to New Haven to live with an aunt in a small three-room house next to her uncle's plumbing- and heating-supply shop. Rahel's older sister went to work immediately in a hat store. Rahel was expected to pursue a business curriculum in high school so that she, too, could contribute to the family support. Instead, over the protestations of both her mother and sister, Rahel took college-preparatory courses and then embarked upon four years of university education, working whenever possible at various factory and business jobs. Upon graduation, despite great hopes of becoming a writer or teacher, Rahel found herself unemployed. She was forced to move back to her mother's house with her now-married sister and to depend on them again for support. "To my family," she wrote, "I was no doubt a great disappointment":

> Not only did I not become a writer, but I didn't even get a teaching position. During this period I worked at odd jobs, such as tutoring and typing. I was able to contribute a little toward our home, but very little indeed. This was a very miserable period. Finally I got a job as a typist and earned twelve dollars a week, but even this did not last long.[35]

A job on the Writers Project in New Haven finally ended this long period of "hopeless and useless" unemployment. During the months that followed Rahel wrote a long, eloquent autobiography and recorded numerous life histories, including many of New Haven Jews and Ukrainians.[36]

As one reads the files of the Connecticut Ethnic Survey, one gets to know the interviewers as well as the interviewees. The life histories are not uniformly useful, nor were all project employees dedicated or inspired. Most fieldworkers like Frazzetta, Russo, and Mittelstein energetically pursued family, community, and labor networks to locate informants; others simply knocked on doors in their assigned areas or talked to proprietors of small businesses or leaders of ethnic institutions. Some stayed in the office to clip newspapers or edit and type; others loafed, signed in, and then went to the movies.[37] One worker in the New Haven office submitted as her interview of a Jewish woman a portion of Mary Antin's autobiographical novel, *They Who Knock at Our Gates.*[38]

The WPA life histories are records of all the factors that went into their making: the interests and experiences of both interviewers and informants and the dynamic process of the interview itself. This rather long excerpt captures Pearl Russo's self-conscious attempt to overcome the social distance created by the interview situation as well as the tension of such encounters:

> We walked up a dark flight of stairs to the door of an apartment above a vacant store. The hallway, originally painted bright blue, was streaked and dirty; the stairs were narrow and worn. At the top of the stairs, a narrow hall led to a bathroom at one end, and to the door of the apartment at the other.... A woman's voice answered our knock with a call to "come in."...
>
> She asked us to be seated, and cleared two chairs of crumbs for us. She seemed to accept our entrance and right to ask questions—we distinctly had the impression that she thought we came with some authority to do so. This submissiveness, let us say (for want of a more precise word), while it created a feeling of uneasiness in ourselves, and some embarrassment—was quickly dispelled when we had a chance to "chat" with her. We first discussed the relative merits of corn breads. . . .
>
> She stood by the table, looking down at us as we asked our questions, for some time. She seemed unconscious that she was doing so until we asked her to be seated. She sat at the table, and during the early part of the first interview, until we managed to engage her in reminiscences, her hand kept wandering restlessly, without conscious purpose, to the collection of utensils, cloths, etc., on the table—picking them up, putting them down again in the same place.... Later she sat still, with one arm across her protruding abdomen, holding her hand close to her body—almost hugging it; this, we noticed, was an habitual relaxed position. Mrs. B. told us she was thirty-three years old, and had been married for thirteen years.[39]

Federal Writers Project directives encouraged interviewers to make their informants feel important, to be "a good listener with a good ear for recording, or remembering both what is said and how it is said, to take down everything you hear just as you hear it without adding, taking away or altering a syllable. Your business is to record, not correct or improve."[40] Without the aid of tape recorders, writers on the Connecticut project tried to remember accurately and reproduce not just the content of what was said but the grammar and patterns of speech as well. Vincent Frazzetta, one of the project's most prolific interviewers, recalled his strategy many years later: "I absorbed the words of my subject and (when) I returned to the project office, I felt the empathy of their words as I ran them on the typewriter."[41] Pearl Russo's technique was to take copious notes in "a stenographer's notebook." "I'd come right back to the office and write up the stories, remembering what wasn't in the notes. We talked to people and tried to come back with the story as realistically written as we could possibly reproduce it."[42]

The processes by which life stories are constructed are broadly collaborative. Even when tape-recorded an oral history has two authors; it is the product of the interaction between two people. Aware that the questions asked in an interview influenced the answers that were given, Koenig and Rodnick urged fieldworkers to be flexible and to allow, as much as possible, the informant's view of his or her own life to organize the formal structure of their life histories. Although WPA interviewers were provided with uniform and detailed questions, respondents were asked to talk freely, following the natural association of ideas and memories. The fieldworkers manual cautioned:

> The questions contained in this outline are intended to be merely suggestive, and are to be utilized by the field worker as preparation for this interview, not as a ready set of questions to be rigidly adhered to at the time of the interview. (They are a guide) as to what information is relevant, what data should be obtained.[43]

Questions could be changed or reformulated at any time in response to the information narrated, and since the interview guide itself constituted a synthesis of what had been learned, it was periodically revised to incorporate new areas of investigation.

A recent critic, who worked on the now-famous North Carolina project, has challenged the accuracy of many of the published Federal Writers Project oral histories, arguing that interviewers were often "persons who considered themselves creative writers," more concerned with producing a complete or convincing story than with recording an informant's unpolished narrative. Additionally, he claims, biographies were censored and retouched by supervisors and editors before publication.[44]

In contrast, most fieldworkers on the Connecticut project had no literary pretentions or training. Ironically, decreasing funding and the precipitous demise of the ethnic survey meant that life histories suffered little alteration from the complex process of editing and censorship that normally preceded publication. The original rough typescript pages handed in by the interviewers were ignominiously stored in barrels to gather dust in the basement of the state library in Hartford. "We hoped we would have a book, but nothing ever came of it," Pearl Russo explained. "All these years I didn't even know where my interviews were, I thought they had been destroyed."[45]

❧

Like all documentary sources, life histories are socially produced and must be analyzed in terms of their specific historical and contextual meanings.[46] The processes by which elements of their form and content are extrapolated and transformed into facts involves a complex dialectic of past and present. But while these processes are often invisible for traditional historical sources, they are less easily ignored in life histories.[47]

In the reading of life histories the events of the narrative allow us to see social relations in action and to anchor our understanding of culture in its concrete behavioral manifestations. The language used reveals the ideological structures that confer meaning to social realities and shape the way social relations are perceived. Because these structures are most often experienced unconsciously, close textual analysis of life histories can reveal processes hidden even from the actors themselves. The selectivity of recollection itself becomes a source of historical knowledge, providing important clues to social attitudes and behaviors. In the interpretation of oral histories, the historian attempts to "listen beyond," to hear "in the words of a given person the speech of a culture."[48]

The value of the WPA life histories lies, therefore, not just in the light they can shed on what happened but also on their ability to disclose the various ways immigrants organized their understanding of past experiences. For example, underlying Mildred Hecht's narration of her story the reader can detect the interplay between the reality of the moment described and that in which the recollection occurred. On December 12, 1939, when she was interviewed by Rahel Mittelstein, Mildred Hecht worked in a garment factory; her husband was unemployed. "Nothing has become better for me," she explained, "the house is cold and poor." From this vantage she described the circumstances and feelings that surrounded her coming to America:

> My father and mother wanted to go to America to the other children. I didn't want to go. I was a tailor in Russia and a good one, too. I liked my work. I liked it like a painter likes his work. When I used to finish making a coat it was good, and I would get much pleasure from it. I would look at it and feel good all over like I made a beautiful sculpture. I used to think that in America human beings are like machines, and I wasn't fooled. In America, when I went to work in a factory, I felt like a machine. Here is a bigger speed-up, hurry up. I wasn't enthusiastic about going to America. My heart must have told me that things wouldn't be so good for me here."[49]

As this excerpt illustrates, a life history is more than a collection of events in an individual's life; it is a selection of structured self-images, mobilized to make an argument about the way society operates. The past is more or less unconsciously ideologized, as events are reshaped and reevaluated according to the present life circumstances of the respondent. This rearrangement allows the individual to incorporate her or his own past into the strategy or "script" of the present.[50]

In a recent interview, Pearl Russo described this interactive process of recollection: "You can't restrain the subjective impulse to put your present self in it. It's not a conscious distortion; years go by and you can't remember the thing as it was at the time."[51] Since the WPA life histories were recorded while both narrators and interviewers lived in first-generation ethnic communities, the "memory culture" that they access becomes a valuable guide to the ideological structures through which immigrants understood and influenced the social conditions of their existence.[52]

To unravel the many elements in each retold event, the analyst must utilize the form as well as the content of the story. The words chosen can give important clues to the processes of cultural persistence and change. Take for example Mary Huda, a Slovak woman employed for 25 years as a domestic and as a factory benchworker in Bridgeport. Although she vividly recalled 14-hour days of hard labor as a young woman in Europe, Mrs. Huda told the WPA interviewer that she "hadn't worked" before she came to America: "In the old country . . . (I) . . . was a farmer-woman," she explained.[53] Work, in the language of her new American home, had become synonymous with paid labor. Maryan Petraitis responded similarly to an interviewer's query: "I don't work in Lithuania, we're only farmers. . . . But when I came here . . . I start to work right away. I work in Ives Toy when I come from Europe."[54]

In the course of her oral history, Agnes Bonsza, a Hungarian immigrant and CIO activist, described her persistent disagreement with a friend, who in times of economic distress increased her own workload and never complained. The mixture of rural and industrial images contained in the metaphors Bonsza creates to tell this story suggests the congruence of preindustrial and left trade-unionist values in her radicalism:

> I always tell her, "If all the people was like you, the capitalists give the people hay." I tell her, "Sure if everybody be like you, the capitalists be glad. Then they never had to give the people anything."[55]

The language used in Anna Navakowsky's life history is revealing in a different way. Describing her widowed mother's decision to allow her to leave Poland for New Britain, Anna chooses these words: "She smiled tenderly and a little ruefully: 'Very well, then, you may go . . .' I looked with tear filled eyes for the last time at Rupin, peaceful and picturesque in the early light of morning, little realizing I was never to see it again."[56] In this instance, the stilted language suggests that the cultural context of the original event has been lost; the daughter's memory first distorted it and then restructured it within the value system informing the moment of recollection. It was then again reconstructed by Stan Dabkowsky's transcription of her words. The flowery, abstract mode of expression is the joint product of the daughter and the interviewer who reinterpreted the past from the viewpoint of a younger generation living in America some 30 years after the act.

These same processes probably removed any discordant note of personal discontinuity or discomfort from a Polish woman's nostalgic recollection of her early years in America:

> No sooner would we come from work at night, when we ate supper hurriedly, did the dishes even faster, and then all of us would gather in one house. All the young people who knew each other came. Here we could talk gossip, laugh, tell jokes, often quoting American phrases like "go home," "upstairs," "where you work," etc. Always there was laughter and merriment.[57]

To interpret this passage requires that the information it contains about patterns of ethnic communality and strategies of adjustment be disentangled from the narrator's characterization of her feelings, remembered from the distance of 40 intervening years. The original behavior and later recollection reveal different timebound aspects of first-generation immigrant experience.

Such anachronistically jarring language warns the historian to use these oral histories critically. But the clash of past and present values also highlights the internalization of differing and sometimes conflicting interpretations of experience. This segment from Julia Karbowski's life history, for example, signifies her struggle to justify the familial decision that sent her away from home within the context of a contemporary American preoccupation with parental love:

> Then one day we talked about America. My parents thought it would be a good idea if I went there, to make some money, and then, eventually to return. You mustn't get the wrong impression about their wishing me to go. You mustn't think that just because your parents wanted you to go that they didn't love you. Oh, no. Underneath, they were thinking of me and of the entire family's welfare. It is something to contend with when you grow older.[58]

❧

Although the value of oral history is generally advocated by those who stress the importance of subjectivity, the WPA narratives also disclose social "facts" that were recorded only in the memory of those who lived them. By analyzing many oral histories and checking them against each other, the historian can move beyond questions of motive and psychology to unravel the changing or stable webs of relationships that underlie daily processes. Although they seldom fulfill the prerequisites of representative samples, when many life histories support and reinforce each other and new biographies add little to the portrait that has emerged, we can extract patterns of group behavior from cumulative individual experience. In the words of French sociologist Daniel Bertaux, "The story can then begin to be told. The line between narration and theory breaks down."[59]

For example, tabulations from WPA life histories indicate that 78 percent of the immigrants interviewed entered the American job market through kin and friendship networks; 84 percent of new arrivals lodged with relatives or friends from Europe.[60] Although these oral histories were not scientifically sampled, nor was their number large enough to support precise measurements of mobility or class position, the striking similarities in the information they contain and the detailed nature of the case histories themselves allow us to perceive the patterns of recruitment to different occupational groups and to analyze the processes that produced them. They demonstrate that job recruitment through kin produced contradictory effects and that unequal resources and skills in Europe could determine divergent levels of attainment in the U.S. economy.[61] Kinship ties mediated the entrance of artisans and peasants from preindustrial cultures into urban industrial life and permitted the transmission of communal values of mutual support into ethnic solidarity at work. At the same time, they facilitated the fragmentation of the work force by employers and created a material basis for ethnic competition and hostility.

Because WPA oral histories also disclose the ideological frameworks within which immigrants interpreted this experience, they provide insight into the subtle ways prejudice operates. Pasquale Gruci, who emigrated to Bridgeport in 1882, recalled how ethnic conflicts were created by the structural segregation of the work force, which cast new immigrants into low-paid labor, while earlier arrivals monopolized the better jobs:

> Some of the Italians were afraid to live on the East Side because the Irish would always pick a fight. The Irish thought the Italians were cheap laborers. On one occasion, I remember a bunch of Irish and Germans, about 50 of them, went to Water St. where some of the Italians boarded, and armed with clubs, axes and sticks began to fight with the Italians.[62]

The overwhelming experience of ethnic segregation and job segmentation often masked the complex structural forces that produced it, giving credence to voluntaristic theories that blamed job clustering on immigrant values and cultural preferences. To many immigrants ethnic stereotypes seemed to explain job tracking. For example, George Victoria, a Polish worker, was convinced that foundry work was forced upon Poles and Slovaks because of Italian preferences for the outdoors.

> Like you take the Italian people; maybe some when they come here they get jobs in the shops, but pretty soon the boss in the shops find out that the Italian man don't like to work on the inside because he says that it's too hot. . . . So somebody have to work on these hard jobs, so the bosses take the Polish people and the Slovak people to work in the foundry.[63]

These perceptions conferred meanings to experience that undermined intergroup solidarity and created a partial and confused understanding of discrimination. Similarly, the angry illogic of this Slovak worker's testimony reveals the strain married women's work placed upon traditional role relationships and the success of employer practices that pitted male against female workers, causing this discomfort to erupt into overt hostility. The sexist stereotypes this worker embraces blind him to his own manipulation, subverting the possibility of resistance. The interpretive framework he endorses fails to account for the complexity of his situation, providing a focus for his fears but no adequate solutions.

> The shop started to transfer women and 'broads' over to our department. This burned up a lot of the old-timers like myself. . . . After a couple of weeks, we found out that some of the men in our department were getting knocked off and they were putting the broads in the places. The men were sent home a little at a time, and the press jobs were done by the women after that. A couple of old-timers like myself stayed there on the job, and

> the whole thing dragged on like that for a couple of years. . . . A while after the women came . . . prices on all the piece work jobs went down. The few men that were left in this department started to see that it was the fault of the women working for cheaper money. The lousy part about it was that the women were starting to do more work than the men ever did when they were working on the same jobs. And they got less money for it. . . . When the women started to come on they put in newer machines that could go faster. . . . I don't mind that a broad has to work in a shop, but why the Christ does a married woman have to work. Their business is to take care of the house. . . .
>
> Now that you ask me what the reason is that people are out of work . . . women are the fault . . . and the lousy shops too. They ought to make a law that no married woman should work in the shop.[64]

These dogmas pervade WPA oral histories proclaimed by men and sometimes echoed by women: "The husband is the boss of the house and . . . everything he says is to be obeyed," "the man in the family should be the only worker," "the woman is not made for work."[65] But they do not reflect the actions of immigrants described in the same narratives. WPA oral histories highlight this often contradictory relationship between articulated values and actual behavior. They also reveal how inherited cultural traditions were translated into new strategies of adjustment and how these strategies, in turn, altered the old values themselves. For example, Lucia Salanto justified her decision to continue working in a laundry after her marriage as a continuation of Italian customs and practices: "In Italy when the husband don't make enough money, the wife she have to work hard."[66] She later rationalized her return to work when her child was only three years old in similar terms: "Italian girls . . . are always knowing that they have 'responsibilita' of the house and they want to help. When my husband was lay off, I go to look for a job myself, nobody tells me."[67]

But if the "responsibilita" of women in traditional Italian culture provided a value system within which Mrs. Salanto could adapt to her new industrial environment, the experience of work itself transformed these attitudes. She refused to stop working when her husband got a better job, claiming that she now would stay on to ease bill paying. While she began her employment at the laundry to ensure the family's subsistence, by the late 1930s she was working to improve their standard of living.

In other instances, WPA oral histories describe how wage work, entered into within the familial values of traditional patriarchal culture, had the potential to subvert that culture. Although Mildred Hecht bitterly complained of her dual exploitation as a working wife in Connecticut ("If a woman has housework to do, it's enough for her"), she did not want to quit her job. "Still there is advantage to working," she explained:

> It makes me independent. You see, I am a hot communist and my husband isn't and is against communists. . . . He reads the *Forward,* that's the trouble. I read the *Freiheit.* . . . I got angry and told him he can't stop me from going where I want to go. I couldn't talk like that if I wasn't working.[68]

Mary Rauci Young took a factory job to support her children, but once there she became active in the CIO and participated in one of Bridgeport's first sit-down strikes, led by immigrant women. Family need and traditions of the legitimacy of female labor sent women into the paid work force in immigrant households not yet affected by the possibilities of single-income support or Victorian domesticity. At the same time participation in industry and in unions strengthened their voices, extending the realm of women's activities beyond the household and ethnic neighborhood.[69]

WPA life histories also disclose the often hidden arenas of acculturation, focusing attention on the subtle mechanisms of cultural transmission and transformation underlying daily events. This 60-year-old construction worker's description of the evolution of street-corner conversation in Bridgeport's Italian east side reveals the changing character of ethnic communities as places where immigrants transmitted old values, forged fresh identities, and developed collective responses using the tools of past experience to confront new problems.

> Then, all the Italians were feeling like they were in the old country and they used to meet on the corner every time that they could get a chance . . . to talk about Italy and how they got letters from there . . . they used to do this at that time because they miss their country, and they wanted to remember it some way. Then they used to meet people from the other parts of Italy and they used to compare one place with the other. This was what they talked about in the early times, but after a little bit they used to

> talk more about the work that they used to do in the shop and on the gangs where they worked.[70]

The richness of the Connecticut Ethnic Survey as a historical source arises in part from the large number of women's narratives it contains. Most oral histories, even from the Federal Writers Project itself, record only the stories of male industrial workers.[71] The perspective of women that emerges from the WPA life histories reveals the collective and familial context of immigrant life, focusing attention on the ways individual experience is embedded in complex fabrics of social organization. The women interviewed by the Connecticut Federal Writers Project spoke of the people around them and of their relationships to those people, contextualizing social processes in a way that men did not. From women's narratives emerged the outlines of biographies of husbands, children, neighbors, and more distant kin as well as the relational networks that tied them together.[72]

In contrast, men more frequently spoke about their actions and decisions as solely their own. For example, Morris Shapiro, a Jewish immigrant to Hartford in 1923, described his migration as a series of self-induced events. "For the first time in my life," he claimed, "I was actually on my own. No family, no relations and very few friends."[73] Yet he made the journey from Russia to Hartford with money from his father and assistance from his sister, who had preceded him. Upon his arrival in New York he was met by an aunt, who directed him to Hartford where he went to live with his sister and brother-in-law. They in turn settled him in a place to live and helped him find a job.[74]

Interviews with couples often brought out clashes in their accounts and interpretations of the past. A case in point was the joint interview with a Hungarian couple, Mr. and Mrs. Carpati.[75] Asserting the prevalent patriarchal dogma, Mr. Carpati assured the interviewer that he had forced his wife to quit work when they got married. Mrs. Carpati then corrected him, reminding her husband that she had in fact been laid off from her job and had subsequently returned to work.

By providing a glimpse of the entire life cycle, WPA life histories reveal the crucial economic role of women in immigrant households and the integration of the spheres of unpaid family labor and wage work in women's lives. They detail the varying strategies mothers organized to achieve family subsistence, coordinating and alternating their own labor (paid and unpaid, inside and outside the household) with their husbands' and children's wage contributions. Whereas cross-sectional tabulations of the percentage of women who worked at any one time mask the significance of paid labor outside the home for immigrant women, WPA oral histories show that women were seldom isolated from the world of wage labor.[76] Ninety-two percent of the women interviewed who were single when they arrived in the United States worked outside the home before they were married. A majority continued to work until the birth of their first child. Although most remained at home while their children were young, 40 percent of first-generation wives and mothers performed income-generating work within their households, tending boarders and lodgers, washing clothes, doing piecework, and "helping" in family stores. Furthermore, 65 percent of these women, including those who were married in Europe, returned to paid employment outside the home for substantial periods in their later lives.[77]

WPA oral histories demonstrate that the varying work choices of immigrant women from diverse ethnic groups cannot be contained within the simple rubric of cultural preference. Different patterns of work emerged from the complex interaction of many factors: male income; available employment opportunities; inherited skills and traditions; life-cycle stage; and the existence of familial, friendship, or ethnic ties to specific jobs. Mary Huda, for example, described how the particular opportunities for paid labor in American cities altered southern and eastern European work preferences. When she first came to Bridgeport, Mrs. Huda, like many single Slovak women, followed European traditions and networks into domestic service, but later she worked at various factory jobs. She explained:

> When I would get home (from her job as a cleaning woman), I used to have my lady friend in the next house come to my house and we would talk about her work and my work. She used to tell me that she worked in the Corset Co., on bench work . . . that it would be better if I worked in the factory instead of house work. She said that the work wasn't hard and that in the night time you were like free. I told her that in Europe . . . when there was a chance for a young girl to work in the house of some rich people, it was like being in the family and everybody used to like to do housework on the side. I said Slovak people think that there is more

> respect to work in the house instead to work in the factory. She said that the old country was the old country, and in this country the people think it is better for the woman to work in the factory.[78]

WPA oral histories show women as active agents of their own fates, but they also provide striking evidence of the sometimes stultifying limitations patriarchal values and employer practices placed on women's lives. An immigrant mother of seven, for example, described the tragic consequences of her desperate self-sacrifice in an attempt to stretch her husband's meager earnings:

> (My youngest child) is a year old now, and doesn't make any attempt to get up. I wasn't getting the proper nourishment when I was carrying her. What I had, I gave to my husband and the children, and didn't take it for myself. . . . I cheated her to feed the others. Somehow you don't think of the one that isn't there yet.[79]

Pearl Russo, who recorded this life history, recalled the distinct perspective of WPA fieldworkers that led them not only to focus on the strengths of immigrant families but also to detail the constraints under which they labored:

> We could not be nostalgic about the lives of our neighbors. Why would we, when we lived them? In your generation you see this sort of roseate picture. . . . It's not true at all. These (actions) were the exigencies that the situation demanded and they came naturally to you because you came from poor people.[80]

Remaking their lives in Connecticut cities, southern and eastern European immigrants fashioned a means of survival and even betterment under conditions that they did not create and could not entirely control. The WPA life histories allow the historian to analyze specific choices and actions together with the networks of social relations that allowed them to take place. "One can see through life histories," wrote Isabelle Bertaux Wiame, "how social relations permeate private life, and how each person in their own way internalized them as part of their own self consciousness. . . . It takes a keen observation of the particular to show us the way to the universal."[81] Ultimately the view of immigrant life in Connecticut contained in the WPA narratives provides a glimpse of the usually invisible connections that integrate family experience into the broader networks that constitute the social reproduction of a society and the history of its class relations.

❧

By the last years of the Depression, the Federal Writers Project, along with its companion programs in theatre and art, was under heavy attack from conservatives who opposed the New Deal. Although there had always been red-baiting (Pearl Russo and Vincent Frazzetta recalled anonymous letters accusing them of being Communists), the project was invulnerable in the optimistic atmosphere of the early New Deal. In the period preceding World War II, however, the assault gathered new momentum and credibility. The new House Committee on UnAmerican Activities (popularly known as the Dies Committee after its chair) and the Woodrum Committee (a subcommittee of the House Appropriations Committee) pioneered tactics later made famous by Senator Joseph McCarthy in their intensified attacks on the Federal Arts Projects, singling out the Theater and Writers Projects for special vendettas.[82]

In 1939 Congress terminated appropriations for the Theater Project and called for massive budget reductions and the decentralization of the Writers Project, which was now required to seek state sponsorship. Simultaneously, the entire WPA lost its independent status, becoming the Works Projects Administration under the Federal Works Administration. A new law in 1940 forbade government employment of communists, fascists, and Nazis. As a result, some of the most effective interviewers left the Federal Workers Project, refusing to sign the new loyalty oath.[83]

Although most state programs successfully found local support, newly developed social and ethnic studies were usually abandoned in favor of "no-risk projects like fact books and recreation guides."[84] The workers on the Connecticut Ethnic Survey, however, remained at first undaunted. They continued to collect life histories and other data on immigrant life under state sponsorship. But finally the vitriolic assaults of the Dies and Woodrum committees, cutbacks in funding, and the war in Europe ended their jobs and dreams for the project.

Samuel Koenig and David Rodnick subsequently published several articles in obscure academic journals. But these scholarly pieces were based mainly on institutional and statistical data collected by the ethnic survey; the life histories played little part in their conception. A much longer and more ambitious manuscript by Koenig and Rodnick, analyzing the ethnic composition of Connecticut's industries and cities, including a preliminary presentation of the life histories, remained buried in the project's archives for more than 30 years.[85]

In the four years from 1935 to 1939, the Federal Writers Project produced 320 publications and 100 full-sized books, mainly guides but also ethnic studies, folklore, and even zoology.[86] More than 600 other books were left in various stages of completion.[87] Nevertheless, the promise to "give back to the people what we have taken from them" was never fulfilled. Morton Royce's vision, that the more than 160 investigations conducted by his social and ethnic studies unit would provide data for a major work entitled "Composite America," disintegrated in the confusion and cutbacks of the final years of the WPA.[88] Virtually none of the projects conceived by Alsberg, Royce, and Botkin came to fruition. Only one book, *The Albanian Struggle in the Old World and the New,* published by the Massachusetts Project in 1930, had Royce's imprint.[89] Two other books, published after the project closed down, have become classics of the documentary genre: *Lay My Burden Down,* a collection of ex-slave narratives edited by Botkin himself, and *These Are Our Lives,* interviews with both black and white southerners from the North Carolina Project, under the direction of W.T. Couch. Two recent anthologies have retrieved some of the manuscript pages deposited in the Federal Writers Project Archives in the Library of Congress.[90] But the vast majority of the estimated 10,000 narratives have been lost or remain submerged in archives, barely accessible to scholars let alone the general public.[91]

Yet an important part of the WPA social and ethnic studies has survived in the Connecticut Ethnic Survey's narratives of immigrants, and most uniquely of immigrant women. Another fragment of the legacy left to us by the Federal Writers Project can now be reclaimed as the contents of these unedited life histories are interwoven with subsequent historical research into a new and more complete portrait of immigrant life in the first decades of the twentieth century.

Notes

1. The Works Projects Administration Connecticut Ethnic Survey, including all the life histories quoted in this paper, is housed in the archives room of the University of Connecticut library at Storrs. I wish to thank William D'Antonio, Bruce Staves, Vaneta D'Andrea, and Rand Jimerson for facilitating my use of this material. A larger microfilmed collection of Connecticut WPA materials can be found in the state library in Hartford, but it is not usefully cataloged. A hand list of the Storrs collection is provided in Appendix I of my Ph.D. dissertation: Laura Anker Schwartz, "Immigrant Voices from Home, Work and Community: Women and Family in the Migration Process 1890–1938" (SUNY, Stony Brook, 1983), 780–816. Some material from this article was published in Laura Anker, "Women and Migration: Southern Italian and Eastern European Immigrant Families in Urban Connecticut," *Polish American Studies* (Winter 1988), 23–49, and "Family, Work and Community: Southern and Eastern European Immigrant Women Speak from the Connecticut Federal Writers Project," in Dorothy O. Helly and Susan M. Reverby, eds., *Gendered Domains: Rethinking Public and Private in Women's Lives* (Ithaca, N.Y., 1992).
2. Few documentary sources exist that reflect the perspectives, concerns, or speech of ordinary people. The WPA oral histories and block and ethnic-group studies offer the possibility of applying the methods of intellectual and cultural history to the narratives of working-class immigrant men and women. Professor William R. Taylor, my dissertation advisor, shared my enthusiasm for these sources and was involved in this project at every stage in its evolution. As his student I learned to approach sources as texts to be carefully and critically analyzed in all their dimensions, paying close attention to voice and structure as well as to content. His keen eye directed me to find fresh meanings in the language of the WPA narratives and in their ordering of experience; his sensitive ear helped me to listen more acutely to the immigrant voices that echoed from their pages.
3. The Connecticut WPA Ethnic Survey also includes interviews with Irish, Swedish, Norwegian, Cape Verdian, French Canadian, and German immigrants as well as with African-Americans. My analysis of southern and eastern European immigrant narratives has benefited from extensive discussions with two surviving interviewers from the Bridgeport staff, Pearl Kosby Russo and Vincent Frazzetta, who collected a disproportionate number of the best life histories and block and ethnic-group studies.
4. Louise Lamphere argues this point in *From Working Daughters to Working Mothers; Immigrant Women in a New England Industrial Community* (Ithaca, N.Y., 1987), ch. I and II, 15–91. See also, among others, Elizabeth Ewen, *Immigrant Women in the Land of Dollars: Life and Culture on the Lower East Side, 1890–1925* (New York, 1985) and Judith Smith, *Family Connections: A History of Italian and Jewish Immigrant Lives in Providence, Rhode Island 1900–1940* (New York, 1985). For a focus on one group see Virginia Yans-McLaughlin, *Family and Community: Italian Immigrants to Buffalo, 1890–1930* (Ithaca, N.Y., 1978) and Sidney Weinberg, *The World of Our Mothers: The Lives of Jewish American Women* (Chapel Hill, N.C., 1988).

5. Author's interview with Pearl K. Russo, Brookline, Mass., February 16, 1983. I am particularly indebted to Pearl Russo not only for her wonderful oral histories but also for the memories and analysis of the Connecticut Ethnic Survey that she has shared with me in many hours of discussion over the last few years. For a more detailed discussion of the significance, history, politics, and methodology of the Connecticut WPA Ethnic Survey, see Schwartz, "Immigrant Voices," especially ch. III.
6. Works Projects Administration, Connecticut Ethnic Survey, "Ethnic Groups in Connecticut: A Study of Their Adjustment and Acculturation: Plan of Study" (box 30; 120:20; 30p); see also Ann Banks, ed., *First Person America: Life History Narratives from the Archives of the Federal Writers Project* (New York, 1980).
7. The WPA was at first called the Works Progress Administration; the name was changed in 1939, shortly after the activation of the Connecticut Ethnic Survey.
8. Jerre Mangione, *The Dream and the Deal: The Federal Writers Project 1935–1943* (Boston, 1972), 42. Mangione was coordinating editor of the Federal Writers Project and has become its leading historian. See also by the same author, *An Ethnic at Large: A Memoir of America in the Thirties and Forties* (New York, 1978). Unless otherwise noted, the chronology presented here is taken from his accounts.
9. Mangione, *The Dream and the Deal*, 56. See also Monty Noam Penkower, *The Federal Writers Project: A Study in Government Patronage of the Arts* (Urbana, Ill., 1977), 18–19. Alsberg's book was entitled *Letters from Russian Prisoners*.
10. Penkower, *The Federal Writers Project*, 238; author's interview with Vincent Frazzetta, Bridgeport, Conn., November 13, 1983; Russo interviews, February 26, 1983, and June 18, 1983. See also Mangione, *The Dream and the Deal;* Banks, *First Person America*. Both Samuel Koenig, the sociologist who served as director of the Connecticut Ethnic Survey, and David Rodnick, the anthropologist who served as assistant director, published in academic journals before and after their involvement.
11. Fifty state guides were published, one for each of the 48 continental states, Alaska, and Puerto Rico. All but one were still in print in 1973. There were also five regional guides and various city guides. See Arthur Scharf, "Selected Publications of the WPA Federal Writers Project and the Writers Program," in Mangione, *The Dream and the Deal*, 375–98. *The WPA Guide to New York City* was republished by Pantheon in 1982 and, although the editor left out some of the most interesting essays, it became a virtual best seller.
12. Mangione, *The Dream and the Deal*, 193–94. Each state guide was mandated to "survey the state's geology, climate, racial composition, industries, folklore, social life and culture to describe in detail every city, mile by mile, every town and village, and every major road and every landmark in between," William Scott, *Documentary Expression and Thirties America* (New York, 1973), 11. The requirement to say something about each community was intended to force writers to record nuances of what they found and thus

reveal what the editor of the Minnesota guide called "an America that neither historians nor imaginative writers of the past had discovered," Mable Ulrich, "Salvaging Culture for the WPA," *Harper's* (May 1939), 656. See also Alfred H. Jones, "The Search for a Usable American Past in The New Deal Era," *American Quarterly* 23 (December 1971), 710–24, and Scott, *Documentary Expression,* 110–12.

13. Mangione, *The Dream and the Deal,* 44–50; see also Mangione, "The Federal Writers Project" (paper delivered to Symposium on the Arts During the Depression, Brooklyn College, N.Y., April 18, 1983).
14. The project had already published *The Italians of New York* (in English and Italian), *The Jewish Landsmanschaften of New York* (in Yiddish), *The Armenians of Massachusetts,* and *The Swedes and Finns of New Jersey,* but these books were written from secondary sources and from the perspective of individual personalities and contributions.
15. Morton Royce, quoted in Banks, *First Person America,* xv.
16. Benjamin Botkin, quoted in Mangione, *The Dream and the Deal,* 279. A native Bostonian who spent his undergraduate years at Columbia and Harvard, Botkin had already compiled regional folklore and edited a journal called *Folksay* when he received his Ph.D. from the University of Nebraska in 1932.
17. Benjamin Botkin, quoted in Mangione, *The Dream and the Deal,* 278.
18. Ibid.
19. Benjamin A. Botkin, "We Called It 'Living Lore,'" *New York Folklore Quarterly* 14 (Autumn 1958), 196. See also by the same author, "The WPA and Folklore Research: Bread and Song," *Southern Folklore Quarterly* 3 (March 1939), 1–20; *Lay My Burden Down: A Folk History of Slavery* (Chicago, 1945); "Living Lore on the New York City Writers Project," *New York Folklore Quarterly* 2 (November 1946); "Applied Folklore: Creating Understanding Through Folklore," *Southern Folklore Quarterly* 14 (September 1953), 203.
20. Mangione, *The Dream and the Deal,* 279–80.
21. WPA Federal Writers Project, Connecticut Ethnic Survey, "Ethnic Groups in Connecticut: A Study of Their Adjustment and Acculturation: Plan of Study" (box 30; folder 120:2; 7p), 3.
22. Ibid., 2–3.
23. Ibid., 7.
24. Ibid., 1.
25. Russo interview, February 16, 1983.
26. Works Projects Administration, "Ethnic Groups in Connecticut," 2.
27. WPA Federal Writers Project, Connecticut Ethnic Survey, "The Guiding Outline for Obtaining Life Histories of Immigrants of the First and Second Generation." Part IV of "A Field Workers Manual for the Study of Life Histories of First and Second Generation Immigrants" (New Haven, Conn., November 1938; box 30; folder 120:2), 1–4, reprinted in Schwartz, "Immigrant Voices," App. 2.

28. Frazzetta interview, October 1982; Russo interview, February 16, 1983. Federal Writers Project regulations required that 90 percent of employees pass the means test; only 10 percent of the employees could be hired solely on the basis of professional qualifications.

29. This biography is based on material from Frazzetta interview, October 1982, and "Frazzetta Family" by Vincent Frazzetta, Connecticut Ethnic Survey Archives (box 23, folder 109:13b; 13p).

30. See Vincent Frazzetta, "Italians in Bridgeport" (box 22; folder 109:13a; 99p); "The Polish Community in Bridgeport" (box 25, folder 109:19; 117p); "Slovak Community in Bridgeport" (box 18; folder 109:4; 80p); "Growth of Bridgeport" (obtained from Frazzetta, 5p); "Sicilians in Bridgeport" (obtained from Frazzetta, 5p); "Survey of an East Side Block, Hallett St. and Pembroke St. (box 27; folder 109:23b; 15p); "Block Survey with Supplementary Interviews of Italians in Bridgeport" (box 27; folder 109:23b; 15p); "Block Survey with Supplementary Interviews of Italians in Bridgeport" (box 27; folder 109:23b; 26p); "Survey of the Hallett St. Block of the East Side with Supplementary Interviews of Slovaks in Bridgeport Life" (box 27; folder 109:23b; 37p). In our discussions, Vincent Frazzetta spoke proudly of this work and of his many commendations from project directors as well as now-prominent writers (like Louis Adamic) who used his interviews in their published works. He talked only reluctantly of his subsequent return to blue-collar employment.

31. This biography is based on interviews with Russo on February 26, 1983, and June 18, 1983.

32. Russo interview, February 26, 1983.

33. See for example M.G. Sayers and P.K. Russo, "Clinton Avenue Survey" (Bridgeport; including 10 life histories; box 27; folder 109:23d; 14p); "Survey of Remington City with Interviews" (box 27; folder 109:23b; 8p); "Miss Y" (Alice Mackenzie, pseud.; box 21; 109:21; 9p). See also the following interviews by Pearl Russo: "Mrs. C" (Mrs. Bella Chornoy, pseud.; box 21; 109:11; 41p); "Mrs. Z" (Mrs. Mary Rauci Young, pseud.; box 21; 109:11; 12p); "Miss A" (Hermina Lovasz, pseud.; box 21; 109:11; 19p); "Mr. and Mrs. C" (Mr. and Mrs. Carpati, pseud.; box 25; 109:19; 13p).

34. This biography is taken from Rahel Mittelstein's autobiography (box 62; 157:3; 43p).

35. Ibid., 42.

36. Ibid., 41–43; see for example "Benjamin Egal" (box 62; 175:3; 6p); "K.G." (Kalya Rivkin Greenberg, pseud.; box 61; 1571e; 14p); "S.G." (Sara Gosden, pseud.; box 61; 157:1e, 5).

37. Russo interview, February 16, 1983; Frazzetta interview, October 1982. I have cross-checked interviews against each other and against other sources and analyzed the internal consistency of long biographies narrated over several sessions.

38. An anonymous worker submitted a portion of Mary Antin's autobiographical novel, *They Who Knock at Our Gates, A Complete Gospel of Immigration* (New

York, 1914), as the biography of Mrs. David Goldberg (box 62; folder 152:3; 11p).

39. Mrs. B. (French-Canadian; Marie Bretagne, pseud.; box 62; folder 152:3; 11p), 1. Many of the subjects of WPA life histories are identified solely by initials. I have assigned them fictional names to facilitate references to them in the text. These pseudonyms, composites I created from Bridgeport city directories of the period, are provided after their initials. See Schwartz, "Immigrant Voices," bibliography, Section I, 726–37, for the complete cross-reference of pseudonyms.

40. Quoted in Banks, *First Person America,* xx.

41. Vincent Frazzetta, personal communication with author, April 12, 1982. I interviewed Frazzetta at his home in Bridgeport, Conn., both in April and a second time in October, 1982.

42. Russo interview, February 16, 1983.

43. Works Projects Administration (WPA), Federal Writers Project, Ethnic Group Studies, "The Guiding Outline for Obtaining Life Histories of Immigrants of the First and Second Generation" (part IV of "A Field Workers Manual for the Study of Life Histories of First and Second Generation Immigrants," New Haven, Conn., 1938; box 30; folder 120:2; 35p), 1.

44. Leonard Rapport, "How Valid Are the Federal Writers Project Life Stories: An Iconoclast Among the True Believers," *The Oral History Review* (1979), 6–17. Rapport's criticisms are directed mainly at WPA, Federal Writers Project, *These Are Our Lives* (Chapel Hill, N.C., 1939).

45. Russo interview, February 16, 1983.

46. Statistics, journalists' reports, private letters, or published biographies also include a perceptual bias whose social meaning must be evaluated. Behind each census report, newspaper article, or public document stand a cultural context, administrative purpose, and interpretive framework that shape the factual material presented. See Peter Friedlander, *The Emergence of UAW Local, 1936–39: A Study in Class Culture* (Pittsburgh, Penn., 1975), xx–xxii. See also Paul Thompson, *The Voice of the Past, Oral History* (New York, 1978) and "Life Histories and the Analysis of Social Change," in Daniel Bertaux, ed., *Biography and Society* (Beverly Hills, Calif., 1981); June Namias, *First Generation: In the Words of Twentieth Century American Immigrants* (Boston, 1978).

47. See Paul Thompson, "Life Histories and the Analysis of Social Change," in Bertaux, *Biography and Society,* 290. See also in the same volume Maurizio Catani, "Social-Life History as Ritualized Oral Exchange," 211–24, and Martin Kohli, "Biography: Account, Text Method," 61–76.

48. Isabelle Bertaux-Wiame, "The Life History Approach to the Study of Internal Migration," in Bertaux, *Biography and Society,* 266.

49. M.H. (Jewish, Mildred Hecht, pseud.), interviewed by Rahel Mittelstein (box 61; 157:1e), 3.

50. For detailed discussions of this point see Daniel Bertaux, "From the Life History Approach to the Transformation of Sociological Practice," in Bertaux,

Biography and Society; Jeremy Brecher (with the Work Relations Group), "Uncovering the Hidden History of the American Workplace," *Review of Radical Political Economy* 10 (Winter 1978), 11–23; Ron Grele, ed., *Envelopes of Sound: Six Practitioners Discuss the Method, Theory, and Practice of Oral History and Oral Testimony* (Chicago, 1975) and "Can Anyone Over Thirty Be Trusted: A Friendly Critique of Oral History," *Oral History Review* (1978), 36–44; Agnes Hankiss, "Anthologies of the Self: On the Mythological Rearranging of One's Life History," in Bertaux, *Biography and Society*, 203–10; Kohli, "Biography Account, Text, Method," in the same volume; and Paul Thompson, *The Voice of the Past.*

51. Pearl Kosby Russo and Michelangelo Russo, interview with author, February 16, 1983.

52. Nicole Gagnon, "On the Analysis of Life Accounts," in Bertaux, *Biography and Society*; Robert F. Hainey, "Men Without Women: Italian Migrants in Canada 1885–1930," in Betty B. Caroli, Robert F. Harney, and Lydio F. Tomasi, *The Italian Immigrant Women in North America* (Toronto, 1978), 94.

53. Mrs. Mary Huda (Slovak) interviewed by Vincent Frazzetta (obtained from Frazzetta, 10p), 1. This interview is missing from the Connecticut Ethnic Survey Archive in Storrs.

54. Mr. and Mrs. H. (Lithuanian, Petraitis, pseud.), interviewed by P.K. Russo (box 17; 109:11), 3.

55. Mrs. B. (Hungarian; Agnes Bonsza, pseud.), interviewed by P.K. Russo (box 21; 109:11; 21p), 3–4.

56. "N Family" (Polish; Navakowsky, pseud.), interviewed by Stan Dabkowski (box 87; 187:76; 28p), 13.

57. "Polish Woman #3" (Mrs. Carrie Lesiaski, pseud.), interviewed by Stan Dabkowski (box 87; 187:4; 6p), 4.

58. "Polish Woman #1" (Julia Karbowski, pseud.), interviewed by Stan Dabkowski (box 87; 187:4; 6p), 4.

59. Daniel Bertaux, "From the Life History Approach to the Transformation of Sociological Practice," in Bertaux, *Biography and Society*, 34.

60. Schwartz, "Immigrant Voices," 382–90; see also ch. 7, 453–506. The WPA oral histories suggest the existence of a rigid tracking system by which European class standing was transmitted to Connecticut, reinforcing the findings of some recent historians that class origins in Europe were the best predictors of economic success for American immigrants. Of 11 well-to-do immigrants whose life histories are included in the Connecticut Ethnic Survey, all but one had been prosperous in Europe; of 24 middle-class families, 14 had been artisans. In Europe, three had been well-to-do, one had been a prosperous farmer, and one had been a shopkeeper. Only five, all small farmers in Europe, had risen into the middle class. Among the working class, 33 of 39, or 85 percent of the total, had traded subsistence farming in Europe for wage labor in America; four had been artisans and two had been well-to-do. See also Josef Barton, *Peasants and Strangers: Italians, Rumanians and Slovaks in an*

American City, 1890–1950 (Cambridge, Mass., 1975); John W. Briggs, *An Italian Passage: Immigrants to Three American Cities, 1890–1930* (New Haven, Conn., 1978); John Bodnar, Roger Simon, and Michael P. Weber, *Lives of Our Own: Blacks, Italians and Poles in Pittsburgh, 1900–1960* (Urbana, Ill., 1982) and "Migration, Kinship and Urban Adaptation: Blacks and Poles in Pittsburgh, 1900–1930," *Journal of American History* 66 (December 1979), 548–65; Thomas Kessner, *The Golden Door: Italian and Jewish Immigrant Mobility in New York City, 1880–1915* (New York, 1977).

61. John Bodnar, *The Transplanted, A History of Immigrants in Urban America* (Bloomington, Ind., 1985), 207.

62. Pasquale Gruci (Italian), interviewed by Vincent Frazzetta (box 23; 109:13b; 18p), 4.

63. Mr. Victoria (Polish; George, pseud.), interviewed by Vincent Frazzetta (box 25; 109:19; 14), 3.

64. Slovak man, quoted by Vincent Frazzetta, "Slovak Community in Bridgeport" (box 18; folder 109:4; 80p), 57–59. For an incisive discussion of this issue see Hal Benenson, "Skill, Degradation, Industrial Change and the Family and Community Bases of U.S. Working Class Response," paper delivered to 9th Annual Meeting of Social Science History Association (Bloomington, Ind., November 1982), 12.

65. Pasquale Gruci interview, 8.

66. Mrs. L. Salanto (Lucia), interviewed by Vincent Frazzetta (box 23, 109: 13b), 2.

67. Ibid., 2–3.

68. M.H. (Jewish; Mildred Hecht, pseud.) interview, 3. Marie Esposito (Jewish), interviewed by William J. Becker (box 22; 109:1a; 11p), 9.

69. Mrs. Z. (Hungarian; Mary Rauci Young, pseud.), interviewed by P.K. Russo (box 21; 109:13b; 9p), 6. Susan Glenn makes a similar point in her superb study of Jewish immigrant women, *Daughters of the Shtetl: Life and Labor in the Immigrant Generation* (Ithaca, N.Y., 1990). She argues that the renegotiation of gender roles began in the Old World, which was itself in a state of flux, and accelerated in the New. But the WPA interviews demonstrate that this analysis does not apply only to Jewish immigrants.

70. Italian worker, quoted in Vincent Frazzetta, "Italian Community in Bridgeport," 39.

71. See for example the oral histories of Ann Banks, *First Person America.*

72. See for example Marie Maddelena Zambiello, interviewed by Emil Napolitano (box 23, 109:13b; 9p), 1. For a fuller discussion of this point, see Schwartz, "Immigrant Voices," especially ch. 3. See also Bertaux-Wiame, 257–60.

73. Morris Shapiro, interviewed by Morris Tonkin (box 61; 157:1e; 25p), 12.

74. Ibid.

75. Mr. and Mrs. C. (Mr. and Mrs. Carpati, pseud.), interviewed by M. Sayers and P.K. Russo (box 25; 109:19; 13p). See also Mr. and Mrs. Gergely, interviewed by P.K. Russo (box 21; 109:11; Mr. Gergely, 12p, Mrs. Gergely, 25p).

76. Statistical sources indicate that 26 percent of all Connecticut women were working in 1929. Although immigrant women were always more likely to be in the work force than their native-born sisters, these numbers still do not capture the reality of women's work experience. Joseph Hill, *Women in Gainful Occupations 1870–1920* (Census Monograph 9; Washington, D.C., 1929), 13, 19, 67, 105, 123; Harold Bingham, *History of Connecticut,* Vol. II (New York, 1962), 850; Joan Younger Dickinson, "The Role of the Immigrant Woman in the U.S. Labor Force, 1890–1910" (Ph.D. diss., University of Pennsylvania, 1975); Loraine Pruette, *Women Workers Through the Depression* (New York, 1932).

77. This is an underestimate, since women were counted as not working if no such work was mentioned. Schwartz, "Immigrant Voices," ch. 10, 636–86. Quantitative data alone also tells us nothing of how families made decisions about work or residence or how these decisions were understood, evaluated, and activated by the actors themselves. For a particularly useful discussion of these problems, see the introduction to Judith E. Smith, "Remaking Their Lives: Italian and Jewish Immigrants: Family, Work and Community in Providence, Rhode Island, 1900–1946" (Ph.D. diss., Brown University, 1981).

78. Mary Huda interview, 2–3.

79. Mrs. B. (French-Canadian; Marie Bretagne, pseud.), 2.

80. Russo interview, February 26, 1983.

81. Bertaux-Wiame, 253.

82. David Caute, *The Great Fear: The Anti-Communist Purge under Truman and Eisenhower* (New York, 1978).

83. Russo interview, February 26, 1983.

84. Mangione, *The Dream and the Deal,* 348.

85. Samuel Koenig and David Rodick, "Ethnic Factors in Connecticut Life" (book manuscript, box 40; folder 137:1; 350p).

86. See Scharf for a complete listing.

87. Mangione, *The Dream and the Deal,* 8.

88. Ibid., 279–80.

89. Federal Writers Project, Massachusetts, *The Albanian Struggle in the Old World and the New* (Boston, 1939).

90. A relative handful of the estimated 10,000 oral histories have been published in Banks, *First Person America,* and George Rawick, ed., *Slave Narratives: A Folk History of Slavery in the U.S. from Interviews with Former Slaves, 1936–1938* (17 volumes; St. Clair Shores, Mich., 1972).

91. Banks, xx. Some documents are also deposited in other locations of the Library of Congress, the National Archive, the Schonberg Collection in New York, and in a few local and state libraries.

The Comedy of Love and the *Querelle des Femmes*: Aristocratic Satire on Marriage

Christopher Lasch

FEMINISM AND THE CONTROVERSY ABOUT FEMINISM ARE "ETERNAL," WE ARE told; they rise and fall in cycles "with the rise and fall of civilization and with fluctuations in public morality," wearing "masks so varied that it is necessary to look closely in order to recognize beneath them the same face." These words appear in the introduction to a study of French feminism, so called, in the time of Molière. Another of the older studies of early modern "feminism" opens with the same kind of assertion: "the quarrel of the sexes is eternal." Still another announces, in the very first paragraph: "In all times, and in almost all countries, there has been a Querelle des Femmes." Many of the works in this vein treat Christine de Pisan as the "first of our feminists," thus tracing modern feminism all the way back to the beginning of the fifteenth century.[1]

Recent scholarship, strongly influenced by the feminism of our own day, perpetuates this way of thinking. In *The Second Sex*, which launched a new wave of feminist speculation in 1949, Simone de Beauvoir declared that "society has always been male," that "political power has always been in the hands of men," and that the "quarrel" between men and women, accordingly, "will go on as long as men and women fail to recognize each other as peers." Since "patriarchal society . . . goes back as far as recorded history," as Eva Figes argued in 1970, it follows that "patriarchal attitudes"—the belief that women belong in the kitchen, the treatment of women as instruments of men's pleasure—have a history as old as history. Strictly speaking, they have no history at all, since they never change. "In all periods of history," writes Katharine Rogers in her study of misogyny, "there has been a dark stream of attacks on women," and the substance of this indictment, her book leads us to believe, remains unchanged over the centuries. Joan Kelly's recent study of the *querelle des femmes*—the literary controversy about women conducted in late medieval and early modern Europe—tries to establish a "400-year-old tradition of women thinking about women and sexual politics" before the French revolution, in the course of which "their understanding of misogyny and gender led many feminists to a universalistic outlook that transcended the accepted value systems of the time." The early feminists, beginning with Christine de Pisan, understood that the "sexes are culturally, and not just biologically, formed," and their "rewriting of history," according to Kelly, provided an "utterly feminist . . . critique of culture."[2]

This anachronistic interpretation of an earlier dispute about women, by transforming defenders of women's "honor" into modern feminists, obscures the nature and significance of the *querelle des femmes* and makes it impossible, moreover, to identify what was original and historically unprecedented in feminism itself. Modern feminism, until recently at least, promised not to intensify sexual warfare but to bring about a new era of sexual peace in which men and women could meet each other as equals, not as antagonists. The earlier controversies about women, on the other hand, took sexual antagonism for granted. More precisely, they took for granted the contradiction between love, which rested on sexual equality, and marriage, a hierarchical arrangement in which a wife was expected to submit to her husband's authority. The *querelle des femmes* had its material roots in aristocratic customs governing marriage, which defined marriage as a dynastic institution, not as an expression of sexual attraction. In late medieval and early modern Europe—a society newly conscious of the power of sexual attraction and inclined to surround it, moreover, with an elaborately idealized body of imagery and conventions, to exalt romantic passion as the most intense emotion available to mankind—the contradiction between marriage and passion became almost unbearable. Poetry and satire registered this contradiction and attempted to relieve it with tears and laughter. Until the eighteenth century, however, no one gave much thought to the possibility of overcoming it altogether.

The *querelle des femmes* is usually dated from the second part of the *Roman de la Rose,* written by Jean de Meun between 1275 and 1280. Incongruously grafted onto Guillaume de Lorris's lyrical tribute to courtly love, this celebrated work presented a kind of symposium on love, which juxtaposed various positions and put them in the mouths of stock characters immediately recognizable to a knowledgeable audience. As Pierre Col pointed out in reply to critics of the poem, Jean de Meun spoke through "personnaiges" and "fait chascun personnaige parler selonc qui luy appartient."[3] The highly conventionalized speeches assigned to these characters combined themes drawn from courtly romance with themes drawn from satirical stories of marriage and everyday life (*fabliaux*) in which young wives and their lovers foil a jealous husband in the attempt to monopolize his wife's affections. The courtly veneration of womanhood had as its obverse a certain uneasiness about female sexuality, which betrayed itself in a deeply rooted conviction of woman's inconstancy. *La donna è mobile.* Jean de Meun's disputation on love scandalized his audience, in all likelihood, because for the first time it brought courtly lyricism and low comedy together in the same work, thereby hinting at their underlying identity.[4] In deliberately violating the conventional separation of genres, the *Roman de la Rose* opened the way for the *Decameron* and the *Canterbury Tales.* Yet in many ways it looked back to the twelfth century, to the first courtly poets and also to the twelfth-century revival of classical learning—the most important influence on the humanism of Jean de Meun. The courtly lyric itself owed something to classical traditions, the meaning of which, however, medieval authors completely transformed.[5] The recovery of the classics not only revived old arguments, pro and con, about the "art of love" but also encouraged the spirit of disputation in general, exemplified in its most compelling form in Abelard's *Sic et Non.* The love of contradictions, not the hatred of women, furnished the real inspiration behind the *Roman de la Rose.* Jean's poem explored the *sic et non* of love and marriage. Just as Abelard produced arguments on both sides of theological and philosophical questions, Jean de Meun argued both sides of the question of Eros.

Its critics found the poem disrespectful of women, coarse, and obscene. In her *Epistle to the God of Love,* Christine de Pisan demanded that detractors of women be banished from his court. Jean de Montreuil replied with a long defense of the "profound and famous work of Master Jean de Meun." Other worthies entered the fray on both sides. Much of the contention centered on passages—naively assumed by critics and sometimes even by defenders of the poem to represent the opinions of the author himself—that celebrated fecundity and upheld the propagation of the human race as an inescapable obligation enjoined both by nature and by the gods. When Jean's followers claimed that he upheld marriage, condemned adultery, and aimed merely to show young women how to defend themselves against seduction, Christine replied indignantly that his poem addressed itself to those who laid siege to the castle, not to its beleaguered defenders.[6]

The *querelle de la rose* eventually subsided, but the *querelle des femmes* continued for another three centuries. Works like Alain Chartier's *La Belle Dame sans Merci* and the anonymous *Les Quinze Joyes de Mariage*—the latter depicting the misfortunes of a young husband beset with a nagging, extravagant, unfaithful wife—carried the tradition of the *Roman de la Rose* and the *fabliaux* into the fifteenth century. Rabelais's *Gargantua and Pantagruel* is often regarded as having revived it a century later, the discussion of marriage in Book III, according to one author, recalling the "old dispute begun in the *Roman de la Rose*" and at the same time looking ahead to Molière, who allegedly shared with Rabelais the prejudice that a "woman's place is in the home."[7]

Together with works by Boccaccio, Chaucer, and Erasmus, often cited as belonging to the same genre of abusive commentary on women, these stand out as major landmarks in a literary tradition carried on for the most part by minor writers and therefore distinguished by stylized and repetitive arguments on either side. Certain authors seem to have taken part on both sides of the debate—another indication of the stylized, ritualistic quality of the literary abuse and defense of womanhood.[8] In many tracts, as in the *Roman de la Rose* itself—the progenitor of this genre—arguments for and against women appeared side by side. By the end of the sixteenth century, the *querelle des femmes* had degenerated into formulaic diatribes against women, countered by equally conventional and predictable arguments in defense of women. Yet the subjects around which it revolved—jealousy, adultery, and sexual combat—continued to serve as a source of fresh inspiration not only to Molière but also to the Restoration dramatists in England. It was only in the eighteenth century that the old debate about women gave way to a new debate founded on wholly different premises.

Eighteenth-century feminists began to argue for the first time that masculinity and femininity are social conventions alterable by education. Those who took part in the *querelle des femmes* took it for granted, on the other hand, that people grow up into sexual roles. It would never have occurred to them that a woman can be, or ought to be, anything other than what she is—what she is destined to become. They defined virtue as conduct appropriate to one's station, which included social rank and gender. Those who debated the pros and cons of womanhood did not concern themselves with the abstract question of whether nature makes one sex superior to the other. Such a question would have seemed completely meaningless to the medieval and early modern mind. The issue that presented itself to those times was not whether woman is equal to man in the abstract but rather in what social relationships is she his equal, in what relations his subordinate?

Strictly speaking, the *querelle des femmes* was not a dispute about women at all, but a dispute about marriage. Should a man marry? If he does, does he marry anything but trouble? Do the pleasures of marriage outweigh its innumerable irritations and inconveniences? Do husbands have the right to be jealous of their wives' lovers? Are they justified in accusing the female sex of inconstancy, calculating seductiveness, and insatiable lust? Was it male lust, on the contrary, that lured women into adultery and fornication? Should adultery and fornication be condemned in the first place? Isn't the free union of adulterous lovers morally superior to the forced union of husband and wife? "Antifeminist" invective directed itself not to the abstract question of whether women are naturally submissive, passive, and inferior—issues that figured prominently in later debates about women—but to the concrete miseries and dangers of marriage. Denunciation of women and denunciation of marriage went hand in hand. Satire directed itself not against women as such but against the contrast between their status as lovers and their status as wives.

In marriage, a wife was expected to defer to her husband's judgment and to obey his orders. Marriage meant the end of sexual equality, hence also the end of love. In the words of the arch-"antifeminist" himself, Jean de Meun, "There's no companionship twixt love and siegneury."[9] Heloise advanced the same kind of argument against Abelard's ill-conceived proposal of marriage, "preferring love to wedlock," as she later wrote, "and freedom to chains."[10] The incompatibility of love and marriage was the central premise that underlay both of the literary traditions the juxtaposition of which made up the medieval dialectic of love. Courtly poetry glorified adultery on the grounds that equality, and therefore erotic passion, can have no place in marriage. The stylistic antithesis of courtly romance—the comic satire against marriage exemplified in the *fabliaux* and given lasting expression by Chaucer, Boccaccio, and Rabelais—either deplored or maliciously celebrated the refusal of wives to accept their subordinate status with good grace. Instead of submitting demurely to their fate, wives berate their husbands, dress up in expensive clothes designed to show off their figures, and enjoy love affairs with younger men. The insubordinate wife makes her husband an object of ridicule and crowns her career by crowning him with horns—the climactic indictment of matrimony, to which medieval and early modern satire returned with obsessive interest.

At a time when social ridicule—institutionalized in such popular customs as the *charivari*—served as the most effective sanction with which to enforce everyday morality, the fear of ridicule dominated discussion of marriage. The comic figure of the jealous husband personified this fear. It is he who usually gives voice both to the stock criticism of marriage and to the stock vilification of women; and since he is himself an object of conventional satire, the satire against women also contained a satire against the male in his capacity as householder, husband, and cuckold. Far from giving vent to "antifeminist" prejudices, aristocratic satire rested on criticism of marriage and more specifically of jealousy, rightly believed to dominate relations not founded on the principle of voluntary, reciprocal submission. The courtly lover swears to serve his mistress—a word people of the Middle Ages still used with an awareness of its political overtones—in the same way that a vassal swears homage to his lord. *Frauendienst* becomes the erotic equivalent of feudalism: a bond between the free and equal. The jealous husband, on the other hand, demands from his wife a subordination to which he is legally entitled but which he is powerless to enforce.

One of the most durable among the many misunderstandings surrounding medieval literary traditions is that courtly poetry, in its refined idealization of love, developed in opposition to a "bourgeois" and ecclesiastical literature that made fun of marriage and treated women with contempt. Thus it is said of the Chevalier de la Tour-Landy, one of the fifteenth-century "misogynists" who entered the debate about women, that his attitude was "thoroughly bourgeois as regards the position of women and, no doubt, reflects the viewpoint of a large part of the lesser nobility, which was never closely in touch with the movement of chivalrous gallantry and female supremacy."[11] In his classic study of the *fabliaux*, Joseph Bédier described these ribald narratives as the expression of a "bourgeois Dionysian myth," a bourgeois vision of earthly abundance. According to Bédier, aristocratic exaltation of womanhood gave rise to a contemptuous bourgeois reply, "*préciosité* to *gauloiserie*, the dream to derision, courtesy to villainy, the cult of the lady to . . . bantering scorn and . . . raillery." In their rivalry, each class developed characteristic attitudes about women, formalized in rival genres.[12]

Yet Bédier himself noted that the *fabliaux*, like the courtly lyrics and romances, were composed by wandering scholars, minstrels, and *jongleurs*, not by bourgeois authors, and that they found favor with the same aristocratic audience that delighted in the myth of courtly love. Bédier pointed out that both types of stories, moreover, share important structural features. In both genres, he wrote, the family is "singularly reduced," consisting of the husband, his wife, and her young lover. Nor did it escape his attention that a reader is no more likely to meet a young unmarried girl in the *fabliaux* than in the *chansons d'amour.*[13] Both genres, in other words, deal with illicit love for a lady. If Bédier had allowed himself to speculate about the reasons for this uniformity of content, he would have found it hard to avoid the conclusion that both genres uphold adultery against marriage and that both, indeed, tell the same story. The only difference is that in the comic version, the lovers outwit the stupid, gullible husband, whereas in the courtly version, the forces of social order (marital, ecclesiastical, and dynastic) usually prevail, leaving the lovers to seek union only in death.

It should not surprise us that the aristocratic literature of love, whether comic or courtly, revolved around the triangle composed of the jealous husband, his beautiful young wife, and the wife's lover, often depicted as a kinsman, vassal, or retainer of the husband, as if to highlight the Oedipal rivalries underlying this three-cornered sexual comedy. As long as marital alliances played a central part in the consolidation and transmission of landed property and in the continuity of the aristocratic house or lineage, marriages continued to be arranged without regard to romantic passion or to the wishes of the young. Such conditions naturally discouraged any inclination to identify love with marriage. The aristocratic marriage system, moreover, often paired older husbands with young wives, since men found it hard to marry before coming into an inheritance.[14] Courtly romance and its comic antithesis, the "misogynistic," "antifeminist" satire against marriage, sprang from matrimonial arrangements that required the subordination of wives and children. Literary students of domestic conflict never questioned the necessity of those arrangements, but they insisted that heads of households, especially if they marry high-spirited women much younger than themselves, find it hard to exercise their rightful authority in a just and even-handed way. Instead these men fall prey to jealousy and suspicion. They become either hateful tyrants or figures of fun. If they indulge their wives, they soon regret it. If they beat them, they fare no better in the end. In medieval and early modern satire, physical force merely represents, as usual, the last refuge of failed authority. It gives the jealous husband no comfort. He remains obsessed by the fear—by the certainty—that in spite of his beating and his jealous supervision, his wife will dishonor him. In the end he allows himself to be dominated not by a mistress to whom he has voluntarily sworn submission, not even by an insubordinate, domineering wife, but by his own obsession, which consumes him.

In the hands of a master, the underlying pathos of the jealous patriarch became fully explicit. Thus Shakespeare saw the psychological truth beneath the conventional mockery of marriage and the misogynistic attitudes associated with it: that the misogynist makes himself his own victim. In *Othello,* he raised the jealous husband to the level of a tragic hero. Here and elsewhere, he gave new life to another theme associated with anti-marriage satire, the woman falsely accused. In the satirical tradition, wives do not always outwit their husbands by taking lovers. Sometimes they suffer patiently, like Griselda, under reproaches that have no foundation in fact. Shakespeare endowed Griselda with a tragic dignity in the person of Desdemona or again in Cordelia, another victim of jealous patriarchal authority. A certain spiritual kinship unites these long-suffering wives and daughters and also unites the men who unreasonably accuse them of disloyalty, patriarchs based on the familiar figure of the jealous husband or the more pathetic figure of the father at odds with his favorite daughter. In his eagerness to believe the worst of those who love him, Lear is cousin to Othello.

The *querelles des femmes* unfolded in an age that delighted in dialectics and carried to a high pitch of refinement the art of verbal disputation. Like the tournament—to which it was often compared—stylized disputation sublimated warfare, just as courtly love sublimated lust. On one side, the literary controversy about women owed something to the ritual warfare of the joust: the champions of woman's honor saw themselves as knights riding to her defense against detractors. On the other side, it breathed the air of the schools, where dialecticians sought to overwhelm opponents with dazzling logic and impressive displays of learning. The quarrel about women took the form of a ritual contest in which clearly identifiable disputants take positions inseparable from their social roles. In the *Roman de la Rose,* the most notorious "antifeminist" tirades are delivered not by the author (who never speaks in his own voice) but by the young lover's Friend, by the Jealous Husband, and by another stock figure of medieval satire, the Vieille or Duenna, who teaches young women the ways of the world. The Friend advises the lover, against the precepts of courtly love, to use every artifice in pursuit of his goal and to seize it by force if necessary. The Jealous Husband accuses women of extravagance, vanity, insubordination, and infidelity. He lectures the lover on the dangers of marriage, pointing to the well-documented truth that no woman resists for long (even if she happens to be married to someone else) the siege of a determined lover. He caps the case against marriage by recalling the unhappy history of Heloise and Abelard. Their troubles began when they married, overriding Heloise's better judgment. Abelard's fate—emasculation—awaits every husband: such is the burden of the Jealous Husband's monologue. But that monologue is immediately followed, it should be noted, by a passage in which the Friend draws a different moral, one that contradicts the cynical advice he himself gave earlier. A jealous husband tyrannizes over his wife, the Friend points out, whereas lovers "are emancipated, frank, and free." This explains why love usually dies with marriage: he who once swore himself woman's slave now sets himself up as her lord and master.[15]

The Duenna's coarse, cynical speech, which answers the complaint of the Jealous Husband, consists of advice to young women by a woman of the world. It represents another form of satire on marriage, which takes the wife's side against a husband who tries to monopolize her affections. The Duenna lists all the things a lady has to do in order to find the right kind of lovers. Dress so as to conceal your defects and show off your charms. Wipe your mouth before drinking; don't go to sleep at the table; don't get drunk—for a "drunken woman is without defense." Carry yourself seductively in the street. Avoid poor men and proud men alike. Don't lose yourself in love; calculate. Don't give your heart away, make him pay for it. Don't give it to one man alone: witness the fate of Dido and Medea. All women love the "game" of love and have a right to play it, the Duenna insists; jealous husbands should suffer in silence. "Every female longs for every male, and each gives free consent."[16]

The assertion of woman's sexual freedom and the mockery of marriage, one might suppose, should have commended itself to female readers of the *Roman de la Rose.* It was precisely these passages, however, together with a few others, that provoked the most important criticism of the poem advanced by Christine de Pisan. The entire second half of the *Roman,* she argued—like Ovid's *Art of Love,* on which it was modeled—had no other purpose than to instruct men in the military science of seduction. In Christine's eyes, the poem's libel of womanhood lay in the claim that women not only provoke sexual encounters but seek them so ardently that they can seldom rise to the demands of loyalty or wifely submission. She tried to show that Jean de Meun contradicted himself when he outlined elaborate strategies with which to capture a stronghold allegedly on the verge of surrender. If women are as weak as their detractors claim, why do men devise such complicated schemes to overcome their resistance? In order to enter a captured castle, you don't need to start a war.[17]

Some historians of the *querelle des femmes* claim that the grounds of debate shifted over the centuries. Whereas medieval polemics addressed the question of which sex was superior, seventeenth-century "feminists" advanced the more radical claim that woman is man's equal.[18]

But even the boldest claims advanced in the seventeenth century for the most part still adhered to the old terms of debate. The *querelle des femmes,* refined and elaborated in the writing of the *précieuses,* in the plays of Molière, in Restoration comedy, in the novel of worldiness, and in the heated discussions about women that enlivened the salons of London and Paris, remained a debate about marriage, in which both sides started from the same premise: that marriage is incompatible with sexual equality.[19] This premise could lead to an increasingly cynical defense of adultery or, on the other hand, to a defense of a single life not only for men but for women as well. In the Age of Reason, a number of prominent women joined men in upholding the advantages of independence, and it is the anti-marriage arguments articulated by women that make seventeenth-century "feminism" look modern. The context of those arguments, however, still links them to older traditions.

Consider the claims advanced by the high-minded women who asserted their right to remain single in seventeenth-century England. Most of these women were Catholics or high-church Anglicans unreconciled to the Protestant celebration of married life and resentful of the growing contempt for spinsters. In reply, they sought to restore the moral esteem formerly reserved for virginity. They deplored the dissolution of monasteries in England and sought to provide single women with a substitute for these useful institutions. Mary Ward, a Catholic, established a foundation for single women with the help of Queen Henrietta Maria. She did not deny that "women are to be subjected to their husbands," nor did she question the social conventions according to which "men are head of the church, women are not to administer sacraments, nor preach in public churches." She insisted, however, that women were the intellectual equals of men and that a life devoted to piety and learning had as much value as marriage.[20] "The belief that virginity is the noblest ideal of life did not entirely die with the nunneries," according to one scholar; "in high church circles it survived throughout the 17th century."[21] In the 1630s, two sisters, Anne and Mary Collett, managed to found a kind of Protestant convent at Gedding in Huntingtonshire, in spite of the opposition of their bishop, who advised them to marry in order "that they might not be led into temptation." In a letter written to her uncle in 1631, Anne Collett expressed a strong desire to remain single. "Touching my condition of life, such content do I find, I neither wish nor desire any change in it; but as God may please, with my Parents' leave, to give me grace and strength, that I may spend the remainder of my days without greater encumbrances of this world, which do of necessity accompany a married Estate." In 1641, a Puritan pamphlet demanded a Parliamentary investigation of the "nunnery" established by the Collett sisters.[22]

The most prominent advocate of a Protestant version of monasticism, Mary Astell, noted that "very good Protestants" continued to complain, even at the end of the seventeenth century, that "monasteries were Abolished instead of being Reform'd." She called for the creation of a "monastery or if you will (to avoid giving offence to the scrupulous and injudicious) . . . we will call it a Religious Retirement," designed to provide a "retreat from the World for those who desire that advantage." She ridiculed the widespread fear of "dispeopling the World" and extolled the virtue of a single life.[23] The daughter of a high-church, mercantile family in Newcastle, Astell opposed the admission of occasional conformists to public office, condemned immoral novels and plays, and upheld the divine right of kings. Although she is often mentioned as a precursor of Mary Wollstonecraft, there is no evidence that her writings had any influence on Wollstonecraft; nor is there any reason to endorse the claim that "it was a hundred and fifty years before her vision . . . was fulfilled" by the establishment of the first women's colleges at Oxford and Cambridge.[24] Far from being ahead of her time, she was hopelessly behind it. Her ideas appealed principally to conservatives like John Evelyn, who shared her wish that "at the first Reformation in this Kingdom, some of these demolished Religious Foundations had been spared both for Men and Women; where single persons devoutly inclined might have retired and lived without Reproach, or ensnaring Vows."[25]

It was not only the economic realities underlying matrimonial arrangements that made it difficult for aristocrats and religious conservatives to take a fresh look at marriage and courtship but the persistence of long-established conventions associated with the "art of love" and the verbal battle of the sexes. The courtship ritual of agonistic insult proved so durable and satisfying, as a literary convention, that it must have drawn not only on current experience—which suggested to many observers, in the sixteenth and seventeenth centuries, that match-making had become increasingly cynical and mercenary—but also on ancestral memories of the rivalry underlying all forms of marriage and courtship.[26] In *The Taming of the Shrew,* Shakespeare made the art of sexual insult, elevated to a new level of verbal refinement, bear the whole weight of the dramatic action. Witty exchanges between courting couples figure in many of his other comedies as well. Beaumont and Fletcher used this convention so freely—in *The Woman's Prize, or The Tamer Tame'd* (1611), *The Scornful Lady* (1613), *The Wild Goose Chase* (1621), and *Rule a Wife and Have a Wife* (1624)—that their comedies created a whole vogue of plays built on the "combat between the sexes," as one critic describes it, having as central characters the "wild gallant and his witty mistress" and taking a "cynical attitude toward marriage and sex."[27] In Restoration comedy, the ritual antagonism of the sexes becomes a matter of obsessive fascination. In Congreve's *Love for Love,* Angelica replies to those who abuse women with the familiar argument that men, not women, initiate sexual hostilities by professing a devotion they do not feel. " 'Tis an unreasonable accusation, that you lay upon our sex: you tax us with injustice, only to cover up your own want of merit. . . . Men are generally hypocrites and infidels, they pretend to worship, but have neither zeal nor faith." A favorite plot, used by one Restoration playwright after another, depicts a woman-hater and shrew-tamer himself tamed by a witty woman, in the course of verbal duels that rehearse the conventional themes of sexual antagonism and misogyny. In Cavendish's *Humorous Lovers* (1677), Boldman, a self-professed "despiser of Love," advises a friend to avoid that "sickly, whining, and unmanly humour; a Man is good for nothing while he has the fit upon him." "I fear the wed-lock Ring," he goes on, "more than the Bear do's the Ring in his Nose. Oh! the torment to be tied to the stake of Matrimony, and to be baited all the dayes of a Man's life by a Wife." Here as in Dryden's *Secret Love,* the misogynist eventually falls in love with a witty heroine, "so horribly much," in the words of Dryden's Celadon, "that contrary to my own Maxims, I think in my conscience I could marry you." Heartfree, the protagonist of John Vanbrugh's *Provok'd Wife* (1697), delivers himself of a tirade against marriage, with the usual references to Eve, to women's "tricks," and to their pride, vanity, covetousness, indiscretion, and malice. When he fails to make a misogynist of his friend Constant, Heartfree resolves to provide him with the skills with which to bring his mistress to bed. "Since I can't bring you quite off of her, I'll endeavor to bring you quite on, for a whining lover is the damnedest companion upon earth." In the end, Heartfree himself succumbs to Bellinda, not without reminding himself that marriage is a lottery, a "great leap in the dark."[28]

Colley Cibber's *Careless Husband* (1704), a comedy built entirely around the erotic battle of wits, shows how little the terms of debate had altered over the centuries. Lady Easy, unhappily married to a womanizer, makes speeches that combine criticism of current marital fashions with the age-old accusation that men have reduced the art of love to a technique of sexual conquest. "Nowadays one hardly ever hears of such a thing as a man of quality in love with the women he would marry. To be in love now is only having a design upon a woman, a modish way of declaring war against her virtue." The advice given to a naive young lover by her husband and his fellow-tutor, Lord Foppington, shows the justice of this complaint. "Courage is the whole mystery of love," according to Lord Foppington, "and more use than conduct is in war." Sir Charles Easy believes that "women are only cold . . . from the modesty or fear of those that attack 'em." The courtship of Lady Betty Modish by their "pupil," Lord Morelove, consists of verbal fencing.

Morelove learns to play the part of a misogynist, not very eloquently imitating his masters in vituperation: "The mischiefs skulking behind a beauteous form give no warning." Lady Betty, a coquette who believes (or professes to believe) that "sincerity in love is as much out of fashion as sweet snuff," sees through Morelove's disguise without difficulty. Her verbal triumphs elicit Lord Foppington's admiration. "Your ladyship pushed like a fencing master; that last thrust was a *coup de grâce*, I believe." Only when Sir Charles convinces her that Morelove is determined to have nothing further to do with her does Lady Betty, regretting her "giddy woman's slights," renounce "gallantry" and apologize to her long-suffering lover. Meanwhile Sir Charles has undergone a similar change of heart. Finding that his wife has suffered his own infidelities with the patience of a Griselda—infidelities he had imagined undiscovered—he promises constancy henceforth.

> In all my past experience of the sex I found even among the better sort so much of folly, pride, malice, passion, and irresolute desire, that I concluded thee but of the foremost rank, and therefore scarce worthy my concern. But thou has stirred me with so severe a proof of thy exalted virtue, it gives me wonder equal to my love.[29]

As always, the example of a virtuous wife counters the record of woman's wiles, shames men who abuse women, and brings the *querelle des femmes* to a provisional but satisfyingly symmetrical resolution, in which both sexes admit their faults and vow to mend their ways.

In emphasizing the persistence of certain themes and conventions associated with the ritual battle of the sexes, I do not mean to deny that every age adapts old conventions to its own purposes. Thus in seventeenth-century England, many playwrights revived conventional satire against courtly love in order to ridicule the vogue of Platonic love, itself a revival of courtly traditions, introduced by Henrietta Maria in the 1630s.[30] In France, the counter-courtly tradition served to enliven ridicule of the *précieuses*, many of whom celebrated Platonic attachments. But the comic playwrights and novelists of the seventeenth century, French and English alike, directed most of their criticism, as did the *précieuses* themselves, against a more important and in the long run more threatening object than platonic love: the competing sexual morality that was beginning to emerge among the middle classes. As merchants and professional men grew more wealthy and self-assertive, more insistent than before on the need for strict standards of sexual propriety in marriage, and more emphatic in their attacks on fashionable license, aristocratic satirists launched a counterattack on middle-class marriage. The critique of sexual jealousy and jealous husbands, always an important ingredient both in the courtly tradition and in the satire it called forth in rebuttal, now took on broader implications as part of a new ethic of worldly civility, advanced in opposition to the sexual enslavement of women allegedly practiced in bourgeois circles and to the unenlightened sexual attitudes among the more rustic members of the nobility. Aristocrats in the age of Louis XIV regarded a rational code of sexual morality as one of their principal achievements. But in their eagerness to distinguish themselves not only from their social inferiors but also from the "barbarous" past, they minimized their indebtedness to earlier traditions. The concept of honor, always central to an aristocratic code of conduct, continued to dominate speculation about love and marriage in the seventeenth and eighteenth centuries. A revised ideal of honor—not, as some interpreters have argued, a shift from an external system of emotional regulation to an internal one—informed the new code of "civility" and the aristocratic feminism so often associated with it.[31] Thus the "terrible indictment of marriage" drawn up by the "feminist logicians" of the salons, as one historian refers to it, carried one step further the traditional mockery of jealous husbands.[32] A wife's infidelity should no longer be considered a disgrace to her husband, according to the *précieuses.* Jealousy itself was the disgrace; and even if a husband found himself faced with a rival, his honor lay in avoiding any public display of emotion. The conventions now widely accepted in polite society accounted a husband "wiser when he knows how to suffer than when he has found the means of avenging himself" on an unfaithful wife and her lover.

> It is the first lesson one gives to those who marry, to defend themselves against suspicion and jealousy. . . . We live without constraint, even before our husbands, and . . . they do not dare to exclude or rebuke us. A husband has to put up with the most hateful countenances, approve the

desires and designs of his wife, and know how to bend to debauches and diversions, and discommode himself or interrupt his own affairs sooner than obstructing his wife's parties or interfering with her walks or conversations.[33]

The *précieuses* not only denounced jealousy in husbands but insisted that a woman should not be expected to submit to the advances of a man who disgusted her. They condemned men who kept their wives pregnant all the time and defended women's right to remain single, on the grounds that love seldom survives the "long enslavement" of marriage. Sappho, the heroine of Madeleine de Scudéry's novel *Le Grand Cyrus,* knows men, she says, "who deserve my esteem and could even win a part of my friendship," but as soon as she thinks of them as husbands, she finds that she "regards them as masters so near to becoming tyrants that it is impossible for me not to hate them from that instant."[34] In another novel based on the ideas of the *précieuses,* one of the characters finds it impossible to conceive of a "tyranny in the world more cruel, more severe, more unbearable than that of these shackles lasting right up to the tomb." A wife, she declares,

has to support an insupportable thing; and—what, to my mind, is the epitome of the tyranny of marriage—she is obliged, I say, to take to her frozen breast the ardors of her husband, to endure the caresses of a man who displeases her, who is horrible to her mind and heart. She finds herself in his arms, she receives his kisses, and no matter what obstacle her aversion and pain can discover, she is constrained to submit and to receive the law of the conqueror.[35]

The *précieuses* attacked the double standard of sexual morality by demanding the same privileges for women that men wished to monopolize. Bourgeois morality, on the other hand—however imperfectly realized in practice—implied a very different kind of attack on the double standard: monogamy for men and women alike. Modern feminism, already implicit in the new conception of domestic life that was beginning to emerge in the seventeenth and eighteenth centuries, attempted to reconcile marriage with sexual equality. From a worldly point of view, this was a utopian undertaking. Criticism of marriage resembled Catholic criticism of monasticism. It assumed the immutability of the institution under attack.

Just as writers like Erasmus and Rabelais had denounced corrupt and lascivious monks as bitterly as any Protestant, but without calling into question the institution of monasticism itself, critics of marriage—often the very same writers—took it for granted that marriage would always represent a union of fortunes and lineages, not the union of lovers, and that it would therefore lead, in the normal course of things, to emotional suffering on both sides, to adultery and sexual intrigue, to jealousy and suspicion, and to the contest for sexual supremacy, in short, the nuances of which these writers described, at their best, with such an abundance of carefully observed psychological details.

Feminism, beginning with Poullain de la Barre and Mary Wollstonecraft, rested on the belief that social institutions can be redesigned according to principles accessible to human reason. Just as science promised control over nature, economics and a new understanding of history promised control over social relations, hitherto shaped by accident and historical drift. Even the relations between men and women, seemingly ordained by biology, could be reordered once they were perceived as the product of custom, "prejudice," law, and education. Such was the hope that gave birth to modern feminism: a new sexual dispensation based on human intelligence and rational design, not on the irrational irrelevance of gender.

More specifically, the climate of opinion in which feminist ideas took root was shaped by the Cartesian revolution in philosophy, quite directly in the case of Poullain de la Barre. The Cartesian proclamation of the mind's independence of the body made it possible to argue that mind has no sex, as feminists used to say. According to one account of the unceasing, unchanging controversy between men and women, as it mistakenly appears to so many modern historians, this was one of "two directly opposite lines of thought" that had persisted "throughout the centuries," the other being the dogma that "woman's special province is the home."[36] In fact, however, the disembodied character of mind is a distinctively modern idea, as is the disembodied, presocial conception of selfhood according to which individuals owe nothing to society, flourish fully formed in a state of nature, and enter into the social contract only to secure the inalienable rights they already enjoy. Only when men and women began to abstract mind from body and the self from its social roles was it possible to envision a fundamental modification of the conventions hitherto governing courtship, marriage, and the position of women in society.

One other influence on feminism might be mentioned: the waning of the play-element in the battle of the sexes. It is the highly stylized character of this competition, more than anything else, that distinguishes modern sexual polemics from the "age-old game of attraction and repulsion played by young men and girls," celebrated both in the courtly tradition and, more robustly, in the aristocratic tradition of erotic comedy that found expression in the *fabliaux*, on the Restoration stage, and in the works of Rabelais and Molière. Only when "civilization as a whole becomes more serious," in Huizinga's words—when not only "law and war, commerce, technics and science" but love itself "lose touch with play; and even ritual . . . seems to share the process of dissociation"—does the old game of love begin to look deadly serious.[37] At that point, it becomes difficult to remember that it was ever anything else.

Notes

1. Francis Baumal, *Le féminisme au temps de Molière* (Paris, n.d. [ca. 1923]), 8–10; Blanche Hinman Dow, *The Varying Attitude toward Women in French Literature of the Fifteenth Century* (New York, 1936), 48; Gustave Reynier, *La femme au XVIIe siècle* (Paris, 1929), 2–3. See also Theodore Joran, *Les féministes avant le féminisme* (Paris, 1910).

2. Simone de Beauvoir, *The Second Sex*, H.M. Parshley, trans. (New York, 1961), 65, 676; Eva Figes, *Patriarchal Attitudes* (New York, 1970), 25; Katharine M. Rogers, *The Troublesome Helpmate: A History of Misogyny in Literature* (Seattle, 1966), ix; Joan Kelly, "Early Feminist Theory and the *Querelle des Femmes*, 1400–1789," *Signs* 8 (1982), 5, 7, 18, 20.

3. Francis Lee Utley, *The Crooked Rib: An Analytical Index to the Argument about Women in English and Scots Literature to the End of the Year 1568* (Columbus, Ohio, 1944), 20. On the *Roman de la Rose* and the controversy it set off, see Alan M.F. Gunn, *The Mirror of Love* (Lubbock, Tex., 1952); Lionel J. Friedman, "'Jean de Meung,' Antifeminism, and 'Bourgeois Realism,'" *Modern Philology* 57 (1959), 13–23; Lula McDowell Richardson, *The Forerunners of Feminism in French Literature of the Renaissance from Christine de Pisan to Marie de Gournay* (Baltimore, 1929); Dow, *Women in French Literature;* Marguerite Favier, *Christine de Pisan: Muse des cours souveraines* (Lausanne, 1967); and Charles Frederick Ward, "The Epistles on the *Romance of the Rose* and Other Documents in the Debate" (Ph.D. diss., University of Chicago, 1911). I am indebted to Vivian Folkenflik for help in translating key documents in the Ward collection from the Old French.

4. On the separation of styles, see Erich Auerbach, *Mimesis: The Representation of Reality in Western Literature,* Willard Trask, trans. (Princeton, N.J., 1953), especially ch. 9.

5. C.S. Lewis, *The Allegory of Love* (Oxford, 1936). For a sampling of the vast body of scholarship on courtly love, see Moshe Lazar, *Amour courtois et fin' amors dans la littérature du XIIe siècle* (Paris, 1964); John C. Moore, *Love in Twelfth-Century France* (Philadelphia, 1972); A.J. Denomy, *The Heresy of Courtly Love* (New York, 1947); F.X. Newman, ed., *The Meaning of Courtly Love* (Binghamton, N.Y., 1967); Aldo D. Scaglione, *Nature and Love in the Late Middle Ages* (Berkeley, Calif., 1963); and Denis de Rougemont, *Love in the Western World,* Montgomery Belgion, trans. (New York, 1956).

6. "Christine's Reply to Pierre Col" (in Ward, "Epistles on the *Romance of the Rose*"), lines 676–747.

7. For a useful corrective to this view of Rabelais, see M.A. Screech, *The Rabelaisian Marriage* (London, 1958), who shows that the *Tiers Livre* cannot be reduced "to the trivial status of an admittedly learned intervention into the *Querelle des Femmes* on the side of extreme antifeminism" (p. 2).

8. Thus Edward Gosynhill, to whom is usually attributed the scurrilous diatribe against women, *The School House of Women* (1541), replied to *The School House* a few years later in *The Praise of All Women.* In some works—for instance, in C. Pyrre's *Praise and Dispraise of Women, Very Fruitful to the Well Disposed Mind, and Delectable to the Readers Thereof* (ca. 1563)—arguments for and against women appeared side by side.

9. *The Romance of the Rose,* Harry W. Robbins, trans. (New York, 1962), lines 8452–53.

10. *The Letters of Abelard and Héloise.* Betty Radice, trans. (Harmondsworth, 1974), 114.

11. Raymond Lincoln Kilgour, *The Decline of Chivalry* (Cambridge, Mass., 1937), 116. "The bourgeois temperament," according to Kilgour (p. 358), "is at odds with the refinements of courtly love." See also Helen Waddell, *The Wandering Scholars* (London, 1927), 198, 210, in which Jean de Meun is described as "the *vrai bourgeois.*"

12. Joseph Bédier, *Les fabliaux: Etudes de littérature populaire et d'histoire littéraire du moyen âge* (Paris, 1925), 363–65.

13. Ibid., 322, 370, 378, 382, 385, 392.

14. Georges Duby, *Medieval Marriage,* Elborg Forster, trans. (Baltimore, 1978), 3–15, and "The 'Youth' in 12th-Century Aristocratic Society," in Fredric L. Cheyette, ed., *Lordship and Community in Medieval Europe* (New York, 1968), 198–209; J. Hajnal, "European Marriage Patterns in Perspective," in D.V. Glass and D.E.C. Eversley, eds., *Population in History* (London, 1965), 101–43.

15. *Romance of the Rose,* lines 9413–23; for the speeches in question, see lines 7231–10,005 (the Friend); lines 8464–9360 (the Jealous Husband); and lines 12,541–14,546 (the Duenna).

16. Ibid., lines 14,029–30.
17. "Epistle of the God of Love" (in Ward, "Epistles on the *Romance of the Rose*"), lines 348–406.
18. Richardson, *Forerunners of Feminism,* 155; Emile Telle, *L'Oeuvre de Marguerite d'Angoulême, Reine de Navarre, et la querelle des femmes* (Geneva, 1969), 379–80; Marjorie Henry Ilsley, *A Daughter of the Renaissance: Marie le Jars de Gournay, Her Life and Works* (The Hague, 1963), 201 and passim; Jacob Bouten, *Mary Wollstonecraft and the Beginnings of Female Emancipation in France and England* (Amsterdam, [1923]), 22–23.
19. On the seventeenth-century controversy about women and marriage—the writings of the *précieuses* in particular—see Baumal, *Le féminisme au temps de Molière;* Reynier, *La Femme au XVIIe siècle;* S.A. Richards, *Feminist Writers of the Seventeenth Century* (London, 1914); Carolyn C. Lougee, *Le Paradis des Femmes: Women, Salons, and Social Stratification in Seventeenth-Century France* (Princeton, N.J., 1976); Jean-Michel Pelous, *Amour précieux, amour galant, 1654–1675: Essai sur la répresentation de l'amour dans la littérature et la société mondaine* (Paris, 1980); Hilda L. Smith, *Reason's Disciples: Seventeenth-Century English Feminists* (Urbana, Ill., 1982); Peter Brooks, *The Novel of Worldiness* (Princeton, N.J., 1969).
20. Florence M. Smith, *Mary Astell* (New York, 1916), 62–63, note 37.
21. Ibid., 63.
22. Ibid., 64–66.
23. Ibid., 23, 52.
24. Ibid., 76. Smith herself admits that "there seems no proof that Mary Astell's writings had any direct influence on Mary Wollstonecraft" (p. 165). Cf. Hilda Smith, *Reason's Disciples,* 207: "Astell's writings . . . apparently had no direct influence on later feminist thinkers." One reason for this, surely—although Astell's admirers ignore it, and indeed persistently try to link her ideas to a later feminist tradition in spite of their own evidence—is that her monastic ideal of education was of little use in the world of the eighteenth and nineteenth centuries, in which education commended itself as preventive exposure to the world, not as a refuge from it.
25. Smith, *Mary Astell,* 74.
26. All over the world, peasant cultures have observed the changing seasons with games and festivals in which groups of young men and women exchange playful insults. In ancient China, these "courteous rivalries" celebrated the "imperious law of union to which [the sexes] were subject," according to Marcel Granet. "But, as representatives of their sex and their clan, weighted with the spirit of the soil, full of domestic pride and sexual egoism, [men and women] felt themselves at first to be rivals. The courteous struggle which was to bring them together opened with a tone of bravado and mistrust." Rhymed couplets, "invented to suit the rhythm of the dance" and flung back and forth "according to the rules of traditional improvisation," elaborated a

"whole cycle of venerable analogies." At the feasts of Demeter and Apollo in ancient Greece, "men and women chanted songs of mutual derision"; and this ritual, in the opinion of Johan Huizinga, "may have given rise to the literary theme of the diatribe against womankind." Even in western Europe, the ceremonial rivalry of the sexes, conducted by organized groups of young men and women, continued well into the nineteenth century to play a large part in peasant courtship, itself still linked to seasonal festivities organized in large part by sexually segregated peer groups. Festivals celebrated sexual fecundity in the context of seasonal change—the reawakening of the land in the spring, the fall harvest—but surrounded the union of the sexes with reminders of their opposition: verbal insults, games pitting men against women, and masquerades in which men and women exchanged roles for the purpose of satire and ridicule.

This ritual antagonism of the sexes, which seems to be a universal feature of the neolithic village culture that persists in some peasant societies right down to our own day, reveals a sense of life as the conflict of opposites. A search for the foundations of this antagonism would take us back to the dawn of culture itself. See Marcel Granet, *Chinese Civilization*, Kathleen E. Innes and Mabel R. Brailsford, trans. (New York, 1930), 159–64; Johan Huizinga, *Homo Ludens* (Boston, 1955), 68, 122; Edward Shorter, *The Making of the Modern Family* (New York, 1975), 121–46; Frank J. Warnke, *Versions of Baroque: European Literature in the 17th Century* (New Haven, Conn., 1972), 92–93.

27. John H. Wilson, *The Influence of Beaumont and Fletcher on Restoration Drama* (Columbus, Ohio, 1928), 116–17. See also John Wilcox, *The Relation of Molière to Restoration Comedy* (New York, 1938), 200–201, and John Harrington Smith, *The Gay Couple in Restoration Comedy* (Cambridge, Mass., 1948), 9–13. The following three examples come from Smith's engaging analysis of this theme: Congreve (p. 157), Cavendish (pp. 53–54), and Dryden (p. 56).

28. John Vanbrugh, *The Provoked Wife*, Curt A. Zimansky, ed. (Lincoln, Neb., 1969), 27–28 (act II, scene 1, lines 155–82), 32 (act II, scene 1, lines 304–7, 107 (act V, scene 5, line 67).

29. Colley Cibber, *The Careless Husband*, William W. Appleton, ed. (Lincoln, Neb., 1966), 31 (act II, scene 1, lines 91–95), 43 (act II, scene 2, lines 218–20), 45 (act II, scene 2, lines 285–86), 60 (act III, lines 345–46), 65 (act III, lines 476–77), 66 (act III, lines 497–98), 113 (act V, scene 7, lines 184–89), 118 (act V, scene 7, lines 317–26).

30. Smith, *The Gay Couple*, ch. 2; see also Kathleen M. Lynch, *The Social Mode of Restoration Comedy* (New York, 1926), ch. 5; Jefferson Butler Fletcher, "*Précieuses* at the Court of Charles I," *Journal of Comparative Literature* 1 (1903), 120–53; and Fletcher, *The Religion of Beauty in Women* (New York, 1911).

31. Norbert Elias, *The Civilizing Process: The History of Manners*, Edmund Jephcott, trans. (New York, 1978) argues that the new "civility" reflected the internalization of social constraints and, more generally, a "renunciation of instinctual gratification" (p. 134).

32. Baumal, *Le féminisme au temps de Molière,* 37, 92. In Baumal's view, no "modern George Sand" stated the case against marriage "with more vigor or apparent logic." *Préciosité* "had become *un veritable foyer de révendications féministes*" (p. 49). Madeline de Scudéry in particular, with her "spirit of independence" and her "strong taste for liberty"—whose "disdain for marriage" rested on "an extreme concern for personal liberty"—"appears to deserve the name of feminist in the modern sense of the word" (pp. 77–80).

33. Baumal (ibid., 27–29), quoting from the seventeenth-century novel by the Abbé de Pure, *La prétieuse, ou les mystères des ruelles*—a satire of preciosity that nevertheless gave an accurate account, according to Baumal, of what emancipated women were talking about at the time.

34. Quoted in Baumal, *Le féminisme au temps de Molière,* 77–80.

35. Bouten, *Mary Wollstonecraft,* 4–7.

36. Ibid.

37. Huizinga, *Homo Ludens,* 122, 134.